LUXURY TRAINS

George Behrend

MA (Oxon), FRGS, MCIT

LUXURY TRAINS

FROM THE ORIENT EXPRESS TO THE TGV

The Vendome Press

New York   Paris

For Philip Jefford

Designed by Ronald Sautebin

First published in 1982 in Great Britain
by the Transport Publishing Company, Glossop,
in association with Jersey Artists, St. Martin, Jersey

French edition copyright © 1977 Office du Livre,
Fribourg, Switzerland

Copyright © The Vendome Press
Published in the United States of America and Canada
by The Vendome Press, 515 Madison Avenue, New York, N.Y. 10022

Distributed in the United States of America
by The Viking Press, 625 Madison Avenue, New York, N.Y. 10022
Distributed in Canada by Methuen Publications
All rights reserved

Library of Congress Cataloging in Publication Data
Behrend, George
    Luxury trains
    Bibliography: p.
    1. Railroads—Express-trains.   I. Title.
TF573.B43   385′.37   81-10366
                       AACR2
ISBN 0-86565-016-0
Printed and bound in Italy

Contents

APPENDICES

Preface and Acknowledgements

Orient Express! It is astonishing what romantic dreams are associated with those two words, and also how they seem to be forever linked with the evocative destination board 'Paris-Lausanne-Istanbul', rather than with any other service.

By the time this book appears, the last regular sleeping car of the International Sleeping Car Co. (Wagon-Lits) will have run from Paris to Istanbul, though the Orient Express from Paris-Est to Munich, Vienna, Budapest and Bucharest will remain, still with its sleeper staffed by private enterprise even in Communist Hungary and Roumania, thirty years after Wagon-Lits had to withdraw its other services from those countries. In 1983 the Orient Express will celebrate its centenary.

In an age when very few people are both old enough and lucky enough to have experienced comfortable railway travel, when suspicion of foreigners is growing, all the while that officially the objective is for friendly co-operation, this book takes a look at the art of travelling in a civilized manner, at a deliberate rather than frantic pace, with excellent plumbing, clean sheets and fine meals along the way, with a rich, cosmopolitan taste for a complex and contradictory world.

The current preoccupation with deserts and backward countries, the prevalence of discontent and envy, the absence of pride in one's work, the failure of will to improve the environment—none of these issues has been addressed in this book. Instead, we have wanted to show the young that, along with two world wars, they have also missed the marvel of steam trains in profusion and of high, luxurious style while moving about on rails. And the exciting thing is that the young seem to be interested in the details of a life—slower, more dignified and comfortable, more trustworthy—that existed before television, communication satellites, supersonic air travel, the computer and the sophisticated criminal who can now, as always, move about even faster than everybody else.

Partly for security reasons, partly for publicity purposes, the truth about Trains de Luxe was not always told at the time these services went into effect, all of which has caused historians to go astray. It also accounted for much of the 'mystique' of Trains de Luxe, which yields to rational analysis once the language barriers have been broken, disclosing the long-held secrets of what actually happened beyond the frontiers. The facts that could never be properly verified enabled thriller-writers to add even more spice to the romantic life aboard the international trains. If anyone knew the truth, he refused to reveal it, since all the folklore that gathered about Trains de Luxe was undoubtedly good for business.

Needless to say, the opinions in this book are the author's own, but we should add that the opportunity to produce a history of Trains de Luxe came with the framework wherein it had to be delivered. The reason your favourite Pullman or train, or favourite country, may not get a mention is simple—lack of space. Except for this sentence, the author's own favourite train, the Oberland Express (Calais-Laon-Rheims-Chaumont-Belfort-DELLE-Berne-Spiez-Interlaken) gets no mention either. But there is no through service this way today, so *tant pis*!

Your first journey across more than one country by through train will not be the same as the rail journeys of yore. But if you enjoy it, perhaps you will think the experience as magnificent and sumptuous and pleasant a way of life as was travelling on the Oberland Express—in 1929. That will be splendid, because you will arrive feeling happier than when you started, which is what this book is all about.

Acknowledgements

The author wishes to thank all those mentioned below, and any others who may have been inadvertently omitted, either officials or

friends of 25 to 30 years' acquaintance, for their generous help and for the use of their collections of photographs and plans.

He would thank, first of all, M. Jean Hirschen of Office du Livre, the originating publishers, M. Hirschen's most understanding editor, M. Dominique Guisan, and, in particular, his young designer Mr. Ronald Sautebin, for his creation worthy of the style of the Trains de Luxe. The author also wishes to thank his wife, Jon, for her great patience over four years, despite very grave illness, and her understanding of the upheavals caused by the editing of this work. M. Jean des Cars of *Paris Match* must not be forgotten either, but for whom this book would have been perhaps very different! Also M. Roger Commault, whose help and friendship have been continuous for over 30 years.

The author acknowledges a debt of gratitude to Mr. Alexis Gregory and his staff of The Vendome Press, New York, publishers of the American edition; Mr. John Senior of Transport Publishing Company, publisher and editor of the English edition, and his understanding staff; and Mr. John Price, editor of the Thomas Cook International Timetable at Peterborough (England), for his great assistance in many ways extending over 25 years, but especially in regard to both the English edition and the original French edition of this book. The author also extends his thanks to Mr. Walter Köpfli of Orell Füssli Verlag, Zurich, which published the German edition, and Mr. Kurt Schuyt of Schuyt & Co., Haarlem, the sponsor of the Dutch edition.

The author further expresses his appreciation to: Mary Adshead; Jean Albertini; Chef du Service Extérieur, SNFC, Paris; John Alves; Alex Amstein, Chief of Public Relations, SBB, Bern; Jacques Azoulay, Orient Express Restaurant, St. Cyr-Ecole; Michael Bailiss, Director, West Somerset Railway; Heather Batchelor, Publicity Department, French Railways, London; Paul Bianchini, Editions Orient Express, Paris; R. Black, Speyside Railway Association; Marie-Thérèse Bonnet, Service Presse, CIWLT, Paris; David Boyers, SAR/SAS Travel Bureau, London; Dr. H. Büchler, DB Representative, London; Juan Cabrera; Jean-Paul Caracalla, Inspecteur-Général, Chef des Services Extérieurs, CIWLT, Paris; D. J. Carson; J. Church, Sales Controller, BR Supply Directorate, Derby; Dr. John Coiley, Keeper, National Railway Museum, York; Bill Coo, VIA Canada, Montreal; R. Copson, VVM Hamburg; Gérard Coudert; Paul Delacroix, Directeur, La Vie du Rail, Paris; William Devitt, formerly Railway Engineering Dept., Sea Containers Services Ltd., London; David Dine, Tenterden; Marcel Doerr, Directeur French National Railway Museum, Mulhouse; Arthur D. Dubin; Maurice Earley; Michael Edge; T. Edgington, NRM, York; Roy Edwards, BR (SR); Friedhelm Ernst, Freundeskreis Eisenbahn, Cologne; Keith Faulkner, lately General Manager, Nene Valley Railway, Peterborough; Walter Finkböhner, SBB Representative, Milan: F. M. Fontan, Chief Engineer, CIWLT, Paris; Viscount Garnock; Count Giansanti-Colluzzi, Fulgurex, Lausanne; Armando Giliberti, Chef du Service Commercial, CIWLT, Rome; Albert Glatt, President, Intraflug AG, Zurich; Frank Gutteridge, CBE; Brian Heath, VIA Canada, Montreal; David Hewings, BMOT, Brighton; J. B. Hodford, Midland Railway Trust, Derby; I. G. Holland, Publicity Manager, New Zealand Railways, Wellington; Richard Hope, Editor, and Murray Hughes, *Railway Gazette*, London; J. T. Howard Turner; Sebastian Jacobi, CFF, Berne; David Jenkinson, Education Officer, NRM, York; Dennis Joiner, Chief Press Officer, BR Board, London; R. W. Kidner; L. Kieni, Managing Director, SSG, Olten; Albert Kunz, Director, and Jurg Schmid, Chief of Publicity, SNTO/SBB, London; Charlotte and Robert Lambert; J. Liddiard, VIA Canada, London; Raymond Martin and Maurice Mertens, Railphot, Paris; Alan Milton, OBE, Director of Supply, BR Board, Derby; Baron Montagu of Beaulieu; C. R. Pennycook, Deputy Travel Commissioner, New Zealand High Commission, London; John Pentlow, General Manager, Nene Valley Railway, Peterborough; Peter Prior, Chairman, H. P. Bulmer Ltd., Hereford; S. C. Pritchard, Chairman, Peco Ltd., Seaton; Ray Privett, BRSR; Peter Punt, Public Relations Officer, UIC, Paris; Roland de Quatrebarbes; Dr. P. Ransome Wallis; R. C. Riley; Timothy Robbins, Train Manager, Sea Containers Ltd.; Claude Roche; Michael Sedgwick; James Sherwood, President, Sea Containers Ltd., London; A. J. Simpson, Head of Operations, Travellers Fare–BTH, London; J.L. Smith, Lens of Sutton; Werner Sölch; Robert Spark, Editor and Publisher, *European Railways Magazine*, Cobham; William Spirit, FCA, Secretary, Jersey Artists Ltd., Jersey, CI; N. Stevens, Public Affairs Officer, Sealink UK Ltd., London; Thelma Stevenson, Public Relations Officer, Sea Containers Atlantic Services Ltd., London; Dr. Fritz Stökl; Edmund Swinglehurst, Press Officer, Thomas Cook Group, London; C. Thompson Walker, Public Relations Officer, Sealink UK Ltd., London; Dr. A. Waldis, Director, Swiss National Transport Museum, Lucerne; Dr. W. A. C. Wendelaar; Kenneth Westcott Jones; Patrick Whitehorse, Director, Birmingham Railway Museum, Betty Wijsmuller; D. Wilson, Tenterden Railway Co.; Neil Wooler, Information Officer, Travellers Fare BTH, London; Ian Yearsley; Edy Züger, Vice-President, Intraflug AG, Zurich.

I must also cite the Directors of the London Tourist Offices of Australia, Japan and South Africa; the Press Officers of the British Railways Board; the Public Relations Officers of BLS (Berner Alpenbahn Bern Lötschberg Simplon), Bern; FS Italia (Dr. A. Ciambricco), Rome; Linke Hofmann-Busch AG, Salzgitter; London Transport (K. G. Pope); MOB (Montreux-Oberland Bernois), Montreux; OeBB (Oensingen Balsthal Bahn), Balsthal; SAR/SAS

opposite: 1. The Nostalgic Orient Express of Intraflug with Lx16-type sleeping cars, in 1977.

above left: 2. The last steam all-Pullman train in Great Britain, in 1957. Bulleid SR Merchant Navy Pacific No. 35017 'Belgian Marine' on the *Bournemouth Belle* at Worting Junction, near Basingstoke. The former *Devon Belle* route passes under the bridge (left).

above right: 3. The Bulmer Cider Train near Hereford, in October 1971. BR 4-6-0 No. 6000 'King George', ex-Great Western Railway, at the head of Pullman Cars *Aquila* and Nos. 36, 83 and 76. Note the engine's bell, presented by the Baltimore & Ohio Railroad in 1927, when the locomotive led the centenary procession.

left: 4. The *Flèche d'Or* at Calais Maritime, waiting to leave for Paris after the maiden voyage of the *Canterbury* in 1929. Nord 4-6-2 Pacific No. 3, 1227.

(South African Railways), Johannesburg; Schindler AG, Pratteln and Zurich; the Librarian (Mrs. Southgate) of the Chartered Institute of Transport, London.

For permission to reproduce songs, the author wishes to thank: Mme Jeanne Boyer for the chorus of *Le Pyjama Présidentiel* by Lucien Boyer (p. 66); Charles Clegg for 'The Ballad of the Twentieth Century' by Lucius Beebe (p. 76); Faber & Faber, London, for 'The Railway Cat', from *Old Possum's Book of Practical Cats* by T.S. Eliot (p. 164); Editions Gallimard, Paris, for 'Ode' by Valérie Larbaud, extracted from *Les Poésies de A.G. Barnabooth* (p. 28); and Veronica Music, London, for Bud Flannagan's theme song to 'Dad's Army' (p. 25).

I

THE TIME OF THE PIONEERS

1. The Origins of Trains de Luxe

Pullman! The name conjures up vistas of exciting journeys in exotic railway cars, replete with porter, butler, valet, and chef, a world of gracious living in elegant drawing rooms, in sleeping berths and spacious dining saloons aboard the trains used by the wealthy for travel around America in the days when the only means of transport were the railways or the horse and buggy.

Even rail travel, often for several days and nights on end, was rough; sometimes even dangerous. Though the primitive sleeping car is said to have started running on the Cumberland Valley Railway (now part of Penn Central) as early as 1837, when George Mortimer Pullman was just six years old, it was Pullman who saw the need to provide comfortable accommodation with washing facilities and proper beds at night.

Pullman cars were massive constructions, sumptuously furnished with velvet drapes and plush-upholstered pairs of armchairs that pulled together to make a sleeping berth, whilst upper berths let down from the roof, an arrangement known as a 'section'. There were proper sheets, pillows and blankets, hot water for washing and for heating the cars. For each car Pullman provided an attendant, a porter, that is, who kept watch while the passengers slept. Pullman charged a supplementary fare for the use of his cars, which were switched from one railroad to another, while menial passengers had to change trains. Dining cars soon followed, resplendent with silver service and extensive bills of fare at reasonable prices, so different from the hastily swallowed, exceedingly bad but very expensive meals that were snatched at stops along the way. Pullman's sleeping and dining cars ran regularly in the ordinary trains for the general public who chose to pay the extra fare. Eventually they could be found throughout the American continent, though at this time it was not yet possible to cross all America by train, since the railroads were not completed.

Let us not forget the novelty of it all. Motor cars and aircraft did not exist; they were conveyances of the future. Hotels in western America were primitive in the extreme, and not particularly safe for wealthy visitors. So the rich bought their own vehicles from Pullman, or sometimes they hired them from his fleet of 'private' cars. When the Grand Hotels began to be built later on, they were equipped with special sidings, on which these private cars could be parked, like the Cadillacs or Rolls-Royces of today. Gradually, the Pullman system of sleeping, dining and 'hotel' cars (which combined sleeping and dining) grew in numbers, until in the 1930s when some 30 million people per year were travelling in about 9,000 Pullman cars in the United States alone!

George Mortimer Pullman

George Mortimer Pullman was born in Brockton, New York, on 3rd March 1831, the third of ten children. His father was a general mechanic. His elder brother Albert, a carpenter, also played a part in the luxury railroad-car business. In 1845 George Pullman left school and got a job in a farm-supply store, but three years later he moved to Albion and began roving about the country, selling the cabinets and other furniture manufactured by his brother Albert. Is this perhaps the origin of the marquetry work that many Pullman cars made famous?

In 1853 Pullman travelled from Buffalo to Westfield, a mere 58 miles (70 kilometres) but taking all night! Lighting was by candles. Heating? It did not exist. A further journey two years later, from Chicago to New York, made him more determined than ever to do something about uncomfortable railway travel.

Pullman had by now become a contractor in Chicago, specializing in the removal of badly sited buildings by jacking them up and shifting them bodily. One such project was the Tremont House Hotel, a four-storey building threatened with demolition because it was in a low-lying swamp and unable to cope with that American speciality—the plumbing. Pullman jacked it up so successfully, ap-

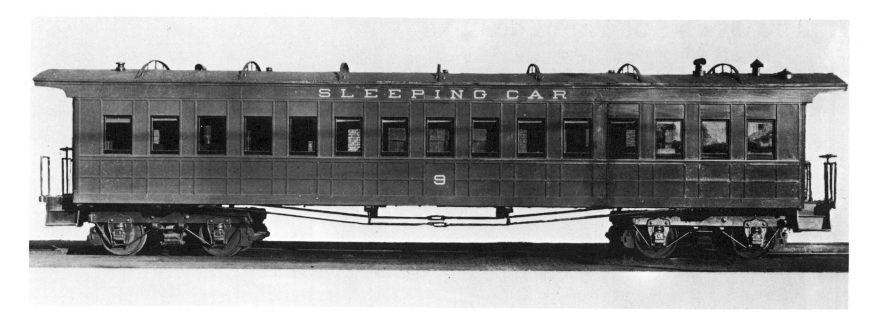

5. The first sleeping car, adapted from an ordinary day saloon by Pullman in 1859. A reproduction of the Chicago & Alton Railroad's No. 9. (The original was destroyed by fire in 1897.)

parently without the place closing, and without breaking a pane of glass or causing the chamber maids to smash the china they were carrying, that what was to become the criterion of Pullman travel got its first mention: even whilst being moved on wheels, people in the Tremont could drink their beer without spilling it.

Now flush with money and prestige, Pullman borrowed two of the Chicago, Alton & St. Louis Railroad's twelve coaches, Nos. 9 and 19, which were 44 feet long, with the usual open-end entrances but with something not seen in Europe—bogies or trucks. The remodelling of the inside cost $2,000 (a lot of money in those days) so that the backs of the reversible seats would let down, to form longitudinal beds. Pullman did most of this himself. There were no plans or blueprints or anything fastidious like that; Pullman was a self-made, self-taught man. He had a carpenter named Leonard Seibert as assistant. Although Pullman cars were to change out of all recognition in the subsequent century, two items stand out as characteristic: plush upholstery, associated with all Pullmans up to the mid 20th century; and the employment of the first Pullman porter, Mr. Johnathan L. Barnes, who was in charge of the car. The porters not only gave status to the Pullman cars; they also gave status to American blacks after 1870.

Mr. Barnes, however, was one of Pullman's white conductors. He lived to a ripe old age of 85, garrulously recounting his trip as the first porter on the first Pullman service, which ran on 1st September 1859 from Bloomington to Chicago through the state of Illinois. Although there were oil lamps, they apparently did not

work, for lighting was still by candle. But there was a box-stove for heating the three fare-paying passengers, who went to bed in their boots! Barnes had to insist that they take them off.

Pullman was, first and foremost, interested in making money. He knew he was onto a good thing, and when Barnes, at the end of a trip, deferentially remarked that No. 9 was a fine car, Pullman gruffly replied that it ought to be, it had cost enough. Just to convert cars for the Chicago & Alton Railroad was not enough. On the New York Central, rival Webster Wagner would soon be doing the same for the Vanderbilts. Pullman wanted to build his own cars and run them about for his own profit. The supplement between Bloomington and Chicago was only fifty cents, and the equipment did not include sheets.

But Pullman's plans for the future were to be interrupted by the American Civil War. The Unionists requisitioned all the C&A rolling stock, and Pullman found himself short of money and out of business. Whilst his future rival, Colonel William d'Alton Mann, was busy under General Custer giving the US Cavalry a name for bravery by frontal charges with much loss of life, without any victorious outcome over the Confederate enemy, Pullman put as big a distance as possible between himself and the war. Settling at a gold-rush camp called 'Pike's Peak or Bust', near Gregory Gulch, Colorado, he made a lot of money, not by prospecting, but by selling high-priced supplies of food and materials to the prospectors, who themselves had little luck. He returned to Chicago at the end of the war with $20,000, which he spent on his first Pullman car, appropriately named *Pioneer*.

Pullman built the car as he wished, without regard for anybody else. Other people's cars cost about $4,000, and they conformed to the requirements of the railway. Pullman's massive vehicle, mounted on bogies each with four axles instead of the usual two, cost in all $20,170 and was too big for what the railways call the 'loading gauge', that is, the width and height beyond which any vehicle would

6. Pullman Car *Pioneer* of 1864. The first sleeping car built entirely by Pullman, shown here in its 1865 style with standard Pullman bogies.

hit things like platforms, bridges, trees, cuttings or even wagons on adjacent tracks. Pullman learnt such technical terms the hard way. When in the middle of 1864, about a year after being built, his *Pioneer* was at last 'ready to roll', it stuck! It had to be put away in a shed, where it got a new name, 'Pullman's Folly'. What ex-New York Senator Ben Field, Pullman's partner, called it is not recorded. C. Hamilton Ellis has described Pullman as 1 per cent inventor, 9 per cent improver, and 90 per cent business man.

In April 1865, all America was horrified by the assassination of President Abraham Lincoln. His funeral train was arranged to run from Chicago to Springfield. The president of the Third National Bank of Chicago, where Pullman had his account, was Colonel Bowen, who assumed responsibility for the funeral arrangements. Only the best seemed good enough for Lincoln's last journey, but it was stuck in a shed.

The Chicago & Alton Railroad was thus forced to take *Pioneer* and alter its loading gauge to accommodate the huge car. Large numbers of people turned out to watch the train pass on 2nd May 1865, giving Pullman the publicity he needed. And now the C&A, having worked night and day adjusting platforms, cuttings, etc., was always available for *Pioneer* to run on.

The new President was General Grant, and Pullman again offered his car for the Presidential conveyance, this time over the Michigan Central Railroad, which also had to alter its loading gauge. This publicity gave Pullman the edge over his rivals, many of whom were actively producing sleeping cars. Fifty-eight feet long, its floor high above the ground, *Pioneer* was certainly impressive, and the fact that it weighed over 27 tons was not to be complained about when the car had been deemed fit for a President. Other cars followed fast.

The difficulties were no longer physical but competitive. Exclusive contracts became the thing, and if this could not be attained, then an association had to be formed with the various railways,

sharing the profits, but keeping the rivals off the line. Webster Wagner was the greatest of these, starting his New York Central Sleeping Car Co. in 1865, financed largely by the Vanderbilt family, owners of the New York Central. Pullman obtained an association arrangement with fourteen railroad companies that hitherto had no sleeping-car services, but many railroads established their own sleeping-car services, which Pullman gradually took over.

In the days of wooden coaches with steel or cast-iron under-frames (or chassis), there was always a danger of 'telescoping'. The steel chassis did just that when an accident occurred, smashing the wooden bodies to matchwood and crushing the unfortunates inside. Pullman's integral construction of massive interlocking wooden framework prevented this happening, but the open platforms persisted until the Pullman Vestibule and Gangway was patented in 1887, rather better than the European-type 'concertina' covered passage-way. The Pullman or buck-eye centre coupling has long been adopted on American railroads and also used in Britain, where side buffers and centre-screw couplings are now kept on coaches only for attachment to locomotives, or older, non-equipped vehicles, making a clever arrangement that permits the Pullman buck-eye coupling to be dropped down and the buffers pulled out from the ends of the coaches.

By 1867, George Pullman had forty-eight cars in service and created the Pullman Co., which took them over from his personal ownership. The Pullman Co. had a number of subsidiaries, notably the Pullman Standard Car Co., to manufacture carriages, and the

7. The town of Pullman, Illinois, constructed by Pullman in 1880 to house his workmen.

8. Typical interior of Pullman Cars in the United States. This is *Australia,* built for Pullman service on the Union Pacific and Central Pacific railroads.

Pullman Palace Car Co. Inc., the operating firm whose activities in Europe (which we shall pursue further) were tiny compared to the services in the United States.

In the same year, Pullman first expanded over the United States border to Canada, and then to Mexico in 1889.

In 1867 the first Pullman sleeping cars with catering facilities appeared. Called 'hotel cars', one of the earliest was the *Western World,* operating in Canada on the Grand Trunk Railway, part of the Canadian National from 1923. The first Pullman to be constructed as a dining car was the *Delmonico.* Named after a famous New York restaurant, and running in 1868 on the pioneer Chicago & Alton line, it was a great success.

Now that the golden spike had been driven on 10th May 1869 at Promontory Point, linking the Union Pacific and the Central Pacific railroads, Pullman rail travel soon reached from the Atlantic to the Pacific Coast. Business men were to hire whole trains of Pullman hotel-cars, or buy their own private cars from Pullman.

In 1870 the Pullman firm began to build its own cars in its own Detroit works. The demand outstripped the size of these shops. Between 1867 and 1881, 282 cars were built for Pullman by railroad companies and other car-building firms.

Thus, Pullman decided to construct a huge works at Lake Calumet, America's first planned industrial city, 14 miles south of Chicago. Designed by the architect Spencer Beman, it contained, in addition to houses, an hotel for visitors, a water tower, and a large administrative building housing the steam power plant. The whole

town was, of course, called Pullman, and, after completion in 1881, it occupied 3,600 acres of land.

Life at Pullman was strict. The position, as well as the size and shape, of the houses allocated to the workmen varied according to the grade and station of the employee-occupant. Pullman offered splendid parks, but idling in them was forbidden. Also banned were saloons!

The same architect put up Pullman's headquarters building in the heart of Chicago, which was pulled down in 1956, and Chicago's Grand Central Station, demolished in 1969.

2. The Train de Luxe Comes to Europe

With the development of more luxurious carriages in America, the phenomenon arose that the New World had something to offer the Old World. Among the visitors from Europe was Georges Nagelmackers, a young Belgian banker who had trained as a mining engineer. He arrived in 1868 from Liège.

Georges Nagelmackers

A greater contrast to George Pullman could hardly be imagined. Rich and gentlemanly, Georges Nagelmackers was steeped in the traditions of a family that had sent him to America to forget a love affair. There, on the rebound, he fell in love again, this time with the Pullman system, whose elegant dining cars with proper napery and service were unheard of in Europe. Nor did through sleeping cars running without change from one country to another exist in Europe as they did between the United States and Canada. If such comfort and convenience were possible in the New World, why not in the Old? asked Nagelmackers.

Nagelmackers knew why. Railways in Europe were military assets, not connecting properly at frontiers. To prevent a potential enemy from using any captured rolling stock to help their cause, couplings were not made to fit each other, and buffers of coaches of different nationalities would sometimes lock on curves, causing accidents.

Yet in 1863, young Nagelmackers had been able to see Europe's first international train at his own local station, Liège, running over four different railways from Basle in Switzerland, through France, Luxembourg, Belgium and Holland to Rotterdam, operated by the French Est Railway. Only large-scale bankers like the Rothschilds or Baron Maurice de Hirsch, who fixed up the Est's service through financial stakes in all the lines concerned, put business interests above nationalism.

Nagelmackers foresaw that an international company was needed in Europe, offering Pullman-style services and vehicles that suited the requirements of all the railways over which they would run. But he also realized that progress would be slow; thus, on return to Europe early in 1870, he joined the Mines and Blast Furnaces of Vesdre, the Luxembourg Blast Furnaces and the United Cheratte Coal mines as general manager of all three, living quietly with his family at Liège. Meanwhile, he spent all his spare time on his 'secret' project, publishing on 20th April 1870 his *Projet de l'installation de wagons-lits sur les chemins de fers du continent*.

La Compagnie Internationale des Wagons-Lits

After the Franco-Prussian War, Nagelmackers set up the Compagnie Internationale de Wagons-Lits at Liège on 4th October 1872 and signed his first contract with the Belgian State and Dutch Rhenish railways three weeks later, to operate from Ostend to Cologne. Soon afterwards he had a contract from Vienna to Munich, and from Ostend to Berlin, with further contracts in Germany.

Nagelmackers' contracts differed widely from those of Pullman. Often valid for short periods only, terminable at a month's notice, they specified the size and weight of the cars to be used. Four 4-wheeled cars had been supplied from Austria, costing 20,000 Belgian francs each, for the Paris-Vienna route, but only two of them were needed for the Munich-Vienna portion, which was already in service. The Germans specified 6-wheeled cars, so four more had to be ordered, from Germany.

Colonel William d'Alton Mann

Nagelmackers' family then behaved as bankers always do; they withdrew support when the entrepreneur needed it most, and he was forced to seek money elsewhere. Naturally he turned to England, for London in those days was the world's centre of wealth, and here he encountered the American Colonel William d'Alton Mann.

Like Pullman, Mann believed in patenting things. Leaving the army, he patented military equipment and sold the patents to the US forces, with the help of old comrades still in the service. With the money he tried to start sleeping cars, having patented 'boudoir' cars with real compartments, instead of Pullman's sections, which Europeans found immoral. However, Mann discovered he could not compete with Pullman and came to England.

The upshot was an alliance. On 4th January 1873, the CIWL name was changed to Mann's Railway Sleeping Carriage Co. Ltd., registered in London instead of Liège. The new cars had 'Mann Boudoir Sleeping Car' on them, with a big 'M' engraved on the window panes, and they were painted royal blue. Mann was delighted. He was also quite happy to leave the running of the company to Nagelmackers, and even to leave the old name and address on the letter heading, along with the new one. J. Staats Forbes of the LC&DR was on his board.

Nagelmackers continued to seek contracts, and signed his first French one on 19th February 1873 with the Est Railway, between Paris and Avricourt. This was the French portion of the Paris-Vienna route. Mann Car No. 3 went on show at the Vienna exhibition from May until October. On 30th June Nagelmackers obtained a trial contract of just one year, terminable at a moment's notice, with the Rothschild-controlled Nord Railway of France (and the subsidiary Nord-Belge), for its portion of the route from Paris to Cologne and Berlin, as well as for its Paris-Calais line.

While Nagelmackers was busy negotiating, Mann succeeded in putting one of his cars at the disposal of the Prince of Wales (later Edward VII), who was travelling to Berlin, and on to the Russian frontier for his brother's wedding in St. Petersburg. (Prince Alfred, Duke of Edinburgh, married Tzar Alexander II's daughter Marie on 4th January 1874.) This attracted wide publicity and enabled the Paris-Vienna service to be started. The Paris-Vienna was a great success, profitable and very popular, generating demands for further services to be operated from Vienna in other directions.

Meanwhile, in 1872, Pullman had another visitor. This was James (later Sir James) Allport, who was travelling round America on sabbatical leave from his job as general manager of the go-ahead Midland Railway, one of the largest railway companies in England, with headquarters at Derby, the heart of the Midlands. Allport also saw the advantage of a special company to operate over more than one railway (since the Midland already had plans to run through trains to Scotland). He invited George Pullman to address the Midland shareholders at the 1873 annual general meeting in Derby. Whereas Nagelmackers' contracts were tentative, terminable at any time or at a month's notice, Pullman was invited for *fifteen years!* Derby was to become the advance base from which, to quote the London *Times:* 'Pullman Hotel Cars would run all over Europe'.

9. Georges Nagelmackers (1845–1905), founder of the Compagnie Internationale des Wagons-Lits (CIWL).

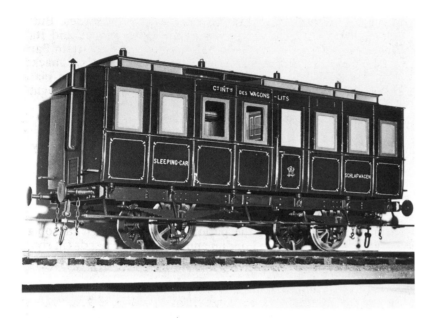

10. Model of the first sleeper (No. 1 of 1872) of the Compagnie Internationale des Wagons-Lits (CIWL).

It was not quite like that, however, for the faithful Rhenish Railway and the Belgian State Railways gave Nagelmackers ten-year contracts at the end of 1873, at last making his undertaking look like a viable one.

Pullman installed John Miller in the Pullman London office (76 Cheapside) and Colonel Charles Gourand in the Paris office (1 Rue du Quatre Septembre) as managers, and sent Mr. Rapp, a Pullman (Detroit) engineer, to supervise the Derby assembly of the parts sent over from America. The first Pullman (named of course *Midland*) was ready on 25th January 1874, a second on 15th February. The third car, *Victoria,* was the first Pullman parlour car ever to run in either the United States or Great Britain! It had two private rooms with side corridor and seventeen revolving armchairs in the main saloon (nineteen armchairs had been intended).

On 21st March 1874 a trial trip was made from London to Bedford and back, during which cold luncheon was provided, the first meal ever served in a British train. The engine was Kirtley-built MR2-4-0 No. 906, the first of several Midland engines whose tenders were altered to take the special central Miller buck-eye coupling. Only two days later, one of the sleepers was landed at Dunkerque, to be shown off in Paris. Because of its awkward central coupling, it took four days by slow goods train to reach La Chapelle (just outside the Gare du Nord), where it was displayed. Colonel Gourand asked for a Paris-Brussels Pullman contract on 2nd May 1874 but got a cold refusal, which suggested that the open plan of Pullman sections was not suitable for Europe, whereas in America the sharing of beds was not uncommon.

In England Pullman had provided a whole train, the very first to have a corridor, with lavatories in the first- and second-class ordinary coaches, or day cars. A third-class and baggage car was situated at each end; in between were a mixed first- and second-class day car, a sleeping car and a parlour car. Only the last two belonged to the Pullman Co., for which a supplement was charged. The rest were sold, immediately on completion, to the Midland Railway, which upholstered and painted them in its standard livery. They were the first bogie carriages in the United Kingdom.

All Pullman-built cars had central hot-water heating from a Baker heater—a vast improvement on the English footwarmers, which grew cold much too quickly and were rarely replaced by fresh ones.

The train started to run nightly on 1st June 1874 from London to Bradford, returning the following day. The parlour car supplement varied from one to five shillings according to the distance travelled; a sleeper berth cost six shillings any distance. There was 'a courteous conductor' (Mr. J. S. Marks, who became British Pullman manager for many years), assisted by an 'alert domestic'.

The British success of the parlour car led to two more being assembled at Derby in 1874 from parts sent over from Detroit for the London, Brighton & South Coast Railway (LBSCR). This coincided with Pullman's introduction of other parlour cars in the United States in 1875.

But M. Banderali, general manager of the Nord, who came to see the cars in 1874, said they were 'absolutely useless, although the sleeping cars were more popular'. It was the weight that stopped Pullman's advances. The train carried 200 people for an all-up weight of 100 tons, compared to the 50 tons estimated by Banderali as the weight of ordinary coaches needed for 200 people.

As Derby had now assembled two more Pullman sleepers, *Midland* was withdrawn from the Bradford train after only six days and sent on 6th June 1874 to France, once more on show, in the hope of winning contracts, preferably exclusive ones, for Pullman in France and Italy, especially since Naglemackers' Nord contract was to run out on June 30th.

Pullman's First European Success

On June 20th, Gourand secured Pullman's first European success, with the Upper Italian Railways (Società delle Ferrovie d'Alta Italia—SFAI), which worked the Mont Cenis Tunnel and the Riviera line, from the French border to north-west Italy. Three Pullman Cars had to be delivered to Turin as soon as possible or at least within a year, which caused Mr. Rapp to go off to Turin where the Pullmans were assembled from parts shipped direct from the United States to Genoa. A rather pathetic address in rhyme, presumably written by the interpreter, survives from the time the men were laid off in 1875, after the cars had been assembled:

TO
PULLMAN ESQUIRE, THE GREAT INVENTOR
OF THE
SALOON COMFORTABLE CARRIAGES
AND
MASTER RAPP THE CIVIL ENGINEER DIRECTOR
OF THE MANUFACTURE OF THE SAME

THE ITALIAN WORKMEN
BEG TO UMILIATE (*sic*)

Welcome, Welcome Master Pullman
The great inventor of the Saloon Carriages,
Italy will be thankful to the man
For now and ever, for ages and ages.
To Master Rapp we men are thankful,
Cause of his kindness and adviser sages,
Our hearts of true gladness is full:
And we shall remember him for ages.
Should Master Pullman ever succeed
To continue his work in Italy
What we wish to him indeed,
We hope to be chosen
To finish the work, and work as a man,
To show our gratitude to Master Pullman.

Turin, 1875

FINO AND HIS FRIENDS

Pullman does not seem to have taken up the 'exclusive rights for fifteen years, if wanted' offered by the SFAI. Or perhaps the railway 'forgot' this clause, for by 1879, Nagelmackers was able to bring his Indian Mail sleepers to Bologna. But there the Brindisi-bound passengers had to change, because Pullman's exclusive rights for twelve years, negotiated in 1874 with the Italian Southern Railway (Strade Ferrate Meridionali), were rigidly adhered to.

During 1874, the Mann fleet of boudoir sleeping cars grew from 16 to 42, with one Wagon-Salon, No. 43, built at the LC&DR works at Longhedge, London, and run on their line between London and Dover. It had a special compartment for honeymooners! Colonel Mann amused himself with sleeper No. 42, also built in the LC&DR shops to his own very bad design, in which passengers' beds were placed across the entrance doors. The draughts must have been howling!

But in 1875 Mann became bored with operating sleeping cars. No. 42 was on trial with the Great Northern Railway, running to Scotland on the East Coast route described in Chapter 8. Meanwhile, he lounged about in London's Langham Hotel, telling war stories, eating enormous breakfasts of mutton chops and champagne and ignoring Georges Nagelmackers' urgent correspondence. In the summer, he resigned as chairman and handed the entire control of the Mann Co. to Nagelmackers, who returned to Belgium determined to set up his own company once more. This time it would be in Brussels, with King Leopold II of the Belgians as his principal shareholder, and with permission to use the Royal Belgian Lions in his company's emblem.

On 4th December 1876, the present Compagnie Internationale des Wagons-Lits (CIWL) was founded at Brussels. It bought out Colonel Mann, taking over 53 cars and 22 contracts, and adding another the next day—Paris-Bordeaux. This gave access to Spain and turned the flank of the Rothschild-controlled Paris, Lyons & Mediterranean Railway, which meanwhile provided services to the Riviera and the Swiss and Italian frontiers. Unchallenged by Pullman in Germany and Austria, Wagons-Lits offered services radiating from Berlin and Vienna, with one in Roumania from Bucharest to Suczawa on the Austrian-Hungarian border. But rivalry between the two companies continued in France and Italy, Wagons-Lits trying to reach Rome, Pullman eager to attain Paris.

Pullman reigned supreme in England, where Nagelmackers immediately withdrew his two cars, and in 1875, Pullman placed parlour cars in the London-Brighton trains of the London, Brighton & South Coast Railway (LBSCR), which became a staunch ally. In 1876, the Pullman sleepers on the Midland were extended over its new line high across the Pennines to Carlisle, and thence over the North British Railway to Edinburgh, and to Glasgow, by way of the Glasgow & South Western Railway.

The First Dining Car in Britain

At this time both companies introduced dining cars. Pullman did so in 1879 by converting the parlour car *Ohio,* which ran on the Great Northern between London and Bradford or Leeds (in rivalry to the Midland route). *Ohio,* now named *Prince of Wales,* was thus the first bogie dining car in Europe.

In 1881, Pullman entered France with a saloon-dining car running over the Ouest Railway between Paris and Le Havre, the point of disembarkation for liners from America. Wagons-Lits had started some dining-car experiments on the Berlin-Anhalter Railway in Germany, and in 1881 they hastily introduced their first dining car on the French Riviera. This was a 6-wheeler (No. 107).

The Centenary of the first dining car in Britain, Pullman's *Prince of Wales,* originally the *Ohio,* was marked on 13th September 1979 by the 'Centenary Express' from Leeds to Kings Cross Station, London. The special menus and wine labels prepared for the oc-

11. CIWL No. 60, built in 1876. Toilet with compartments in day and night positions.

19

above left: 12. The special label for the wine served on the *Centenary Express* run from Leeds to London on 13th September 1979 to mark the centenary of the first dining car in Great Britain.

above centre: 13. The special menu prepared for the *Centenary Express*.

above right: 14. The Centenary Express Cake, a towering structure with the model *Flying Scotsman* running round and round it.

left: 15. The *Centenary Express* crossing Arlington Viaduct.

casion are reproduced here. Meeting the train on its arrival, Sir Peter Parker, chairman of the board for British Railways, cut the British Transport Hotels Centenary Express Cake. Thereafter came

seventeen days of excursions and static displays in various parts of Great Britain. The menu reproduced here served for the Southampton excursion.

3. Europe's First Train de Luxe: The *Brighton Belle*

Compared to the enormous journey of the *Orient Express,* the 53 miles (82 kilometres) from London to Brighton are nothing at all. They take the traveller to the seaside resort nearest London, on England's South Coast. One of the LBSCR's single-driver 2-2-2 engines (No. 334 'Petworth') designed by William Stroudley (the line's famous steam locomotive engineer) hauled the 'Pullman Limited Express', as the *Brighton Belle* was called at the time, on its inaugural run the 5th December 1881. The service was to last for 91 years until British Rail finally stopped it on 1st May 1972.

The train ran every day, twice in both directions. It outraged the church-going Victorian public and badly damaged its patronage by making the first of its regular round trips on Sunday. Would there not be dashing young gentlemen with loose morals, lurking in the smoking room, ready to sneak across into the drawing-room car and make importunate advances to the young ladies, despite their chaperones?

There were four Pullmans in the train. *Louise* and *Maud* (ex-*Ariel* and *Ceres*) ran at each end. They had a sliding-door luggage compartment, a guard's compartment and a servant's compartment. *Victoria* (formerly *Adonis*) had a small pantry buffet and was the gentlemen's smoker. *Beatrice,* now called a drawing-room car, for the ladies to withdraw into, was believed to be the first railway carriage in the world to be electrically lit. The twelve electric Edison lights, with bamboo-filtered incandescent bulbs, illuminated the car that used to be called *Globe!* In 1881, most people used candles or oil lamps at home. Argand kerosene lamps were the usual Pullman lighting, and *Beatrice* carried these, in case the batteries ran out.

London by then was so enormous a place that the London, Brighton & South Coast Railway (LBSCR) already had two termini: London Bridge, just across the Thames from the City of London; and Victoria, to the west over the Thames this time, close to Buckingham Palace and the Houses of Parliament. The London,

Chatham & Dover Railway shared this station, which today is London's starting point for Europe via the Straits of Dover. Here a specially installed steam engine drove a dynamo to recharge the Pullman train's batteries comprising a total of thirty-two cells installed underneath the floor of the car *Beatrice.*

A trial trip was made with the press on 14th October 1881. Messrs Pincaffe and Lachlan, engineers of France's Fauré Accumulator Co., switched on the lights in the first tunnel and kept them on all the way back from Brighton to London. Since the special made several unadvertised stops, the Frenchmen rather feared that the lights would go out before the train could arrive. This did not happen, much to the annoyance of some invited gas engineers, who reckoned the cost was four times that of the gas supply needed for such a train. They overlooked the fact that escaping gas turned railway accidents into infernos, by setting the smashed woodwork of the carriages ablaze.

It was a triumph for Monsieur Fauré of France, who designed the equipment, and also for George Pullman, who naturally introduced electric lighting into American Pullmans soon afterwards.

When new Pullman Cars arrived in Britain from the USA in 1888, built with Pullman's 1887 patent vestibule mentioned earlier, the whole train was lit by electricity. The power came from a specially built van supplied by the LBSCR and equipped with an axle-driven dynamo designed by Stroudley. The staff christened these vans 'Pullman Pups'. The success of the train was really Pullman's salvation, for the Midland Railway (of Great Britain) did not renew its fifteen-year contract. The American was forced to sell the MR fleet and remove his base to the LBSCR works at Brighton.

To the west of Southampton, the London & South Western Railway was building from nothing a new coastal resort, called Bournemouth, to rival Brighton on, if possible, a more elegant scale.

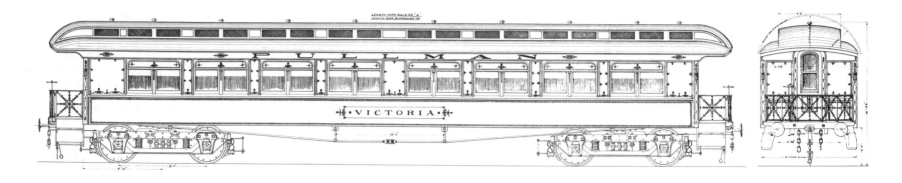

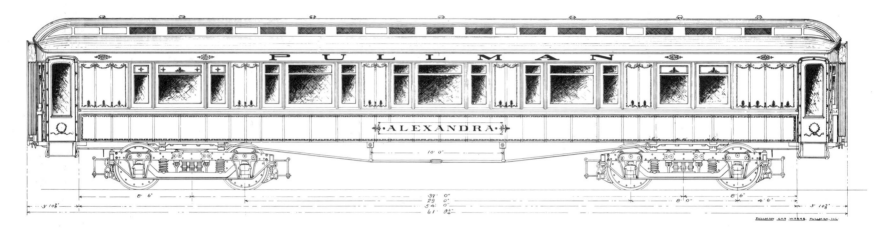

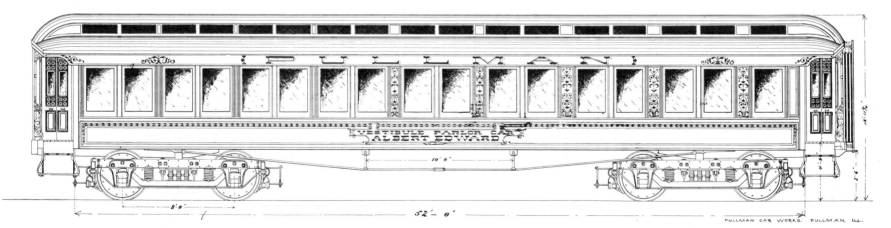

Since there was no more resplendent way to travel by day than in Pullman Cars, two new Pullmans (named *Duchess of Albany* and *Duchess of Fife*) were assembled at the Brighton works. On 21st April 1890 they began running, usually as single cars, not a Train de Luxe, from London to Bournemouth. One departed from the South Western's London terminus (Waterloo), at what became the traditional time for the *Bournemouth Belle*: 12:30 p.m. This was the last steam-hauled British all-Pullman train, and it continued in service until the line was electrified in 1960. Though lasting only from 1890 to 1912, the two Pullmans have gone down in history thanks

top: 16. Pullman Car *Victoria*, formerly *Adonis*, as remodelled at Derby in 1881. Vestibules added in 1889.

centre: 17. Pullman Car *Alexandria* (1889) with vestibules. Used in Pullman Limited Express (*Brighton Belle*).

bottom: 18. Pullman Car *Albert Edward* (1889), also used in the Pullman Limited Express.

to a pair of 'VIP' passengers for whom Sir Arthur Conan Doyle arranged tickets from Winchester to London. During their journey, Sherlock Holmes clears up for Dr. Watson the last vestiges of mystery in the case of the race horse 'Silver Blaze'.

The American depression of 1893 caused George Pullman to lay off four thousand men at Pullman, Illinois, and this was followed in 1894 by a major strike. So serious was the labor disruption that it had to be broken by army troops, the first time force had been used for such a purpose in the United States. The strike also broke George Pullman's health. He had a heart attack and died in Chicago suddenly, on 19th October 1897, at the age of sixty-six. His family continued to operate the firm. In a spirit of conciliation, Robert Todd Lincoln, son of the late President Lincoln, was selected as president of the company after Pullman's death.

On 2nd October 1898, the 'Pullman Limited Express' was re-introduced on the Brighton line as the 'Sunday Pullman Limited', after which the trains were called 'Limited' because the number of people carried was restricted to the seating. Some say 'Limited' referred to the number of stops made. The train now ran on Sundays only, and in 1899 its name was changed again to 'Brighton Limited'. Services in Great Britain gradually fell away, as the various railways preferred to run their own sleeping cars. By 1907 there were just two small Pullman sleeping cars left, working on the remote Highland Railway in Scotland, and the Pullman parlour cars on the LSWR and the Brighton Co.'s line. These comprised several individual cars as well as the 'Brighton Limited'.

In 1908, the assets of the British Pullman Palace Car Co., which in 1882 had been spun off as a subsidiary of Pullman USA, rather than maintained as part of the Pullman Palace Car Co. (Europe), were bought by Sir Davidson Dalziel, later Lord Dalziel of Wooler, to be operated as his own private company. He financed the purchase of new rolling stock through another of his companies, the Drawing Room Cars Co.

Lord Dalziel's first action was to restore the 'Brighton Limited' to daily runs, and it became very popular for trips to the Brighton Races. Next he ordered new Pullman Cars—the first such cars not manufactured in America. They were mounted on British-built 6-wheel (3-axle) bogies, like the last ones to be imported from the United States. Instead of the all-over umber paint that had always covered the bodyworks, the new equipment sported the famous cream upperworks, first introduced on the last three imported Pullmans, which had arrived from America in 1906, while Dalziel was in the middle of his delicate negotiations.

Built at Lancaster by the Metropolitan Amalgamated Carriage and Wagon Co. (whose name, Metro, has long been associated with Pullman construction), the British cars ceased to display the American-style clerestories. But because of Dalziel's authentic ownership, they retained Pullman's famous oval lavatory window with its segmented, leaded, frosted panes, a window that has remained the hallmark of veteran cars decades after the break with American Pullman.

A new train, a new owner and a new, dashing Edwardian age needed a new name for the 'Brighton Limited', which became the *Southern Belle*. And *Southern Belle* it stayed, until the final rake of electric Pullmans went into service on what had become, in 1922, the Southern Railway.

On the inaugural run of 8th November 1908, the engine was a 4-4-2 H1-class Atlantic, built by March and very similar in appearance to the Atlantics of H. A. Ivatt of the Great Northern Railway (of England). Later, however, 4-4-2T tank engines were used, which, although close in size, seemed to give this splendid train a second-rate, suburban look. Dalziel was more interested in profit than anything else, and though the *Southern Belle* continued to offer its famed comfort, esprit de corps and long service, the same mixture disappeared elsewhere as soon as it resulted in a loss. The *Southern Belle* was a money-spinner, even after the First World War broke out, when a run down to Brighton in Pullman ease was a way of shutting oneself off from the horrors.

In 1909, the Great Central Railway, which used the tracks of the Metropolitan Railway's extension line to Aylesbury, negotiated for Pullman cars in their London trains. Though this was cancelled, the Metropolitan, not to be outdone, made a thirty-year contract with Lord Dalziel in 1910 for two cars, *Mayflower* and *Galatea*. These not only ran to Baker Street; they also went round the Inner Circle Underground line of the Metropolitan to Liverpool Street or Aldgate. As you squeeze into your rush-hour London Transport train, do you dream of the egg and bacon breakfasts or evening whiskies once enjoyed by the nineteen lucky occupants of those spacious armchairs? The Pullmans, which had no gangways—since none existed on any other Metropolitan coach—were the first to be electrically hauled. Wealthy bankers and others travelled by this means between their City offices and their homes near Amersham or Aylesbury—Sir John Betjeman's 'Metroland', but in 1910 pure country where the Rothschild family had several large houses. Hot snacks had to be cooked on primus stoves instead of the usual Pullman range, since cooking was forbidden on the Underground, where the lavatories too had to be kept locked. *Mayflower* and *Galatea* continued to run under London Transport from 1933 to 1939; but no Pullman ever graced New York's subway!

On 30th September 1915, the Pullman Car Co. Ltd. was officially formed as a public company in the United Kingdom, to take over all the assets which Dalziel had acquired privately. The acquisition was done with great secrecy, with the result that little was known about who actually owned the Pullman Car Co. from 1908 to 1962. George Pullman's executors would probably not have sold out to Wagons-Lits. If you asked, you were told that the Pullman Car Co. was the British counterpart of the American Pullman. And so it was, for Lord Dalziel had not only bought the vehicles and the contracts, he also bought the right to use the word 'Pullman' on his trains, which by this time stood for 'super, the best', and was a household word in English, on both sides of the Atlantic. So the cars in Great Britain bore the word on the cantrail in typeface identical to that in the United States. If you persisted in suggesting that there was some connection with Wagons-Lits, you were in later years told that, yes, there was friendly co-operation between the two concerns, especially in regard to the *Golden Arrow,* since it extended into France. But if anyone pointed to the Wagons-Lits maps, they were vociferously declared to be a 'mistake'. (These were used outside Britain for a foreign public, and showed all the Pullman services as their own.)

There was already a new type of customer who wanted a treat, and who felt out of place in first class, among the regular travellers.

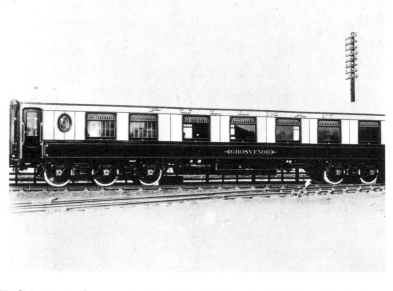

19. The all-Pullman *Southern Belle* at Stoat's Nest, near Croydon. LBSCR 13 class 4-42T No. 24 (built by Billinton).

20. Pullman car *Grosvenor* built in 1908, withdrawn in 1960. One of the first cars constructed in England, for the *Southern Belle*.

Thus, Dalziel introduced third-class Pullman cars. Their standard of comfort was the same as that which passes as first class today, with a single high-backed seat on one side of the gangway and two on the other. Since this was the only difference from the single armchairs of first class, the new Pullmans caused a sensation when they appeared in 1915.

You could travel in them with a third-class ticket, even on all the many cheap day excursions from London to Brighton offered for the masses, but once installed in one of the roomy seats, the excursionist could, for a supplementary fare of one shilling and sixpence, enjoy the same impeccable service as that in first class, where the supplement was now two shillings. Although third-class cars did not have the dignity of names, they were painted like first-class cars, with the name space occupied by the car number and 'Third Class' in big letters. At this period there was no second-class travel in Great Britain, except on boat trains.

After the Great War, while Lord Dalziel struggled with the demand for more Pullmans on other routes, the *Southern Belle* was ready to run again, steadfastly making its double return journey, this time behind the London, Brighton & South Coast Railway's 4-6-4T–class tank engines. One of them was named 'Remembrance', which made it a travelling war memorial bearing a tablet to fallen LBSCR staff.

The *Belle* was one of the few trains unaffected by the compulsory grouping together of British railway companies in 1922.

The 1908 cars continued in service on the *Belle* until 1924, but they were not withdrawn altogether until ten years later. Even then, one car remained. This was *Grosvenor*, designated a buffet car throughout its long life and twice reprieved from the scrap-heap at

the last moment, because it had a kitchen. *Grosvenor* was last seen running in traffic as late as 29th June 1960 (still called a buffet car, though it had been rebuilt in 1936 with a long bar counter), on a boat train of ordinary carriages conveying passengers from Southampton docks to London. It was being used to provide refreshments with Pullman staff, but without Pullman supplement.

The engine now hauling the *Southern Belle*, with 'Southern' on its tender, was one of the famous 'King Arthur' class, developed from the former London & South Western type of 4-6-0 and available once the even more powerful 'Lord Nelson' 4-6-0 engines went into service on the former LSWR routes. The engine power was not really a part of the Trains de Luxe, for different administrations supplied the locomotives for their respective parts of the journey.

There are exceptions to every rule, and the *Southern Belle*, whose journey was so short that it was virtually suburban, and whose many 'firsts' entitled it to pride of place among Trains de Luxe in this book, became the first Pullman in Britain capable of moving itself about. Beginning in 1933, it could draw power from a third 'live' rail, through the end coaches of each set of five Pullman cars.

The 'Southern Electric', as the system was snappily called, evolved under the direction of Sir Herbert Walker, general manager of the London & South Western Railway, who was appointed general manager of the new Southern Railway. Disregarding those who worried about foxhounds, he pushed the suburban trains out to the coast in 1933, but Brighton was not to be deprived of its *Southern Belle*, after over half a century of profitable service.

Lord Dalziel ordered new Pullmans, which came from Metro-Cammell of Birmingham (successors to the Lancaster concern mentioned earlier). From the front, the end third-class (motor) cars looked just like the Southern Electrics used elsewhere in the line, since they had no through corridors; but they were finished in Pullman chocolate-umber and bore the Pullman badge below the driver's windows. These cars also had luggage compartments, for in 1933 people still travelled with trunks and heavy fitted suitcases, handled of course by porters. Such pieces were far too large to go in the Pullman hand-baggage bays, which were situated close to the vestibule so that no baggage whatever should spoil the elegance of the interior décor. The three centre (trailer) cars of each rake comprised two first-class cars with kitchen and one third-class car without kitchen.

One last change in name occurred in the long history of the train, when the Mayor of Brighton (at that time a lady, Miss M. Hardy) renamed it *Brighton Belle* on 29th June 1934. By then the Southern Railway's dynamic management had introduced the *Bournemouth Belle* to the West and the *Kentish Belle* to the South East Coast resorts of Margate and Ramsgate. The Brighton train was to outlive all the other *Belles*.

The reason for the *Brighton Belle*'s long life can be found in its wartime history. After a first short withdrawal in the interests of sacrifice, during what was called 'the national emergency', the *Brighton Belle* began running again in 1940, albeit with rationed food and customers as well as staff who had been up all night in the Home Guard. The Home Guard has been lampooned in a popular 1970s television series 'Dad's Army', but perhaps not all viewers realized that it is the *Belle* that is really immortalized in Bud Flannagan's signature song:

Mr. Brown goes up to Town on the 8:21,
But he comes back each evening and he's ready with his gun.

While viewers may have recalled that Flannagan was the leading member of a group of comedians called the 'Crazy Gang', they forgot that the Gang lived in Brighton, which was why they always insisted on appearing at London's Victoria Palace Theatre, handy for the last train home. The *Belle* continued to run through that fateful summer, until hit by a bomb on 9th October 1940 at Victoria's No. 17 platform.

The bombing made it necessary to withdraw the cars and hide them in unlikely places, such as the Crystal Palace in outer London, where there were some spare sidings. The war went on for another five years, after which the Socialists returned to power and nationalized the railways. The Pullman Car Co. said nothing, and to everybody's surprise, it was not included in the list of companies forcibly taken over. Moreover, the Bill agreed to honour all contracts entered into by the old companies prior to nationalization, in order not to disrupt supplies of various items to the nationalized British Rail during the changeover. After the Bill became law, Pullmans suddenly reappeared on the lines, well patronized, like other forms of public transport, because petrol was rationed and the supply of new motor cars severely restricted.

The *Belle* was forced to run for a year coupled to a rake of ordinary coaches, with one composite first- and third-class Pullman (such as had run to Eastbourne, Hastings, Littlehampton, etc., since electrification in 1933), while the damaged rake of coaches was

21. The *Brighton Belle* electric all-Pullman train in the Sussex countryside in 1933. Withdrawn in 1972 after forty years of service.

being repaired at Birmingham. But in 1947 here she was again, in all her pre-war glory, running as usual three times a day and with a contract not expiring until 1962!

On the platform would be the conductor, resplendent in blue uniform and gold-braided peaked hat. He greeted his travellers and issued reservations to those who had not previously obtained them. At the door of each car, the white-coated attendant ushered you to your seat and placed the ladies' wraps and gentlemen's bowler hats on the gleaming brass rack above the window; your umbrella went in the small lower part of this special double rack. A lamp with a gold satin shade (later plastic) stood on every table. If it was the evening trip, a white terylene cloth would cover the glass table-top. The Pullman Car Co. had its own language for food, quite different from other people's. So there were 'oven-crisp rolls', and there was 'curled butter', while the Pullman Cold Collation meant ham and tongue.

By now somebody was blowing whistles outside the window, the attendant had disappeared to close the inward-opening doors, which only Pullmans had in Britain, while the *Brighton Belle* stole effortlessly out of the station up over the bridge across the Thames. The sparkle of the glasses and silver beneath the table lamps contrasted with the grime without. One of the dark-looking sheds, down below on the left, next to Pullman's Battersea victualling depot, housed the rake of *Brighton Belle* Pullmans reserved for minor repairs and major replenishment of stores, ready for changeover every three days. Then the *Belle* passed Clapham Junction, said to be the largest junction in England.

After Croydon and the longish tunnel at Redhill, the *Belle*'s shining passage full tilt through Gatwick Station usually attracted airline passengers in the adjoining waiting lounge. At last in the splendid Sussex countryside, it seemed a permanent part of the South English scene. The noble viaduct at Balcombe and Haywards Heath stations caught your eye, as the conductor appeared and handed you the Pullman check for your supplement. There was something exhilarating in the motion, the rhythm of the wheels lurching over crossings as you explored what lay behind the famous frosted-glass window, and found an elegant toilet whose scented soap was so identical to that encountered elsewhere in Europe that it nearly betrayed the great Pullman ownership secret! On this occasion there was a coffee stain on the spotless napery, but small print on the menu read: 'Our staff take every possible care and precaution in the service of refreshments, and the Company cannot be held responsible for minor accidents of spillage, etc., which may occur on account of excessive movement of the train'. The *Brighton Belle* was showing its age, and £70,000 was spent renewing its bogies in 1955 to try to ease 'the excessive movement of the train'.

The attendant hovered with the bill, the train slowed down. Then came a squeal of wheel flange against rail as the *Brighton Belle* drew into Brighton's curiously curved platforms. In an hour you had arrived, and non-stop, unlike any BR train today, between London and Brighton!

In the cutting to the right stood Pullman's workshops at Preston Park, opened in 1928, which were closed on 1st January 1964. Here the *Belle* would snooze each day between afternoon tea at 4:00 and redeparture for London at 5:25, arriving there in time for dinner. One day during the pause at Brighton a young lady chose to commit suicide in one of the *Belle*'s lavatories. The press never disclosed whether the motive bore any relation to the curious name of the siding: 'Lover's Walk'.

Having been bought up in 1954 by the nationalized British Railways, the Pullman Car Co. Ltd. ceased to exist when its contracts expired at the end of 1962. Not until 1976 did a Wagons-Lits internal document come to light, showing how Pullman had been totally owned by CIWL since 1935.

In 1967 British Rail—which sometime earlier had painted out the proud Pullman badge with a large yellow warning panel, carried on the front of all non-steam trains for safety—repainted the cars, obliterating their names: *Hazel, Audrey, Gwen, Doris, Mona* and *Vera*. The *Brighton Belles* disappeared under the standard BR blue-and-white livery, but with their title still set forth on the straight sides of cars, thereby giving the train an air of difference. All British Rail's standard-size coaches have curved sides.

The *Brighton Belle*'s popularity persisted. Laurence Olivier, the famous British actor whose name adorns part of the new National Theatre (the part called the 'Olivier Theatre'), was among those who fought hard for its retention.

Until 1972 the *Brighton Belle* stood out like a sore thumb of private enterprise, gliding out of London every day of the year, and arriving at Brighton's imposing terminus exactly one hour later, almost always on time. Many of the staff had been with the train since before the Second World War, and they passed on the tradition of service. Perhaps more than any other train, the *Brighton Belle* showed a new generation of ordinary folk what Train de Luxe travel was like.

By the time BR managed finally to destroy the last service offered by former private coaches in its ownership, there were nostalgic people ready to pay to stop the proud carriages from going to the breakers, twenty-five years after the Southern Railway had been nationalized. Most of the cars have become pubs or cafés. Two motor-coaches and one on loan from Travellers-Fare are preserved by the Brighton Pullman Association, located appropriately enough in the former Preston Park Pullman Works. Two other cars, *Audrey* and No. 286, have been bought by Sea Containers for their London-Venice Orient Express and converted to locomotive haulage. They were not permitted to run on British Railways in time to commemorate the Centenary of the Pullman Limited Express, with a trip from London to Brighton on 5th December 1981. They went in April 1982, the centenary of George M. Pullman's visit to Brighton.

II

THE TRIUMPHS OF PROGRESS

4. The Orient Express

Lend me your great noise, your grand allure so soft,
Your nightly flit across lit-up Europe,
O Train de Luxe! And the squeaky music,
Which wails along your shiny leather-panelled corridors,
Whilst behind the lacquered doors with heavy brass locks
The millionaires sleep.

Singing, I traverse your corridors
And I follow your run to Vienna and Budapest,
Blending my voice to your hundred thousand voices,
O Harmonious Train!

(*Prête-moi ton grand bruit, ta grande allure si douce,*
Ton glissement nocturne à travers l'Europe illuminée,
O Train de Luxe! Et l'angoissante musique,
Que bruit le long de tes couloirs de cuir dorée,
Tandis que derrière les portes laquées, aux loquets de cuivre lourd
Dorment les millionaires.

Je parcours en chantonnant tes couloirs
Et je suis ta course vers Vienne et Budapest,
Melant ma voix à tes cent mille voix
O Harmonika-Zug!)

Valéry Larbaud, *Ode*

Yes, probably you have seen the poem before. If you know any French, you may even have read it aloud to yourself, and marvelled how the rhythm of the rails corresponds so perfectly to Monsieur Larbaud's stanzas. Somehow the elan or 'zing' of the Orient Express is all contained there: the sudden lapse into German for the last line; the creaking of the mahogany round the leather panels of the corridor, as the sleeping car snakes across the points; the hiss of escaping steam; the roar like a waterfall, which for some reason seems to envelop non-air-conditioned cars, particularly the diners. These are just some of the 'hundred thousand voices'.

Murder on the Orient Express had a fabulous success in 1974. The film of Agatha Christie's novel was seen by millions of viewers who probably had never previously given the Orient Express a second thought. The steam engine vied with the rest of the all-star cast for top billing, and the 1930s Wagons-Lits cars gave added authenticity to the atmosphere of intrigue and mystery long associated with the real train.

The Orient Express passengers were always thought to be special, though many were only wealthy tourists just enjoying the fabled journey, daringly novel when the Orient Express first started, in 1883. Business men and bankers, opera stars and orchestral conductors, government couriers with their valises chained to their wrists—all became regular travellers well known to the staff. Berths were permanently reserved for their couriers by both the British and French governments, whether used or not. From time to time, some 'bankers' proved to be a bit less genuine than others, transporting smuggled gold or stolen bearer bonds. Along with them came secret-service agents or plain spies disguised as various other kinds of traveller; and reserved, mysterious gentlemen of noble birth, who turned out to be kings travelling incognito or politicians, often fleeing their own countries. Over the years refugees seemed never to be in short supply.

Undoubtedly fares were high in the 1880s, and only the rich could afford to go. First-class rail tickets were obligatory, and with the supplement for Wagons-Lits, the cost totalled around £60 (60 pounds sterling). For the price of a round trip to Istanbul for two, you could rent a decent home in a smart part of London for about a year. There were specially reduced supplements for servants travelling with their masters, £15 less, and servants' compartments at the end of the cars for them to travel in. The valet's fare was roughly equal to his annual wage at the time!

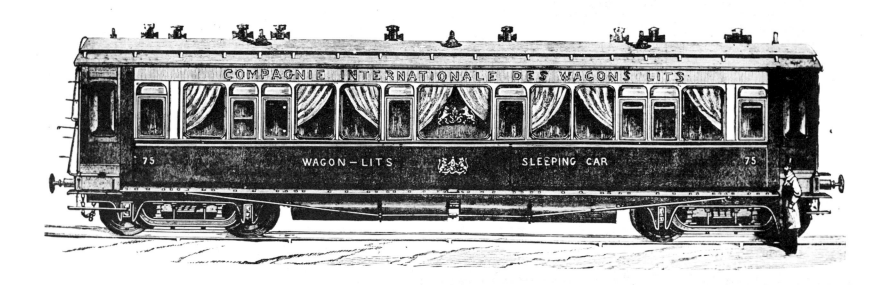

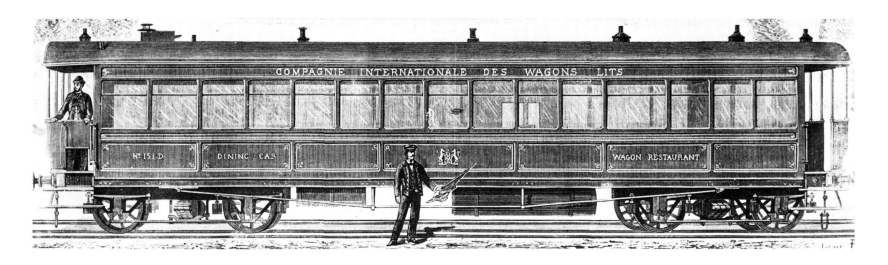

top: 22. CIWL No. 75 (1882), the first bogie sleeping car built for the company. Used in the Orient Express. (Georges Nagelmackers on extreme right.)

above: 23. CIWL No. 151 (1883), the first bogie dining car built for the company. Used in the Orient Express.

One of the earliest regular travellers on the Orient Express was Sir Basil Zaharoff, who first began his international arms-dealing career about 1885. He lived permanently in hotels, and in Istanbul used the Pera Palace, which Nagelmackers had built specially for Orient Express clients, as there were no Western-style hotels at all in Istanbul when the train started. A second hotel, the Therapia Summer Palace, followed soon afterwards.

Sir Basil was born in Turkey, and in his early years he operated as an Istanbul 'guide' (or, rather, pimp). He also served in the city's fire brigade, although arsonist or salvage expert would perhaps be a better description than fireman. In later years, when Sir Basil had received his English knighthood for arms-buying services during World War I, he used to say that he started on his international career as a sleeping-car conductor. This does not seem to have been recorded officially, or even by those journalists eager to recount his love affair in the Orient Express with a beautiful Spaniard, the Duchess of Marchena. She escaped from her mad husband by eloping into Zaharoff's compartment (always No. 7) whilst on her honeymoon! After the Duke's death Zaharoff finally married her, thirty-eight years later.

29

24. The Orient Express timetable effective as of 1st November 1883.

The idea of joining Vienna to Constantinople by railway had been actively pursued since 1869, when Baron Maurice de Hirsch obtained the concession to build the Oriental Railways (CO or Chemins de Fer Orientaux). Because of his long and very prosperous involvement, Hirsch became known as Türkenhirsch. Starting separately but simultaneously to build inland from the Turkish ports of Constantinople (Istanbul), Dedeagatch (Alexandropolis) and Salonica, he had by 1873 built a line from the first two places through Edirne towards Sofia, as far as Tatar Pazardjik, in what is now Bulgaria, but what was then the autonomous Turkish province of Eastern Roumelia.

The non-completion of the line was due to Russian intrigue. In 1878 Bulgaria, aided by Russia, broke away from Turkey, thereby delaying railway construction. So the Orient Express then linked Paris only with Munich, Vienna, Budapest and Bucharest, and you can still travel in it now, nightly to Vienna, going on to Bucharest three times a week.

The Russians did not want Germany and Austria to have easy rail access to Constantinople; neither did the British, whose sea trade would be damaged. Lines going inland from ports were another matter. The first of these was from Varna on the Black Sea to Rustchuck (now Rusé) on the south side of the Danube. Built across north-east Bulgaria, then a Turkish province, and known as the Austrian Eastern Railway, it cut off a great loop that the Danube makes before entering the Black Sea. Here was another of Baron de Hirsch's enterprises, this one completed in 1870 (before the Oriental Railways were ready). So the first route to Constantinople was by railway from Bucharest south to Giurgewo (now Giurgiu), where a bridge now replaces the ferry that in those days took travellers from Roumania across to Rustchuck in Bulgaria.

By 1882, the Paris-Vienna traffic had become so heavy that the railways found it necessary to run trains of sleeping and dining cars only. This in turn created great possibilities for time-saving, since it eliminated the need to stop for meals. Moreover, with a small number of first-class, important passengers, who had only hand baggage for inspection, delays at frontiers could be shortened. Heavy luggage, called 'Registered Baggage', could be sealed in the van and examined on arrival.

Agreement was reached for a trial run, and on 10th October 1882, the very first International Train de Luxe of Wagons-Lits carriages only, with a van provided by the Est Railway, was to be seen in Paris' Gare de Strasbourg, as the Gare de l'Est was then called. A large crowd had gathered to see it start, at nine minutes to seven in the evening.

The Est supplied one of their '500' class 2-4-0 engines, built in 1875. Behind it came No. 75, CIWL's first bogie sleeping car, the first bogie carriage built in Europe, outside Great Britain. Then followed CIWL's first diner, No. 107, and two 6-wheeled sleepers, of which one (No. 77) was brand new and making its first run. Details of these cars are in the Appendices.

For the generations of Hungarian or Roumanian workers who regularly watched it pass, though they knew they would never set foot in it, even a glimpse of the elegant interior of the Orient Express would bring its moment of excitement. It is easy to forget that railways were once a novelty, and it took several years to complete the Orient Express all the way to Istanbul (then known as Constantinople).

In the decade before the Orient Express, the railways revolutionized Eastern European journeys. Hitherto, travel had been a nightmare of hazardous, bandit-prone stages over roads thick with mud or dust, from one flea-ridden inn to another, where no one spoke any comprehensible language, save a few words of broken German or French. Important travellers often had to have escorts of Austrian Imperial troops. Now they could roll by safely in the comfort of a modern train.

opposite: 25. The Orient Express winter timetable for 1888–89, the first year of direct running to Istanbul. Note: no passports required; also rival routes to Paris: SER via Boulogne and LCDR via Calais.

above left: 26. The Orient Express in Turkey about 1910. Two sleeping cars, one dining.

above right: 27. The Ostend-Vienna Express at Ostend about 1910. SNCB 4-4-0, of Scottish design.

left: 28. The Orient Express near Vienna in 1913. Golsdorf 4-4-2 locomotive.

From Paris to Avricourt, the maximum speed was 65–75 kilometres per hour. Here the Est engine came off, and one from the Imperial Management of the Alsace-Lorraine Railway came on. Speed in this part of Germany was lower than in France. Between Ulm and Munich it averaged 57 kilometres per hour, but the Bavarian Railways increased it to 60 kilometres per hour on their line to Simbach, where the Royal Austrian State Railways Co. took over. For some reason, they stopped 3 times on the way to Vienna, but even so the train saved between 3 and 4 hours over the ordinary time, taking 27 hours 53 minutes for the 1,350-kilometre journey and arriving just before midnight on 11th October. The overall average speed was 48.7 kilometres per hour, the weight was 101 tons, and half of the 20 axles on the train were not equipped with any braking gear.

After a day in the Austrian capital, the sleeping-car train came to life again and slowly drew out of Vienna. This time there were several extra stops and slowings in Austria, but presently Deutsch-Avricourt was reached, where the Est 2-4-0 stood ready and waiting. The speed rose, and when the engine tore down the bank between Loxeville and Bar-le-Duc, it reached 98 kilometres per hour. So they drew into the Gare de Strasbourg early, at an overall speed of 48 kilometres per hour. Enthusiasm abounded, and a conference was arranged in Constantinople for February 1883, at which all interested parties would meet to discuss the service.

The conference proved a great success. The weight limit of the train was agreed at 110 tons between Paris and Vienna, and 88 tons beyond, achieved by detaching one of the train's two vans. Normally there would be two Wagons-Lits with a wagon-salon-restaurant between them; extra sleepers could be run if required, up to the weight limit. The contract was drawn up by CIWL with the railway representatives, whose administrations ratified it, each by turn, between 2nd March and 2nd May 1883. Those concerned were:

The Management of the Est Railway Co. of France;

The Imperial Management of the Alsace Lorraine Railways, Berlin;

The General Management of the State Railways of the Grand Duchy of Baden;

right: 29. The Orient Express diverted through Switzerland, near Wettingen (Zurich), in 1919. SBB 4-6-0 No. 721.

below: 30. The Orient Express in July 1959, leaving Munich by the original route. Diverted via Simbach instead of Salzburg. It has to be steam-hauled, by DB 01 class Pacific No. 01-052.

The General Management of the Kingdom of Würtemberg State Railways;

The General Management of the Lines of Communication of the Kingdom of Bavaria;

The Imperial and Royal Management for the Operation of the State Railways, Vienna;

The Imperial and Royal Austrian State Railways Co.;

The Royal General Management of the Roumanian Railways.

All was now ready—except the new bogie sleeping and dining cars. So the 6-wheeled sleeping cars, the 6-wheeled diner and the only bogie sleeper were the ones that made the trial, when the 'Express d'Orient' made its first run, on 5th June 1883. There was no official inauguration. By October, Rathgeber had delivered the sleeping cars from their Munich factory, and the recently opened Wagons-Lits works at Marly-les-Valenciennes near Paris built the first of the bogie diners (No. 151).

On 4th October 1883 the Orient Express took aboard 'the most unlikely' fraternity of some forty state officials, engineers, execu-

tives and publicists, as one of the latter, Edmond About, a French writer, described them in his book *De Pontoise à Constantinople*. England was represented by Otto de Blowitz, the illustrious Paris correspondent of the *Times*, bent (successfully) on interviewing the Sultan of Turkey. (This had never been achieved before by any Western newspaper. De Blowitz 'Interviews' had something of to-day's TV commentator's personalized cross-examination of heads of states.)

Among the nineteen Frenchmen on board was *Figaro*'s Georges Boyer, journalist almost as eminent as de Blowitz. Also present were Germans, Austrians (whose ladies came aboard at Strasbourg), a Dutchman and a Turkish Effendi, one of those cosmo-

31. Filming *Murder on the Orient Express* at Landy Carriage Shed, Paris (Nord). SNCF 230; G 353 4-6-0; F 1283; WR 4271; WL 3504; WP 4163.

politan officials of perfect grace and manners, fluent in many languages, who seem to have vanished forever in the more democratic days of post-World War II. Lastly there came a large group of Belgians, among them, Nagelmackers himself.

All were overwhelmed by the splendour of the dining car, with its Genoese velvet curtains, its Gobelins tapestries on the walls, its engraved silverware and sparkling crystal goblets on the tables. And they had a high old time, for the Lucullan meals were worthy of the surroundings. Nothing like this had ever been seen before on such a lengthy journey.

The subtle changing of identity within the very same luxury coaches, whenever the track changed nationality, gave these cars a compelling fascination, out of all proportion to the actual splendour of their physical appointments, though they were far more comfortable than anything yet seen on rails in Central Europe, where Pullman never penetrated. The captivating charm of the ever-shifting surroundings of the train seemed somehow to rub off on some of the Europeans on board, notably the Wagons-Lits Co.'s sleeping-car conductors, whose chameleonic ability to adapt totally to each succeeding country through which the train passed has become legendary. This bewitching transmutation was coupled to courteous service as well as to knowledge of three languages.

The appointments of the sleepers, with soft wall-to-wall carpeting and plush upholstery, with running water and WCs in the toilets, and crisp white linen on the beds, were more appreciated after Rusé, where the passengers jolted in 4-wheeled carriages, while meals became picnics of uneatably tough fowls and weird Turkish pastries. Bulgarian bandits pillaged one station, gagging the station-master and setting fire to the buildings, just before the train arrived. From Varna to Istanbul and back the illustrious trav-

32. Filming *Murder on the Orient Express*. Dinner in Pullman Car No. 4163. (On the right, Sir John Gielgud, doyen of British Shakespearean actors.)

ellers used an Austrian Lloyd liner. Eventually they all returned safely to Rusé, and home again to Paris, bowled over by the Wagons-Lits Co.'s plenitudinous hospitality.

But Vienna was still unconnected to Constantinople. From Vienna, the Royal Austrian State Railways Co.'s line through Budapest continued as far as Orsova, on the Roumanian frontier near the Iron Gates, beside the Danube. In 1876 the line met the Roumanian Railways, which the Austrian State Railways operated by agreement, running through Craiova to Bucharest and Giurgiu.

The Royal Austrian State Railways was a company set up with French capital to buy and operate the state-owned main lines in Austria and Hungary from 1850 onwards. Then in 1869 the Hungarian government formed the Royal Hungarian State Railways to take over various privately owned lines in Hungary. The Hungarians did not like the Austrian company, since it was French-owned and under Austrian jurisdiction. They resisted attempts by the company to link Budapest with Belgrade (the capital of Serbia), and in 1882 built their own line from Budapest to Subotica in Serbia. The Serbian line on to Belgrade, with the bridge across the River Sava, was ready in 1883.

On 3rd September 1884 the Belgrade-Nis railway began operations, and in 1885 the Orient Express initiated service once a week from Budapest to Belgrade and Nis. From Nis to Sofia and to Tatar Pazadjik, there was a frightful horse diligence, organized by Wagons-Lits. The ferocious coachman named Brankovits, well able to withstand any bandit assaults, thought nothing of starting at three in the morning. The roadside halts were extremely unpleasant and the food revolting. Instead of just walking, the passengers had to push through the mud in wet weather. This went on for three years, partly because of the terrain, but mostly because the Russians were in no hurry to see the Bulgars complete the line. The guide-book painted a rosy picture, prompting a critic to remark that it only followed the route one way, since no one ever returned by this road. Passengers preferred to go by ship to Varna!

Nagelmackers sent Viscount de Richemont to obtain King Ferdinand's signature for railway operations in Bulgaria. Etiquette was strict, uniform essential, but de Richemont, because of the privations of Brankovits' coach, had not got one with him and thus appeared before the King dressed as a captain of his own police. 'What a ridiculous country', said the King, as he signed the contract. De Richemont was rewarded with the direction of Wagons-Lits in Spain.

Wagons-Lits cars first ran through to Istanbul in 1888. This saved over 14 hours compared to the Varna route. Because local time was not synchronized in Europe in those days, the trip took about 81 hours going east but only 77 going west. The Austrians used two times at once, that of Vienna and Budapest. Thus, the dining-car clock was kept to Paris time.

From 1900 to 1902 the Paris cars were joined by a Berlin-Constantinople sleeper at Budapest. The Orient ceased to operate during World War I, though the Germans ran a military 'Balkanzug' that also took privileged civilians, from Berlin to Istanbul.

Restarted after World War I as a military train between Paris and Vienna (then continuing to Warsaw), the Orient Express was not fully restored as a Train de Luxe until 1932, and it ceased to be exclusively sleepers and diners again in 1939. Its place was taken in 1919 by the Simplon Orient Express (Paris-Venice-Istanbul) described in Chapter 12. The Simplon route has been the only one used by the regular Paris-Istanbul sleeper since World War II, and this service finally ended on 22nd May 1977.

Apart from a short break in 1962, the Orient Express sleeper from Paris to Bucharest has continued to run, regularly crossing the Iron Curtain. It is still staffed by Wagons-Lits, changing the Austrian conductor at Vienna for a Hungarian.

5. The Rome Express and the *Palatino*

On his return from America, Nagelmackers' first endeavour was to make arrangements to take passengers on the Indian Mail postal train, running between Ostend and Brindisi via the Brenner Pass. The Franco-Prussian War of 1870 delayed matters, and no sooner was it over than the General Post Office of Great Britain abandoned the route, in favour of the shorter one from Calais by way of Modane and the Mont Cenis Tunnel from France to Italy, opened in 1871.

The Index to the 1879 Wagons-Lits pocket timetable listed the Paris-Modane sleeper, and the timetable inside showed the train going to Turin—at the whims and fancies of the SFAI (Upper Italian Railways). From 31st May 1879, SFAI permitted the Calais-Modane sleepers, included in the once-weekly Indian Mail which Nagelmackers had at last supplied to the P&O Steam Navigation Co.'s special train, to work through to Bologna. Here the P&O passengers had to change into a Pullman in order to reach Brindisi Marittima, as we saw in Chapter 2.

In 1882, George Pullman, it seems, visited Europe, where he saw the electric lighting in his Brighton train and had a long discussion with Nagelmackers on a suggested amalgamation. The enterprise was to be called Compagnie des Wagons-Lits et des Wagons-Salons and registered in London, while all rolling stock was to be bought from the Pullman works at Pullman, Illinois, and shipped over from the USA. This would not have appealed to Nagelmackers, who had previously experienced the problems of controlling his Continental operations (through Colonel Mann) from a faraway London office. And he was already having enough trouble getting the Orient Express cars delivered from Germany, let alone shipped across the Atlantic.

Against the Wagons-Lits fleet of 110 cars, Pullman had 12 sleepers in Italy, 4 saloon restaurant services scattered about Europe, and 45 assorted sleepers and parlour cars in England, not all of which were needed there. The fusion was to be on a 50/50 basis, despite the small size of Pullman's Continental activity. Nagel-

mackers turned Pullman down and planned a third Train de Luxe from Paris to Trouville-Deauville of wagons-salons in 1884, to thwart Pullman, who was still operating between Paris and Le Havre, but not between Paris and Caen, a route that CIWL had secured, along with the Trouville-Deauville service. But so short was the supply of cars that in order to equip the Trouville Express Train de Luxe, CIWL had to buy those in the Austrian Imperial train, which they converted.

Wagons-Lits had, Nagelmackers declared on the 28th February 1883, spent a mad amount of money in Italy for relatively poor results. Meanwhile, at Derby, five refurbished Pullmans were standing idle, surplus to requirements but ready to reinforce the twelve in Italy. Pullman sought an ally to help him move the cars to Italy, with passengers to pay the cost, instead of having to pay to run them all that way empty. And a powerful ally appeared in the person of Thomas Cook, who ever since the famous Leicester excursion of 1856 had reigned supreme as a booking agent for foreign travel. In 1879 Wagons-Lits began booking, in addition to sleeper berths and hotel reservations, further travel facilities, doing so in response to their passengers' requests, though the first Wagons-Lits Travel Office was not opened until 1886 at the Bazar de Voyage, 3 Place de l'Opéra, Paris.

When Rome staged its Italian Fine Arts Exhibition in 1883, Thomas Cook became the general passenger agent. Together, in the greatest secrecy, Cook and Pullman planned a special Train de Luxe, to leave Calais on 23rd February 1883, which was of course a Friday, the very day the Indian Mail ran. Naturally the route went via the Mont Cenis and Bologna to Rome, which permitted passengers for Brindisi to change into the regular Pullman train waiting at Bologna.

On the last day in his office at Brussels, before starting for the Constantinople conference, Nagelmackers came across a little notice in the London *Times*. It was the first he knew about any special

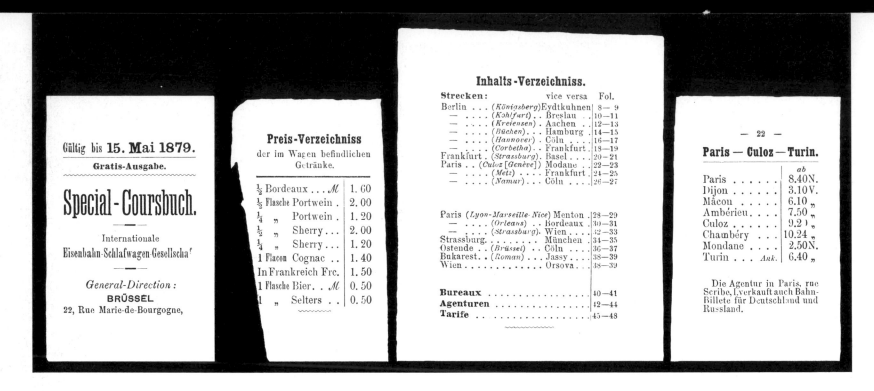

Gültig bis **15. Mai 1879.**

Gratis-Ausgabe.

Special-Coursbuch.

Internationale
Eisenbahn-Schlafwagen-Gesellschaf'

General-Direction :
BRÜSSEL
22, Rue Marie-de-Bourgogne,

Preis-Verzeichniss
der im Wagen befindlichen
Getränke.

½ Bordeaux . . .	ℳ	1. 60
½ Flasche Portwein .		2. 00
¼ „ Portwein .		1. 20
½ „ Sherry . . .		2. 00
¼ „ Sherry . . .		1. 20
1 Flacon Cognac . .		1. 40
In Frankreich Frc.		1. 50
1 Flasche Bier. .	ℳ	0. 50
1 „ Selters . .		0. 50

— 22 —

Paris — Culoz — Turin.

	ab
Paris	8.40 N.
Dijon	3.10 V.
Mâcou	6.10 „
Ambérieu	7.50 „
Culoz	9.2) „
Chambéry . . .	10.24 „
Mondane	2.50 N.
Turin . . . Ank.	6.40 „

Die Agentur in Paris, rue
Scribe, I. verkauft auch Bahn-
Billete für Deutschland und
Russland.

33. CIWL pocket timetable of 1879. Note the Paris-Modane service, extended to Turin.

train from Calais to Rome, which was in flagrant breach of the Wagons-Lits exclusive rights on the Nord and PLM. Nagelmackers wrote urgently to his 'dear colleague' Napoleon Schroeder, who presided over the Paris headquarters, for at this time there was a sort of 'dual monarchy' in the Wagons-Lits organization, rather like the Hapsburgs' arrangements for Austria-Hungary. He enclosed the Wagons-Lits copies of the contracts, always kept at Brussels, so Schroeder could see the extent of the infringement by 'our enemies, Cook and Pullman'. He may also have forwarded the copy of the offending handbill reproduced here (but not in facsimile since it is too faded to photograph) and believed to be the only one to survive Hitler's bombs, which destroyed the Pullman records at London's Victoria Station, along with the *Brighton Belle*.

ITALIAN FINE ARTS EXHIBITION
SPECIAL PULLMAN CAR TRAIN TO ROME
Friday February 23rd 1883

THOS. COOK & SON

Have pleasure in announcing that they have arranged with the Pullman Car Company and with the various Continental Railways for a Special Train, composed of Pullman Drawing-room and Sleeping Cars of the newest pattern, to be run from Calais to Rome, without change. Passengers for the Indian Mail will change at Bologna. Passengers holding ordinary First-class Through Return or Circular Tickets will be allowed to travel by this train if provided with Pullman Car Supplementary Tickets, which will be issued only at THOS. COOK & SON'S Chief Office, Ludgate Circus, or their Branch Offices, 35, Piccadilly, or 445, West Strand, at the following rates:

Use of Drawing-room and Sleeping Car (reserved berth):

*Calais to Bologna, Florence, or Rome	£2.16.0
*Paris to Bologna, Florence, or Rome	£2. 0.0
*Paris to Turin	£1.18.0
*Calais or Paris to Brindisi	£2.17.6
*Turin or Bologna to Rome	16.10

*In addition to first-class fare.

A representative of Thos. Cook & Son will accompany the train throughout.

Passengers by this train will be conveyed by
SPECIAL STEAMER FROM DOVER TO CALAIS.

Ample time will be allowed for meals at the various buffets en route.
Passengers will leave London on Friday, Feb. 23rd, at the following times:

HOLBORN VIADUCT, 9.55 a.m.; LUDGATE HILL 9.56 a.m.
VICTORIA 10 a.m.

The following is the Time-table of the Train:

Leave	London	9.55 a.m.
Leave	Dover	12.00 noon
Leave	Calais	2.26 p.m. by special Pullman train
Leave	Boulogne	3.35 p.m.
Leave	Amiens	5.36 p.m.
Arrive	Paris (P.L.M. Station)	
Leave	Paris (P.L.M. Station)	10.25 p.m.
Arrive	Dijon	5.06 a.m.
Leave	Dijon	5.17 a.m.
Arrive	Macon	7.50 a.m.
Leave	Macon	7.55 a.m.
Arrive	Culoz	10.36 a.m.
		breakfast
Leave	Culoz	11.14 a.m.

34. Grand Luxe from London to Paris, 1889–93, in the Club Train. The severance of Pullman from his English base on the Midland Railway in 1888—combined with the opening of the direct line, which permitted Calais-Paris trains to avoid reversal at Boulogne Ville—made Nagelmackers believe that the time was ripe to re-enter the English scene. Resentment towards supplements prompted Midland Railway to take over all Pullman's diners and parlour cars running on its line in 1883, and not to renew the sleeper contract after 1888. It seemed that the 1889 Paris Exhibition, complete with a section called 'The Means of Transport', would prove to be enough of an attraction to cause the London smart-set to fill a special Train de Luxe and make popping off to Paris in the late afternoon their latest escapade.

'The Paris Limited Mail' was to be a prestigious London-Dover train with supplementary fare and four brand-new wagons-salons from Belgium, sheathed in shiny green paint instead of gloomy old varnished teak. And if the gentlemen wished to smoke, they could do so in the luggage van, in order not to pollute the atmosphere for the 'grandes dames' travelling in these sumptuous saloons. Accordingly, the 'fourgons-fumoirs', as the vans were called, had bogies, a smoking compartment and a kitchen as well as the guard's look-out.

For the French train, Wagons-Lits ordered eight wagons-salons, because two rakes would probably be needed. These were built in France and constituted Wagons-Lits' first large French order for saloons.

John Staats Forbes, the chairman of the LC&DR, was persuaded to build a special ship, the *Calais-Douvres* (the second of that name) so as to have the edge over the rival South Eastern Railway from London to Dover, which ran via Folkestone and operated the Folkestone-Boulogne ships exclusively.

As there was a pool of cross-Channel facilities, the SER's chairman, Sir Edward Watkin, arch-enemy of Forbes, declared that the LC&DR exclusiveness was a breach of their pool agreement and insisted on his own 'Continental Club Train', for which Wagons-Lits supplied three more saloons.

Unfortunately the service was far from a financial success and thus became the first Train de Luxe to be taken off, for in reality the service proved less magical than it had set out to be.

Here an English couple board the boat at Calais, while a French porter in traditional blue humps their port-manteau, watched by the steward dressed in a Wagons-Lits uniform. Perhaps the English conductors crossed the Channel to meet them, as would those of the *Golden Arrow* at a later date.

35. The Rome Express from Paris, entering Genoa in July 1930. Lx-type sleeping cars. Note: overhead wires 3000V DC (centre) currently used, and the 3-phase current originally used; the current change-over point in background.

Arrive	Modane	3.35 p.m.
		dinner
Leave	Modane	5.40 p.m.
Arrive	Turin	9.20 p.m.
Leave	Turin	9.40 p.m.
Arrive	Bologna	5.27 a.m.
Leave	Bologna	5.41 a.m.
Arrive	Florence	10.00 a.m.
		breakfast
Leave	Florence	10.30 a.m.
Arrive	Rome	7.15 p.m.

As a limited number of tickets only will be issued, early application is necessary to Thos. Cook & Son.

Through Registration of Baggage from London to Turin, Bologna, Brindisi, Florence and Rome.

Indian Mail passengers can remain at Bologna until 9.20 a.m. on Sunday morning, leaving by Pullman Express for Brindisi.

FIRST-CLASS ORDINARY SINGLE-JOURNEY FARES:

	£	s.	d
London to Turin	6	19	9
Bologna	8	15	1
Brindisi	12	1	9
Florence	9	6	3
Rome	10	16	9

To the above fares must be added the supplemental charge for travelling by the Special Pullman Express as given on the other side.

Hand luggage only allowed in the Cars. All other luggage must be registered at the station of departure.

All communications to be addressed to:

THOS. COOK & SON

Specially appointed by H.R.H. the Prince of Wales; Passenger Agents for the Royal British Commission: Vienna 1873; Philadelphia 1876; and Paris 1878; General Passenger Agents to the Rome Fine Arts Exhibition, 1883.

CHIEF OFFICE—Ludgate Circus, London
West End Office—35 Piccadilly (opposite St. James's Church)
Strand Office—445 West Strand
Euston Road Office—In Front of St. Pancras Station
Crystal Palace—Tourist Court

BRANCH OFFICES

(There followed 30 offices including Dublin, Paris [2], Nice, Cologne, Brussels, Geneva, Rome, Naples, Malta, Cairo [Shepheards Hotel], Alexandria and Jaffa, New York, Bombay, Melbourne, Auckland, Algiers [Agent], plus 10 English & 2 Scottish Offices.)

For information regarding this train apply also to the General Office of the Pullman Car Company St. Pancras Station.*

Despite protests, the single special Pullman journey ran, as advertised, in February 1883. What rankled most were the write-ups in the British press, suggesting that the service would be regular, or should be. The *Times* said 'there was no equally complete service in Europe', which of course was true at that precise moment! (The Orient Express did not start until June 1883, and the Rome Express began in December of the same year.) But Mr. Pullman was not allowed to run any more through trains from the Channel ports to Italy, although the British preferred Pullman, where everybody spoke English, to Wagons-Lits. The P&O's passengers hated changing at Bologna and wanted an all-British train, not one in which the compartments would suddenly fill with mysterious foreigners, who no less unexpectedly disappeared at intermediate places. Most of all, the British have never ceased to resent paying supplements, especially high ones. Between 1883 and 1890 the first-class fare from Calais to Brindisi rose by just 6d (6 pence in English money). The Wagons-Lits supplement, after getting control of the service, was an enormous £1. 14s. 6d. more than that charged on the special train as shown on the handbill!

Less than two months after the return of the Orient Express press party, described by the London *Times* as a 'revolution in train travel', Nagelmackers launched his second Train de Luxe, on 8th December 1883, linking Calais (London) and Paris with Rome. It was far from easy because of Pullman's powerful position in Italy. To get to Rome, Wagons-Lits had to go round by the Riviera.

Wagons-Lits' Calais-Nice-Rome Train de Luxe was a great success, better than even the most optimistic had hoped for. Nagel-

---

*St. Pancras was the Midland Railway's London Terminus.

---

opposite: 36. Lx10-type sleeper No. 3532 at St. Denis CIWL works in 1976. Preserved at Mulhouse National Railway Museum.

mackers ordered his first sleeping cars in Italy, from Savigliano, which were fitted out at the Marly WL works. He also added the words 'et des Grands Express Européens' to the company title, which lasted until 1967.

In 1885, the Italian Railway companies came together as a group, and by paying heavily, Nagelmackers managed to secure the contracts previously held by Pullman, taking over the Pullman cars when his rights expired. Nagelmackers did so in the nick of time, for in 1885 Prussia began to make difficulties for the Wagons-Lits cars radiating from Berlin.

Beginning in 1890, the Calais-Nice-Rome express was supplemented by Wagons-Lits sleepers running from Calais and Paris to Rome via Modane. The Calais car was for a period attached, between that port and Paris, to the Club Train de Luxe, whose wagons-salons ran between Paris and London from 1889 to 1893.

From 1897 the Rome Express became a Train de Luxe, running once weekly via Modane. The Calais-Nice Train was named the Meditérannée Express (see Chapter 9). An inaugural Rome Express trip on 15th November 1897 included two English journalists, who were seen off at Calais by the station-master, M. Favre, and the Wagons-Lits representative, Mr. Richardson, who, like the sleeping car's conductor, was English. In those days there were no tiresome national trade-union restrictions, and the main condition of Wagons-Lits employment was the ability to speak three languages fluently.

French Customs formalities took place on board the Trains de Luxe, instead of in the draughty Customs House, which greatly impressed the travellers of that period. Departing Calais at 12:49 p.m., the passengers just had time to leave their coats in their compartments before luncheon was served. The menu consisted of:

Hors d'oeuvres variés	Petits pois à l'Anglaise
Filets de Sole au vin blanc	Galantine de volaille
Cotelettes de Mouton à la Mont	Langue escarlate
Cenis	Fromage Fruits
Café et Liqueurs	

All this was described as 'simple and wholesome'! But fresh peas in the middle of November—simple? There were, of course, no tins in those pioneer days. Wagons-Lits performed such miracles by buying peas from Corfu in the Brindisi market and sending them to Calais on the Indian Mail, which had arrived the day before. The bill for all this was a mere four shillings, with wine and liqueurs extra.

After a damp, drizzling London, and an unpleasant, icy crossing, passengers liked the sleeping car's 65°F heating. They also enjoyed lingering over coffee, and they were all ready for that British institution, afternoon tea, served in the diner once the train had left Paris' Gare du Nord. The Rome Express took the Grande Ceinture line, avoiding the Gare de Lyons. Now among the inaugural passengers were a Frenchman, an Italian baritone and his wife, some members of the Russian Imperial family and a British attaché of the Rome embassy returning to his work. Let us follow them to their 5/6d (5 shillings, 6 pence English money) dinner, the same price as that which had been charged on the club train, and there described as 'very expensive':

Hors d'oeuvres	Poulet de Grains
Consommé à la Duchesse	Salades
Barbue, Sauce Hollandaise	Soufflé à la Rome Express
Aloyau de boeuf rôti	Glaces
Haricots Verts	Fromages Dessert
Café Liqueurs	

Nine courses for 5/6d or 7 francs does not seem so expensive! After a rubber of whist in the diner's smoking room, our journalists remarked that they walked on the platform at Macon 'while the engine was being changed'. In reality, at that time, the Rome Express ran this far coupled to the rear of the Meditérranée Express.

Next morning, before Turin, breakfast was served in the compartment, with complimentary morning newspaper. With luncheon ready in the dining car after Genoa, Rome was reached late in the evening at 22:45.

During World War I, the Rome Express sleepers and diner continued to run, though in a train with other coaches, for the benefit of those in high places wishing to travel between the three capitals of the Allies. Between the wars the Rome Express reverted to a Train de Luxe.

In 1932 the Calais-Rome and Calais-Meditérranée sleeping cars were attached to the Flèche d'Or Pullman train from Calais to Paris. The Flèche d'Or at that time left Calais at 14:30, and sleeping-car passengers could enjoy the Pullman luxury for lunch or afternoon tea, without paying a supplement. After the bustle of the Channel crossing, the struggle on and off the boat, up and down gangways, finding a seat, wondering if it would be rough, the peace and security of this train seemed even more satisfying.

The conductor would follow the French police inspection of people bound for Italy, again asking for passports but this time placing them, with the tickets, in his bag for the frontier crossing at Modane, at 04:25 in the morning, so that normally sleeper passengers would not be disturbed.

There was something particularly thrilling about rushing along at express speed, behind one of M. Chapelon's most successful 4-6-2 Pacific engines, shut away from the world almost with the isolation of a ship and without the fear of disruption by telephone calls or urgent requests to take action. After three and a half hours the Flèche d'Or deposited its passengers at the Gare du Nord in Paris. But sleeper passengers could simply stay snugly in their cabin, while one of the Nord's 040TG-class 0-8-OT shunting-tank engines hitched itself to the rear of the great train. The shunters, clinging to the impressive array of steps, would blow their plaintive brass horns. A sigh of escaping air from the brakes, and the Train de Jonction was ready to depart round the Petite Ceinture, with its glimpses of Parisian roofs, between tunnels, a momentary sight of the great Est main line, by which the Orient Express left Paris, an old canal, and then a large bridge across the innumerable lines outside the Gare de Lyons, where the train arrived a full seventy minutes before the Rome Express proper was due to depart.

You could simply leave everything in your compartment and take a stroll on the platform, safe and sound, whilst others struggled with their luggage or fumbled for their tickets. You could also watch the great blocks of ice being loaded into the dining car, or go and buy magazines and newspapers for the journey ahead.

But it was unwise to leave the sleeper too long. You could never be quite certain that it would still be where you left it on your return, whatever the timetable told you about its hour of departure. One passenger found this out in Naples, where dressed in his waistcoat, as it was a hot day, and in slippers for comfort, he returned to the platform of the Central Station to find the sleeper gone, with money, jacket, passport, everything. He had to dash madly down some steps to the Piazza Garibaldi Station underneath, where fortunately the train had stopped again.

The great PLM Pacifics, class 231 H in the SNCF category, which were extremely spirited performers, would back stealthily onto the train, for French engines, burning soft coal, made little

right: 37. Modane International station about 1950. Three-phase overhead wires used by the Italian Railways (FS) and third rail used by French (SNCF) engines. Both now superseded.

below: 38. CET (Compagnie Européenne de Tourisme) Paris-Dobiacco (Toblach). One of the last steam-hauled, all-WL trains in Italy, 8th March 1970. Three Lx sleepers and FS 741 class 2-8-0 No. 124, with Franco-Crosti boiler.

blast from their chimneys, unlike English or German ones. One minute the train would be just waiting; the next there would be the great engine, ready to whisk the cars off to Laroche-Migennes, where it would hand them over to another Pacific, perhaps 231G this time, for the run on to Dijon.

So you climbed back into your sleeper, and no sooner had the Rome Express disappeared into the murky gloom of the Parisian suburb named Villeneuve, with its great marshalling yard, than the dinner bell rang. The diner was shiny, and French. It ran only to Dijon, returning in the morning with the Simplon Orient Express. Advertisements adorned its interior partitions, altogether far more brash and functional than the ornate Pullman at tea time.

While you were at dinner, the deft conductor of the sleeper would be making the bed by revolving the seat and lifting up the back to make the upper berth. There was a drugget on the floor so you need not step barefoot onto the carpet. Also present was a three-step folding ladder, in which everyone all over Europe pinched their fingers, no matter what service the Wagons-Lits car might be running on. Only with later cars was this replaced by a light, upholstered ladder, clipped to the compartment wall or fastened against the upper berth.

The route from Dijon was via Louhans to Bourg en Bresse, avoiding Macon. After Bourg, no stop was shown in the timetable until Aix-les-Bains, in Savoy, but a service stop occurred at Culoz, the junction for Geneva, for here steam gave way to electricity. The engines used were the very long PLM 2-C-C-2 type, operating on 1,500 volts and fitted with both overhead pantograph and third-rail pick-up shoes. Until 1974 third rail prevailed between the stations from Chambéry to the frontier at Modane, climbing up the steep valley of the Maurienne. From Culoz to Chambéry, overhead wires served throughout. During World War II, the main PLM line was electrified from Paris to Lyons, as were the branches from Macon to Culoz, which made it possible for the modern engines to run through to Chambéry without difficulty.

But back in the 1930s Modane station had 1,500 volts DC French electrification (SNCF) and 3,700 volts at 16.7 cycles per second, 3-phase AC Italian electrification (FS). Since the latter

39. Sleeping car of the T2 type.

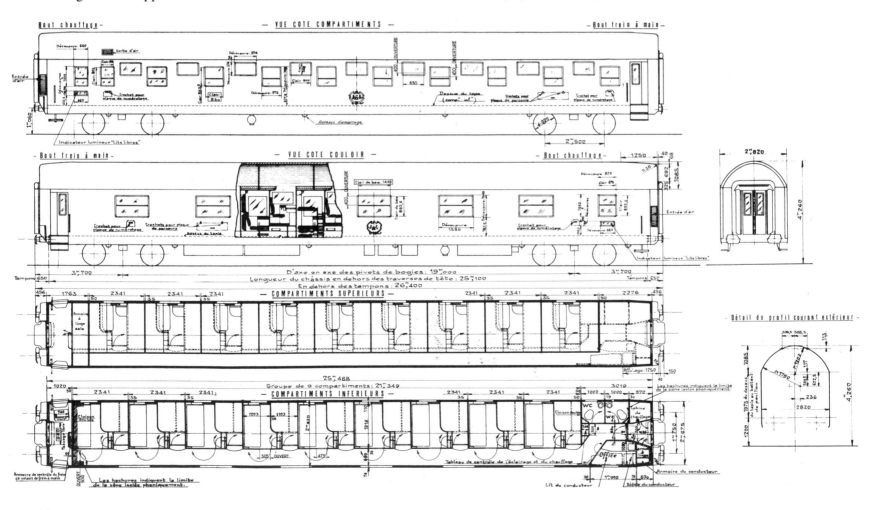

system had double wires, one for each of two phases, it took up all the overhead space, so the station had third rail for the SNCF trains. By 1964 this had been done away with, and FS engines today use the standard 3,000 volts DC of the rest of Italy's electric network, operating at half-power over the SNCF 1,500-volt wires in the frontier station.

The third-rail equipment was not particularly suitable for an area with heavy snowfall, and either very long engines, or engines used in pairs, had to be provided so that at least one shoe would be in contact with the live rail. Thus, the old system became more and more a bottleneck for the increased freight traffic caused by the creation of the Common Market.

Leaving Modane, the train climbed the Mont Cenis pass and tunnel behind an FS 550 class (AC), 'a little giant of Jove', so-called from the engine's first introduction on the steeply graded pass down which the train later ran, from Turin, to reach Genoa at almost sea level. The Rome Express reversed at Turin, where the Wagons-Lits diner came on. Originally the diners worked right through, an arduous task for the crews (one French, one Italian), sleeping every other night in hammocks, one night in lodgings and every fourth night at home.

For the run down the coast to Pisa, with stops at La Spezia, Rapallo and Viareggio, 1-D-1–class electrics were used, jagged-looking engines with great poles sticking out fore and aft to catch the current. Here in 1937 the Rome Express turned inland, with steam haulage from Pisa to Florence, where the faster, 3,000-volt DC wires were already linked to Rome, although the coastal electrification would not be ready until 1938.

After another reversal, the Rome Express glided away from the Santa Maria Novella Station in Florence, behind a 428 class 2-Bo-Bo-2 engine, new in 1937. It ran non-stop to Rome through the Chianti fields, past Arezzo, unless someone wished to alight at Chiusi for the Baths of Cianciano.

Luncheon was the appetizing meal which Wagons-Lits Italian chefs, who seem very individualistic, somehow managed to make out of ordinary fare. The train sped non-stop through Orvieto and Orte onto the four tracks beginning at Setti Bagni. In the 1930s the

40. FS 444 ('Flying Tortoise') class BB electric locomotive, as used on the *Palatino*.

Rome Express drew into Roma Termini station in the late afternoon, about 18:00.

That the *Palatino* Train de Luxe should have started at all in 1969 is something to be excited about, for this train of sleepers, diners and couchettes only, with an all-inclusive fare for rail ticket, dinner, breakfast and sleeper supplement, and still running every night between Rome and Paris, came at a time when the Rome Express had been demoted from a Train de Luxe. Slowed and diverted via Switzerland because of the heavy traffic over the Mont Cenis and deprived of its Calais-Rome sleeper, which had been replaced by a couchette, the Rome Express seemed a target for extinction in the 1960s. Instead it has survived and was renamed 'Napoli Express' in 1978 to emphasize its through coaches to Naples.

As far as Turin the engine of the *Palatino* was, until perhaps superseded by the 1979 FS 633 class, one of the 444 class Bo-Bo engines. Since the latter were the fastest express engines on the FS, Italian humourists dubbed them the *Tartarugas* or (Flying) 'Tortoises'. A portion of the train that now runs from Florence through Bologna to Turin was in 1969 attached at Pisa, the only stop between Rome and Genoa. When the train started, a 656-class Bo-Bo–articulated electric engine was used. From Modane it is pulled by one of the SNCF 6500 CC engines built in 1970, or a 7200 BB built in 1980, covering the 596 kilometres from Chambéry to Paris in about five hours, with one stop at Dijon.

There is no doubt that the M or Modern class of sleeping car, introduced in 1964, gives a more comfortable ride than the Lx class of 1929. The beds are longer and wider, there are foam-rubber mattresses, air-conditioning and upward-opening windows that make it extremely hard to lean out. These cars only run in or to and from Italy. All others are the MU class, which have the 'Universal' arrangement in their similar compartments, allowing them to be used as first-class single or double, or tourist T3 (three-berth) class.

On the *Palatino,* there is an air of rapturous abandon. The young Wagons-Lits conductors wear their kepis perched at curious angles over shocks of thick, rather long hair. They also take an enormous pride in their job, and it is Roman pride, somehow different from the deft efficiency of the impeccable French Wagons-Lits conductors. The Italians function *con brio;* the French, *à la mode.* In the morning there will be one of the SNCF's red self-service diners, called 'Gril-Express', attached with a first-class coach at Chambéry to serve breakfast to the couchette passengers. Thereafter dinner is made up of tray meals, called 'Plateaux Express', assembled in the bar car, which is detached at Genoa. The SNCF couchette cars on this train have Italian Wagons-Lits attendants.

Perhaps the most moving sight in the 1969 *Palatino* was the dining car, fitted with new bogies for fast *Palatino* running. The car had something familiar about it, exuding a smell of roasting veal, mixed with the sulphurous fumes of its kitchen chimney, in Roma Termini before departure. Neon strip-lighting had replaced the former solid-brass ceiling lights, but apart from these modifications, it was indeed the same car (No. 2869) found on the Rome Express of thirty-two years earlier!

below: 42. Plan and sections of saloon car No. 155, believed to have been the first Pullman parlour car *Victoria.* Early in 1883, the Dutch State Railways asked Wagons-Lits to start a wagon-salon service between Amsterdam and Rotterdam, and WL promptly ordered two wagons-salons from Rathgeber in Munich. Owing to the pressure of work and the priority for the Orient Express cars, Rathgeber could not make an early delivery of the equipment, and the Dutch Railways threatened that if the service did not start by 19th February 1884, they would give the contract to Pullman. Nagelmackers pleaded for an extension until 1st May, but even so, the cars were not finally ready until 1885. Thus, Wagons-Lits had to buy a parlour car from Pullman. It had two private rooms with side corridor and seventeen revolving armchairs in the main saloon (two less than may have been intended).

Thanks to Hitler, it is impossible to prove that the diagram of CIWL's No. 155 is actually that of the first Pullman parlour car, *Victoria,* which had run as Alexandria on the London & South Railway until 1882, but then seems to vanish from the scant records in Britain.

The Italian Fine Arts Special Train handbill of 1883 reproduced on pages 38 and 40 mentions a drawing-room car going to Italy, yet none was taken over there by Wagons-Lits in 1886. If definietly had open platforms. And surely Pullman would have sold their very oldest car?

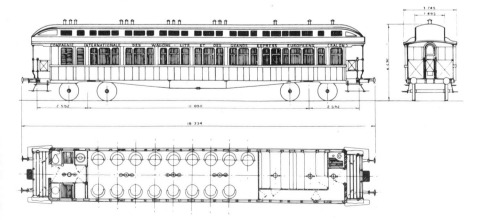

6. The Nord Express and the Audacious Trans-Siberian Express

In remote Russia, the Tsar had come to the conclusion that more comfort was needed on the best train linking Kiev with Odessa, and as early as 1864 the service began offering primitive bed carriages with armchairs in which passengers could lie down. There were also primitive bathrooms, made possible by large numbers of servants used to heat water and pour it into the tubs.

Nagelmackers' early success in linking Belgium with Germany (Ostend-Berlin) was soon followed by an extension to the Russian frontier of East Prussia, but there he had to contend with the different rail gauge. A visit to St. Petersburg in November 1877 failed to solve the problem. Internal railways were one thing; foreigners operating services to make Russia easy of access quite another.

In February 1882, Nagelmackers sent the Count de Chazelles to negotiate with the Russians. This resulted in an agreement permitting Wagons-Lits vehicles to run over the Russian State Railways from Wirballen (the German frontier station) to St. Petersburg, as part of through Wagons-Lits service from Paris, on which the bogies would be changed from one gauge to the other at the Russian frontier. Nagelmackers decided these cars should run right through south-west from St. Petersburg to Lisbon. Why stop at Paris when the same expensive wheel-changing arrangement for Russia could be used to make through sleeping cars possible on the different gauges of France and Spain?

Thus, in 1884 Nagelmackers' Nord-Sud Express was born. It would run in one train from St. Petersburg to his home town, Liège. Here the second, smaller portion would run to Brussels and Ostend, with a special boat to Dover, providing a quick link to London, while the main train carried on to Paris, Irun, Madrid and Lisbon. Nagelmackers was in advance of his time. There would be no through bogie-changing Wagons-Lits sleeping cars between Paris and Madrid until 1969!

The idea of the Prussian State Railways being used by a foreign operator as a transit line from France to Russia was more than Bismarck and his Emperor could stand. In 1885, when they discovered that Nagelmackers planned to run his cars right through to St. Petersburg, the Prussians cancelled their contracts with him and suspended the Wagons-Lits services. Thus, in 1887, Wagons-Lits managed to link St. Petersburg and Warsaw, and then the latter city with Vienna by means of a further sleeper service, for which the passengers changed from one car to the other at the point where the two different rail gauges met. Wagons-Lits' Austrian Division conductors worked right through with their passengers, changing cars with them and leaving the other cars in charge of cleaners at Warsaw. (French conductors did the same on the Sud Express at Irun up to 1926.)

Wagons-Lits was thus established in Russia before 17th March 1891 when Tsar Alexander III signed the decree creating the Great Siberian Railway. As is well known, the Russians were quite determined to do everything themselves on their new railway, which they began to build simultaneously from Moscow eastwards and Vladivostok westwards.

Pressure, brought by royalty and others, persuaded the Prussians at last—after eleven years—to allow the Nord Express to begin running on 9th May 1896. But the service still entailed a change of sleeping car at the gauge break, where the birch logs in the Russian tenders contrasted with the coal-burning Prussian engines.

All conductors had to be German, preferably Prussian, on the through sleepers from Wirballen/Eydtkuhnen to Paris and Ostend, while Russian conductors worked St. Petersburg–Wirballen. The staff of the Ostend-Eydtkuhnen diner, which ran coupled to a four-gon-fumoir of the English Club Train (see Chapter 5), were Belgian, and it was suggested that they should work through to the Russian

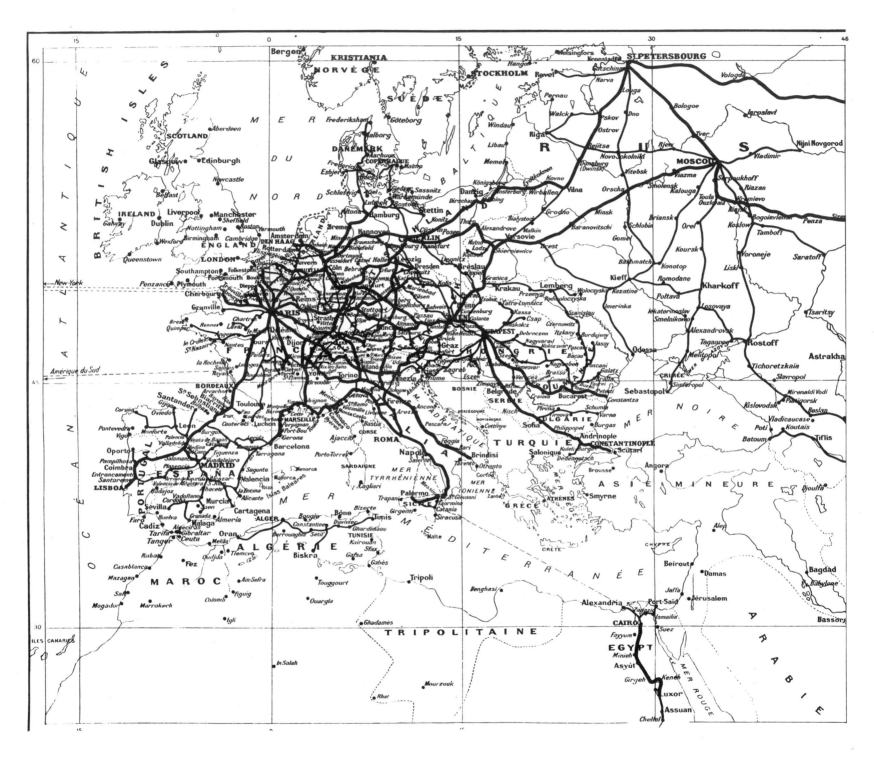

capital, owing to the difficulty of getting suitable Russian personnel for the St. Petersburg diner.

The Wagons-Lits were forced to charge low supplements on the Prussian portion of the journey: £1.8s.7d. for Ostend–Berlin and £3.17s.6d. for Ostend–St. Petersburg. The exclusive use of a two-berth compartment cost only one and a half supplements between Ostend and Eydtkuhnen. The objective was to minimize competition with the Prussian State Railways' own sleeping-car network.

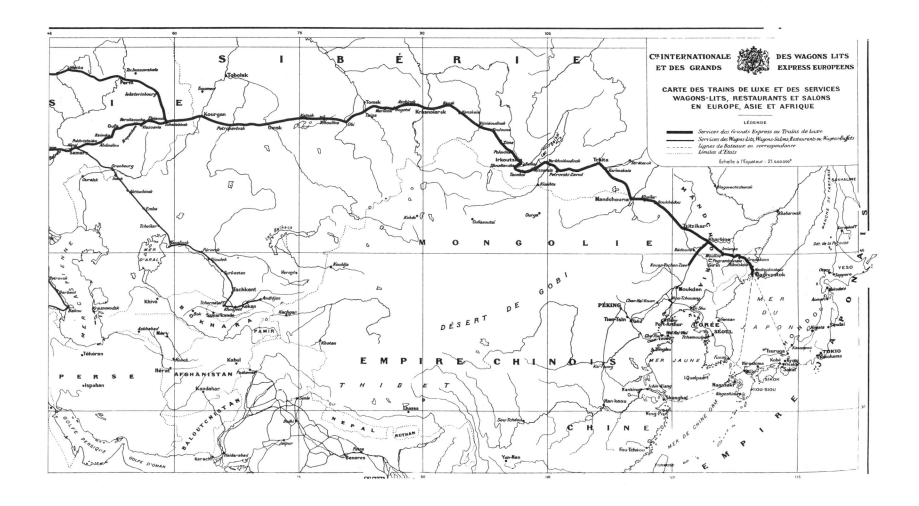

The Silver Jubilee of Nagelmackers' first operations, in 1898, was celebrated with the inauguration, on 15th November, of the St. Petersburg–Nice–Cannes Express and, on 3rd December, the Siberian Express between Moscow and Tomsk. The official opening date for the Russian line was 17th June 1898. On the St. Petersburg–Cannes train, dressing for dinner was de rigeur, and some grandees had their valets place silk sheets over Wagons-Lits' regulation linen ones. In addition to taking Russian and Austrian aristocrats to the Riviera, Wagons-Lits had also built the resort at Opatija, then called Abbazzia, on the Istrian Peninsula, near Fiume (present-day Rijeka).

The Siberian Express took six nights to reach Tomsk, arriving at two in the morning and leaving again the same day, with Moscow reached seven days later. Supplementary fares were 9.25 gold francs for first class, 7.50 gold francs for second class or 2.50 and 2 gold francs respectively for each night on the train. On 14th January the service was extended to Kransnoiarsk and then, towards the end of the year, to Irkutsk, near the shore of Lake Baikal, which passengers could reach on their own by ordinary train over the 60 miles to Listvennitschnaya.

A short way beyond the town station, trains were loaded aboard the ice-breaker ferry for the trip across Lake Baikal to Missovaia. The ferry, called of course *Baikal,* was built by Armstrongs in England, taken in sections to the lake and assembled there. It had four funnels and entrances at bow and stern. Although only the *Baikal* took on rolling stock, the Russian lake could also be crossed on passenger steamers.

From Missovaia, the Trans-Baikal Railway was laid through Varnihudinsk, Nikolsk and Chita—headquarters of the railway—to Stratensk. From here the rivers Shilka and Amur made a navigable waterway eastward to Kharbarovsk, the northern terminus of the Oussuri Railway leading south to Vladivostok. Some idea of the difficulties encountered by the engineers and construction workers can be gained from a contemporary account written by a Welshman who took a month, going west, to get from Kharbarovsk to Stratensk, thanks to the frequent grounding of steamers. Stern-wheel steamers were used to reduce their draught. On one occasion the food ran out, and only the arrival of another ship saved the passengers from starvation in mid-stream. On other occasions they had to disembark and walk along the bank to lighten the vessel.

43. Inaugural Nord Express Poster of 1896, featuring Moscow, St. Petersburg and Berlin.

The Amur (meaning 'Love', with all its implications) forms the border between Russia and China. With its easier topography, it offered a very much shorter route from Nikolsk to Vladivostok, going due east across Chinese territory. The Russians obtained a concession to build a line not only here, a line called the Chinese Eastern Railway, but also one going south from Harbin to Manchuria to Mukden and Dalni, on the Manchurian coast, where they established a whole new settlement. This line was completed in late 1900, four years before Harbin and Vladivostok could be finally linked.

44. The St. Petersburg–Vienna–Cannes Express leaving Wien Westbahnhof for Cannes. Golsdorf 2-6-4 locomotive.

Although built with heavier materials, the Trans-Baikal sank into the bog at some points, where the intense heat of the sun combined with poorly constructed rail-joints to cause rail-buckling. But slowly the line was improved. During 1900–03 the Trans-Baikal was very dependent on the Russian-operated Chinese Eastern Railway, which provided most of the rolling stock for both lines. The rails were laid by Chinese coolies, by Russians and Tartars (local Muslims) who were often political exiles and thus prisoners, or by local peasants 'indentured without pay' (a polite term meaning slave labour).

Thus, in 1900 the 'Trans-Siberian' did not exist—except at the Paris Exhibition! This event was very largely organized and run by Wagons-Lits, which issued 25,000 tickets for combined entry and accommodation. A CIWL subsidiary completed the Elysée Palace Hotel in time for the fair, along with other, less costly hotels built at the Trocadéro. Wagons-Lits paid for many attractions, including a huge reconstruction model of 'Old Paris' and the 'Palais de l'Optique', which showed off the moon as though it were 'a yard away'. Almost every country's pavilion had a Wagons-Lits at its stand.

The Belgian Pavilion displayed No. 1 (actually No. 8 of 1873). The Italian Pavilion had No. 759, a diner, and No. 760, a mixed sleeping car and saloon, both Italian-built replacements for the old Pullmans. The Austrian stand offered Austrian-built Nos. 680 (WL) and 681, a diner with a smoking compartment. The French Pavilion had No. 778, a sleeping car built for Egypt, and a notice explaining that the Trans-Siberian exhibit had been constructed by the French. In the first-class Trans-Siberian sleeper the upper berth was slung

45. CIWL Russian menu cover for the St. Petersburg–Dwinsk and Dwinsk–Warsaw service.

46. Icebreaker–Train Ferry *Baikal* on Lake Baikal in 1902. Built in England and assembled at the lakeside.

from the roof of the extra-large cabins, Pullman style, at right angles to the lower berth.

The main features of the train were the sumptuous saloons, Nos. 724 and 725. One had rose silk with blue hangings and gold buttons on green plush, all in Louis XVI style. Mouldings concealed every screw and nut. This car also boasted a piano and a hairdressing saloon panelled in sycamore.

The other saloon, a moorish-style Louis XV smoking room done up in leather, with red and blue armchairs garlanded with flowers and rococo flounces, provided a double-locking safe for valuables. With one key held by the passenger and the other by the chef du train, the safe could be opened only by both at once. A gymnasium and a bathroom were in the fourgon of the train.

Passengers entered a special dining car past whose windows unfurled a diorama of the scenery from Moscow to Irkutsk, four different portions of it passing at different speeds, to represent foreground, middle-ground and background. An attendant in white, dressed like a Tartar with jacinth sash, invited guests to taste *borsch* (beet soup), zakouskis, caviar and sturgeon from the Neva River. After three-quarters of an hour the diorama ended, and the 'pas-

COMPAGNIE INTERNATIONALE DES WAGONS-LITS
DIVISION SUISSE
Centralbahnplatz 7 - BALE - Téléphone 24 08 26

Pilatus

BASEL – WIEN
INTERNATIONALE SCHLAFWAGEN GESELLSCHAFT
WIEN I, AKADEMIESTRASSE 2

Bei Beschwerden ersuchen wir
diese Note anzufügen.
En cas de contestation prière
de joindre cette note.

Datum

Brigade: ....

Österr. Linien

520222

O. K. Sta...

№ 101219

Cⁱᵉ INTⁱˢ DES WAGONS-LITS
40, Rue de l'Arcade - PARIS-8ᵉ
R. C. Seine 55 B 9027

BAR
BREDOUX II
28 AOUT 1966
M...

COMPLET		
PAIN		
BISCOTTES	CROISSANT	BRIOCHE
CONFITURE	BEURRE	POTAGE	ŒUF DUR

INTERNACIONAL DE COCHES-CAMAS
ESPAÑA 5?3079
Marqués de Urquijo, 28

En caso de disconformidad se ruega unir la nota.
En cas de contestation prière de joindre cette note.

Fecha
Date

INT. SCHLAFWAGEN-GESELLSCHAFT
DIREKTION FRANKFURT AM MAIN
Arndtstraße 33
COMPAGNIE INTERNATIONALE
DES WAGONS LITS

Bei Rek...

DATUM
DATE
DIENST ... MAI 1961
LIGNE ...

E

023912

A. Madsen

Café		Thé
weiß	komplett	
au lait	complet	

Gr. Tasse	Früh-	Kräuter-
Kaffee	stück	tee
Simple	Complet	Infusion

WAGONS-LITS   15946 EN

Strækning:

Brigade 4 MAI 196

A. Madsen

Ved evt. bemærkninger adr. til selskabets kontor,
VESTERBROGADE 2 B, KØBENHAVN V,
bedes regningen vedlagt.

У случају рекламације молимо да се приложи овај лист.
En cas de contestation prière de joindre ce relevé.

W ...

... SERVICE

Международное Общество Спальныхъ Вагоновъ
и Европейскихъ Скорыхъ Поѣздовъ.
Międzynarodowe Towarzystwo Wagonów Sypialnych
i Expresów Europejskich.

Serie F.

Общество прос...
въ Правленіе С.-...
Towarzystwo uprasza pp. ...
S.-Petersburg, Newski, 22.

Ansio
Linja

№ 14092

Compagnia Carrozze-Letti
Direzione per l'Italia
Nizza, 128 - ROMA

o 386983

11 MAI 1981

Cⁱᵉ INTERNATIONALE
DES WAGONS-LITS
40, RUE DE L'ARCADE - PARIS (8ᵉ)
REGISTRE DU COMMERCE ...

DATE : 18 DEC. 19... LIGNE :

HOTE	Déjeuner	Diner	Café	Simple	Complet	Afternan	Déjeuner

KOMPANİ ENTERNASYONAL
DE VAGON-Lİ
Cie. INTERNATIONALE
DES WAGONS-LITS

ISTANBUL
HAYDARPAŞA   HESAP PUSULASI

TARİH
DATE   8/?/?...

HAT
LIGNE

ŞİKÂYET BİLDİRİLDİĞİ TAKDİRDE İŞBU NOTUN RAPTEDİLMESİ
EN CAS DE RECLAMATION PRIERE DE JOINDRE CETTE NOTE

TABLDOT YEMEK	ÖĞLE YEMEĞİ DEJEUNER	AKŞAM YEMEĞİ DINER	KAH-VALTI COMPLET	ALATURKA KAHVE CAFE TURC	SEMPL SIMPLE			
	17,5	50	70	75	90	100	125	175	200	250	275
ALAKART YEMEK	500		60						

| MEŞRUBAT CONSOMMATIONS | BEYAZ ŞARAP VIN BLANC | SİYAH ŞARAP VIN ROUGE | MENBA SULARI EAUX MINERALES | LİMONATA 1/4 | AFYON KARAHİSAR | SODA 1/2 | TABİİ SODA SODA NATURELLE | BİRA BIERE | PORTAKAL SUYU JUS D'ORANGE | ELMA SUYU JUS DE POMME | DOMATES SUYU |

LİKÖRLER

| 75 | 75 | 75 | 100 | 110 | 120 | 225 | 275 | 1140 |

1265

YEKÛN
SERVİS
VERİLECEK MEBLAĞ YEKÛNU

№ 865452

HOTEL TERMINUS MARITIME & BUFFET-RESTAU...
STATION OOSTENDE KAAI
Tél. 72027

Beheerd door de
Internationale Slaapwagens
Maatschappij (N.M.)

Gérés par
Compagnie Inte...
des Wagons-L...

Handelsregister Brussel
Registre du Commerce Bruxelles   5205

In geval van klacht, gelieve
deze nota bij te voegen

En cas de conte...
prière de joindre

Oostende, le 21/10 9.3. № 19

1	Middagmaal - Déjeuner - Lunch
	Avondmaal - Diner - Dinner
	Ontbijt - Petit Déjeuner - Breakfast
	Koffie - Café - Coffee
	Thee - Thé - Tea
1	Bier - Bière - Beer
1	Water - Eau

BEDRAG — MONTANT
Bediening - Service 10 %

TOTAAL BEDRAG
MONTANT A PAYER

PERL
Vloeibaar Fruit
Sinas - Cassis - Cerise
Frambozen en Grape Fruit
GEZOND - VERFRISSEND

Cⁱᵉ INTⁱˢ DES WAGONS-LITS
et des Grands Express Européens

AMSTERDAM, Centraal Station
Kantooretage, Kamer 44

030053

NEDERLAND

Eventuele klachten te richten
aan nevenstaand adres onder
bijvoeging der nota

Datum:
Dienst:
Oberkellner:

Ontbijt	Lunch	Diner	Plat du jour	Koffie/Thee	
A la Carte			1		6,—
				1	3...
DRANKEN					
Aperitifs Likeuren					
Sigaren Sigaretten					

BEDRAG .... 6 3...
BEDIENING 15 %
Minimum f 0.05
TOTAAL ....

21.02.175 (HOLLAND) 9-59

sengers' got out at the other end of the train, where a pavilion arranged like Peking Station had a Chinese restaurant, said to be the first in Paris worthy of that name.

After the exhibition, the train went to Russia where No. 724 became a dining car in 1903, and No. 725, so sumptuous it took the visitor's breath away, was kept for private hire. It cost so much that only someone as rich as a Vanderbilt could afford to hire it, as he did on a visit, but it was, in consequence, very little used! Incidentally, the famous piano did not travel to Russia but remained at St. Denis CIWL repair works in Paris.

The first Russian-built Wagons-Lits (in 1887 Nos. 211–215 for St. Petersburg–Warsaw) came from the Russian-Baltic Wagon works at Riga, which, together with the Upper Volga Wagon works at Twer (now Kalinin), supplied some 50 vehicles, mostly sleepers with some diners, to CIWL. An observation car built at Riga bore the number 221, which caused it to be mistaken for one of the ex-Pullmans given the same number in Italy.

All these cars enabled CIWL to set up a further train, in 1903, based at Harbin and running west to Missovaia, a train whose conductors spoke Chinese as well as Russian, German, French and English. Both services were called 'Trans-Siberian' at last, and the Moscow-based one extended from Irkutsk to the western shore of Lake Baikal. But hardly had it started when war broke out against Japan, so that passengers, after years of travelling only by Russian military permit in second-, third- or fourth-class ordinary cars, now found that the nice new Train de Luxe had been taken off. Only the Irkutsk train remained. The Baikal ferry became a bottle-neck, and in the winter of 1904 the Russians laid tracks across the frozen lake to speed supplies to the war. But the Japanese won on land at Mukden, as well as at sea when Admiral Togo sank the Russians'

top left: 49. CIWL smoking saloon for the Trans-Siberian Express at the Paris Exhibition of 1900.

top right: 50. CIWL dining car for the Trans-Siberian Express at the Paris Exhibition of 1900. The space between the tables (allowed by the Russian gauge) is notable.

above: 51. Diorama of the Nord Express at the Paris Exhibition of 1898.

Baltic fleet off Vladivostok, after the ships had sailed there via Africa!

In October 1903 the London-Shanghai fare was just under £70. On 1st May 1904 the Grand Hôtel des Wagons-Lits opened at Peking, remaining a rendezvous for 'old China hands' (Europeans living in China) for many years after Wagons-Lits had ceased to run it. The poet Blaise Cendrars made the journey in the first train to go round the newly built line through the mountains surrounding the southern shore of Lake Baikal. Later, somewhat after the manner of poets, he became a washer-up in the Peking Hotel, where he even named his chow 'Wagon-Li'!

In 1906, the Wagons-Lits director for Russia, M. Widhoff, made a new twelve-year contract with the Chinese Eastern Railway, which placed nine trains a month on the Trans-Siberian run. Wagons-Lits worked three per month, while the Russian State Railways' own sleeping-car trains ran the others. The latter had no washing facilities.

In 1908, the Russian government handed over the entire operation of all Trains de Luxe on the Trans-Siberian to Wagons-Lits and began building new workshops at St. Petersburg and Vladivostok, to supplement those at Harbin and Fokrova, Moscow. A special repair shed, for running repairs, was set up at the Koursk Station at Moscow, the starting point of the Trans-Siberian Express, though some through cars were processed at the Brest Station if the Trans-Siberian was late, as it often was. Passengers could sleep in the cars for three roubles and have dinner in the diner, instead of staying overnight in hotels, preparatory to catching the Moscow-Warsaw Nord Express. At Warsaw the train connected with the St. Petersburg–Cannes service and with a special part of the Nord Express to Berlin and Ostend.

The Wagons-Lits guide of 1909 informs us that one and a half railway tickets and speed (*vitesse*) supplements, plus two sleeper supplements, could secure the exclusive use of a pair of double-berth first-class compartments, with a lavatory shared between them. The second-class had some two-berth, but mostly four-berth, compartments. The train had lighting, and 'the cars were heated in winter' (a slight understatement of Siberian conditions!). One conductor was a barber, another a trained infirmary nurse, with access to a medicine chest on board. A doctor could be telegraphed to meet the train en route, at principal stops.

The Trans-Siberian had a staff of seventeen, including a fitter locksmith. An electrician looked after the dynamo in the baggage van, 'where dogs could travel if properly muzzled and on a chain, but the Company would take no responsibility, and each animal must be fed and looked after by its owner'. Their only recreation was to bark at passengers using the bath, which had hot and cold water and was also in the baggage van, along with the chef du train's compartment. This contained only four berths, so the staff had to sleep where they could during the nine-day journey. Over one hundred books in four languages filled the train's library, where passengers could talk freely, though Article 15 of the regulations stated that French, the language of the Russian court, must in general be spoken on the trains! Also available were games of chess

52. To emphasize the direct service to China, Wagons-Lits omitted the word 'European' from their title on this Trans-Siberian inauguration poster of 1903.

and dominoes. There was even a series of telegraphed news bulletins sent over the Russian State Railways wires by—no less!—the *New York Times*.

Breakfast was usually taken in the sleeper compartments, from 7 to 10. Luncheon came at noon and dinner at 6 p.m. The *table d'hôte* offered two prices (6/- and 9/- English, depending on the number of courses taken), but one could also select à la carte, the dining car being open from 7 a.m. to 11 p.m. 'for the service of Refreshments, for Smoking, etc.'. (What visions of Maurice Dekobra's *Madonna des Sleepings* are conjured up by that 'etc.', though of course the book was not written until the 1920s!)

Eight days' notice was enough to reserve sleeping-car places and book baggage through to the principal towns of China and Japan, also to America. The general agent in the Sleeping-Car Building at the junction of Fifth Avenue and Thirtieth Street, New York City, was significantly called the 'General Eastern Agent'. London-bound travellers nonetheless started off by going west through Chicago to San Francisco, then by ship to Yokohama, where they could choose to go via Fusan and Korea (the shortest sea route, a mere eleven hours). The Korean Chosen Railways offered "Good Accommodation, Best Attendance and Moderate Charges' in their Train de Luxe to Chang Chun, between Mukden and Harbin, the change-of-gauge point. It was also possible to travel via Dairen to Chang Chun; or go by Russian steamer to Vladivostok where, in 1914, the Trans-Siberian at last began to run through to Moscow without change. The service had been speeded up, and was now quicker than the P&O liners between England and China, even when P&O's special Brindisi and Marseilles Express services of Wagons-Lits cars were used to shorten the journey. The first through Trans-Siberian left on 13th May 1914. The St. Petersburg portion of the train was attached or detached at Cheliabinsk.

In 1914 the Tsar decided that relying on a railway run through someone else's territory was not very satisfactory, and so the present line linking Stratensk with Kharbarovsk was started and then finished in 1917, just in time for the Revolution.

In 1919 Wagons-Lits were forced to withdraw their foreign personnel and forfeit 161 cars, without compensation. A handful of the Russian fleet survived in Latvia, reinforced by a few broad-gauge cars built in the 1920s. Some also survived in China, where in 1923 Wagons-Lits ran the Trans-Manchurian Express from Manchoulie on the Manchurian frontier through to Vladivostok, using cars taken over from the old Oussuri Railway and modernized. Soon they were forced to stop at Pogronistchnaia, the Chinese frontier west of Vladivostok. Standard gauge was extended from Chang Chun (or Kwanchedzee as it appears in old timetables) to Harbin, where the Wagons-Lits Far East Division was established and lasted until 1948. The fleet comprised 67 cars in 1923, including stock taken over from the Chinese railways in 1910. They ran on the standard gauge previously operated by the Chinese themselves. Some CIWL cars had their bogies changed to standard gauge.

The China fleet was reinforced with teak cars sent from Europe. These had been made redundant by the new regulations permitting only all-steel stock. Among the rejects were some of the dining cars of the series that included the 1918 Armistice Car, No. 2419. Others of this series went to Finland, where dining cars continued to be run by Wagons-Lits until 1959.

In the 1930s, the Soviet Union once again opened the Trans-Siberian to foreigners, the classes of travel being hard, soft and international. The latter meant ex-CIWL sleepers. The conductors, like the cars, had an air of being left over from pre-revolutionary days. Even Wagons-Lits called them *provodniks*, according to Baedeker. One contemporary work speaks of 'the two opulent black bottles of some unthinkable wine, on the dining-car tables, never opened and rarely dusted, that might contain the elixir of life; or, alternatively, ink!'

In 1934 bandits attacked the Trans-Manchurian Express, as the 1923 broad-gauge train was called, and set it on fire, leaving five cars gutted. After the Japanese had established the Manchukuo State, the joint Russo-Chinese management of the Chinese Eastern Railway ended, sending the Russian personnel back to the Soviet Union, where they were not well treated under Stalin. Wagons-Lits gave up operating the broad-gauge cars, but single Wagons-Lits, each with White Russian conductor, Chinese tea boy and samovar, ran on such routes as Peking-Shanghai until World War II. Two *Golden Arrow* Pullman cars were shipped to Hong Kong to run to Canton (Kwangchow), but Nos. 4062 and 4065 never entered service and were sold after the war. One was photographed in 1981, still in service as an ordinary coach at Kowloon.

The Great Siberian Railway nowadays has the same amount of daily traffic as was carried in one year in 1902. A goods train rolls out every 20 minutes. There used to be 18 different steam engines on the *Russia*—the present Trans-Siberian Express—plus the spectacle of 3 great engines hauling and pushing the train up the mountains to Lake Baikal (where in early days 'reversing stations' were necessary, as in South America, for climbing the mountains zig-zag fashion). Now double track goes the whole way, and the line is electrified for some 6,400 of its 9,297 kilometres and 548 stations, 91 of which are served by the present train. The Wagons-Lits Trains de Luxe called at 249. Stops varied from 1 hour to 3 minutes.

Today there are only hard- and soft-class compartments turning into bunks. Before World War II the units were cleaned by sweeping debris through a hole in the floor covered by a trap.

Vladivostok is no longer open to tourists, who must change and wait a day at Kharborovsk. To connect with Russian ships to Japan, a special train, with an air-conditioned sleeping car, runs to a point 70 miles from Vladivostok, where it turns east, over a new, 130-mile line to Nahodka, allowing passengers to embark at the Tikhookeanskaya Station.

---

opposite above left: 53. The Trans-Manchurian Express of 1924 (after CIWL had been obliged to withdraw from the Trans-Siberian) ready to leave Manchuria (Russo-Chinese frontier) for Vladivostok.

opposite above right: 54. CIWL dining car and Chinese crew on the Trans-Manchurian Express in 1923.

opposite below: 55. The Trans-Manchurian Express at Harbin in 1923, with CIWL staff. Russian G-class 4-6-0s continued to be used on the Chinese Eastern Railway.

Two through sleeping-car services join Moscow with Peking, one through Mongolia past Ulan Bator—the capital—over a new line. This reduces the distance to 7,865 kilometres instead of 9,001 kilometres by the old route via Harbin (Pinkiang), still followed by the second service.

Though regular Trains de Luxe no longer serve Russia, there are through USSR sleeping cars linking Moscow with Paris, a service started in 1962. Shortly afterwards a similar service began running to Ostend, with a change of bogies at Brest Litvosk, the present frontier, as Nagelmackers envisaged.

In 1977 Intraflug of Zurich organized a Trans-Siberian Special Limited, of USSR sleeping and dining cars only, from Moscow to Kharbarovsk and back, with onward tours to and from Japan. In 1982 this service will run twice, and there will be a Caucasus-Crimea Express as well (started 1981). The special train carries a crew of 45 to look after 90 passengers!

56. WR 2426 (VR No. 2018) on Russian-gauge bogies in Finland at Turku Harbour. The series was identical to the present replica of the Armistice Car, but with shutters for crossing Porkkala Zone, Finland, which in 1950 was a USSR naval base.

7. Trains of Kings and Kings of Trains: Some Royal and Presidential Journeys

When it came to Royal Trains, no elegance, grandeur, comfort, advanced engineering, safety or magnificence possible in the design and manufacture of railway carriages was spared in creating prestigious vehicles worthy of the crowned heads who were to travel in them.

Nowadays, when royalty are disrespectfully referred to as 'royals' and the most powerful states of the world have long ago dispensed with monarchs, it is difficult to remember that regal opulence used to give pleasure to *everyone*, including (not least) the artisans who crafted it.

Perhaps ordinary folk should be more sympathetic towards royal journeys, since, for all their splendour, they are somewhat arduous. Become involved in a royal procession, and you will find your departure time narrowed down to the last half-minute, unlike travel on ordinary trains. Most of us are less punctual.

Queen Victoria was persuaded to make her first train journey in 1842, from Windsor to London by Great Western Railway (a company considered by many rail buffs to have had the best service in Britain). Thereafter she travelled often by rail, particularly to Scotland from the Isle of Wight. By contrast, Louis-Phillippe was not allowed on board a train, on orders from the French government, which feared for his safety. Consequently, he made his first railway journey in 1844—in an English royal train on a state visit to Great Britain!

By the 1860s many sovereigns had royal carriages, and often complete trains. Among the latter was the royal train of King Max of Bavaria, whose heir, Ludwig II (he of all those astonishing castles), added a magnificent saloon, now in Nüremberg Museum. Its blue-and-gold décor is perhaps the most sumptuous to be found in any of the surviving royal coaches.

Queen Victoria had a pair of 6-wheeled royal saloons built for her by the London & North Western Railway with a bellows connection. Her Majesty disliked the bellows and refused to walk through it whilst the train was in motion. She also had a similar pair of coaches built and maintained for her in Brussels, albeit kept mostly at Calais (an arrangement that persisted even though she preferred to travel in her yacht to Cherbourg from Osborne in the Isle of Wight, and start from there on her royal journeys). In 1897 the English pair of coaches were mounted on a single frame with bogies. The Continental coaches seem to have remained as they were, at least until the Queen's journey to Nice. Later these too were placed together on a bogie-borne chassis. King Edward VII had a royal saloon built for him in 1883 by Sir Edward Watkin's Manchester Sheffield & Lincoln Railway (later Great Central) but assigned to his South Eastern Railway (see Chapter 5) and actually kept in Calais! He seems to have had Wagons-Lits servants as well as royal ones. As Prince of Wales, he made many journeys in it.

France also had its Imperial Train, but lost it in 1871 as a result of the Franco-Prussian War and the collapse of the Second Empire (though one of the coaches has recently been restored for preservation in the Mulhouse Museum). The Russian government bought the train at Napoleon III's bankruptcy sale and adapted the bogies to the Russian gauge. In 1881, while aboard the Imperial Train, Tsar Alexander II had a narrow escape between the Crimea and Moscow. One of the multitudinous 0-8-0 tender engines used for goods and passenger traffic alike had been attached as pilot to the small 2-4-0 royal engine to get over the hills in southern Russia, and, while making a descent, the train ran away. The 0-8-0 derailed, causing a nasty smash that killed 22 people and injured more than 30.

Ringhoffer of Prague were the great royal train builders of Central Europe. In 1891 they created a whole train for the Austrian Emperor: baggage/generator car, diner, kitchen car (bogie), Emperor's saloon and saloon for the suite. Not to be outdone, the

NE PAS SE PENCHER AU DEHORS

NICHT HINAUSLEHNEN

È PERICOLOSO SPORGERSI

ΜΗ ΚΥΠΤΕΤΕ ΕΞΩ

A NU SE PLECA IN AFARA

NIE WYCHYLAĆ SIĘ

ES PELIGROSO ASOMARSE

НЕ НАГИЊИ СЕ КРОЗ ПРОЗОР

DANGEROUS TO LEAN OUT

É PERIGOSO DEBRUÇAR-SE

PENÇEREDEN SARKMAK YASAKTIR

НЕ СЕ НАВЕЖДАИТЕ НАВЪН !

NE IŠSILENKTI

NIETS BUITENSTEKEN

LÆN DEM IKKE UD

NENAHÝBEJTE SE Z OKEN

KIHAJOLNI VESZÉLYES

Hungarians provided a saloon of their own, with 6-wheeled bogie. Ringhoffer also built a saloon for the King of Roumania in 1896. A Bulgarian royal train, with a 6-wheeler, appeared in 1887, followed by a bogie royal saloon for King Ferdinand in 1908. But the Bulgarian monarch's favourite place to travel was the footplate, a preference he shared with his son Boris, whose exploits on the engine of the Simplon Orient Express are legendary.

Pope Pius IX had an audience car and travelling carriage, both 4-wheelers, for visiting Civitavecchia on the Pio Centrale Railway. He owned an even more magnificent bogie car with an observation platform, built by the Pio Latina Railway (Rome-Frascati) in 1858. But with the loss of the Papal States, the Popes gave up travelling by train for almost a century. The Vatican State acquired its station only in 1929, and it continues to be used mostly for goods trains. A roller shutter let down to close the breach in the wall made for the branch. The first passenger train to depart from this station was Pope Pius XII's funeral train to Venice in 1959. |John XXIII was the first living Pontiff to use the terminal, which now serves the present Pope.|

After Britain in 1923 grouped its many railway companies into four large companies, the former LNWR Royal Train became the one most favoured for the monarch's overnight journeys. The day saloons of the LNER, built by the NER&GNR, were the usual rake for the journey from London to Wolferton, the local station serving Sandringham in East Anglia. This station had royal waiting rooms on both the departure and arrival platforms, since royalty often came to the station to greet their friends. (These Royal Waiting Rooms are now open to the public, having been bought by an enterprising railwayman at the time the Kings Lynn–Hunstanton branch was closed. Now HM Queen Elizabeth, like everyone else, must drive to Kings Lynn to catch the London train.)

On the Southern Railway, Pullman cars often serve for short royal journeys, such as to the Derby Day races at Epsom. At Portsmouth, royal specials usually start on a light-weight wood-planked jetty belonging to the Admiralty (Royal Navy), as a result of which antediluvian engines had to be used, instead of the heavier modern ones that normally hauled royal Pullman specials to or from Gatwick Airport or the Channel Ports.

After Britain survived without being invaded in 1940, HM King George VI had a pair of new coaches provided for his frequent troop and war-damage inspections. Built by the LMS Wolverton works of the former London & North Western Railway, they served for thirty-five years, the very last coaches on British Rail to have wooden bodies. Their interiors, which originated in a time of austerity, were brightened up considerably in 1952. A new saloon for the royal children came in 1955, a dining car in 1956 and a new saloon for the Queen's private secretary and members of the Royal Household in 1957.

57. 'Do not lean out' brass plates for opening windows of CIWL cars, in different languages: 1) French; 2) German; 3) Italian; 4) Greek; 5) Roumanian; 6) Polish; 7) Spanish; 8) Serbian; 9) English; 10) Portuguese; 11) Turkish; 12) Bulgarian; 13) Lithuanian; 14) Dutch; 15) Danish; 16) Czech; 17) Hungarian.

In the next twenty years BR gradually changed over from vacuum to air brakes and abandoned steam. In 1976 they introduced the high-speed trains described in the next chapter, running about twice as fast as the speed permitted by the royal train. Thus, two prototype coaches for the HSTs, built at Derby in 1972, were reconstructed at BR's Wolverton works, where the royal train is always kept, and made ready in time for Her Majesty's Silver Jubilee in 1977.

Once altered, the second-class prototype became the Queen's saloon, comprising a large double vestibule entrance, sitting room, bedroom and bathroom, a combined bedroom/bathroom for the

right: 58. King Leopold II of Belgium, a big CIWL shareholder, arrives on the Côte d'Azur by Wagons-Lits special train.

below: 59. The arrival of the German Emperor by Wagons-Lits special train at Bari, Italy. The royal car (back view) is a Mercedes-Benz.

opposite: 61. Interior of the London & North Western Railway's saloon built in 1869 for HM Queen Victoria.

above: 62. Sixteen-year-old King Farouk of Egypt, at about the time of his accession in 1936, emerging from his white-and-gold Royal Train, a confection dating from 1909. Note the open veranda behind the monarch.

left: 63. Interior of one of the two cars built in 1899 for Don Porfirio Diaz, President of Mexico. Note the emblematic eagle interwined with 'RM' (for República de México).

below: 64. The two cars for the President of Mexico, built in Chicago in 1899 by the Pullman Co.

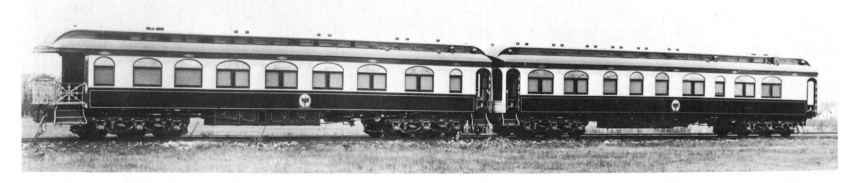

above left: 64. A rare photograph, taken at Wiesbaden in 1911, of the two 6-wheel Continental Royal Saloons prepared for HM Queen Victoria, as later re-mounted on a single-bogie underframe.

above right: 65. A rare photograph, taken at Wiesbaden in 1911, of HM King Edward VII's Continental Royal Saloon. Built in 1883, this carriage nominally belonged to the South Eastern Railway, but was stored at Calais in a special shed. It was frequently used by the British Monarch for his Continental journeys.

left: 66. Dining car of the French Presidential Train, with Wagons-Lits crew, ready for use by Soviet Premier Kruschev, during his visit to France.

Queen's dresser and a further vestibule. Prints of former royal journeys decorate the walls in a blue-and-white décor chosen by Her Majesty.

A similar vehicle serves for HRH the Duke of Edinburgh's saloon, which includes entrance vestibule, lounge/dining room, bed-room and bath, bedroom/bathroom for His Royal Highness' valet and a combined kitchen and staff vestibule, for use when the saloon is running independently of the royal train. The kitchen can provide full meals for up to ten people, the dining table has an amber leather top (doubling as a desk), and there are cane-seated chrome dining chairs for five.

To accommodate the kitchen, the Duke's sitting room is smaller than that in the Queen's saloon, and his bathroom has a shower,

opposite: 67. Marshal Foch of France and Governor Hart of Washington State, on the *Olympian*, during a visit to the United States, shortly after World War I, en route between Chicago and Seattle.

with special electric pumps to maintain high pressure at the spray head. Yellow-bordered green curtains and a brown-patterned carpet complete the décor of the lounge.

The rest of the royal train was updated, including ordinary cars called 'semi-royal', such as the power car with guard's compartment at each end, since the whole of the rake stays permanently together. The diesel generator takes over during overnight stops, when no locomotive is coupled to the train.

Her Majesty first used the new royal train on 16th May 1977 for an overnight journey from London (Euston) to Glasgow at the start of the Silver Jubilee progress through Great Britain. It travelled over the West Coast main line, which in 1966 was electrified at 25,000 volts AC. In that same Jubilee year a number of former royal railway carriages went into retirement at York Museum, which now has nine royal coaches in its charge, more than any other museum.

Some Presidential Journeys*

He had not damaged his pyjamas,
Its amazing, but it's like that!
He has not damaged his pyjamas,
They're embroidered 'Chief of State'!

(Il n'a pas abîmé son pyjama
C'est épatant mais c'est comm' ça!
Il n'a pas abîmé son pyjama,
Il est verni, l'chef de l'Etat!)

Paul Deschanel, surely the most extraordinary of all French Presidents, managed on 23rd May 1920 to fall out of the window

*Lucien Boyer: 'The President's Pyjamas, Express Song' (chorus).

68. President Truman and Sir Winston Churchill on a Baltimore & Ohio Railroad special train, shortly after World War II.

69. Royal Train near the entrance to Otira Tunnel, New Zealand. Locomotives built by English Electric.

of his Presidential Train! The special train left the Gare de Lyons at half past nine in the evening; Deschanel was suffering from over-tiredness and nerves. It was hot; he opened the window wide. . . .

Deschanel was discovered by a ganger between Mignières-Gondreville and Corcy-Corbeille, 110 kilometres from Paris, near Montargis, and taken to a level-crossing–keeper's house. Because of extreme swelling in his face he was not recognized. But otherwise the President had not suffered much injury, since, fortunately, he had fallen on soft earth while the train was going very slowly over tracks under repair.

At first the doctor sent for by the Montargis station staff refused to believe the astonishing story. But when he returned in the morning for another look at his patient, the swelling had gone down, and the President was recognizable. The Sub-Prefect of Montargis took

right: 70. CIWL dining-car royal luncheon menu for HM King George VI's state visit to Paris on 28th July 1938.

below: 71. Royal Train for the Derby, at Hackbridge near Epsom. LBSCR B4 class (unrebuilt Billinton) 4-4-0.

VINS	DÉJEUNER
—	—
Mumm Cordon Rouge 1928	Homard à la Française Sauce Tartare
Veuve Cliquot brut 1928	Selle d'Agneau Renaissance
	Fonds d'Artichauts Colbert
	Poularde à la Gelée d'Estragon
	Cœurs de Laitue Maison d'Or
	Pêches à l'Impératrice
	Petits Fours Glacés
	Corbeille de Fruits

Deschanel to the Prefecture, where his wife and the President of the Council, M. Millarand, brought him back to Paris—by car.

In the meantime, the train swept on overnight, stopping for engine water at various places along the way. Two minutes to five in the morning, at Moulins, the station-master woke up the PLM engineer in charge of the train—a man who rejoiced in the name of M. Prudent—to say that somebody had fallen out of the train. M. Prudent thought the message was a mistake and did not take much notice.

At Saint-Germain des Fossés around half-past five there was another message. This time M. Prudent woke up everybody—except the President, whom he did not like to disturb. So the party of senators and pressmen went on. The President, upon retiring at ten, had said firmly not to wake him before seven, as he was feeling poorly and had taken a sedative. At five past seven the train stopped at Roanne. The President's bedroom gave onto an antechamber occupied by a commandant, who swore no one had gone in or out. The window was open, curtains flapping; otherwise the entire suite—bedroom, bathroom, study—was empty.

Now it was necessary to telephone to Paris, but of course French telephones moved into the 20th century only during the

opposite: 72. Interior of HM Queen Elizabeth II's royal saloon, built in 1977 for the Silver Jubilee of her accession to the throne. The prints are of HM Queen Victoria's royal journeys.

below left: 73. Royal dining saloon of the British Royal Train. Built in 1956, the car includes a kitchen.

below right: 74. HRH the Duke of Edinburgh's royal saloon, built in 1977 for the Silver Jubilee (25th anniversary) of HM Queen Elizabeth II's accession to the British Throne.

1970s. And to make matters worse, the government had passed a new law closing down long-distance telephones on Sundays and bank holidays, effective as of 24th May 1920, which happened to be Whit Monday! So the Minister of the Interior, who was with the party, deputized at the function the President should have attended at Montbrison.

In the United States, no political vignette is more famous than that of a Presidential candidate electioneering from the observation platform at the rear end of a private train taken on a whistle-stop tour of the American hinterland. And once elected, Presidents have made endless use of the rails for their private pleasure. Today, Air Force One has taken the American Commander-in-Chief off the tracks forever, but as recently as 1958 President Eisenhower made a trip to Monterey, California, on board *Sunset*, the Southern Pacific Railroad's private car. Naturally, he went to play golf at the famous Hotel del Monte.

The corporate jet has also made the private railroad car practically extinct, but just before the 1929 Crash, the robber barons' private carriages were unparallelled. Railroad presidents managed to travel free in private cars, usually called 'business cars', a favour they exchanged with one another from line to line. Large numbers of them used to visit Florida at the turn of the century. The Pullman Car Co. had a whole fleet of private cars available for hire by those who did not want permanent ownership of their own individual carriage. The late Lucius Beebe owned the last private car, *Virginia City,* in the old tradition. Now, however, at least fifty private Pullmans have been restored for use as passenger vehicles. SIC TRANSIT GLORIA!

8. The *Flying Scotsman,* the *Queen of Scots* Pullman, the *Twentieth Century Limited,* the Trains de Luxe of Mexico and Egypt

The *Flying Scotsman*

The *Flying Scotsman* departs London's King's Cross Station every morning at 10 o'clock for Edinburgh. It has been leaving at this time for 120 years, but it has never charged a supplementary fare, nor included any Pullman cars, and so really it is not a Train de Luxe at all. On the other hand, its accommodation is limited, and at one time it had various luxury features. In 1979, moreover, it was one of the fastest-running trains in the world.

The train started as the 'Special Scotch Express' in 1862, running over the great Northern Railway almost to York, the North Eastern Railway on to the Scottish border and the North British Railway from Berwick-on-Tweed to Edinburgh.

The great rival was the West Coast route, which from London (Euston) to Carlisle belonged to the London & North Western Railway, a company that refused to have any Pullman cars on its lines. At Carlisle, the LNWR met the Caledonian (Roman name for Scottish) Railway from Glasgow, with a branch from Edinburgh (Princes Street) joining the Glasgow line at Carstairs. The third rival, the Midland Railway, which we met in Chapter 1, started from London's St. Pancras Station but shared Carlisle Station with eleven other railways, and sent its trains, including through Pullman sleeping cars (until 1888), on to Edinburgh by the North British Railway, across the Cheviot Hills on what was known as the 'Waverly Route', now torn up.

All these railways, except the North British, were amalgamated in 1923 into the London Midland & Scottish Railway, which like the LNWR detested Pullman cars. The Pullman Car Co. nevertheless had a base at Glasgow and supplied dining cars without supplementary fare to the Caledonian, the Glasgow & South Western and also the Highland Railways. The Pullmans continued to run on these lines, even after LMS took over, until the contracts expired in 1934. Pullman also operated a supplementary-fare car, the *Maid of Morven,* on the Glasgow-Oban Caledonian line. This service began in 1923, although the carriage had been built in 1914 and then set aside, owing to World War I and its financial consequences.

In 1888 the East and West Coast rivals started racing, hence the nickname *Flying Scotsman.* As a result, the previous 9-hour journey was cut to 7 hours 15 minutes. Parliament then began to receive frightening accounts of rough riding at high speed; thus, the rivals agreed to a speed restriction of 8 hours 15 minutes. This lasted for 44 years! It also led to various improvements in comfort, as a means of competition.

Although the Great Northern Railway ran the first dining-car service between London and Leeds in 1879, using Pullman's *Prince of Wales* (see Chapter 2), there was no diner on the *Flying Scotsman* until 1900! Maybe the North Eastern Railway liked the lengthy lunch stop at its York headquarters, which catered for everybody (instead of the few able to use a diner). The *Flying Scotsman* started carrying third-class passengers in 1887.

Six-wheeled coaches disappeared from the train in 1900, when at last a diner was introduced. The Great Northern's Stirling Single 4-2-2 engines gave way to Ivatt-built 4-4-2 Atlantics, followed in turn by the first Pacific engines built in quantity in Great Britain. Sir Nigel Gresley began producing them for the LNER in 1923. Before amalgamation, the North Eastern also supplanted their 4-4-0 engines with 4-4-2s and later a couple of 4-6-2s. For many years their engines hauled the *Flying Scotsman* through to Edinburgh over the North British line as well as their own.

Most famous of the many Gresley Pacifics were the A1, later A3, class, of which No. 4472 was named after the *Flying Scotsman.* It is now preserved. These enabled heavier coaches to be used, including a triple-articulated dining set with kitchen car in the middle, supported on the two bogies of the dining saloons. The first-class saloon had three-a-side moveable armchairs.

At this time the *Flying Scotsman* provided reserved seats in the first-class dining saloon throughout the journey, as did the LMS rival *Royal Scot*. In 1928 it began running non-stop from London to Edinburgh, the 392.5-mile journey easily becoming the world's longest unbroken run. The engine drivers and firemen changed over half-way by means of a corridor in the tender, unique in the world, spending the other half of the journey in a reserved compartment at the head of the train. Water troughs were commonplace in Britain but not in the United States or on the Continent (though the État Railway of France used them to compete on the Paris-Bordeaux run with the Paris-Orléans Railway). Tenders fitted with a retractable scoop drew water from troughs between the rails, thus avoiding water stops.

By 1930 the *Flying Scotsman* had a ladies' retiring room and a hair-dressing saloon. A cocktail bar was added in 1932, the year when the LNER decided to abandon the speed restriction, and by 1937 the transit time had been reduced to seven hours. However, at the same time that the barber had given place to a mere ladies' maid, the *Flying Scotsman* had been eclipsed by the first streamlined

train in Britain, the LNER's *Silver Jubilee* of 1935.* It ran between London and Newcastle for a supplementary fare of 5/- first and 3/- (5 shillings and 3 shillings English) third class, which paid for the train in two years. Northern business men for the first time could make a day trip to London with two hours for work there.

World War II saw the end of these streamliners, but the *Flying Scotsman* continued, running in two portions to accommodate the many troops on leave from Scotland, and sometimes with 23 coaches

---

*To mark the 25th anniversary of HM Queen Elizabeth II's accession, the name *Silver Jubilee* was given on 8th June 1977 to the 07:45 express leaving London for Edinburgh and the express leaving Edinburgh for London at 15:00. The name ceased to be used in 1978.

75. Up (London-bound) West Riding Pullman leaving Stoke Tunnel in 1932. LNER Gresley Atlantic No. 3284.

on a single train, now worked by the A4 streamlined 4-6-2s. The service included many additional intermediate stops, but once again became non-stop in 1948. A new alteration, however, came in 1949 when the new non-stop *Capitals Limited* was started by British Rail.

In 1962, Deltic class diesel-electric engines took over the train, at once reducing the overall time to about 6 hours. The restaurant facilities were now cut down to a single diner and a mini buffet. The train had limited capacity and carried about 180 first-class and 378 second-class passengers (third class became second in 1956) in some 12 coaches. The journey with one stop (Newcastle) took 5 hours 43 minutes.

right: 76. Gresley A3 4-6-2 No. 4476 'Royal Lancer' at the head of the *Flying Scotsman* in 1927.

below: 77. Gresley streamlined A4 Pacific No. 4492 'Dominion of New Zealand' near Grantham, en route for Edinburgh in 1937.

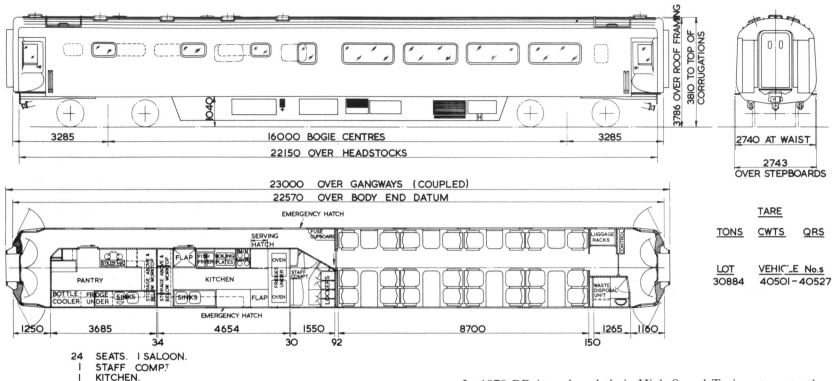

3786 OVER ROOF FRAMING
3810 TO TOP OF CORRUGATIONS

3285   16000 BOGIE CENTRES   3285
22150 OVER HEADSTOCKS

2740 AT WAIST
2743 OVER STEPBOARDS

23000 OVER GANGWAYS (COUPLED)
22570 OVER BODY END DATUM

EMERGENCY HATCH

SERVING HATCH
FUSE CUPBOARD
LUGGAGE RACKS
CONTROL

PANTRY   KITCHEN   STAFF COMPT.   WASTE DISPOSAL UNIT

BOTTLE COOLER   FRIDGE UNDER   SINKS   FLAP   OVEN   LOCKERS

EMERGENCY HATCH

1250   3685   4654   1550   8700   1265   1160
34   30   92   150

24   SEATS. I SALOON.
1   STAFF COMP.T
1   KITCHEN.
1   PANTRY.

TARE		
TONS	CWTS	QRS

LOT	VEHICLE No.s
30884	40501 – 40527

78. British Rail air-conditioned restaurant car, 1st/2nd class (unclassified), for running on HST sets working the *Flying Scotsman*.

79. HST *Flying Scotsman,* without headboard, passing York Minster.

In 1978 BR introduced their High Speed Train sets onto the *Flying Scotsman*. These sets offer limited accommodation in first and second classes, with restaurant car, and hold the world speed record for trains powered by diesel-electric engines. The time to Edinburgh has been cut to 4 hours 7 minutes, and since the train runs during lunch-time, the 'Travellers-Fare' (BR Catering Services) 'Main Line' menu is offered. All seats are reservable on the train, which is made up of 8 cars. The journey time includes a 2-minute stop at Newcastle and takes 1 minute less in the 'up', or London-bound, direction. These trains have full air-conditioning in BR's Mark III type coaches, and no supplementary fare at present. But the famous name appears only in the timetable, because the headboard has been dropped.

The *Queen of Scots*

When the London & North Eastern Railway was formed, it moved all the Pullman cars from the Great Eastern Railway to the Great Northern Railway lines, which it had just absorbed, except for the London-Harwich boat trains. These began running from London to Leeds and Harrogate, a northern spa. In 1928, new all-steel Pullman first- and third-class cars were built by Metro-Cammell, Birmingham, and the London-Harrogate Pullman was extended to Scotland. Called the *Queen of Scots,* the train ran 451 miles, since the Leeds route is longer than the direct line through York (taken by the *Flying Scotsman*), and the Pullman train travelled to and from Glasgow, beyond Edinburgh.

Two ten-car trains were needed, but two Pullmans were detached from the north-bound train at Leeds and collected by the train returning to London from Glasgow later the same day. The

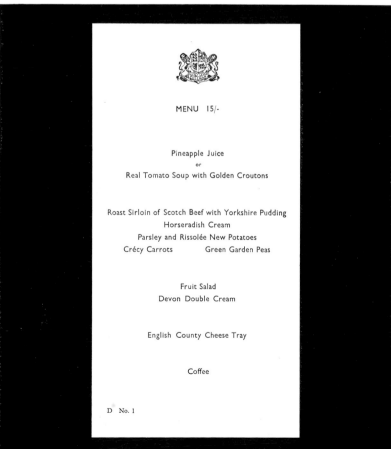

MENU 15/-

Pineapple Juice
or
Real Tomato Soup with Golden Croutons

Roast Sirloin of Scotch Beef with Yorkshire Pudding
Horseradish Cream
Parsley and Rissolée New Potatoes
Crécy Carrots   Green Garden Peas

Fruit Salad
Devon Double Cream

English County Cheese Tray

Coffee

D No. 1

below: 82. *Queen of Scots* Pullman at Edinburgh-Waverly. BR Eastern Region 4-6-2 No. 60519 'Honeyway', 1959.

supplementary fare was 7/6d or 4/- (7 shillings, 6 pence or 4 shillings) third from London to Leeds, 10/- or 5/6d (10 shillings or 5 shillings, 6 pence) to Newcastle (much higher than the *Silver Jubilee*) and 12/- or 7/- (12 shillings or 7 shillings) to Scottish stations. The train called at Leeds, Harrogate, Darlington, Newcastle, Drem, Edinburgh and Falkirk, or at Polmont instead of Falkirk when starting from Glasgow. Supplies for the trains went aboard at both London and Glasgow for the nine-hour journey, during which luncheon, tea, dinner and refreshments were served.

The *Queen of Scots* offered the longest Pullman service in Great Britain and needed little advertising, being well patronized by nobility, large landowners, business men, visitors to Harrogate and sportsmen going for shoots on the Yorkshire moors and in the Scottish Lowland, for whom the Drem stop was provided. The attendants came to know many of the patrons and their special requirements. For those with through tickets from stations on the LNER going to Europe, a special mini-bus (Road Motor Saloon) was provided from King's Cross Station to Victoria Station in London. The train was usually hauled by a 4-6-2 Pacific with a change of engine at Leeds. It was a particularly comfortable way to the north in winter, snug and warm inside against the sleet and snow outside.

Life on board was staid. The train provided nothing like a bar or club car; indeed, the older clients would probably still have talked of 'American bars'. Still, many of the regulars knew each other, which created a convivial atmosphere. There was much demand for the coupé compartments at the car ends, where business could be discussed in privacy. The menus had a distinctive Northern flavour, offering Yorkshire pudding at dinner and grilled royal kippers at 'high tea'.

In 1928, at the time the Harrogate Pullman was transformed into the Scottish train, a second London-Leeds Pullman train was altered to run up to London from Leeds in the morning and return in the evening. This was called the 'West Riding', and later the 'Yorkshire Pullman'.

The Pullmans had to be withdrawn during World War II, at which time many of the third-class cars became ordinary LNER coaches, painted in their colours. This made it difficult to restore the train, as did a strike at the Birmingham factory, where the cars were overhauled.

The *Queen of Scots* Pullman continued running as before, with much the same exclusive kind of passengers and service, until the Pullman Car Co.'s contract expired in 1962. It lasted two years longer but finally ended in 1964.

Pullman cars continued until 1978 to run on weekdays between Harrogate, Leeds and London in the Yorkshire Pullman, which had second-class ordinary coaches and a diner in its formation. British Rail does not like exclusive supplementary-fare trains and allows the new High Speed Trains to be run without any supplement. In 1978 BR withdrew all Pullman services out of London King's Cross when HSTs were introduced between London and Leeds. Some ran on to Harrogate. Also withdrawn in 1978 was the Hull Pullman, which originally had been a section of the Yorkshire Pullman detached at Doncaster but later became a separate Pullman train to and from London. Only the London (Euston)–Manchester Pullman runs today.

The *Queens of Scots'* post-war dinner was:

Menu 15/-
Pineapple Juice
or
Real Tomato Soup with Golden Croutons
Roast Sirloin of Scotch Beef with Yorkshire Pudding
Horseradish Cream
Parsley and Rissolée Potatoes
Crécy Carrots Green Garden Peas
Fruit Salad
Devon Double Cream
English County Cheese Tray
Coffee

The *Twentieth Century Limited*

This is the edict above the law,
Without exception, beyond appeal;
The general manager stands in awe
Of the ukase cast from vanadium steel;
In terminal and in wayside station,
Transcending all that the sages knew,
This is the ranking regulation:
'The 20th Century' must go through!

Faint the marker and iced the rail,
This is the writing writ in fire:
Hold the 'Vanderbilt', stab the 'Mail'
Annul 'The Limited', flag 'The Flyer'
Leave 'The Iroquois' in a fix;
This is The Word, revealed and true:
Give green to twenty-five and -six;
'The 20th Century' must go through!

L'Envoi

So, Prince of the Pearly Signal Tower,
Line the celestial interlocking,
On the minute and on the hour,
To keep 'The Century' on its clocking
In Heaven or Albany, THIS MEANS YOU!
'The 20th Century' must go through!

Lucius Beebe

opposite above: 83. A celebrated view of the *Broadway Limited* (left) racing the *Twentieth Century Limited* on parallel tracks outside Chicago, about 1930.

opposite below: 84. The *Twentieth Century Limited* at full speed on the banks of the Hudson, which has given its name to 4-6-4 engines, not just those of the New York Central System, but of the world.

They called it the greatest train on earth, and it functioned for almost seventy years, from 1902 to 1970. Running between New York and Chicago over the New York Central and associated railroads of the Vanderbilt family, the *Twentieth Century* succeeded a Train de Luxe called the *Lake Shore Limited* of 1897. The latter name has been restored by Amtrak to designate the overnight service now covering the same route. There was, of course, the rival route provided by the Pennsylvania Railroad, just as, until 1899, there had been rival suppliers of Trains de Luxe. In that year, however, Pullman bought out the Wagner Palace Car Co., and George H. Daniels, who was the general passenger agent for the NYC from 1889 to 1907, decided that since he had to have Pullmans like the rival railroad, he must also create a new train, called, with brilliant forethought, *The Twentieth Century*. *Limited* was added a few months later.

Only 27 passengers, of the 42 that were possible, made the first trip, which had 2 sleepers, a diner, a buffet with a library, bath and, of course, an observation car. To cover 1,547 kilometres in 20 hours was amazing for those days. And one must not forget that Syracuse, with its famous railway in the middle of the street, slowed down the *Century* for many a decade. It was for places like Syracuse, as

well as for entering stations, that all American engines had bells as well as whistles. The *Twentieth Century* train numbers were 25 to Chicago and 26 for the return journey.

New stock arrived in 1903, including four observation cars, since the train usually ran in two portions, or sections, as they are called in American railroad parlance. To signal that there was another train following, two green flags adorned the engine on either side of the chimney. In the early cars the observation platform was wide; gradually it got smaller until it vanished altogether in the circular end to the observation lounge. Since it is American practice to push trains into termini, the observation platform, or lounge end, is the first thing the customer sees. On its rear brass rail, or at the centre of the rear windows, an illuminated plaque proclaimed the train's name. A special red carpet was unrolled along the platform

85. Inaugural Chicago–New York run of the new, streamlined *Twentieth Century Limited* leaving La Salle Street Station, 15th June 1938. Train designed by Henry Dreyfuss.

86. General Eisenhower, actress Beatrice Lillie and Mayor O'Dwyer of New York City inaugurate the *Twentieth Century Limited* in 1948 after World War II.

87. The *Twentieth Century Limited* of 1948 beside the Hudson River. Note the entirely enclosed observation car.

in both New York and Chicago, to give the train a prestigious environment, and thus a new term entered the American consciousness.

The *Twentieth Century* drew out of New York's Grand Central Station at 14:45, with third-rail electric haulage to Harmon and steam haulage the rest of the route.

Before the whole line became the New York Central, 4-4-2 engines were used on the Central's own portion of the line. Thereafter Lake Shore & Michigan Southern pulled the train with its Prairie engines, which were rather ungainly 2-6-2s but capable of a high turn of speed. These gave way to the K2 and K3 class Pacifics.

All-steel stock was introduced on the train between 1910 and 1912, weighing 25 tons more than the earlier wooden cars.

The *Twentieth Century* began running on the 'Water Level' route, so-called because the tracks followed the Hudson to Albany. There a portion of the train from Boston was attached after having been sent over the Boston & Albany Railroad. Later the *Twentieth Century* ran along the south shore of Lake Ontario and Lake Erie, through Utica, Syracuse, Buffalo, Cleveland, Toledo and Elkhart, often encountering severe snow storms along the route.

World War I, which for the United States lasted little more than a year, hardly seems to have disturbed the *Twentieth Century*. In the 1920s the *Limited* required so many sections that a new Train de Luxe, the *Advance Twentieth Century Limited,* was started. Since it ran one hour earlier from each terminus, the *Advance* had to provide lunch from New York.

Normally three sections were enough. Each section had a club car with baggage and dormitory (eighteen bunks) for crew, eight

sleepers (the old Pullman open type as explained in Chapter 1), a diner and of course the observation car. The dining cars were laid out with two seats on one side and four on the other, which allowed plenty of space down the central corridor, giving access to each table. The potted ferns were something never seen in European dining cars.

Before and after Prohibition, catering on the *Twentieth Century* was partially railway and partially Pullman. The latter firm, we are told, used bottled cocktails, whereas the NYC personnel shook cocktails to order. (What a contrast to the *Queen of Scots,* where whisky predominated, despite the admonition on the menu: 'Better drink Martini sweet or dry'.) Each section of the *Twentieth Century* had a barber, who wielded his cutthroat service at 70 miles an hour. Staffing all these sections at short notice was not easy. Only cars approved by the NYC for the service, marked with an asterisk on the Pullman list, could be used from the pool of available Pullman cars, which at this time totalled nearly 9,000. No privately owned Pullmans could be hitched onto so august a Train de Luxe as the *Twentieth Century* under any circumstances.

One section, and sometimes more, carried the Railway Post Office car, although the *Twentieth Century* included no mail storage cars, except sometimes between Boston and Albany. If the RPO was full, mail could be stored in the baggage compartment in the adjoining club car.

The *Twentieth Century* gained spice and zest from the presence of the *Broadway Limited,* offered by the rival Pennsylvania Railroad throughout the existence of the Central's great Train de Luxe. The *Twentieth Century Limited* pulled out at 12:40 from Chicago's La

88. Pullman Car *Quantzintecomatzin* built in 1902 by the Pullman Co. for the American Tourist Association and used in Mexico. The Aztec name means 'The noble eater of the royal dish'.

Salle Street Station, the same terminal used by the *Broadway*, and at one short period for some miles there used to be races between the two expresses, on parallel tracks! Such was the prestige of the *Century* that it often ran in three sections, whereas the *Broadway Limited,* which competed evenly enough in terms of comfort, needed but a single train.

Good though the Pacific engines were, it is the 4-6-4 class locomotive that will forever be associated with the steam days of the *Century*. Even the type style used for name, familiar all over the world, recalls the Hudson River. The 4-6-4s pulled the train all the way through from Harmon to Chicago. And 24 of them were needed for all the sections run in the service. They made their debut in 1930.

The New York Central could run all these train sections because it had 4 tracks for the 474 miles from Castleton, outside New York City, to Collinwood, just before Cleveland. Engine crews changed from time to time, while gantries at selected points replenished the coal from overhead hoppers. By the middle 1930s, the NYC wanted something more modern, and by 15th June 1938 it had its new *Century* stock ready.

There were 62 new light-weight cars, minus the famous open observation platform but with extremely luxurious master suites termed 'Master Rooms' in the observation cars. The *Twentieth Century* proudly became the first all-room train in the United States, with no archaic open Pullman sections. Ten streamlined Hudson engines led off the sections, and everything from locomotives to coffee cups was designed by Henry Dreyfuss. Something more powerful than the 4-6-4s was needed, and the Niagara 4-8-2 class 'Mohawks' were turned out. They could not be called 'Mountains' as elsewhere, because this word was associated with the hilly Pennsylvania line, whereas NYC advertised 'The Water Level Route—You Can Sleep'.

Steam gave way to diesel about 1945, and in 1948 General Eisenhower himself was called on to assist British actress Beatrice Lillie in the relaunching of the *Twentieth Century Limited*. They broke a champagne bottle over the observation car—the bottle filled, of course, with water from the Hudson River and Lake Erie, the Mohawk River and Lake Michigan.

Although the anti-trust laws had forced the Pullman Co. to sell its operations to the 59 railroads in 1947, operations continued as before, under the famous Pullman name, with Pullman Car conductors as well as head guards (train captains in America) on trains like the *Twentieth Century Limited*. And the full cost of running Pullmans fell on the various railroads, including the NYC.

As more and more patrons took to the air, the Train de Luxe struggled on for another ten years. This brought forth all kinds of ideas, such as merging the *Century* with the Santa Fe's *Super Chief* to give a through train across America, instead of merely switching sleeping cars, as the *Century* had done from time to time.

On 28th April 1958, the Central admitted second-class or coach passengers, scrapping the extra fare (payable on top of the supplement for the sleeping accommodation, depending on the luxury provided). This naturally drove a great many patrons onto the rival *Broadway,* which remained the luxurious, exclusive train it had always been.

Thus in 1962, the train's sixtieth birthday, new rolling stock was provided and great efforts made to advertise luxury at no extra

89. Pullman open panoramic car *Chililitli* built for the American Tourist Association in 1897 and used in Mexico.

cost: orchids for the ladies, buttonholes for the gentlemen, better food, new china, valet service, use of typewriter and electric shaver and complimentary morning paper—to no avail. What ordinary people need are low fares. When they want luxury they also want to be exclusive, for which they will pay.

A typical rake now comprised a Post Office car, a baggage-cum-dormitory car for the crew, an ordinary coach, two 'sleeper' coaches, a second light-weight diner for coach class, plus the traditional 1920s luxury-style Pullmans, with six instead of eight sleeping cars offering roomettes and bedrooms instead of the outdated section. The journey time since the advent of diesels was about sixteen hours or sometimes slightly less.

The New York Central sold some of their older, more luxurious *Century* stock to Mexico, and the enormous inroads into passenger traffic made by the airlines cancelled whatever luxury remained. On 31st December 1968, the Pullmans ceased to operate, and the railways assumed responsibility for sleeper services.

The *Twentieth Century* lasted two more years. By that time many railroads were in financial trouble, and even the Pennsylvania had to amalgamate with its rival, the New York Central. Finally, the American government set up Amtrak, then called 'Railpax', to start working its own trains with its own equipment (bought or leased from the railroads, or bought new).

What most distinguishes American rail travel from similar travel in Europe would seem to be the preference for togetherness.

An absolutely staggering amount of lore grew up around the *Twentieth Century Limited,* where the passengers' names on the train's car diagrams, always called a 'sailing list' in the US, were likened to sailing lists of the *Queen Mary* or the *Mauretania.* There were people who went just for the ride, to Albany and back, calling themselves the 'Twentieth Century Limited Associates'. Anybody who was anybody went on the train, and their wants were well known to the two famous diner stewards, Tommy O'Grady and Tommy Walsh. Most Pullman conductors seem to have had at least thirty years' experience attending to details of courtesy and decorum. Trouser pressing was a matter of course. There is, however, an absolutely splendid story of how an Ambassador was parted from his trousers, due to shunting operations at Albany, where the valet-servicing car somehow got switched from its section to the one behind. Consternation, followed by telegrams, eventually held the first part of the train at Harmon until the second part could arrive, trousers waving in the air from the leading car (which contained barber and valeting compartments), to be caught by the anxious Pullman porter on one of the rear cars of the leading section, where the diplomat waited in his underwear. The story may be apocryphal!

Perhaps nobody has done more to promote Trains de Luxe lore than the late Lucius Beebe, whose name will forever be associated with Trains de Luxe in America, since he was a professional journalist—writing for the *New York Times, Holiday,* the *San Francisco Chronicle* and many others—who combined his passion for trains with his authoritative views on fashion and manners. In 1958 he and his partner Charles Clegg were among the few private individuals in the USA who still maintained private railway cars. As no one else, perhaps, Beebe expressed the esprit de corps felt by passengers privileged to travel on Trains de Luxe. Among the really rich he found himself totally at ease, and he thoroughly enjoyed life. There is no doubt at all that this American interest in the great and pow-

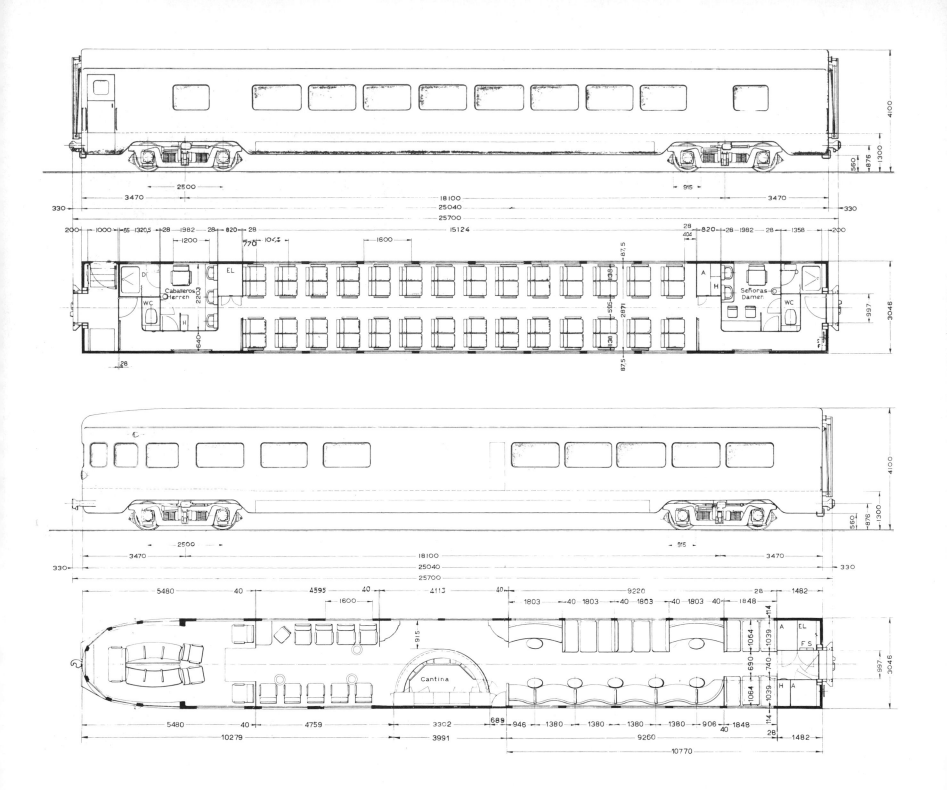

90. *Aztec Eagle* cars top: 1st-class car (gentlemen's WC left; ladies' right). above: Observation car with bar.

erful, who could be glimpsed aboard the liners or the *Century,* while remaining remote from ordinary mortals, did a great deal to keep the *Century* running.

Some Mexican Trains

Mexico once differed from the United States in that its citizens drove considerably fewer motor cars, and for many years good roads were non-existent there. Train or plane provided the only means of transportation to some parts of the country. The railways were built largely with American capital, and through trains from the USA to Mexico flourished.

In 1892 the Pennsylvania tour train made its first trip, with rolling stock offering comfort equal to that on the *Pennsylvania Limited.* The *Montezuma Special,* from New Orleans to Mexico City, started in 1899, put together by Pullman and the Mexican Central, Mexican International and Southern Pacific railroads, long before the Mexican railways had been nationalized to become the Nacional de Mexico (NdeM).

The United States' interest in Central America at the beginning of this century was enhanced by the Panama Canal. The *Panama Limited,* a Train de Luxe started in 1911 between Chicago and New Orleans, and its diner, with 23 entrées on the menu, has gone down in history as one of the finest in the world.

It was, however, the *Sunshine Special* that really began linking the US and Mexico, starting in 1915, when German submarines made crossing the Atlantic a hazardous business, and the Riviera in wartime had become less attractive than the beaches of the New World. This Train de Luxe, or perhaps one should say *Trén de Lujo,* entered service on 5th December 1915 from St. Louis and Memphis. The starting railroad was the Missouri Pacific, whose dining cars worked right through, with US and Mexican personnel. It switched cars at Little Rock and used the lines of Texas Pacific, Southern Pacific and National of Mexico, crossing at Laredo/Nuevo Laredo, unlike the *Montezuma,* which went via El Paso/Ciudad Juárez.

In 1937 came the *City of Mexico,* a once-a-week tourist Train de Luxe described as the finest international train in the world. It got passengers from St. Louis to Mexico City, in 47 hours 30 minutes. Through Trains de Luxe stopped in 1942 during the war.

Attempts in July 1946 to extend the *Sunshine Special* to New York and call it the *Sunshine Eagle* had to be abandoned at the last moment, since the NdeM did not buy its share of Pullmans needed for the joint service. So the train was hastily renamed *Texas Eagle.* No through sleeping cars ran again until 1962, after a twenty-year lapse in service. In 1948 the boss of the Missouri Pacific received the Order of the Aztec Eagle, the highest award given by Mexico to foreigners. Five years later a train named the *Aztec Eagle* began running from Mexico City to Nuevo Laredo. It consisted of three new trains supplied by Schindler of Zurich and a supplement of second-hand US Pullman equipment. The Swiss bogies needed careful looking after because of the poor Mexican track and road-bed, which prompted a change to American-type bogies. Through Pullmans from St. Louis appeared in 1962 with the *Aguila Azteca,* to give it its proper Mexican title, but the advent of Amtrak has imposed an uncomfortable switch at Laredo.

91. CIWL No. 1859, dining car built by Ringhoffer in 1908. It has the same primitive air-conditioning, using blocks of ice, first devised for WR Nos. 763–765.

92. Not what it seems. Pullman Car *Rainbow,* proudly carrying the Pullman Car Co. badge, was never used by the company, but sold to CIWL, which eventually renamed it *Cleopatra* (CIWL No. 58).

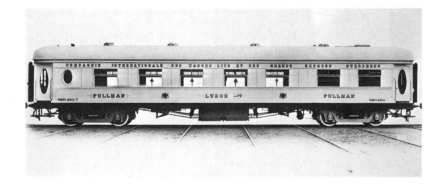

93. Pullman Car *Luxor* (CIWL No. 2914) was built in 1926 with a double roof for Egypt.

94. Mirrors replace marquetry, leather replaces upholstery, but otherwise the interior of *Luxor* is almost identical to that of European Pullman Cars.

95. The *Star of Egypt* arrives at Aswan. Local thieves were so skilled that had the windows been left open like this during the journey, clothes and baggage would have been stolen by means of fishing rods, launched during stops from carriages on the next track.

The *Sunshine Express*

Really it should be remembered as *Le Sunshine Express,* though this Train de Luxe was never called *L'Express de Soleil,* since it ran in neither Britain nor France, nor moreover in either Europe or America. Like so many Trains de Luxe, it was an all-Pullman Wagons-Lits service. The *Sunshine Express* started on 1st November 1929 and lasted just ten years, though its Pullmans survived to run again after World War II—up the Nile!

On board one found the rich who, for the want of time or inclination, preferred to visit the monuments of Luxor by some means other than Cook's Nile steamers, which at this period were part of the Wagon-Lits empire. And many of the passengers went one way by boat. Most were British or American. The Pullman cars they travelled in had ancient Egyptian names or names of Egypt's well-known places or lesser-known oases, from which a few years later the British Long Range Desert Group would set out in American jeeps to harass Rommel's Afrika Corps.

The European-style food was as impeccable as in other Wagons-Lits services. The Levantine, Maltese or even European staff spoke English and French, while Arabic could be heard in the pantry. The passengers had a high old time in the Pullman's clean, sparkling European surroundings, from which they could consider how the other half of the world lived, without having to share its squalor, dirt and noise. Only the appalling lurch as the train couplings tautened after every stop reminded them that the camels and donkeys and beggars outside were real enough, and not part of a diorama like the 'Trans-Siberian-in-Paris'! The staff were amazing in that they never spilt things, for the almighty lurch was always unexpected, never at the precise moment of leaving. The Egyptian Railways' engines did not have the power to start heavy trains unless the couplings were slack, and the same lurching occurred on the Pullmans, which Wagons-Lits also ran to Port Said and Alexandria.

Wagons-Lits first arrived in Cairo in 1894 and four years later began operations on the Egyptian Railways. Nagelmackers' immediate goal was to build hotels and compete with the well-established tourist monopoly of his rival, Thomas Cook. The most famous achievement of the latter had been the use of his Nile steamers for the relief of Khartoum. The establishment of a British garrison in Egypt created a demand for more hotel accommodation. To meet it, Wagons-Lits took over the Khedive's former palace at Gezereh, rearranging its massive furniture with the advice of London's Maple & Co., a firm that had furnished new Wagons-Lits hotels elsewhere.

opposite: 96. Poster (representing Rameses I at Thebes) for the Gezereh Fête, which took place at Cairo in 1896 and cost £2,000. Note the timetable of Trains de Luxe to Trieste, whence the Austrian Lloyd Line sailed to Alexandria. The printer's address is coincidentally that of the CIWL's present Paris central kitchens and stores, the Maison Raoul Dautry, built in 1952.

The Gezereh Palace would become the 'in' place for Western visitors, but Cairo already had a famous hotel, opened more than forty years earlier by the Englishman Shepheard, who ran it until 1860, when he sold Shepheards to a Mr. Zech. The latter's manager, Luigi Steinscheider, seems to have been the top hotelier of his day, and when Wagons-Lits hired him away to run the Gezereh, Shepheards found itself under siege.

To publicize the new Gezereh Palace, Nagelmackers authorized the expenditure of thousands of pounds for the Cairo Fête Committee, which at the Gezereh Sporting Club re-enacted the entry of Rameses I into Thebes, complete with camels, bands and hordes of Egyptians dressed as ancient soldiers.

In the face of such a promotional onslaught, Zech decided he could not continue and sold Shepheards to Wagons-Lits, which ran it with a new manager, Charles Baehler of Switzerland. Now Cook's tourists would have to stay there courtesy of their arch-rival, Wagons-Lits.

Shepheards was an institution of pure luxury. The Sudanese who staffed the hotel were totally honest, unlike the Egyptians of Cairo, and much blacker in complexion. The local touts, dragomen, etc., would loiter endlessly around the entrance of Shepheards, without ever being allowed to mount the steps. Wagons-Lits lost on the hotel and sold out to Baehler himself. Shepheards continued until the 1950s, when it burnt down. A new hotel of the same name occupies a different site.

Having got control of Cairo's two grand hotels in 1898, Wagons-Lits next planned to charter special railway sleepers with double roofs and slats over the windows. Paris supplied the sleepers while Prague sent three dining cars. The diners had a special air-conditioning arrangement worked by ice blocks. Three hundred pounds of ice reduced the temperature inside the cars to 77°F when it was 95° outside. With these cars, Wagons-Lits started the Cairo-Luxor Express, which became the *Star of Egypt* when the train, of sleepers and diners only, was extended beyond Luxor to Aswan, terminating at the El Shallal Station beside the Nile. Here a boat service led on up to Wadi Halfa, terminus of the narrow-gauge Sudan Railways. At one time some sort of through train with bogie changing was envisaged, but nothing came of it.

The cars for Africa were all painted white, and in 1902 Wagons-Lits organized the Tunis-Oran Express, using older, 6-wheeled sleepers on the lighter track. An excursion was offered from Paris via Palermo and back from Algeciras, but owing to the unreliablity of the ships, it was not a success, and these Trains de Luxe ended in 1903. Wagons-Lits worked many other services and hotels in Africa, and the company still staffs some sleeping cars of the Moroccan Railways between Casablanca and Oujia.

Most of the Pullman cars for Egypt, as well as the later steel sleeping cars, were built at Birmingham Railway Carriage & Wagon Co. and shipped direct from England to the Middle East. Two, however, originated in Italy. They had been among the ten supplied for the British Pullman Car Co. but then sold to Wagons-Lits for use until their own steel cars were ready, at which time the other eight returned to England. The Egyptian cars were scrapped in 1937 and replaced by an all-steel car sent from France.

After World War II the *Star of Egypt Express* was restored. In 1950 Wagons-Lits gave up operating Pullmans and diners in Egypt, but the sleepers continued until 1961. There is a stone model of a Pullman in the Cairo Museum.

Travel history, however, repeats itself. In 1976, Wagons-Lits opened the Etap Hotel, at Luxor, which the company built as part of its Etap chain of hotels. Other units in the chain included British Transport Hotels. In 1979 discussions took place between EER and Wagons-Lits regarding the possible staffing and servicing of 60 new sleepers, 12 club cars and 12 generator vans, all newly built by Messerschmidt-Bölkow-Blohm of Donauworth, West Germany, to standard European gauge. The arrangement went into effect in 1981. The cars are painted sand colour, to match the Egyptian desert.

The sleeping cars have 12 2-berth compartments and replace, on the Cairo-Aswan tourist route, Hungarian ones dating from 1962, which in turn had superseded the Wagons-Lits sleepers. Pre-cooked meals, stored in the sleepers' kitchenette/pantries, are served to passengers in their compartments, since there are no facilities at Aswan for servicing the trains. The van contains a refrigerator for supplies, a staff dining saloon with cooker and a baggage compartment. Hot and cold snacks are available, as well as drinks from the bar of the club car, which has 20 chairs, arranged round tables in groups of 4 or 3. The cars ride on Swiss Schlieren bogies, cooled by Swiss Brown Boveri air-conditioning. A 650-horsepower generator with 40 hours independent operation supplies all the electrical requirements, thereby eliminating the need to refuel. Each train can carry up to 240 people in its 18 sleepers, 2 bar cars and a van. The sleepers all have large fold-down tables, and the all-inclusive fare for a double berth is £E28,035 (£E48,45/US $105 for a single). This covers hot dinner, breakfast, sleeper berth and single fare from Cairo to Aswan or vice versa, with break of journey at Luxor and no reduction if the journey is confined to the Cairo-Luxor sector. At present, half the vehicle order has been delivered, so the service runs nightly each way between Cairo and Aswan, where a new line diverges to El Shallal and terminates further south at El Sadd el Ali near the High Dam.

A relief train between Cairo and Luxor runs when required, and when the rest of the vehicles arrive during the year, the growing numbers of groups will be better catered for. Group reservations are handled by Wagons-Lits' Paris headquarters. Though the train is as yet unnamed, the *Star of Egypt* has truly risen again, complete with club-car bars that are the direct successors of the *Sunshine Express*.

III

THE GOLDEN AGE OF LUXURY TRAINS

9. An Aristocrat: *Le Train Bleu*

However dark the times may be,
I oft times in a mirage see
The sleek blue coaches of the Wagons-Lits
That greet the traveller, on Calais Quay.
                                    Kenneth Brown

The famous royal-blue, all-steel sleeping cars of the Wagons-Lits made their debut at Calais on 19th October 1922, running on the weekly Bombay Express, the boat train to Marseilles Docks that once connected with the Peninsular & Oriental Steam Navigation Co.'s liner to India. But only on 9th December 1922 did Lord Dalziel have enough of the forty new sleepers to launch his post-war revamp of the Calais-Méditerranée Express to the Riviera. The campaign included repainting the teak diners and fourgons blue and lining them out in gold to match the sleeping cars.

A whole generation had grown up ignorant of the delights of the Côte d'Azur, whose pre-war splendour had led Wagons-Lits in 1913 to order their first all-steel sleeping car from Pullman in Chicago (Type X, No. 2700). But war caused the order to be cancelled.

The post-war S-class steel sleepers were built by the Leeds Forge Co., a firm that became a virtual pioneer of all-steel railway cars in England. Leeds fitted out the sleeping cars in a special shed at Immingham in north-east England, where the wartime train ferries had been temporarily laid up. From here the carriages moved by ferry toward Calais, since the river at Richborough Port (near Dover), although constantly dredged during the war, had now silted up again and become useless for shipping. The difficulty of transporting the rolling stock across the Channel led directly to the establishment in 1924 of the Harwich-Zeebrugge freight-train ferry, which still runs today between Britain and Belgium.

Nagelmackers' son René, Lord Dalziel's son-in-law, was Wagons-Lits general manager at this time. Together with the Nord and PLM railways, Wagons-Lits invited 150 guests to Nice, in two special trains, one originating in Calais and the other in Paris. The guests included 23 representatives of American and British newspapers, and about 20 from the French press. Within 10 minutes of each other, both trains arrived mid-morning at Nice, where they were met by the Crown Prince of Sweden, the Duke of Connaught and the Mayor of Nice.

Monsieur Margot, general manager of the PLM, declared the cars to be of supreme comfort and premium luxury *(le luxe de bon aloi)*. The *New York Times* said there was nothing in the United States to compare with the sensible arrangements providing maximum comfort and privacy together with economy of cost and space. Forty-four years later the carriages could still give the author a comfortable ride, and their toilets seemed remarkable in remotest eastern Turkey, where by then they formed part of the Dogu Express between Istanbul and Kars.

Success was instantaneous. The Riviera once more became the most fashionable place to spend January and February, and to be seen on board the Calais-Méditerranée was an essential part of the snobbish social round. The smart set immediately christened it the *Blue Train,* and going on it was considered to be the most exciting pastime of the period.

The Côte d'Azur proved no less popular with visiting Americans and the Parisian élite than with the British, and it consequently could attract a full complement of passengers on the Paris-Méditerranée Express, which ran separately from the Calais train each night. Not to be outdone by Monte Carlo, the director of the Deauville casino invited *le tout Paris* to come to his chic Normandy seaside resort, doing so by helping in the relaunch of the Trouville-Deauville Express in June 1923. Four blue sleeping cars in day position were used for this afternoon train, along with a diner converted to a bar and the saloon used by Marshal Foch during the war. The guests included Sergei Diaghilev, who said that this trip inspired him to commission the *Train Bleu* ballet.

97. Poster for the English clientele of the *Blue Train*, about 1929. Note the CIWL monogram with the big 'C', to indicate the acquisition of Thomas Cook.

SUMMER ON THE FRENCH RIVIERA BY THE BLUE TRAIN

above: 98. The first all-steel sleeping car, CIWL S type, in the fitting-out shed at Immingham (Lincs., England). Note the absence of steps, which would have exceeded the English gauge. The cars were painted before being dispatched by train ferry to Calais. The one here is CIWL No. 2641, in 1922.

right: 99. S-type *Blue Train* compartment in day position. Note the marquetry, the glass ventilator panes of the window, the spitoon, the lavabo covered by a hinged table-top. *Sous le lavabo se trouve un vase,* whose cupboard door is very visible.

The S2 had a wider distance than the R type between berth and wash-room door. There were red and black wall-to-wall carpeting and linen droguets to stand on when undressing. Main lighting came from the ceiling hung with a globe containing several bulbs, one of which was blue and could be controlled by a cleverly designed three-way switch. Concealed reading lights, fitted flush to the wall, illuminated when their brass cover was pulled out. A plush-upholstered fob-watch hanger was provided, and a handle, sealed at the end of a tube, operated the alarm system, described in a four-language notice. The coat-hangers all had rubber stops to prevent rattling. Also rattle-proof were folding rings to hold tumblers, or bottles, normally stored in the wash-room cupboard.

For safety reasons, all new rolling stock for France had to be of steel construction. The first French-built steel dining cars appeared in 1926, displacing the wooden ones in the *Blue Train* to less distinguished runs elsewhere. In this, the hey-day of grandiose service, the *Blue Train* became 'the best train to the Riviera', as the travel agents prosaically described it. Agatha Christie wrote of 'the Millionaire's Train' when she first introduced Hercule Poirot and had him investigate a sudden death aboard a Train de Luxe on which he just happened to be travelling. *The Mystery of the Blue Train* was first published in 1928, at a time when lady travellers often had their maids quartered in second class and many young bloods took their valets with them to the Riviera as a matter of course.

After only six years, even grander sleeping cars seemed necessary for the superior *Blue Train*. Lord Dalziel, just before he died in 1928, ordered ninety new cars for the *Blue Train*. A year later the new cars were ready, called Luxe or Lx (x = 10) because they

only had ten large single-berth compartments instead of the more usual twelve of the S class, which were transferred to the Simplon Orient Express in 1929. Thirty of the cars were built in Birmingham, England, and sixty at Aytré, near La Rochelle, France, in a works originally started during World War I to assemble boxcars shipped over from the US for the American Army in 1917. Exclusively first class, the new cars were the acme of comfort, with berths larger than the standard. Inlaid mahogany double doors hid the extra-large wash-basin, which when opened revealed a pair of full-length mirrors. Only a short time after its debut in 1929, the *Blue Train* suffered the same slump that had struck the stock market. Now, a single train to San Remo, combining the Calais- and Paris-Méditerranée, sufficed to serve Marseilles, Cannes, Nice, Monte Carlo and Ventimiglia, the Italian frontier station where most of the cars were detached. The Lx class had to be reconstructed to take second-class travellers in double berths either in all (Lx 20) or in six of their ten compartments (Lx16). And thus they would remain on the *Train Bleu* for over forty years!

Only at the end of 1936 did any Wagons-Lits cars slip in and out of London in the Night Ferry, and then only at hours when few people saw them pass. In England, relatively few people had taken the *Blue Train*, but these thought of it and the Orient Express as epitomizing the Wagons-Lits network. The whole gamut of international operations of Trains de Luxe lay deliberately shrouded in mystery, to ensure swifter and easier passage of the frontiers on their route. World War II marked the end of an era of the grand European expresses, composed exclusively of Wagons-Lits cars, which in September 1939 totalled 1,738, spread over 24 countries, including Britain, where just 12 cars could enter. In 1943 I was moved to write:

> When at last, I reached Algiers,
> I was almost moved to tears!
> Wasted as a transit camp,
> In the sidings, cold and damp,
> That I came so far to see—

> Rows and rows of Wagons-Lits!
> Now, I fear, I never shall
> Sally forth to El Shallal—
> Dim terminus, beyond Aswan
> From Cairo, going to Sudan—
> Blue Train! O symbol of the war,
> That no one here is fighting for,
> What's the good, when Hitler's dead,
> If you stay 'Mitropa' Red?
> (Eighth Army, 1942)

During the war some 845 Wagons-Lits cars were damaged, destroyed or seized by various forces. France alone lost 189. But the Wagons-Lits survived, thanks very largely to their Director General, René Margot Noblemaire, and with just one international Train de Luxe, composed exclusively of CIWL sleeping, dining and fourgon cars, the company recommenced the *Blue Train*. In 1949 the proud name at last reappeared on the destination boards.

For sixty years, discriminating people of means had been escaping from the sea-mists of the Channel, or from a wintry Paris, cold, grey and generally unattractive, to arrive next morning beside a sparkling blue sea, warm and sunny, beset with palms and mimosas. One thing has changed in the second half of the 20th century: it is much colder than it used to be strolling along the Promenade des Anglais in February.

A colossal 0-10-0 tank engine (050TQ) now brought the two Calais sleepers into the Gare de Lyons, the cars hitched, as always,

overleaf left. 101. Lx10 compartment in day position. Note head-cushion, lamp and mirror.

overleaf right: 102. The same compartment in night position. The Lx10 had larger single berths with angle-bracket reading lights on the wall above the settee (which had to be removed when the economic slump of the 1950s forced the introduction of double-berth compartments). The compartments had large wash-basins sunk in a shelf to form a dressing-table, with an adjustable round shaving mirror above it, the whole enclosed by two curved double doors, stretching from floor to cabinet height, which when opened provided two moveable full-length mirrors. The outside of these doors had inlaid marquetry designs and shark-skin panels at the base. Electric razor points appeared in CIWL cabins about 1950. The decorators of these cars are identified in the Appendices.

to the *Golden Arrow*. By 1950 this was the only steam engine to enter the all-electric terminus. An elderly electric shunting engine placed the sleepers at the head of the *Train Bleu*, already in the station. Eventually the post-war demand would be enormous, and up to fourteen cars were permitted in the rake. The whole train ran to Ventimiglia, but only the leading car from Calais proceeded to San Remo.

Suave, warm, inviting and disdaining to welcome you aboard with some horrendous public-address system, like those used for modern trains, the *Blue Train* preserved an authentic 1930s luxury. In 1951 the service acquired its famous bar. 'Passez un moment

above: 103. WR 2975 on arrival from Ostend via Harwich at the Thomas Co headquarters in Peterborough. Bought to commemorate fifty years of associati with Wagons-Lits, the car is seen here on a low loader.

below: 104. From Dijon to Marseilles the *Train Bleu* was hauled by the vast 241P class 4-8-2 engines, which will forever be associated with this train. In 1949 the SNCF began electrification from Laroche to Dijon, and from Paris to Laroche in 1950. The great engines were slowly driven southwards by the overhead wire's advance, and finally off the line altogether in 1962.

opposite: 105. Wine-bottle labels. The perforated letter 'O' indicates the St. Ouen (Paris) cellars of CIWL. Those with letters 'B' and 'S' (for Bordeaux and Strasbourg) could not be obtained for reproduction here. Note the Belgian Division label.

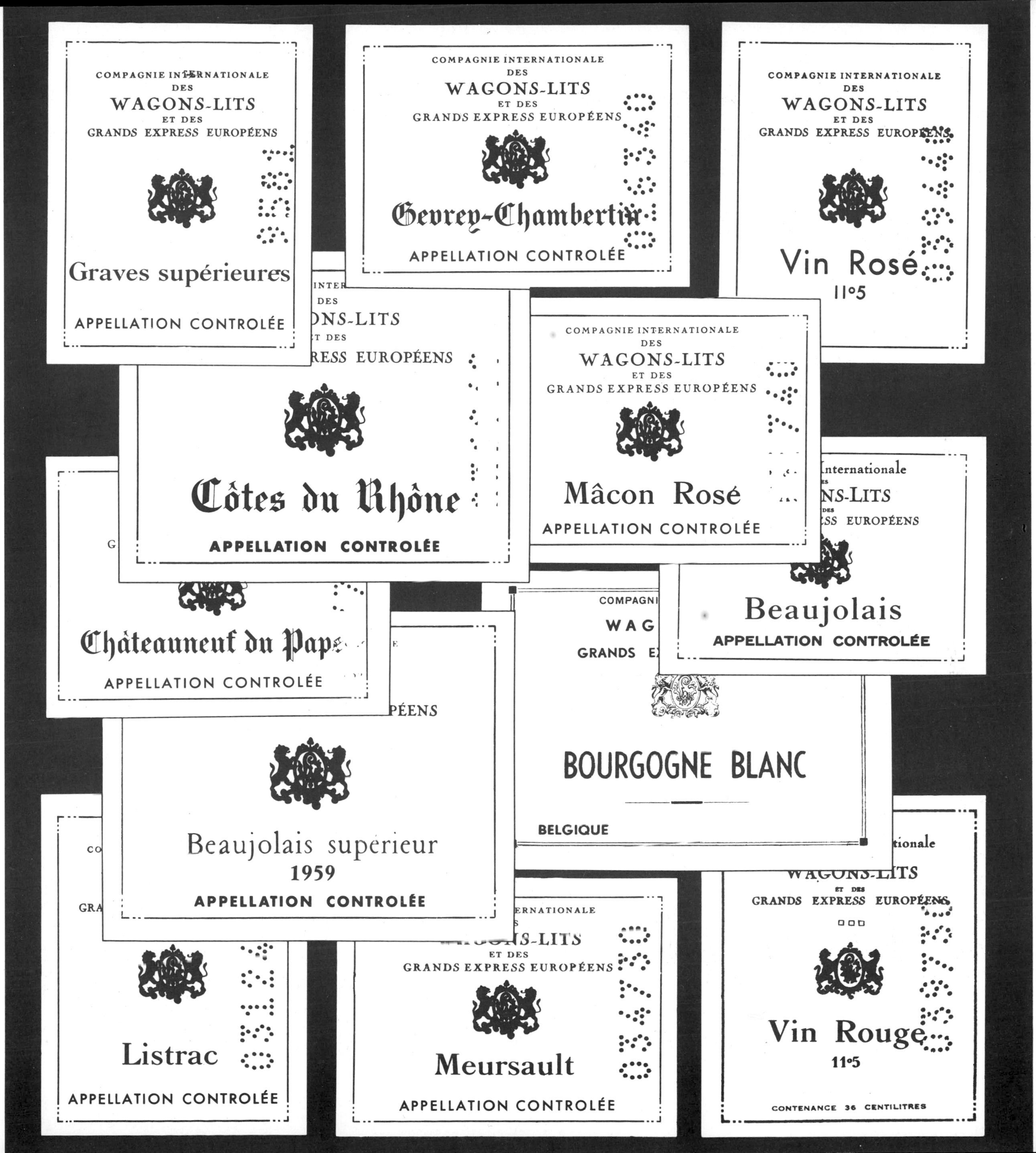

COMPAGNIE INTERNATIONALE
DES
WAGONS-LITS
ET DES
GRANDS EXPRESS EUROPÉENS

Graves supérieures

APPELLATION CONTROLÉE

COMPAGNIE INTERNATIONALE
DES
WAGONS-LITS
ET DES
GRANDS EXPRESS EUROPÉENS

Gevrey-Chambertin

APPELLATION CONTROLÉE

COMPAGNIE INTERNATIONALE
DES
WAGONS-LITS
ET DES
GRANDS EXPRESS EUROPÉENS

Vin Rosé
11°5

Côtes du Rhône

APPELLATION CONTROLÉE

COMPAGNIE INTERNATIONALE
DES
WAGONS-LITS
ET DES
GRANDS EXPRESS EUROPÉENS

Mâcon Rosé

APPELLATION CONTROLÉE

Châteauneuf du Pape

APPELLATION CONTROLÉE

Beaujolais
APPELLATION CONTROLÉE

COMPAGNIE
WAGONS
GRANDS EXPRESS EUROPÉENS

BOURGOGNE BLANC

BELGIQUE

Beaujolais supérieur
1959
APPELLATION CONTROLÉE

Listrac

APPELLATION CONTROLÉE

COMPAGNIE INTERNATIONALE
DES
WAGONS-LITS
ET DES
GRANDS EXPRESS EUROPÉENS

Meursault

APPELLATION CONTROLÉE

WAGONS-LITS
ET DES
GRANDS EXPRESS EUROPÉENS

Vin Rouge
11°5

CONTENANCE 36 CENTILITRES

106. The *Blue Train* in 1967 at San Remo, Italy, with one sleeper from Calais and one ordinary FS coach from Ventimiglia. 341-class diesel No. 2016. After stabling the train, the engine was ready to return to Ventimiglia—with the tail-light board already in place!

agréable', said the advertisement, 'dans la Voiture Salon Bar; rendez-vous des habitués de la Côte'. The *Train Bleu* left at 20:00, and dinner was served immediately thereafter, announced by a handbell tinkled in the corridors of the sleepers. Since the dining car had 42 comfortable armchairs instead of the less comfortable 56 seats, part of the Voiture Salon Bar was turned into an overflow saloon. After the 30 minutes in which half the world met the other half, the habitués would troop into dinner, leaving the inexperienced to discover that the 'moment agréable' lasted all the way to Dijon, with no dinner until after 10 o'clock at night. You learnt the hard way! But when you entered the diner, with its fresh flowers on every table (a preview of tomorrow's carnation nurseries at Ventimiglia), with white crockery instead of blue, and with a gold WL badge instead of dark blue, the long wait was worth it.

The menu, hand-written by the chef de brigade, might be:

> *Consommé Madrilène*
> *Filets de soles Duclère*
> *Poulets cocotte grand-mère*
> *Petits pois à la française*
> *Salade de saison*
> *Fromages variés*
> *Boule de neige*
> *Corbeille de fruits*

On the return journey to Paris, dinner would be served after Nice. One of the barmen was an artist of no mean reputation, no doubt inspired by the Lalique décor and, of course, the view at sunset. And the railway has by far the best view of the Riviera, albeit interrupted by tunnels, where until 1965 the SNCF's 141R class 2-8-2 oil-fired engines emitted terrible black smoke. These famous American- and Canadian-built Mikados were constructed to French design, and for thirty years they formed the backbone or work-horse of every sort of train all over the country, from the *Train Bleu* to the humblest goods train.

When third class was abolished in 1956, one needed a first-class railway ticket in order to occupy a double berth. So P-class cars were added to the train, and spoilt its outward appearance. These unpainted stainless-steel cars, built in 1955 under license from the Budd Co. of the USA, have two levels of small single-berth compartments, for which a lower first-class 'special' supplement was charged. In 1960 the two Calais cars became just one.

Tourist-class passengers were admitted to the *Blue Train* in 1962. Gradually the MU Modern Universal sleepers with one, two or three (tourist) berths replaced the Lx class, though the latter stayed on relief *Blue Trains* until the 1970s. In 1964, electrification made possible a later departure time from Paris, and the Calais–San Remo car was removed altogether. *Le Bleu* now became totally and impeccably French. Since 1972 all the cars belong to the SNCF, though Wagons-Lits still staff, furnish and victual the sleeping cars. If one happens not to be French the train still exudes a benign superiority, for the habitués have always been cosmopolitan, though in the last years of the bar, said to be more elegant than that of the Ritz, one could sense a mild relief that the last remaining sleeper from Calais had been relegated in 1964 to the 'Flandres-Riviera' Express, never a Train de Luxe. The 'voiture salon bar', with its Côte d'Azur Pullman décor, was elegant, but only those who were part of the Parisian *haut monde* really belonged, and by their very presence they made the *Blue Train* more elegant.

The *Blue Train*'s bar disappeared in 1975, along with the Lalique glass décor that had been the service's last link with pre-war magnificence. One of the bar cars can be found in Intraflug's 'Nostalgic Orient Express'. The diner, by now an SNCF red one, ran from Paris to Dijon, but not on the return journey. Still, travellers could have a pre-departure drink in it, if room permitted, when friends came to see them off. And at the end, Wagons-Lits started serving dinners before the train left, even expanding this service on Fridays by means of extra seating added to an ordinary first-class coach with tables. Half the sleeping cars were now detached at Nice, and couchette cars brought from Paris in the Côte d'Azur ordinary overnight express were coupled to the other half of the train continuing to Ventimiglia.

The year 1980 marked the end of an era. The *Blue Train* lost its dining car in the spring, thanks to a 21:46 departure, long after dinner. Before boarding, passengers can dine in the Buffet du Train Bleu at the Gare de Lyons, one of Paris' top restaurants and now a French national monument.

The same dual-voltage 22200-class BB engine, introduced in 1979, is able to run right through to the Riviera without change, which speeds up the service still further. Though pauses are made to change drivers, the first official stop is St. Raphael. Previously, the 9300 BB from Paris was changed to a 25200 dual-voltage BB engine at Marseilles/Blancarde. Now destination boards announce

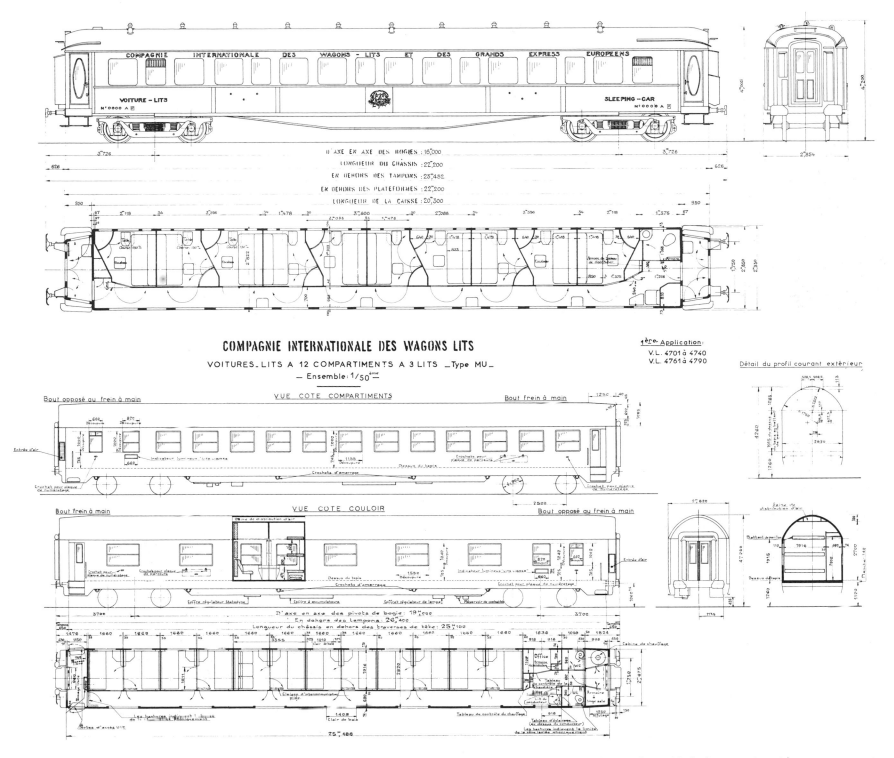

COMPAGNIE INTERNATIONALE DES WAGONS LITS ET DES GRANDS EXPRESS EUROPEENS

VOITURE – LITS N° 0000 A

SLEEPING – CAR N° 0000 A

COMPAGNIE INTERNATIONALE DES WAGONS LITS

VOITURES - LITS A 12 COMPARTIMENTS A 3 LITS _Type MU_

— Ensemble: 1/50ème —

1ère Application:
V.L. 4701 à 4740
V.L. 4761 à 4790

Détail du profil courant extérieur

VUE COTE COMPARTIMENTS

Bout opposé au frein à main   Bout frein à main

VUE COTE COULOIR

Bout frein à main   Bout opposé au frein à main

top: 107. Lx10-type sleeping car (Luxe, 10 single compartments).

above: 108. MU-type sleeping car (Modern Universal with 12 compartments of 1. 2 or 3 berths).

97

above: 109. MU class sleeping cars have been the standard cars of the *Blue Train* since 1977, superseding the Lx class. Rather than left unpainted, the standard MU sleeper was returned to the royal-blue colour scheme. It contains 36 berths in 12 Universal compartments, with 1 vestibule instead of 2, as on the U (reparations) class. Berths already made up let down at night instead of having to be raised. Thick line drawings or blown-up photographs decorate the formica underside of the berths. Three seats, whose back-rests fold flat to make tables by day and a level rest for the lower berth at night, provide spacious day travel. Forced-draught ventilation has given place to air-conditioning on later models. The beds, with foam-rubber mattresses, are longer and wider than pre-war cars.

The Pool also use MU cars, but not the M or Modern class introduced for Italy by Wagons-Lits, with only 2 berths per compartment, all 1st class.

right: 110. The good life in the dining room of the *Blue Train* about 1950.

Train Bleu in much smaller lettering, and couchette cars run all the way in the train. They were added in the autumn of 1979 when a new train, running even later, was put on from Paris to Nice. Called *L'Esterel,* for the hills near Cannes, it too consists of sleeping and couchette cars only. This is the service recommended to travellers for Cannes, where the *Blue Train* now stops at seven in the morning.

The SNCF has officially proclaimed that the era of Trains de Luxe is over, replaced by the age of the *Trains à Grande Vitesse* ('high-speed trains'), which went into service in the autumn of 1981 between Paris and Lyons (see Chapter 15).

But the famous still patronize the *Train Bleu*. Frequent passengers are Prince Rainier and Princess Grace, who arrive from

Paris at Monaco's new station, with its royal waiting room. And in 1983 the *Train Bleu* will be celebrating its centenary, though, as mentioned in Chapter 5, it ran from 1883 to 1889 as the Calais-Nice-Rome Express.

10. Dancing Cars, Radio, Telephones, Bath Cars

People have been dancing their way across Europe in Trains de Luxe for almost a century. No scribe of the Orient Express fails to mention Onady Kahniar and his eleven minstrels serenading the inaugural press party at Szegedin in 1883. When it was time to go, the journalists bundled the musicians into the diner, where they regaled the dancing passengers non-stop for an hour and a half of Hungarian rhapsodies.

The first Wagons-Lits diner fitted with a gramophone ran in 1929 on the Paris–La Rochelle train, followed closely by dancing arrangements in the 1929 Paris-Nice *Côte d'Azur* Pullman. Enhancing the spicy allure of excitement on board was the avant-garde décor of Lalique's glass panels. One of these cars is currently in service with SNCF's weekend special, *Azur 2000,* which also contains a bar, a cinema and couchette as well as sleeping cars. Train hostesses double as baby-sitters and child-minders while the passengers live it up. The *Azur 2000* is jokingly called the train on which the clientele never sleep. Renamed *Alpes 2000* during the winter, it runs to the Savoy at Bourg St. Maurice instead of to Nice. The DSG (see Chapter 11) also have a number of dancing cars for special trains. They are mostly converted dining cars whose kitchens have been retained for snacks and suppers, or even full meals when the cars are fitted up for conferences.

About 1922 experiments with radios began on such long-distance American trains as the *Broadway Limited*. The Chicago, Milwaukee, St. Paul & Pacific Railroad's *Pioneer* at first had headphones for passengers, but by 1927 a radio show was being broadcast in a special car. This railroad also ran a dancing car with six-piece band and even provided a Victrola for use when the band was resting. The proliferation of radios on American trains was partly due to the constraints of prohibition, since the only other on-board entertainment was reading or playing cards! In Britain, during the 1930s the LNER allowed the *Flying Scotsman* to make some radio

experiments—in those days called 'listening-in'. The splendid isolation of the Orient Express, which never had a radio, has been extolled by travellers who rejoiced at being cut off from telephones, arrangements and world news, save for what local newspapers could offer with all the excitement of a different language at almost every stop.

Train stenographers could be found on the *Twentieth Century Limited* as early as 1903, and train secretaries were common on all the American long-distance crack expresses. One of their duties was to supervise the telephones, first installed in the 1920s but usable only at starting points during the half-hour before departure when the train was at the platform. Radio telephones came on board after World War II and could be utilized, for instance, on the *Broadway Limited* for roughly half an hour before and after Newark, Philadelphia, Harrisburg, Pittsburgh and Englewood. Twenty years later Penn Central was advertising its Metroliners between New York and Washington as 'the fastest telephones in the East'.

In Europe, far fewer trains have telephones than in North America, though the German Railways (DB) introduced them on the *Rheingold* in 1963 (see Chapter 15) and have subsequently extended the service throughout the large inter-urban network of business men's trains, which run and connect with each other at regular intervals.

British Railways provide neither telephones nor secretaries on their trains. The German Railways, however, offer train secretaries in large numbers, as do the Austrian Railways' K or Komfort-Wagen, introduced on some business runs after 1955. The *Mistral* TEE had a secretary until the mid-1970s; otherwise, few train secretaries are to be found in France. Telephones did not exist on any of the CIWL cars listed in the Appendices until 1979, when three elderly dining cars were equipped with them for the NS Dutch Railways' Inter-City Plus trains (Maastricht-Amsterdam and Heer-

left: 111. The first radio receiver, aboard the *Pioneer Limited* of the Chicago, Milwaukee & St. Paul Railroad, about 1925.

left below: 112. Bathrooms came early to American trains. Here is the CM&StP's 1912 bathroom on the *Olympian* running between Chicago and Seattle.

below right: 113. This elegant bathroom belongs to the Turkish Presidential Train, constructed for Atatürk by Linke-Hofmann-Busch.

opposite: 114. Pierre Fixmasseau's 1929 poster for the *Côte d'Azur* Pullman, a train that included a dancing car. The prize-winning poster was shown as an example to a generation of art students of all nationalities.

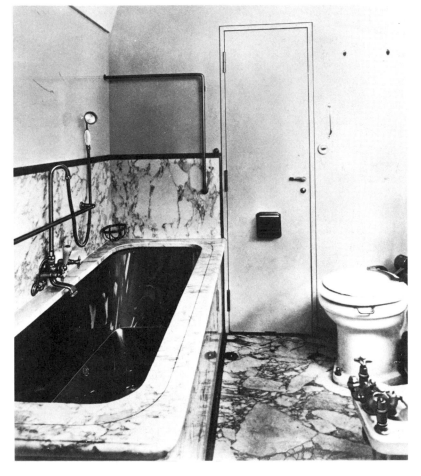

len-Den Haag). NS diners replaced these cars in 1981. In Spain the 6000 series CIWL sleeping cars have internal telephones from the cabins to the conductor's seat.

Because of long distances and climate, lounge or buffet cars with bathing facilities appeared very early on American trains, though private bathrooms in private Pullmans had been in use even earlier. In 1898 the Southern Pacific's *Sunset Limited* included a full-size bath aboard its vestibule-composite Pullman *El Indio*. This 77-foot car also had a baggage room, a barber shop, a buffet and a parlour-saloon with writing desk, small library and sofa, as well as chairs and tables. The 1900 observation car built by Barney & Smith for the Northern Pacific's North Coast Limited also had a full-size bath, and other railroads soon followed suit.

In 1937 Wagons-Lits installed a bath in Lx sleeper No. 3538 for the Duke of Windsor during His Royal Highness' exile on the Continent. French Admiral Darlan used the car in 1940–42, but it was sabotaged in 1944 and remained perched on a broken bridge with one end awash in the Loire for over a year. After repair work lasting two and a half years, the car was restored to its former glory as a standard sleeper without bath. It continues to run in Spain.

Showers in sleeping cars outside Europe are so commonplace that their absence on the Continent is conspicuous. CIWL did not progress beyond a single shower in the fourgon of the Simplon Orient and Rome expresses. And this was a summer facility only, lasting from 1929 to 1939. The element of surprise, which helped to give these trains their romantic air of mystery, spread even to the showers, since they were not always available. One lady discovered this in 1934 when, invited to take a shower, she replied that she would be ready to do so in half an hour. Then, clad only in a dressing-gown, she made her way to the rear sleeper—only to find that the fourgon had disappeared, removed after an axle had run hot. In those days Mussolini's minions delighted in separating passengers from their luggage!

115. Telephone compartment on South Africa's luxurious *Bloutrein*

11. Germany's Mitropa Company

The first Prussian State Railways sleeping car, the *Bromberger,* was started in 1880 between Thorn and Kreuz on the Prussian Ost Bahn, carrying first- and second-class passengers. After the Berlin-Cologne portion of the Wagons-Lits Berlin-Ostend service had shown what possibilities there were, the Prussians (as noted in Chapter 6) suspended their contracts with the CIWL in 1885.

This action forced CIWL to relax its exclusivity of rights on the South German Railways and allow its Berlin routes to be worked with Prussian State sleepers. Meanwhile the CIWL retained their west-east Trains de Luxe, such as the Orient Express, which now included the Calais-Vienna sleeper attached in the outskirts of Paris, inasmuch as the previous route had been cut in two: Calais-Cologne and Mainz-Vienna. The Prussian State's sleepers also ran from Berlin to Basle via Strasbourg and on the Alsace-Lorraine lines, operated by the Imperial Railway Office at Berlin.

By 1882 German dining-car companies were being started to compete with and limit the circulation of CIWL diner services in Germany. The first was the Riffelmann Dining Car Co., followed shortly afterwards by G. Kromey & Son OHG and the Nord West Deutschland Speisewagen Gesellschaft operating in north-west Germany, where the firm also ran station buffets. These buffets, providing luncheon baskets, were themselves extra competition for dining cars.

In 1898 Wagons-Lits started the Deutsche Eisenbahn Speisewagen Gesellschaft, known always as the DSG, not the DESG as modern writers put it, just as the Internationale Eisenbahn Schlafwagen Gesellschaft was always known as ISG long before Wagons-Lits dropped the Eisenbahn from its title in German. The DSG must not be confused with the present-day company bearing the same initials, started some thirty years after the original organization's disappearance.

When royal pressure on Prussia got the Nord Express started in 1896, it was quickly followed by Wagons-Lits' Nord-Sud Brenner Express, running from Berlin through Munich to Verona and soon extended through Milan to Cannes. At this time Wagons-Lits had opened their Riviera Palace Hotel at Cimiez, and trains came to the Riviera from all directions.

There was the Méditerranée Express for the British and the French, the St. Petersburg–Vienna–Cannes service for the Russians and Austrians and the Rome-Cannes run for the Italians. When Queen Victoria came to Nice in 1902 and stayed in the Riviera Palace Hotel, instead of a villa, it set the seal on the establishment. Hitherto, Monte Carlo, with its formidable suicide rate following gambling disasters, had been considered not quite nice. Wagons-Lits built another Riviera Palace Hotel here and brought Luigi Steinscheider from Cairo's Gezereh Palace to run it. The hotel had its own electric tramway, built by Wagons-Lits, running over the steam rack-railway of La Turbie in gauntleted track (tram laid within part of the rack rails). The tram terminated by the terrace of the hotel, which was above Monte Carlo on French territory, about half-way up to La Turbie, whose railway Wagons-Lits had bought.

So prestigious was the Riviera that the Berliners wanted a shorter service than all round by the Brenner. So they allowed Wagons-Lits to start the Riviera Express, serving Frankfurt and then Strasbourg. It proceeded through the length of the Imperial Alsatian line and entered France, reaching Lyons via Besançon, with a wagon-salon running from Lyons to Ventimiglia via Marseilles, Cannes and Nice. The Nord-Sud was soon extended to Rome, Naples and Palermo, using the train ferries to Sicily via Messina, where a sleeper was detached for Syracuse.

Further Trains de Luxe followed. For liner passengers the Lloyd Express began running in 1908 from Hamburg and Berlin, with a branch from Amsterdam to Frankfurt, Basle and Genoa over the Gotthard. It would soon be followed by the Gotthard Express, using the same route but serving ordinary travellers visiting Italy. Another Middle European Train de Luxe was the Berlin-Karlsbad

Express linking with the Vienna-Karlsbad Express, a day train worked with wagons-salons, unlike the Karlsbad Express of sleepers from Paris to that Bohemian resort (now called Karlovy Vary).

Train ferries plied the Baltic, and in Sweden the State Railways (SJ) had developed their network of sleeper services. Before World War I the SJ were working a Stockholm-Berlin sleeper via Malmö. In Denmark Wagons-Lits had exclusive rights over the Danish State Railways, though until 1907, when Wagons-Lits bought the cars, the Hamburg-Copenhagen sleeper was run with Wagons-Lits–built cars and Wagons-Lits conductors and sleeping cars belonging to the Mecklenburg State Railways, which, like the Prussian State Railways, refused to allow CIWL to run on their tracks.

When World War I broke out, all Wagons-Lits vehicles in Germany were stopped and later sequestered. The creation of banking enterprise capital, the Central European Sleeping Car Co., or MSG Mitteleuropäische Schlafwagengesellschaft, was not formed until November 1916, for operation in Germany, Austria and Hungary. It initiated service on 1st January 1917, but in the meantime the well-known Balkanzug came into being as a military train linking Berlin with Constantinople, just as the CIWL's Berlin-Budapest-Orient Express had in 1900–02, running to Budapest via both Breslau and Dresden (in two routes, not worked simultaneously). 'Mitteleuropäische' was shortened to 'Mitropa' as the company name.

The Mitropa took its 116 dining cars from the DSG without payment, and from Wagons-Lits it took 64 dining cars and 35 sleeping cars. But the total Mitropa sleeper fleet was mainly composed of cars from the Prussian and other state railways. With directors from Hapag Lloyd, North German Lloyd and the Deutsche Bank, Mitropa set up several services aiming to serve neutral countries to the east of Germany, but these did not get started before the Armistice was signed (in Wagons-Lits diner No. 2419).

After the war, Wagons-Lits' 35 sleepers were returned in poor condition, but 39 of the 64 diners had disappeared forever, many of them never paid for. The 116 diners of their defunct German subsidiary also vanished without compensation.

A clause in the Versailles Treaty compelled the German railways to accept a Wagons-Lits Train de Luxe from Paris to Vienna and Warsaw, comprising 6 sleepers and a diner, all to be used by military personnel. But the Germans refused to haul the diner, replacing it with a Mitropa one! At this time most of the 14 sleepers and 83 diners in the Mitropa fleet were those of the Prussian State Railways, which on 1st April 1921 amalgamated with and then dominated the other state railways of Germany to form the Deutsches Reichsbahn. Despite DR's determination to save Mitropa, this service could no longer function on the Austrian Railways. Instead Mitropa was asked to run the cabins and catering on the Vienna-Passau Danube steamers, which it did from April 1921 to about 1930, thereby employing the Austrian Mitropa personnel.

Wagons-Lits seem to have been lulled into the belief that the Versailles Treaty would compel Mitropa to amalgamate with them. A negotiation got underway for the purpose of erecting a concern to take over Mitropa. The DR graciously complied with the treaty and allowed the Nord Express to restart, with Wagons-Lits cars, while offering CIWL 20 per cent of the new organization's capital. But Wagons-Lits demanded 51 per cent and walked out, imagining that Mitropa would then collapse. They seem to have reckoned without Herr Renaud, the man who had set up Mitropa and become its first director. With the aid of the Great Eastern Railway of England and the Canadian Pacific Railway, the Société Anonyme Transcontinent was established in Geneva. Now Mitropa handed over 40 per cent of its capital for 20 percent of Transcontinent. Suddenly the firm with its red sleeping cars was no longer wholly German and had come under the supervision of foreign railway companies.

On 1st May 1921, the Paris-Vienna Train de Luxe of Wagons-Lits was once more named the Orient Express. When, two years later, the French occupied the Rhineland, the Reichsbahn took revenge and refused to haul the Orient Express, saying they had no coal. Wagons-Lits were now powerless to hit back at Mitropa. At the last moment the Swiss agreed to take the train through to Austria, as described in the next chapter. Just at this moment the Great Eastern Railway was amalgamated with the London and North Eastern Railway. By backing Transcontinent, the GER's successor soon had its reward, in the form of Mitropa's first Train de Luxe. But first Herr Renaud had to break out of Germany.

Such was the price paid by Wagons-Lits to ensure the revival of the Orient Express in 1924, despite the Versailles Treaty. Mitropa was permitted to run to Holland, Scandinavia and Danzig as well as to restricted places in Switzerland, Austria and Czechoslovakia. Moreover, new arrangements made in 1946 with the Swiss Federal and Bern Lötschberg Simplon Railways made it possible for Mitropa to run sleeping cars to Chur, Lugano, Geneva and Interlaken. But the Mitropa dining cars had to be left behind at Basle because, back in 1903, Wagons-Lits had formed another dining-car subsidiary in partnership with the Swiss Federal Railways, the present SSG Compagnie Suisse des Wagons-Restaurants.

Mitropa had acquired 23 new sleepers in 1923, the first 2 nicknamed *Schwedenwagen* since they ran to Malmö. Mitropa had also taken over the Kaiser's Imperial Train, adapted by Linke Hofmann into saloon cars, with which the first Mitropa Train de Luxe, the Berlin-London Express, ran 3 times a week between Berlin and Hook of Holland, there to connect with the LNER's cross-Channel steamer.

The Wagons-Lits services with wagons-salons and diners were considerably older than the refurbished Imperial Train, and they were no better. Meals at every seat and the prestige of calling the trains Pullman, which would attract American visitors, were the only way to beat the competition. Hence the Pullman invasion described in Chapter 13. Mitropa followed up the Berlin-London service with the Scandinavian-Swiss Express, a 1924 Train de Luxe of sleeping cars running between Warnemunde and Sassnitz and Basle.

In November 1925 the redoubtable Herr Renaud died. His successor, Dr. Kieschke, who came from the Deutsches Reichsbahn, was, if possible, even more dynamic. One German author, using poetic license, suggested that Kieschke loved Mitropa so much he was virtually 'married to it'.

First Kieschke set up food distribution depots at Berlin's Schlesische Bahnhof and Hamburg's Altona. Next he expanded the central drink stores at Berlin's Görlitzer Bahnhof. Then in 1927 he bought the Franz Klein hock (German white wine) cellars at Traben Trarbach. Now Mitropa sleepers and diners had something superior to offer their clients, something that Wagons-Lits could not match.

116. The German Imperial Train was used for the last time to take Kaiser Wilhelm II to Holland at the end of World War I. It then became Mitropa's first Train de Luxe, the Berlin-London Express (Berlin–Hook of Holland). View taken between 1892 and 1900.

117. DSG Wine Cellar on wheels (*Die Rollende Weinkeller*) at Mainz in 1972.

What really prompted the rush to get Pullman cars working on the Continent, even to the point of borrowing them from England, was the discovery that in 1925 only 3 per cent of the capital of the Transcontinent SA remained in Switzerland, and that the Reichsbahn had bought up the other 80 per cent, making the total German stake equal to the 40 per cent of the old Mitropa capital deposited in 1921.

All the prestige of thousands of American Pullman cars lay behind the 1926 inauguration of the *Flèche d'Or* (*Golden Arrow*) service between London and Paris, which marked Wagons-Lits' Golden Jubilee. But Dr. Kieschke decided to go one better, a day Train de Luxe all the way to Switzerland, connecting with the overnight boat from London. Mitropa passengers could of course enjoy Mitropa Gold Top, Silver Top, and Copper Top hock, in half-flasks or splendid full bottles, after it had matured either in the cellars or in the Berlin Görlitzer store. And where better to savour Mitropa hock than along the Rhine? There could be only one possible name for a service of dining saloons lined out in gold: *Rheingold,* already world famous since 1876, thanks to Richard Wagner and his operatic cycle about the Nibelungen.

The train was an instant success, perhaps more popular with the British than with any other nationality. The traveller left London's cavernous Liverpool Street Station, in the north east corner of the city (several miles from the West End), by the Hook Continental, which beginning in 1924 had non-supplement diners as well as the more exclusive first-class Pullman car. After sleeping on the boat, in which berths were far less costly than sleeping cars, passengers would enter the mouth of the Rhine in early morning. On the quay, immediately beside the gangway on the track between the quayside and station, stood the train. *Rheingold* passengers now had only to take a few halting steps across Dutch soil and enter the train's heated saloons. At once the passenger was in Germany, and

only the guard in his Dutch uniform was a reminder that the train had yet to enter the Fatherland.

Customs inspection took place on the train, which comprised luggage van, first-class dining saloon with kitchen and second-class dining saloon without kitchen. Of course, there was second class, for which the supplement was two, instead of three, marks.

Prussian-blue chairs were thick-cushioned and the tables laid with cruets and pots of English marmalade. Unlike the Wagons-Lits staff, whose international language was French and whose English was slight, halting and poorly pronounced, the Germans asked in perfect English what the passenger wished for breakfast (a full one if desired) as the train ponderously moved off beside the canal towards the suburbs of Rotterdam. Destination: 'Mailand'. Only later did 'Milano' also appear. Even so, that first year—1928—the *Rheingold* went only to Lucerne in summer and Basle in winter, just like the *Edelweiss* (see Chapter 13), started one month later as competition for the *Rheingold*.

The Dutch Customs would walk through the train after Utrecht, where the portion from Amsterdam was attached, comprising second-class saloon with kitchen, first class without, first class with kitchen and second class without kitchen.

After Arnhem came Zevenaar, the change-over point for engines in those days. The Reichsbahn would attach one of the Bavarian S 3/6 Pacifics, better known today as the 18 class 4-6-2, which worked the train to Mannheim, nearly 450 kilometres away. Here was the 'top link' shed, where another of the same class took the train on to Basle, 280 kilometres further on. Now the *Rheingold* would run over the joint German/Swiss line across the Rhine to Basle SBB. Here steam engines from Germany were usually put in a corner beside the great No. 1 Platform, along which one could walk to the French piece at the other end—usually pursued by Customs and police.

above left: 118. The FEK *Rheingold* rake (restored by the Railway Friends of Cologne) in May 1971. Hauled by DB 2-10-0 No. 050-001-7.

above right: 119. Interior of 2nd-class *Rheingold* saloon shortly before World War II.

opposite: 120. In the Rhine Valley, the *Rheingold* hauled by Bavarian S 3/6 class Pacific 4-6-2 No. 18529.

below: 121. The *Rheingold* in Cologne Station in 1934. Note the coffee urn and sandwich trolley.

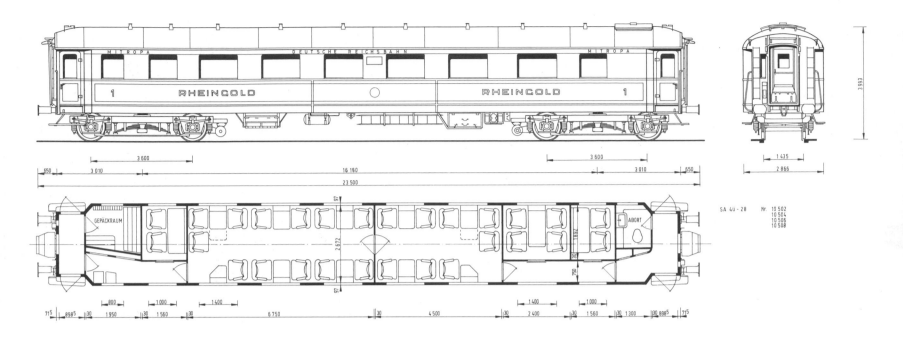

above: 122. Plan and sections of a 1st-class *Rheingold* saloon, built in 1928.

opposite below: 123. The *Edelweiss,* in front, coupled together with the *Rheingold* in 1928, between Basle and Lucerne. With characteristic neutrality, the SBB made sure neither the *Edelweiss* nor the *Rheingold* won the race to Lucerne from Amsterdam, and did so by hauling them together from Basle! Here an SBB Ae 4/7, the standard express engine of 1927 and still in service on secondary trains.

above left: 124. A camouflaged dining car returned to its owners, CIWL, waits to be restored at the St. Denis works (Paris) in 1945. Many CIWL cars were never recovered by CIWL after the war.

above right: 125. Luncheon in a DSG dining car about 1950.

To Dr. Kieschke, a Salonspeisewagen was not a Speisewagen within the meaning of the SBB contract, which said that dining cars from Germany must not go beyond Arth Goldau. The *Rheingold*'s violet-and-white coaches, the largest in Germany, eventually reached Italy over the Gotthard—but in an ordinary train, to be on the safe side. And his Swiss expansion did not stop there, since the agreement governing dining cars said nothing about narrow-gauge ones!

Thus, suddenly there were Swiss-built Mitropa dining cars, running on the Rhätian Railway between Chur and St. Moritz, taking Wagons-Lits passengers off their Engadine Train de Luxe from Paris and Calais and conveying them to the Maloja resort, which Wagons-Lits had built before the war.

Next, Mitropa arranged with the Bernina Bahn, independent of the RhB until during World War II, for yet more dining cars on this spectacular line. Lastly, after the completion in 1930 of the Brig-Visp section of the Visp Zermatt Railway had enabled the Glacier Express to run in summer, from St. Moritz to Zermatt, one of the Rhätian diners was provided with a pinion to work over the rack section of the Furka Oberalp Railway from Disentis to Oberalpsee. Since there was only one diner so fitted and the two expresses passed at this remote Alpine summit, the dining car was solemnly exchanged and returned to St. Moritz. Oberalpsee is the highest station in Europe with a dining-car service. After World War II the Swiss Dining Car Co. (SSG) took over these cars and continues to run them. Their kitchens have been modernized with

micro-ovens, and the meals are largely prepared in advance in the SSG-run station buffet at Chur.

The Germans resorted to all kinds of devices in their attempts to develop armaments that were prohibited under the Versailles Treaty. Apart from making bombs in tram depots, where they could be stored by fascinating, mysterious steam-hauled tramways, they also needed to make and test engines for submarines. So the *Flying Hamburger* was built, which had a Mitropa kitchen and small dining saloon. It ran on Maybach diesel engines and was timed to take 138 minutes for the 178 miles (approximately 500 kilometres) from Berlin to Hamburg, claimed to be the fastest service in the world in 1933. The *Flying Cologner (Fliegender Kölner)* had similar equipment, and in 1938 these railway-Zeppelins were timed to travel at 131 kilometres per hour between Hanover and Hamm en route from Berlin to Cologne.

As Germany advanced so did Mitropa. The Anschluss meant the end of the BB Oestereich, as the Austrian Federal Railways were then called, and the end of Wagons-Lits' contract with them, since, according to the arrangements with the Reichsbahn, any diner running wholly within Germany, which now included Austria, should be operated by Mitropa. Thus, the Vienna-Bregenz sleeper, the only Wagons-Lits service within Austria, quickly changed its destination at Feldkirch and went to Zurich.

With World War II, Mitropa took over 113 Wagons-Lits cars, while other authorities confiscated many more. In order to prevent the requisition of the Italian Wagons-Lits fleet whilst running into

left: 126. The TEE *Rheingold*, with DSG catering, passes above a *Rheingold* car restored by the FEK (Freundeskreis Eisenbahn Köln) at Cologne in 1972.

left below: 127. The TEE *Rheingold* observation car in 1962.

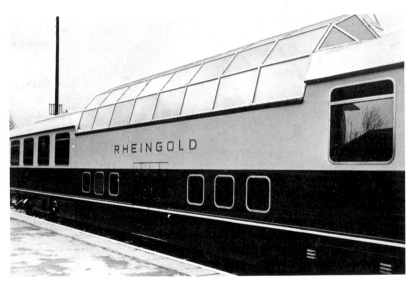

Germany, the cars had 'Deutsch-Italien Dienst' painted on them. From 1945 to 1948 the Russians ran a *Blaue Zug* of Blue Wagons-Lits sleepers and Red Mitropa diners between Berlin and Brest-Litvosk, where the change of gauge occurs.

As of 1949 Mitropa confined its activities to East Germany, except for some through workings to West Germany, where the former Mitropa services became known as the Deutsche Schlaf- und Speisewagen Gesellschaft. Curiously, the eagle badge of the DSG has wings looking remarkably like an M! In 1981 Mitropa once more ran the Berlin–Hook of Holland diner, replacing CIWL's last regular blue international diner from Hook to Hamburg.

The DSG operates the catering in the German Federal Railways series of Inter-City trains, which are the direct successors to the pre-war steam-hauled, fast Henschel-Wegmann train-set that, with Mitropa catering, ran to Berlin each morning from Dresden and returned each evening.

The DSG also staffs a number of the TEE trains, and until the 1960s it operated the Hamburg-Zurich overnight diesel sleeping-car train-set, known as the *Komet*. (This now has standard DSG sleepers.) Beginning in 1954, Wagons-Lits and DSG became allies against the growing threat of competition from air travel, but since 1972 the sleeping-car services have been operated commercially by the railways. DSG staffs all of the services and finds most of the cars, many of them air-conditioned, for runs within Western Germany and for certain international routes, like Munich-Athens.

In Eastern Europe there is really no call for Trains de Luxe, though the *Vindobona* Berlin-Vienna diesel train has Mitropa catering and a supplementary fare for its use.

The *Rheingold*, resuscitated after World War II, when it was operating as an ordinary train with a Wagons-Lits Dutch Division diner between Hook of Holland and Basle, is once more a Train de Luxe, perhaps the best known of all the TEE trains (see Chapter 15). Several of the *Rheingold*'s 1928 cars have been restored by Intraflug and the Friends of the Rheingold of Cologne, who in 1978 ran them in a special Golden Jubilee train from Hook to Lucerne and back to Cologne.

12. The Simplon Orient Express and the Trains de Luxe of Turkey

The Simplon Orient Express began running on 11th April 1919. Almost immediately it became the best known of all the European international Trains de Luxe. Indeed, it was often, but quite incorrectly, thought to be the Orient Express.

Always regarded as something different, the Simplon Orient Express (SOE) came into being at Versailles, a creature of the peace treaty, whose negotiators did not bother to ask the railways for their cooperation, but simply told them to haul the train and gave the route it should follow. The SOE was to run daily and to have an exclusive, ten-year monopoly of luxury-train service from Calais and Paris to Istanbul for the next ten years, running by way of Lausanne (handy for the League of Nations at Geneva), the Simplon Tunnel, Milan, Venice, Trieste, Zagreb, Vinkovci and Belgrade. Thereafter the route to Istanbul would be as described in Chapter 4.

The new 'oriental' was fundamental to a scheme whereby the victorious European allies—Great Britain, France and Italy—could be linked by express to the new Kingdom of Yugoslavia and the enlarged Roumanian Kingdom without the necessity of passing through any German, Austrian or Hungarian territory. While the diplomats adjusted the frontiers to suit their plans, they also asked the Wagons-Lits Co. to provide sleeping and dining cars and arrange the commercial operation of the new train.

Upon their arrival at London's Victoria Station, the London travellers aboard the Dover boat train bound for the Simplon Orient Express discovered three Pullman cars built in 1921 and called *Calais, Milan* and *Padua,* to emphasize their association with the new and already august express. At Calais was the Istanbul sleeping car, together with the Bucharest one, waiting a few steps from the bottom of the ship's gangway. From Paris' Gare du Nord the Simplon Orient sleepers then proceeded round the Petite Ceinture to join the rest of the express at the Gare de Lyons.

From 1919 to 1933 the diner of the Simplon Orient Express ran right through to Istanbul from the Gare de Lyons, where the Paris-Istanbul, Paris-Athens and Paris-Bucharest sleeping cars also hooked into the train.

Simplon Orient passengers experienced the thrill of staying on board the sleeping car for 3 nights in a row, protected by the same conductor all the way. And they never failed to be impressed by his ability to work for 72 hours with very little sleep and converse in the 7 languages needed along the way: French, German, Italian, Serbo-Croat, Bulgarian, Greek and Turkish. But he and his fellow conductors proved no less at home with the various currencies, deftly serving the same size bottle of Vichy water from the same locker for so many francs, lire, dinars, drachmae or Turkish piastres, depending where the train happened to be. In the event of a run on supplies, mineral water fetched from the dining car would be that of the country on whose tracks the train was travelling, and some of the liquid was most peculiar!

At Dijon, one of the PLM's 141E-class Mikado 2-8-2 engines would take over from the similar-looking, elegant Pacific 4-6-2 express engines, which had brought the train from Paris (a run already described in Chapter 5). At Mouchard, a second Mikado would be added as pilot for the climb up into the Jura. And the image of massive great steam engines toiling romantically uphill through the night is one that, for many, will be forever associated with the Simplon Orient Express. By early dawn the train had reached Switzerland, through the smoke-laden Mont d'Or Tunnel.

Only Switzerland had electric traction throughout the country After 1927, the SOE's engine there was one of the SBB's splendid 2-D-1 Ae 4/7 class, which continues to work in large numbers even today. Carefully, it brought the elegant express down to Lausanne at breakfast time, with a gorgeous view of Lake Geneva (Lac Léman) from the diner windows, before calling at the lake-side resort of Montreux. Thereafter the train followed the picturesque Rhone Valley, bordered by high snow-capped peaks, through the Alps to Brig, the only stop where German was the local language. Now the Simplon Orient passed into Italy, through the famous

Simplon Tunnel that joins Brig to Iselle, at the time the longest (12.5 miles) railway tunnel in the world.

On the southern side of the Alps the steep slopes are more verdant. However, trains, even now, make their descent through a spiral tunnel, in a valley so narrow it allows no room for sidings, marshalling yards or engine turntables and depots. So the Swiss run the cars on into Italy as far as Domodossola. Here FS (Ferrovia

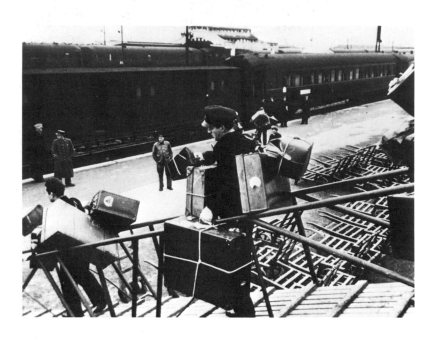

left: 128. The Calais-Istanbul sleeping car of the Simplon Orient Express, alongside the steamer at Calais, about 1930. The porters and ship's stewards use straps to take the luggage down the gangway. Today passengers must carry their own bags, and there are no sleepers to Istanbul.

below: 129. With an SBB Ae 4/7 class 2-D-1 attached at its head, the Simplon Orient Express passes near Chillon Castle, beside Lake Geneva, in 1927. Fifty years later, the same Ae 4/7, still in regular service, can be found heading the Nostalgic Orient Express.

opposite: 130. Wagons-Lits sleeping-car supplement bulletins (never called 'tickets'). Those of Bulgaria and Sweden are rather rare. The bulletins shown here were the last series, withdrawn in 1971.

Compagnie Internationale des
WAGONS-LITS NL Nº 24517
et des Grands Express Européens
« **Spécial** »

03 / 56
LISSONE - LINDEMAN

Bed(den) Lit(s)	W	Rijtuig no Voiture no	5.

Van :
De : Utrecht

Naar :
A : Bellinzona

Op :
Le : 14 juin 19 61
dag - jour
(Nacht van /
(Nuit du : 14/6 op/au 15/6

Uur : 20.37 | Trein
Heure : Train 100.

Datum van uitgifte
Date d'émission

Bedrag per plaats
Montant par place

Aantal plaatsen
Nombre de places perçues

(Te zamen)
(Produits)

TOTAAL
TOTAL

R. V.

Compagnie Internationale des
WAGONS-LITS Nº 49439
et des Grands Express Européens
« **Touriste** » G.B.

03 / 01 / 06

·NM· 27 APR 1961

Berth Nos	3 GENT.	Car Nº	2.

From : PARIS/NORD

To : STOCKHOLM(C)

Date of issue	27/4/61	Fare (including Location Fee)		Service fee
Fare per berth		£4 15 2	7 4	
Number of supplements collected		X	1	
Totals		£4 15 2	7 4	
TOTAL		£5 2	6	

Internationale Schlafwagen Gesellschaft
WAGONS - LITS D Nº 119907
« **Touriste** »
PROLONGATION · MILAN - ROME

Bett(en) nº Lit(s) MODIFIER EN 14	Wagen Nº Voiture No
2	VU

Von :
De : Köln

Nach :
A : Milano

Am :
Le : 1 19 61
Tag - jour
(Nacht ven /
(Nuit du : 4.5. bis/au 5.5.61

Uhr : 20 | Zug
Heure : Zug D69

Compagnie Internationale des
WAGONS-LITS F Nº 736433
et des Grands Express Européens
R. C. Seine 55 B 9927
« **Double** »

04 / 00
PARIS-CAPUCINES

Lit(s) Nº	Voiture Nº
19 Mons	I

De : Paris/Nord

Date d'émission	7/4/60	Suppléments locations et taxes diverses	Droit de service
Montant par place		37,30	3,00
Nombre de places perçues		X	ny
(Produits)			
Total		40,30	
Timbre quittance (payé sur état)			40,30 40,20
TOTAL GÉNÉRAL		40,55	

Compagnie Internationale des
WAGONS-LITS
49012
et des Grands Express Européens
R. C. B. 5202 — H. R. B. 5202 Y

Krevet (i) Br. Lit(s) Nº	Kola Br. Voiture Nº

Od
De Sofia | do
à Istanbul

Dana - Le :
Dan — Jour
(Noć od — Nuit du): | Mesec (slovima)
Mois (en lettres)
do — au; 19

Voz
Train | Sat
Heure

Gospodin — Monsieur
Dama — Dame
Grupa — Groupe Balkanturiste

Le droit de service est compris dans le supplément
Servis

Primerak „Putnik"
Souche «Voyageur»

Datum izdavanja
Date d'Emission

AGENCIJA IZDAVALAC
AGENCE EMETTRICE

Pečat
Code

Classe

SINGLE

SPÉCIAL

DOUBLE

TOURISTE

Broj mesta
Nombre de places

UKUPAN IZNOS
TOTAL GÉNÉRAL

R. V.

George Behrend

Det Internationella Sovvagns-Bolaget
WAGONS-LITS S Nº 112720
„**TOURISTE**"

27179

Bädd(ar) nr. Lit(s) No	20 Mons	Vagn nr. Voiture nº	3

Från
de Copenhagen

Till
à Köln

Den
le 7/5 Maj
mois (en lettres) 19 61

Natten mellan den
Nuit du och
au

Kl.
h. 18.00 | Tåg nr.
Train nº SPE

Namn
Nom Behrend

Utfärdad den Date d'émission	5/5	Sovvagns- och beställ- ningsavgift och div. skatter Suppléments, locations et taxes diverses	Betjänings- avgift Droit de service
Avgift per plats Montant par place		25,80	2,50
Antal platser Nombre de places		X	
SUMMA KR. Produits			
TOTALT Montant total		28,30	

Thos COOK & Son AB
WAGONS-LITS
5 MAJ 1961
Stockholm

AVB. D
RV.
Betjäningsavgift erlagd
Le droit de service EST PERÇU

SE BAKSIDAN
Avis officiel au verso

Den resandes talong
Souche voyageur

dello Stato) steam used to take over, in the shape of a 685-class Prairie 2-6-2, the early models of which were noticeable for the solid disc wheels on the front axle (called 'pony truck'), instead of the more modern and more usual spoked wheels. Only one engine was needed for the downhill run of the Simplon Orient Express to the resorts of Stresa and Arona on beautiful Lake Maggiore, which, like Montreux on Lake Geneva, enticed the SOE's patrons to alight. On the way back to Domodossola, a pair of engines, belching black smoke, were necessary to hoist the heavy sleeping-car train up the heights.

In Italy, the Alpine foothills give way to the flat, steamy Lombard Plain leading to Milan's then new Central Station, with its twenty-one platforms and great overall roof echoing to the terminal's noisy Italian bustle. Here the SOE made only a brief stop, since the new engine could be quickly attached. Another FS 685 Prairie, or later an FS 691–class Breda-built Pacific, would steam slowly across the hot plain of the River Po, stopping beside pretty Lake Garda and then at stations whose names stir the hearts of every Shakespeare fan: Verona and Padua.

The train shimmered under the summer sun, the snug mottled plush of the upholstery seeming almost too warm and the polished marquetry on the compartment walls creaking in the heat of those un-air-conditioned days. There could also be a curious smell, mostly of sulphur, especially if one had been slow to open the window and change the direction of the outside louvre glasses, which would have deflected the smoke when the train reversed in Milan. There was plenty of time to listen to the dignified train's own background music—escaping steam, whistling air brakes, the clank of the brake system mingling with the rail-joint rhythm—until at last the Simplon Orient Express ran slowly over the elegant stone viaduct across the Venetian Lagoon, unparalleled (until the 1930s) by any motor road.

At Venice there might just be time to step outside the Santa Lucia Station to see the gondolas and motor boats drawn up on the

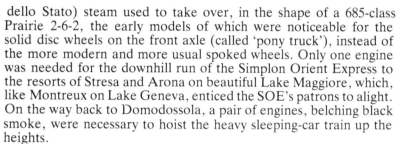

above left: 131. The Simplon Orient Express rake at Athens CIWL works in 1961. The inscriptions on WL No. 2804 (local Athens-Salonika service) and WR No. 4107 (ex-Pullman kitchen car) are in Greek.

above right: 132. The Simplon Orient Express at the Turkish frontier. CIWL Z-type sleeping car No. 3322 is an old faithful—40 years in Orient Express service.

opposite left: 133. Simplon Orient Express and Taurus Express poster of 1930.

opposite right: 134. Pullman Car No. 4158 on the special Simplon Orient Express run by Intraflug in 1976 to mark the CIWL centenary. Note the Lalique glass panels.

Grand Canal at the foot of the steps, where at any other terminal in the world there would have been taxis. But lingering over the sight could be unwise, for FS punctuality is much better remembered as part of Mussolini's regime than his new calendar, which was faithfully used on the dining-car bills.

So far, the train had followed the route of the Simplon Express started by Wagons-Lits as soon as the line through the Simplon Tunnel was completed in 1906. In 1912, CIWL won permission to extend this train to Trieste, an Austrian port until the Treaty of Versailles gave it to Italy. The new Simplon Orient Express also followed this route back across the same viaduct to the large junction at Mestre and then inland to Cervignano, where an FS 626 BBB waited beneath the wires to take over. The line runs romantically above the sea along the side of the cliffs just before Trieste, where the SOE paused for almost an hour so that the dining car could be removed and restocked.

Beginning in 1912, Canadian Pacific liners were met at Trieste by boat trains of the Canadian Pacific Railway's very own parlour cars, built at Vienna or Prague. The first three, named *Canada,*

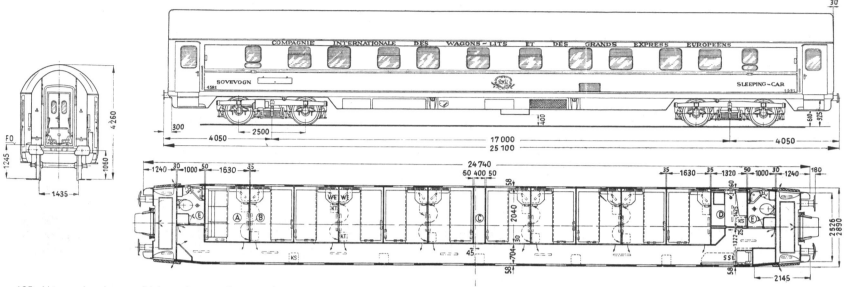

135. U-type sleeping car (Universal, reparations cars).

Europa and *America* (see scale drawing), appeared on 15th January of that year, and the other five, *Austria, Britannia, Australia, Africa* and *Asia,* were ready in 1913. They took tourists on from Vienna to Innsbruck, and all had the Austrian standard vacuum brakes. Some also had air brakes, since they were intended to run to Zurich, but in fact they never entered Switzerland, going instead over the Arlberg pass to the Austrian town of Bregenz on Lake Constance. Several history books have erroneously stated that these trains competed with the Wagons-Lits. Actually, the refreshments served in the CPR cars were all supplied by CIWL diners in the train, also newly built in Austria. The service did not last long, ending in 1914 with the outbreak of World War I. Some of the cars turned up in Italy after the cessation of hostilities.

When the dining car rejoined the Simplon Orient, it had a fresh brigade, ready to serve a succession of prolific repasts for the next thirty-six hours. The crew slept in hammocks slung between the tables. The train now climbed into the harsh, limestone Carso Hills, hauled by another FS 626 to the frontier. Yugoslavian steam (some of it acquired from Austria and Hungary) took over as the passengers turned in for their second night, and in the morning the two front sleeping cars were gone, having been taken off in Vinkovci to go on to Bucharest.

Vinkovci, unlike the other places mentioned on the route, is just a tiny branch junction in the wilds of Yugoslavia, reached during the night. From this point the two Bucharest sleeping cars meandered down the country branch to Subotica, where the dining car from Bucharest stood ready to be attached for its return journey to the Roumanian capital. The train crossed into what was now Roumania at Velika Kikinda and soon afterwards followed the route of the 1883 Orient Express, passing through the Transylvanian mountains beside the spectacular Danube gorge known as the Iron Gates. (On this section of the train in 1940, shortly after World War II had started, a real-life cloak-and-dagger operation is said

to have occurred, involving members of the British Royal Navy and some German agents.) By the time it drew into Belgrade at breakfast, the lordly Simplon Orient Express to Istanbul had been reduced to just three sleepers, the diner and the fourgon (which as of 1929 contained a shower). Thus, beginning in 1932, a grand remarshalling took place at the Yugoslav capital, where three more sleeping cars arrived each morning from Budapest. They came from all over Europe, in the Arlberg-Orient and Orient expresses. None of them ran daily, but converged at Budapest on different days of the week, as shown on the diagram of Orient Express routes.

This made the Simplon Orient that set out from Belgrade every day a palatial express of half a dozen sleeping cars, a diner and two fourgons. At the head of the train would be a huge, black, German-built JDZ-class 05 Pacific 4-6-2. The elegant interior struck a notable contrast to the rural landscape outside, slightly undulating and devoid of any tarred roads or motor traffic. In 1937 it was possible to travel in the SOE all day and see no more than three motor vehicles! So for a gimmick, the makers of the Humber car (now part of Talbot, formerly Chrysler UK) organized an Istanbul-Ostend race with the Ostend-Vienna-Orient Express, which the automobile won.

At Nis, the difference between the modern, sumptuous Simplon Orient Express and the waiting row of antique wooden coaches, with a CIWL teak diner attached, could hardly have been more telling. The rattletrap local cars waited to depart for Athens with the daily pair of sleeping cars next to the SOE's engine, after the rest of the express had reversed out of the station behind another 05 Pacific, bound for the Bulgarian frontier, up the exciting and spectacular Dragoman Pass. The line then climbs on the side of a gorge next to a raging torrent. Agatha Christie, always a stickler for accuracy, arranged for the SOE to become snow-bound here in *Murder on the Orient Express,* which permitted Hercule Poirot to solve the mystery unencumbered by policemen from Nis, the main security post in this part of Yugoslavia.

136. The Simplon Orient Express and Ostend–Vienna–Orient Express at Dragoman, Bulgaria, in 1937. The Humber Snipe car, driven by Dudley Noble for Humber
publicity, raced the train to Ostend, just before the London Motor Show, and won.

Sofia, the Bulgarian capital, is only 30 miles beyond the Bulgarian frontier station of Dragoman. From here to Svilengrad,
nearly 200 miles away on the Greek border, the Bulgarian Railways
gave the SOE regal 2-8-2 Mikados, fit for a king to drive—which
King Boris often did! They were among the fastest and most powerful steam engines ever built by the Swiss Locomotive Works
(SLM) at Winterthur, and they were still hauling the Paris-Istanbul
sleeper to Svilengrad as late as 1966, though by this time part of
the line from Sofia as far as Plovdiv had been electrified.

At Svilengrad the Oriental Railways (CO) took over the SOE
for the rest of its journey to Istanbul. The diplomats at Versailles
had been much less successful here in drawing up the frontiers to
accommodate the railway lines. Consequently, the CO now passed
from Bulgaria at Svilengrad into Greece at Dikkea, into Turkey at
Edirne, where the national wrestling championships are held, then
back into Greece at Pithion, and finally into Turkey once again,
this time at Uzunkopru—all in a space of less than fifty miles!

All these mysterious frontiers were passed in the middle of the
third night, and after 1933, when the Paris-Istanbul diner was cut
back to run only from Lausanne to Svilengrad, CIWL provided a
fourgon-cuisine, or kitchen van, in Turkey so that the sleeping-car
conductors could serve their passengers breakfast in bed. The CO
used French-built 2-8-0s with special low-weight axle-loads for their
poorly laid line, but in Turkey these were superseded by German-
manufactured 4-8-0s, transferred from the former German-owned
Anatolian Railway in Asiatic Turkey, after Atatürk had nationalized the railways (TCDD) in 1937.

The TCDD took over at Pithion but were not allowed to use
the CO's turning triangle there, with the result that their light (that
is, trainless) engines had to run backwards to or from their depot
at Uzunkopru, across the Maritza River's long viaduct. The Turkish
part of the journey is bare and hilly, and in 1929 the Simplon Orient
Express found itself blocked by snow for a week—and on another
occasion attacked by bandits!

After these barren, seemingly endless hills, the last few kilometres provide a welcome change of scene. From Halkali (where
the line is now electrified), the train runs beside the Sea of Marmara,
passing various modern resorts. Exotic Istanbul lies in the distance,
a blaze of light after dark and a seething city by day. The Simplon
Orient Express penetrated the city wall into an indescribable slum,
with the Sultan's Topkapi Palace on the left, towering above the
tracks that end in the Sirkeci Station.

The mosques, the palace treasures, the Bosporus tearing down
from the Black Sea, the hotchpotch of sounds and smells of the
street vendors at the Galata Bridge over the Golden Horn (which
is an inlet of the Bosporus)—all are still there to seduce the tourist.
But in the days of the Simplon Orient Express, there were also
trams galore, and the eerie squeak of their conductors' reed pipes,
a truly Oriental signal for their drivers to move on, has gone forever.

Istanbul's Sirkeci Station, end of the line for the many Orient
Express books, was in reality the starting point of a special 'vedette'
(motorboat ferry) across the Bosporus to Haydarpasa, where the
Taurus Express would be waiting. The advertised interval between
the arrival and departure of the two trains was only an hour and
a half; however, the Thomas Cook Timetable of 1977 advised at
least eight hours minimum.

No description of the Simplon Orient Express would be complete without mention of Athens, which was connected by rail to
the rest of Europe only in 1917, a bare two years before the express
went into service.

At Nis the JDZ 01–class Prairie, with pointed smoke-box décor and weird-looking chimney (smokestack), seemed underpowered compared to the 05 Pacifics on the Istanbul train. Without need to reverse at Nis, the 2-6-2 set off southwards by way of Macedonia, passing through an area where folklore has it that conductors were instructed to pull down the blinds so that passengers would not see local ladies bathing naked in the rivers! Today speed probably takes care of the problem, since the line is electrified as far as Titov Veles.

Eventually the Yugoslav engine staggered into the Greek frontier station (Idomeni), where a lumbering Lambda Beta class 0-10-0 took the train on to Salonica. Here the express reversed for the last time, and the teak Wagons-Lits diner was left behind. To serve breakfast, another CIWL diner with a Greek brigade joined the train during the night at Amfiklia. Wagons-Lits had run this one the previous evening to serve dinner on the way up from Athens. There were now four WL sleepers between Salonica and Athens, two of them teak with Greek lettering (as shown in the Appendices), one with third-class cabins and the other from Istanbul.

When World War II exploded, the Simplon Orient Express continued on its sublime way as long as possible. By that time the cars from Berlin and Paris ran coupled together between Belgrade and Istanbul. 'The enemy's ears are listening', reminded a notice in the French car. Turkish conductors were now used on all three Simplon Orient Express routes, since, being neutral, they could not be interfered with. Queen Marie and King Carol of Roumania, frequent patrons of the Bucharest car, escaped to Switzerland in the SOE, with two Pullmans full of valuables. In peacetime these cars had run to the Black Sea resorts in a Pullman train ironically called *King Carol I*. During World War II Marshal Tito's guerrilla warfare created such delays and disruptions that the Train de Luxe was withdrawn, when in July 1943 CIWL managed to extract half a dozen of its teak sleepers from Yugoslavia and transfer them to neutral Spain.

After the war, the Iron Curtain presented another barrier that had to be surmounted before the train could roll again. Meanwhile, Greece had been cut off by the closed Yugoslav frontier and by the damaged Pithion-Salonica line. However, the old teak Wagons-Lits cars continued to run within Greece itself, almost the last to remain in traffic. (The very last ran in Denmark, between Copenhagen and Esbjerg.) The Simplon Orient Express became a travesty of its former self, composed of ordinary coaches and just one Paris-Istanbul sleeper, which in 1956–57 was barred from crossing the Iron Curtain at Svilengrad. Instead it ran via Salonica, the route followed by James Bond in Ian Fleming's *From Russia with Love*. The film version presented a more authentic image of the train than any previous ones featuring Wagons-Lits service. Rail fans will notice that CIWL's title even appears in Turkish.

In 1962 the sadly reduced Simplon Orient Express was replaced by the Direct Orient Express (later called Direct Orient/Marmara Express), and the Paris-Istanbul car remained one of the 1926 Z class that in pre-war days had worked the Arlberg-Orient services.

138. Souvenir of the 1960s, when CIWL ran Vienna-Istanbul, Haydarpasa-Ankara, and Ankara-Kars sleepers, as well as the Paris-Vienna service, still operating today.

The cabins did not have those temptingly suggestive doors between compartments, as in the S class of the pre-war Simplon Orient. In 1971 the Paris-Istanbul car became part of the TEN Trans Euro Night services operated by the railways Pool of international sleeping cars, though still staffed and serviced by Wagons-Lits. The Paris-Athens car was superseded by the one from Munich, run by the Pool to this day but with a DSG air-conditioned car and DSG staff. The Greek Railways took over the local fleet and bought more cars from Wagons-Lits, which still staff them. One now makes a summer run from Athens to Venice.

In 1976 Intraflug AG of Zurich chartered a Wagons-Lits train from Milan to Istanbul to mark CIWL's centenary. In contrast to the Direct Orient, which provided no diner between Switzerland and the Turkish frontier, this special Train de Luxe had both a diner and the first Pullman car ever to run to Istanbul. Its success has led to Intraflug's Nostalgic Orient Express operation, which has been sending Trains de Luxe to Turkey for over five years. The last regular sleeping car ran in the Direct Orient Express on 19th May 1977. It was the subject of a CBS News *60 Minutes* programme, a BBC documentary and much other coverage by the media.

Sea Containers are implementing a London-Venice Train de Luxe project, conceived in 1977 by that company's US president, James Sherwood. Beginning on 30th May 1982, the Venice Simplon Orient Express will run twice weekly between London and Venice, using the restored UK Pullmans (shown in the Appendices) between London and Folkestone Harbour and the former CIWL cars (also listed in the Appendices) between Boulogne and Venice via Paris and Milan. Special accommodation is to be reserved on the Sealink ship for passengers travelling on this seventeen-car Train de Luxe. From Paris to Venice the service will operate thrice weekly.

The Turkish Trains de Luxe

The Germans started their Anatolian Railway at Istanbul's Haydarpasa Station on the Asiatic shore of the Bosporus and at the end of the line connected it with their better-known Baghdad Railway, still under construction in 1914. Nagelmackers himself directed the now defunct narrow-gauge line that joined the Anatolian Railway to the town of Bursa, even today a popular venue for tourists from Istanbul. He was also director general of the Smyrna, Cassaba & Prolonguements (Extensions) Railway, which the French had built inland from Smyrna (Izmir). That is why you will find Bursa and Smyrna on the Wagons-Lits map (showing the present capital Ankara as Angora, its old name).

After World War I, Kemal Atatürk deposed the Sultan, liberated large tracts of his country from the Allies' occupying forces and moved his capital to the remote, rough, inhospitable village that became Ankara. He disliked Istanbul's atmosphere of foreign intrigue and easy access from Europe by rail and sea. Forced to leave his sumptuous Istanbul Embassy, the powerful British Ambassador spent each week at Ankara in his special Wagons-Lits car. Wagons-Lits had just six cars in traffic in Asiatic Turkey when they obtained a forty-year contract for Turkish services in 1926.

The Anatolia Express was Turkey's first Train de Luxe, linking Ankara overnight with Istanbul. Then in 1930 came the Taurus Express, designed to connect the Simplon Orient Express with Cairo and Baghdad. It ran over the Baghdad Railway through Konya, home of the whirling dervishes, and thus bypassed Ankara until a new line could be readied linking the capital with the summit of the Taurus Pass. Here the *Toros Ekspresi*, as it is still called in Turkish today, drops 1,400 metres to sea level and in steam days required three 2-10-0 engines to struggle up the Taurus in the Istanbul direction. Along the way, it filled the dimly lit sleeper corridor with smoke and smells, to the delight of every rail buff. The low illumination, which gave the train a most romantic air, resulted from the slow speed that prevented the dynamos from fully charging.

More mountains and further steep gradients brought the train from the coast at Adana (close to Cyprus) to the Syrian frontier, a short way from Aleppo, where the train divided. The line to Baghdad ran back into Turkey, recrossed the north-east corner of Syria and petered out at Tel Kotchek on the Iraqi border, where Wagons-Lits ran a rest house. The line reached Baghdad only in 1940. Though the rails all the way to Cairo were actually laid in World War II, through CIWL sleepers never ran farther south than Beirut. Before the war the line ended at Tripoli. Wagons-Lits also operated a teak sleeping car by day from Haifa to Kantara, returning overnight. The Palestine Railways ended in Egypt on the east bank of the Suez Canal, and passengers were obliged to transfer to Kantara West by ferry, since the railway bridge had been dismantled between the wars. For the rest of the journey they travelled by Wagons-Lits Pullman running in the Egyptian Railways trains from Port Said to Cairo, as mentioned in Chapter 8.

From Tripoli in Lebanon to Haifa it was necessary to motor, but 'go by road' is not a veracious description, for the beach was in fact often used. More automobiles were needed to cross the desert from Tel Kotchek to the narrow-gauge Iraqi Railways at Kirkuk. Another two-day motor drive could be arranged for travellers from Khanikin on the Iraqi Railways seeking to reach Teheran.

Both the Anatolia and Taurus expresses continued throughout the war, since Turkey was neutral. By tacit agreement, made to minimize incidents, the Germans used the Anatolia Express and the British and Americans the Taurus Express between Istanbul and Ankara. Through Wagons-Lits sleeper, diner and fourgon carrying the mails ran in the Taurus from Istanbul to Baghdad from 1940 to 1971, though, beginning in the 1950s, the diner functioned only in Turkey. In the 1960s the Turks built a new line through Gaziantep to avoid the Syrian enclave, and for a while the Taurus Express went over both routes to Baghdad, though in different days.

As of 1939 ordinary coaches ran in both the Taurus and the Anatolia expresses, but from 1949 until 1965, when diesel haulage took over, the Anatolia Express became so heavy that the Wagons-Lits portion had to be run separately, as the 'Ankara Express'.

To the end, this Turkish Train de Luxe remained every whit as magnificent as the *Train Bleu* on which it had been modelled, even with ordinary coaches reattached beyond the dining car. Harsh Anatolia might lie outside, but inside the Birmingham-built diner there was the same gleaming silverware on the same spotless napery—even the double racks for hats and umbrellas that we met on the *Brighton Belle*.

CIWL handed over their dining-car operations to TCDD in 1967 and the sleeping cars four years later. Since the sleepers were only leased by TCDD, CIWL later transferred some to Spain.

13. The *Golden Arrow,*
the Trains de Luxe of Iberia, the *Edelweiss*

The *Golden Arrow*

Buoyed by the success of the *Blue Train,* Lord Dalziel set out next to introduce Pullman cars all over Europe, starting with a London-to-Paris service. The purpose of getting the Pullmans onto the tracks as rapidly as possible was to beat the competition of Mitropa, as explained in Chapter 11. By offering meal service at every comfortable armchair seat, instead of in far less comfortable dining cars, and by presenting Pullman parlour cars as an entirely new, improved, British concept, backed by the cachet of a famous name—Pullman—Lord Dalziel hoped to attract many more American and British tourists to the Wagons-Lits network of Trains de Luxe in Europe. It was therefore vitally important not to give any impression that Pullman might be merely a subsidiary of Wagons-Lits, whose wagon-restaurant-salons many English travellers, as we saw in Chapter 3, now regarded as exhorbitant, old-fashioned and 'foreign'.

Single Pullman cars, always painted maroon in south-east England, had run between London and Dover in boat trains since 1911, their conductors crossing the Channel to obtain the Paris reservations for the Dover-London service from Wagons-Lits personnel of the dining cars in the connecting Paris-Calais boat trains.

But the overtures made in 1923 by André Noblemaire, then director general of the Wagons-Lits, were rebuffed by the Nord Railway's director, M. Javary, who said his firm was just reorganizing their boat-train times and could not accommodate a Train de Luxe.

By 1924, conditions on the London-Paris service had, according to a responsible transport journal, become positively nerve-racking because of overcrowded boats, arrival delays of up to three hours, shortage of seats and lavatories and unpleasantness at Customs. To improve matters on the British side of the Channel, the Pullman Car Co. introduced an all-Pullman boat train between London and Dover on 17th November 1924. Lord Dalziel arranged for the equipment to be painted chocolate and pale cream, the livery used on Pullman cars elsewhere in Britain, with the exception of south-east England. The train bore the same name, Continental Express, as the ordinary boat trains, but because of its cream-coloured upper works, the railway staff dubbed it the 'White Pullman'.

New regulations demanded that new Pullman Cars for services based in France should be of all-steel construction. But this kind of manufacture was relatively novel and most of the available capacity fully committed to turning out new sleeping and dining cars for Wagons-Lits. On the other hand, Pullman Cars with wooden bodies, which were perfectly acceptable in Britain or Italy, already existed in plentiful supply. In 1925, Dalziel decided to try out a train of wooden-body Pullman Cars running from Milan to Cannes and thus serving the French Riviera. The decision could be implemented because the cars were based in Italy. His Lordship wished to start rolling at once, and so Wagons-Lits bought ten cars already built for the UK Pullman Car Co. by the Birmingham Railway Carriage & Wagon Co.*

---

*Nos. 2991–3000 were reserved for these cars but never used, since it was decided to return the cars to the Pullman Car Co. when enough steel ones were ready. So they were numbered 51–60 In the Duplicate List (see Appendices). Two of them were sent to Egypt and the other eight returned to England in 1928. They worked in the *Golden Arrow* in 1946. Two have been preserved.

opposite above: 139. *Flèche d'Or* Pullman No. 4018 at St. Denis CIWL works (Paris), restored and ready for preservation at the French National Railway Museum, Mulhouse, the only British-built coach in the collection.

opposite below: 140. Interior of the large saloon of 4018, built at Birmingham in 1926 for the *Flèche d'Or.*

Since the cars had British-type vacuum brakes that could not be used in France or Italy, where compressed-air brakes are standard, they had to travel in a slow goods train from the Zeebrugge (Belgium) freight Train Ferry to Paris' St. Denis CIWL works and there be fitted with air brakes. Whilst this was being done, their chairs were borrowed and placed in two new all-metal diners, Nos. 2700 and 2867, for a trial run, along with S sleepers 2656 and 2657, from Paris to Calais and back. The press reports spoke of nice new, all-steel Pullman cars a whole year before any were built, which puzzled historians for over thirty years until Roger Commault, a veteran of fifty years with Wagons-Lits and now their official historian, happened to discover the facts by chance.

Suitably impressed by the trial, Javary simply stipulated that the new Pullmans be French-built. Lord Dalziel responded in his usual grand manner, for while ordering more Pullmans in France, he also persuaded Javary to accept British-built ones, since French cars could not possibly be ready before 1927. But then the General Strike in Great Britain held up the service from 15th May until 15th September. This was 1926, the Golden Jubilee year of the Wagons-Lits Co., and so Lord Dalziel named the train *Flèche d'Or,* meaning 'Golden Arrow'. To make sure everybody knew it was the Pullman Car Co. rather than Wagons-Lits offering this service, Dalziel had the Continental Pullman Cars painted chocolate and cream to match the UK ones from 1926 until 1932. Silverware and cutlery were ordered from the Pullman Car Co.'s Battersea stores and placed on board the cars at either Birmingham or Harwich before they were shipped to Europe by freight Train Ferry from Harwich to Zeebrugge. The upholstery and carpets used for British Pullman Cars *Marjorie, Sappho, Viking, Medusa* and *Pauline* were the same as those in CIWL Nos. 4001–4030.

The outcome of these arrangements was precisely as planned. Passengers refused to believe they were not carried right through in Pullman Cars by Train Ferry from London to Paris (a project delayed until 1936, when only Night Ferry sleeping cars ran through, not Pullmans). When as a small boy I ventured to point out that a change was necessary at Dover and Calais, I was told that 'little boys should be seen and not heard'.

The Pullman Car Co.'s brochure entitled *The Princely Path to Paris* spoke of 'fastidious passengers in a sybaritic age' whose luggage was whisked into the baggage lockers at the ends of the cars by 'Pullmanic Demigods'. This curious Pullman language helped build the image the company sought to achieve. Filled with colour plates, the brochure evoked the 'Field of the Cloth of Gold', a momentous meeting in 1520 between Henry VIII of England and

left: 141. The *Flèche d'Or* hides the *Blue Train* (roofs visible) at Calais Maritime, alongside the Cross Channel SR Steamer *Canterbury* (foreground), specially built for the *Golden Arrow* service in 1929.

opposite above: 142. Pullman Car No. 34 3rd class, for the *Golden Arrow*.

opposite below: 143. Interior of car no. 34. Compare with the *Rheingold* interior in Plate 119.

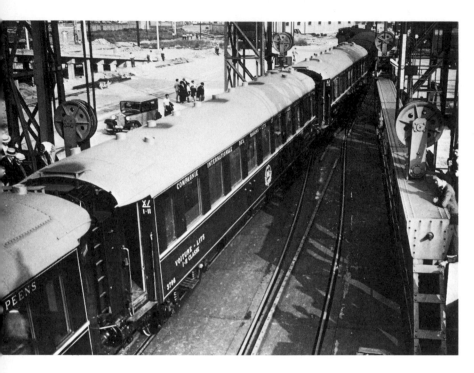

144. Trials of the Night Ferry with the ramp at Dunkirk in 1936. Note the English private car. The train ferries were the first SR ships with an RO/RO garage, above the train deck. Rake of F-type one-vestibule sleeping cars.

Francis I of France at a site near Calais. Thus, Pullman accounted for the name *Golden Arrow* without mentioning the Wagons-Lits jubilee! The publicity sheet went on to remark: 'It is no more difficult to go to Paris now than to, say, Harrogate'. (Few South of England people, prone to popping over to the flesh-pots of Paris, ever spared a thought for Harrogate, but, as readers of Chapter 8 know, Pullman could not waste any opportunity to promote its special service to the remote Yorkshire spa.)

The Pullman Car Co.'s language even found its way into menus. Chicken might be offered daily, but on one occasion it would be 'Roast Surrey Chicken' and on the next, 'Roast Sussex Chicken', the better to convince 'fastidious passengers' that the *Golden Arrow* was 'extra special'. Still, one regular traveller remarked that 'you paid a Pullman Car supplement just to travel in an aroma of boiling cabbage water'!

Many British people believe that the *Golden Arrow* began only in 1929 when the SS *Canterbury* entered the service to cross the Channel and the London-Dover all-Pullman boat train was named *Golden Arrow* for the first time. Before Lord Dalziel's death in March 1928, the SR ordered the vessel to carry Pullman passengers exclusively. At Calais, the Calais-Brussels Pullman waited with the *Flèche d'Or* for the *Canterbury* to arrive. But after 15th May 1931, the effects of the Depression, or 'slump' as it was called in those days, caused the admission of ordinary passengers onto the *Canterbury*. At first, the *Golden Arrow* Pullman train preceded the ordinary one so that the Pullman passengers could obtain the best seats. But to save time for those passengers, the early arrival was abandoned in favour of reserved seats. This worked fairly well, since non-first-class passengers were banished to steerage in those palmy days! As late as 1970, a book appeared explaining everything about the *Golden Arrow* except how the train got its name!

During World War II, the Pullmans were withdrawn and stored in both Britain and France. But by 15th August 1946 the *Golden Arrow* was ready to run again, and from 1947 to 1950 it operated as a Train de Luxe, uncontaminated by ordinary coaches, on both sides of the Channel. For the Festival of Britain in 1951, new *Golden Arrow* Pullmans were built with internal marquetry panels that had been bought before the war and stored (see Appendices for the names of the cars). The post-war engines used for the train in England were normally the Pacifics designed by O. S. Bulleid, the SR's last engineer, and built during the war. British Railways preferred their latest standard 4-6-2s, one of which, specially supplied to the Southern for this prestigious train, is reproduced here. The rest of the series ran on BR's Eastern Region.

The *Flèche d'Or* was more than 'The Princely Path to Paris'; it was also 'La Ligne Luxueuse à Londres'. People in *haute couture,* and fragrant with all the *parfums de Paris,* decorated the Gare du Nord, which has always had a slightly 'Trans-Manche' air about it. Bowler-hatted gentlemen, obviously going home, placed their indispensable umbrellas in the racks, whilst the fitted suitcases, heavy with twin hairbrushes, clothes-brushes and an array of silver-topped glass bottles from Drew & Sons (Piccadilly Circus) were placed in the end luggage racks by the 'demigods' with the assistance of porters.

The passengers could take their ease in the high-backed, heavy but moveable first-class armchairs, as furs dangled below cloche hats. There would be an aperitif, Noilly Prat or perhaps Martini. Along with it came a strong aroma of cigars, or maybe Gitanes cigarettes. The hardier gentlemen could even have been indulging in *papier maïs,* to the ladies' chagrin. Early lunch, served at every seat from the one or two adjoining, kitchen-equipped Pullman Cars (known as Pullman *couplages* or *triplages*), might be:

Potage Cressonière	*Celeris au Madère*
Quennelles de Brochet Lyonnaises	*Fromages Assortis*
Grenadin de Veau Fleuriste	*Coupe Flèche d'Or*
Pommes Anna	*Corbeilles de Fruits*

Café

opposite: 145. The genial warmth prevailing in Pullman Cars is shown in this view of No. 4018's coupé.

THE NIGHT FERRY

FULL BREAKFAST — — 8/-
(Petit Dejeuner Complet)

FIRST COURSE

Chilled Fruit Juices : Tomato Orange Pineapple
(Les Jus de Fruits)

SECOND COURSE Grilled Royal Kippers
(Le Poisson Fumé)

Egg Bacon Tomato Mushrooms Chipolata
(Oeuf avec Bacon Tomate Champignons et Chipolata)

THIRD COURSE Rolls Croissants

Toast Preserves

Tea or Coffee

(Petit Pain Confiture Le thé ou le café **complet**)

CONTINENTAL BREAKFAST — — 4/6
(Petit Dejeuner Française)

Choice of Beverages Toast Rolls Preserves
(Le thé au café complet petits pain et confiture)

A LA CARTE

Two Pan Fried Eggs with Grilled Bacon		5/6
Les Deux Oeuf au le Plat avec Bacon		
Ham Sandwich — —	—	2/6
Sandwich au Jambon		
Biscuits (Sweet) (per portion)	—	9d.
Pot of Coffee (per person)	—	1/6
Le Café Complet		
Pot of Tea (per person)	—	1/6
Le Thé		

i Non Sleeping Car Portion   10.59

Tariff

APERITIFS

Gin and Dubonnet ...	... ...	3/9
Gin and Martini Vermouth, Sweet or Dry	...	3/9
Gin and Lime, Gin and Orange ...	...	3/9
Gin and Bitters	...	3/-
Sandemans Amontillado Sherry ...	...	3/-
Gonzalez Byass Rosa Sherry	...	3/-
Gonzalez Byass Tio Pepe	...	3/6
Sandemans Partners Port	...	3 -
Old Monk Port ...	quarter Bottle	6/-
Martini Vermouth Sweet or Dry ...	...	1/-
Dubonnet	...	1/-

Better drink MARTINI Sweet or Dry !

SPIRITS

Cognac Brandy 'Three Star' (Bisquit Dubouché, Courvoisier Martell)	3/6
Cognac Bisquit Dubouché V.S.O.P.	5/6
Whisky (Ballantine, Black and White, John Haig's	
Gold Label, Johnnie Walker, White Horse, White Label)	3/-
Gin (Booth's, Curtis, Gordon's)	2/9
Jamaica Rum (Lemon Hart) ...	2/9

WINE LIST

Bin		Botts. Hlvs Qtrs.
43 CHAMPAGNE G.H Mumm Cordon Rouge N.V.		36/6 18/6 9/-
63 BORDEAUX RED Médoc (Chaville Freres)		13/- 7/- 4/-
75 BORDEAUX WHITE Graves (Chaville Freres)		13/- 7/- 4/-
88 BURGUNDY RED Macon (Geisweiler and Fils)		13/- 7/- 4/-
90 BURGUNDY WHITE Pouilly Dry Reserve (Bouchard Aîné)		15/- 8/- 4/6
30 HOCK Liebfraumilch Klosterdoctor		15/- 8/- 4/6

BEERS

Bass, Flower's Brewmaster, Double Diamond, Guinness, Worthington	...	2/3
Skol Pilsener Lager, Tuborg Pilsener Lager	...	2/3
Holsten Pilsner	...	2/6

CIDER

Whiteway's "WHIMPLE" brand extra quality	...	2/-
Bulmer's	...	2/-
Babycham	...	2 -

PULLMAN MINIATURES

Courvoisier Brandy XXX	5/-	Drambuie	...	6/-
Whisky, Ballantine ...	6/6	Crème de Menthe	...	5/-
Gin	5/-	Wolfschmidt Kummel	...	5/-
Cointreau	5/-	Grant's Cherry Brandy	...	5/-
Benedictine	5/-	Canadian Club	...	5/-

MINERALS

Vichy Celestins Splits	...	2/-
Apollinaris "Baby Polly"	...	1/6
Schweppes: Ginger Beer Quinine Tonic Soda Water } Baby	10d.
Ginger Ale Lemonade Bitter Lemon Cola } Splits	1/6
Rose's Lime Juice Cordial and Rose's Squashes	1/-
Pineapple Juice ... 1/6 Tomato Juice Cocktail	1/6

CIGARETTES
Piccadilly No. 1   Senior Service   Kingsway   Players
Aspro 6d.

Cigars specially packed for the Pullman Car Company Limited 5/-

G 10/59   O. & C. S.

opposite above left: 146. Special ship *Canterbury* built for *Golden Arrow* service in 1929 by Wm. Denny & Sons, Dumbarton, arriving at Dover Harbour in 1934.

opposite above right: 147. The *Golden Arrow* was hauled by two miniscule 0-6-0 tanks, one of which appeared to have lost most of its cap.

opposite below left: 148. Breakfast menu of the Night Ferry. 'O.&C.S.' at the foot of the tariff means 'Ocean & Channel Services'—Pullman jargon for boat trains.

opposite below right: 149. The Trianon Bar open to all Pullman passengers of the *Golden Arrow*. Designed by Starkie, Gardner & Co., this décor was moved into the second car, used in place of the first Pullman, as the Trianon Bar in the *Golden Arrow*. Note the large Pullman badge on the right.

right: 150. The *Flèche d'Or* at Paris (Nord), ready to leave for Calais Maritime. Chapelon Pacific No. 231 E 37 (from Calais shed).

below: 151. The *Golden Arrow* at Sandling (near Folkestone) in 1952. BR Britannia class 7 Pacific No. 7004 ('William Shakespeare').

GOLDEN ARROW →→→
←←← FLÈCHE D'OR

AFTERNOON TEA 3/6

Toasted Teacake

Buttered Toast   Crumpets & Scones

Fruit Loaf White & Hovis Bread & Butter

Preserves

Teatime Biscuits   Quality Cake

Pot of Tea (Indian or China)

The **TRIANON BAR** in this train

offers a pleasant meeting place.

K 10.59

GOLDEN ARROW →→→
←←← **FLÈCHE D'OR**

APERITIFS
Gin and Dubonnet	...	...	...	3/9
Gin and Martini Vermouth, Sweet or Dry	...	...	3/9
Gin and Lime, Gin and Orange	...	...	...	3/9
Gin and Bitters	...	...	...	3/-
Sandemans Amontillado Sherry	...	...	3/-
Gonzalez Byass Rosa Sherry	...	...	...	3/-
Gonzalez Byass Tio Pepe	...	...	...	3/6
Sandemans Partners Port	...	...	...	3/-
Old Monk Port	...	...	quarter bottle	6/-
Martini Vermouth Sweet or Dry	...	...	1/-
Dubonnet	...	...	...	1/-

Better drink MARTINI Sweet or Dry !

SPIRITS
Cognac Brandy 'Three Star' (Bisquit Dubouché, Courvoisier)	3/6
Cognac Bisquit Dubouché V.S.O.P. Martell's Cordon Bleu	5/6
Whisky (Ballantine, Black and White, John Haig's	
Gold Label, Johnnie Walker, White Horse, White Label)	3/-
Gin (Booth's, Curtis, Gordon's)	...	...	2/9
Jamaica Rum (Lemon Hart)	...	...	2/9

WINE LIST
Bin				Botts.	Hlvs	Qtrs.
43 CHAMPAGNE	G.H Mumm Cordon Rouge N.V.		36/6	18/6	9/-
63 BORDEAUX RED	Médoc (Chaville Freres)		13/-	7/-	4/-
75 BORDEAUX WHITE	Graves (Chaville Freres)		13/-	7/-	4/-
88 BURGUNDY RED	Macon (Geisweiler and Fils)		13/-	7/-	4/-
90 BURGUNDY WHITE	Pouilly Dry Reserve (Bouchard Ainé)	15/-	8/-	4/6
30 HOCK	Liebfraumilch Klosterdoctor		15/-	8/-	4/6

BEERS
Bass, Flower's Brewmaster, Double Diamond, Guinness,			
Worthington	...	...	2/3
Skol Pilsner Lager, Tuborg Pilsener Lager	...	2/3
Holsten Pilsner	...	...	...	2/6

CIDER
Whiteway's "WHIMPLE" brand extra quality	...	2/-
Bulmer's	...	...	...	2/-
Babycham	...	...	...	2/-

IN THE TRIANON BAR
VODKA	...	2/9
Try Vodka and Tonic or Vermouth and Vodka		
UNDERBERG (Miniatures)	...	3/-

MINERALS
Vichy Celestins Splits	...	...	2/-
Apollinaris "Baby Polly"	...	...	1/6
Schweppes: Ginger Beer Quinine Tonic Soda Water	Baby	10d.
Ginger Ale Lemonade Bitter Lemon Cola	Splits	1/6
Rose's Lime Juice Cordial and Rose's Squashes		1/-
Pineapple Juice	1/6	Tomato Juice Cocktail	1/6

PULLMAN MINIATURES
Courvoisier Brandy XXX	5/-	Drambuie			6/-
Whisky, Ballantine	6/6	Crème de Menthe			5/-
Gin	5/-	Wolfschmidt Kummel			5/-
Cointreau	5/-	Grant's Cherry Brandy			5/-
		Benedictine			5/-

PLEASE ASK FOR A BILL

10/59

above: 152. The *Golden Arrow* at Hildenborough (near Tonbridge), en route to Dover in 1961. Third-rail BB Electric class 71 (later 74), No. E5015 originally.

left: 153. *Golden Arrow* menu in 1959.

opposite: 154. For this well-known *Flèche d'Or* poster of 1926, the artist had to draw his inspiration from English Pullmans. Note the English-style high platform, and the CIWL badge, which never appeared on the ends of the cars, as did the Pullman badge on UK cars.

Serving the Iberian Peninsula

It was in 1882 that Spain saw the arrival of the first two Wagons-Lits cars, Nos. 72 and 73. Once running in regular service, they connected with ex-Mann car No. 47 sent from Paris to Irun.

Wagons-Lits services in Portugal began in January 1887 with the Lisbon-Porto Train de Luxe. On 24th October 1887, Nagelmackers had one of his famous launching banquets for the trial trip of the Sud Express, which ran once weekly between Lisbon and Calais via Madrid and Paris. Passengers had to change at Hendaye on the Franco-Spanish frontier when travelling north and at Irun on the way south. The regular service therefore began from Lisbon on 4th November 1887, and from Calais on 5th November, so that the two trains could meet at the frontier and exchange their customers.

Whereas the French Sud Express had plenty of Wagons-Lits cars to draw upon, in the event of delay or difficulty, the Spanish Sud Express arrived at Hendaye from Lisbon at about 5 a.m. and started its return journey from Irun to Lisbon at 7:30 a.m., which left just two and a half hours in which to run the train back empty from Hendaye to Irun and there clean it. Any delay in one direction caused delays in the other, due to the shortage of Wagons-Lits cars in Spain. When breakdowns occurred, ordinary Norte Railway first-class carriages had to be hired. By 1895 the Lisbon sleepers were being separated from the Madrid ones at Medina del Campo, and in 1897 the Madrid portion was extended to Algeciras and called the Gibraltar Express. It perished a year later, for the want of patronage.

When Paris' Gare d'Orsay opened in 1900, the French Sud Express had been speeded up, and sleeping cars were no longer necessary between Paris and Irun. Even so, sleeper conductors continued, until 1926, to travel through from Paris to Madrid and Lisbon, changing cars at the frontier right along with their passengers. In France, Wagons-Lits salons replaced the sleeping cars with wagons-salons, using some of the newly built CIWL cars originally supplied for internal use in Belgium in place of Belgian State Railways first-class coaches (a change not made without a rumpus in the Belgian Parliament). All these cars are listed in the Appendices, but eight of them, Nos. 1546–1553, were definitively allocated to the Sud Express until 1904. Additional new ones joined the Sud Express and the Savoy Express (Paris–Aix Les Bains) during that same year. At a time when gas lighting was normal for most CIWL Trains de Luxe, all these salons had electric lighting. Unlike Pullmans, each car contained one large saloon, several compartments and beautiful appointments. The train enjoyed good patronage. The normal regular run, like that on 14th May 1902, could count among its passengers the Imperial Grand Duke Vladimir of Russia, Prince Albert of Prussia, Count Moltke, Prince Christian of Denmark, the Prince of Monaco, a Marquis, a Count and a Siamese Legation. The suite of all these grandees totalled thirty people, plus servants, according to Roger Commault. One reason for the patronage was the connection at Lisbon with liners to South America.

The train received even better wagons-salons in 1913. Just over a year later, some of these were conscripted into Marshal Foch's and President Clémenceau's special trains, while the rest went into storage for the duration of World War I. Otherwise, the Sud Express continued unaffected in Spain and Portugal. In France it connected with a single wagon-salon, running from Biarritz to Irun.

The salons returned to the Sud Express in France only in 1921, by which time traffic to Biarritz and the Côte d'Argent had become as important as that to Spain. The region began to gain favour during the reign of England's King Edward VII, who preferred it to the Côte d'Azur. Thus, it was to Biarritz and not to Irun that the inaugural Sud Express Pullman ran, on 28th August 1926, the first Train de Luxe in France to be equipped with Pullman Cars. Painted in Pullman's chocolate-and-cream livery, these French-built all-steel cars (Nos. 2737–2748) replaced the teak wagons-salons. They had no Pullman-style lavatory window and only one saloon and several coupé compartments. Moreover, they were joined on the first trip by three 'complementary' cars (2839–2841), each with a kitchen and two saloons. The fourgons were painted chocolate and cream to match.

After the inaugural trip, the French Sud Express continued to run to Irun as before, connecting there with the Spanish and Portuguese Sud Express, which was now a Train de Luxe of sleeping and dining cars but no Pullmans. Beginning in 1926, the French Sud Express rolled under electric power between Paris and Orleans, and by 1927 the Midi Railway's main line from Bordeaux to Irun had also been electrified. But the Orleans-Bordeaux section continued under steam until 1939, after the Paris-Orleans and the Midi had been nationalized.

The Sud Express was repainted in CIWL blue-and-cream Pullman car livery after 22nd May 1932, when *North Star* type second-class Pullmans joined the train. In France at this time the train usually comprised just one *triplage* of Pullman cars (one kitchen, one first-class and one second-class parlour) with fourgon at either end for baggage and post. In this form the service lasted until World War II.

Until the Spanish Civil War stopped it in July 1936, the Spanish Sud Express left Irun with sleepers and fourgon for Lisbon, while the remainder of the train departed for Madrid. The latter divided at Medina del Campo, the diner continuing to Madrid in the main train. A Wagons-Lits Portuguese-division diner, which had arrived at Medina during the night with the Lisbon-Hendaye Sud Express, was attached to the fourgon and sleepers destined for Lisbon and Estoril. A wagon-salon ran to and from Porto in the Lisbon-Pampilhosa train. Restarted a year after the Spanish Civil War, on 25th July 1937, the Lisbon portion of the Sud Express was one of the few Trains de Luxe to continue, albeit by a roundabout route to Salamanca and the Portuguese frontier. It ended at Irun, while the French Sud Express terminated at Hendaye. Passengers therefore had to make their own way across the Franco-Spanish frontier.

For one reason or another, Wagons-Lits declined to supply Pullman Cars to the Andalusian Railway, which, along with the other main companies, became part of the Spanish National Railways (RENFE) after the Civil War. So the Andalusian company itself bought six Pullman Cars from Metro (Birmingham), three with kitchen and three without. At first they were staffed by Wagons-Lits. They even had Parisian coal stoves of a standard pattern. The 'Andalucia Pullman' ran between Seville and Algeciras until 1939. Until 1930 it included a Malaga portion, which was detached at Bobadilla Junction.

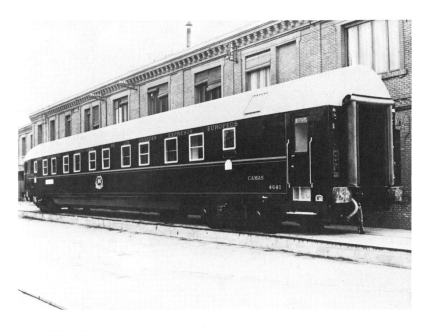

155. CIWL YF-type sleeping car, for Spain. Used on the Costa Vasca Express, amongst others. Note the air intake for the diesel engine that drives the air-conditioner.

156. Changing the bogies of a U-type sleeping car of the *Puerta del Sol,* at Hendaye on the Franco-Spanish frontier. View taken during trials in 1969.

In 1930 Wagons-Lits ordered six teak Pullman cars to be built in Spain for service as single cars in ordinary trains whose diners supplied the refreshments. One became a RENFE cinema coach in 1948 (No. 4165). From 1934 until the outbreak of the Civil War, another ran between Madrid and Hendaye, connecting there with the Pyrennées–Côte d'Argent Express, an overnight Train de Luxe to Paris' Gare d'Orsay, in those days a main-line terminus. The Pyrennées–Côte d'Argent has a successor, called *La Palombe Bleue* ('The Blue Ring-dove'), running from Paris' Austerlitz Station to Hendaye, with a portion to Lourdes and Tarbes. For the first time it passes Bordeaux non-stop. This 690-kilometre run is the longest advertised in France.

After 1939 the Sud Express had ordinary coaches in the train. A first-class Pullman reappeared in the French Sud Express in 1947. At first it operated as part of a *couplage,* but later only the Pullman without kitchen survived, running next to the diner, which supplied the meals served in the Pullman. This car continued to function for almost twenty-five years in the Sud Express, until it was withdrawn on 22nd May 1971, the last regular Pullman in France managed by CIWL. By then the *Puerta del Sol* had been in existence for nearly two years, and Wagons-Lits had given up the commercial operation of sleeping cars, with the exception of those in Portugal.

The Irun-Lisbon Sud Express therefore had the distinction of being the last Western European international sleeping-car service operated commercially by Wagons-Lits that included a Wagons-Lits fourgon to carry the mail, after about a century of such service. Through Paris-Lisbon SNCF couchettes were added to the Sud Express in 1973, with others to Porto and elsewhere following a few years later. In 1978 the Portuguese Railways took over the com-

mercial operation of the sleeping cars, buying the vehicles from CIWL. They also leased the fourgons, which were last observed in 1980, still running in CIWL livery.

The Madrid portion of the Sud Express became so busy that it had to run separately from the Portuguese train. Renamed the Costa Vasca Express, it ends its journey at Irun, while a large section serves Bilbao. Though the French connection at Irun is now good, passengers travelling overnight between Paris and Madrid, or vice versa, are encouraged to use the through Talgo Sleeper Train, started in May 1981 (see Chapter 15).

The third largest of all Wagons-Lits railway operations are still in Spain. The last Train de Luxe, composed exclusively of CIWL cars, was the boat train between Madrid and Algeciras called the 'Castellano Express'. At Algeciras docks it met the liners *Independence* and *Constitution* from New York and lasted until 1964.

But many Spanish trains, such as the Costa Vasca, run three or four sleepers per night in their rake. Usually these comprise one or more Spanish-built YF-type air-conditioned cars, with other P or Lx cars, originally built for service in Europe. Mixed gauge with third rail enters the main CIWL workshops at Irun, to enable cars to be easily transferred from service in France to new service in Spain. The shop has been under the direction of the Berroa family since its inception in 1883. There is a subsidiary works at Aravaca, near Madrid.

After World War II all Wagons-Lits cars carried the company's title in Spanish on one side and in Portuguese on the other, except those for the *Puerta del Sol* train. This was because of the rigorous Customs duties imposed by General Salazar's regime on items renewed at Irun during overhaul. Precisely which cars belonged to the Portuguese or to the Spanish WL fleet was a closely guarded company secret.

Madrid is still linked to Lisbon by a Wagons-Lits Train de Luxe, the *Lusitania Express,* with a bar car travelling throughout the night and also ordinary coaches as well. For many years Portuguese people could make return reservations from Madrid in Lisbon, but only on three days a week when the sleeper was one belonging to the Portuguese division, and the conductor took the reservations with him. Now this Lisbon facility has ended, because the whole service is operated commercially by the Spanish Railways (RENFE), using YF-type air-conditioned WLs built in the 1970s.

The *Puerta del Sol* through sleeping-car train began running from Paris to Madrid in 1969, though Nagelmackers had dreamed of through cars way back in 1884! U-class sleepers, provided by Germany in recompense for some eight hundred sleeping cars lost during World War II, were used in this service, for which Wagons-Lits bought new sets of Spanish-gauge bogies.

High-speed running was a feature of this express, a non-stop train between Paris and Bordeaux. At Hendaye, the sleepers were shunted off (together with the through couchette cars added in 1971), and raised together by jacks in a special shed fitted with four rails, the standard gauge gauntletted inside the Spanish gauge, which placed the bogies of both directly below the car bogie-pins. A special low tractor towed the new bogies into position, pushing the old bogies in front of it. The cars were then lowered and worked away from the opposite end of the shed.

After this the cars joined the RENFE train for Madrid, which alone started from Hendaye, instead of Irun. The CIWL diner was formerly attached there as well, but later this took place at Miranda del Ebro, where electric traction gives way to diesel.

At Burgos, the train took the shorter new route through the hills and Aranda, instead of Medina del Campo. After this line had opened in 1936, heavy fighting occurred in one of the longer, still-uncompleted tunnels.

Breakfast was served in the spacious, heavy, Spanish-built Wagons-Lits diner as the *Puerta del Sol* passed through the arid hills north of Madrid, a landscape that made the interior of the car seem all the more civilized. Then suddenly the train reached its destination, Madrid's new Chamartin Station built in the 1960s as a replacement for the old Delicias Station, now closed. Expresses to or from Irun no longer use Norte either, though this terminal continues to serve other trains. Chamartin is a modern RENFE showpiece with 12 platforms, each 500 metres long and reached by escalators from a raised concourse equipped with the latest electronic announcement technology. A short underground passage connects the station to Atocha, the former starting point for Barcelona, Malaga, Cadiz, Algerciras and, more recently, Lisbon. At one time through trains, such as the Irun-Algeciras Gibraltar Express, had to make a long detour to reach Atocha from Norte.

In May 1981, the *Puerta del Sol* lost its sleeping cars, while retaining its couchette cars and the Miranda-Madrid diner, and has become a car-carrying train. The Paris-Madrid Talgo sleeping-car train, with diner and bar running throughout and a gauge change at Hendaye, is described in Chapter 15. The Paris-Madrid Talgo is pendular, tilting on curves at high speed by means of air bags on columns mounted above the wheels and controlled by an automatic switching system. The arrangement saves about three hours over the entire journey.

The *Edelweiss*

The *Edelweiss* was a splendid International Train de Luxe that began service on 15th June 1928, running from Amsterdam to Basle, in direct competition with the *Rheingold,* which made its first journey between these two cities on 15th May of the same year. The *Edelweiss* traversed more countries than any other Pullman train and after a fortnight's service it went all the way to Lucerne.

Like the *North Star,* the *Edelweiss* was operated by Wagons-Lits' Dutch division. It comprised one first-class Pullman *couplage* and one second-class *couplage* with two WL fourgons. On the way the train called at The Hague, Rotterdam, Antwerp, Brussels, Luxembourg, Metz, Strasbourg and Mulhouse, many of which cities had no other Pullman service.

It started from Amsterdam at 06:50, which was a bit early for tourists, if not for business men, but gradually the start was retarded to 09:29. It took two and a half hours to reach Antwerp, where the train used the Berchem Station. In the first winter of 1928 it began making up at Antwerp, which offered a good connection to and from London via Harwich, thus making the *Edelweiss* all the more competitive with Mitropa's *Rheingold* (see Chapter 11). Holland passengers changed at Antwerp to and from the *Oiseau Bleu.*

In the summer of 1929 the *Edelweiss* was extended from Basle to Zurich, with one first-class Pullman branching off to Lucerne. Then in October 1932 the winter Zurich-Antwerp service was once more extended to The Hague, and finally in 1933 it provided service to and from Amsterdam throughout the year, until the outbreak of World War II in 1939.

After the war the *Edelweiss* was reinstated in the form of a second-class Pullman car attached to a WL diner, running between Brussels and Basle from 1948 to 1952, and first-class Pullmans, in an ordinary train, shuttling between Brussels and Amsterdam from 1947 to 1950.

In 1957 the name was taken over by the *Edelweiss* TEE, operated with diesel sets jointly owned by the Dutch and Swiss railways. For the first time, Wagons-Lits permitted the Compagnie Suisse des Wagons-Restaurants (SSG) to operate outside Switzerland. The SSG provided the catering on this train, which was later, until 1978, electrically powered with former Cis-Alpin Swiss TEE sets. Beginning in May 1977, it was cut back to Brussels-Zurich. In 1978 the train ceased to be a TEE and became an ordinary express with dining car, and since 1980 it has once again been curtailed to run between Brussels and Basle.

On the Narrow Gauge

The Andalusian Railway was not the only Spanish line to buy Pullmans and get Wagons-Lits to staff them. The Vascongados Railway from San Sebastian to Bilbao bought five Pullmans, Nos. 1–3, with kitchen. They were supplied by the Leeds Forge Co. and are metre gauge. They look like miniature Pullmans, though they seem to have lost their oval Pullman windows. The cars remained in service until 1979, labelled 'Coche Salon' or 'Coche Salon Buffet' and seat-

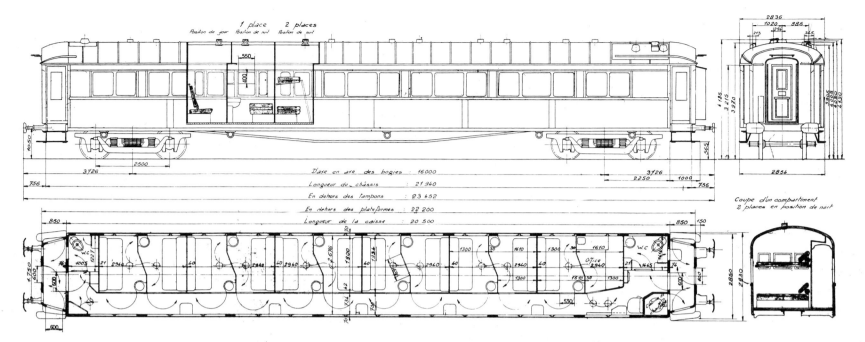

157. Plan and sections of Z0-class sleeping car as rebuilt with Y interior, inter-communicating doors and compartment 12 turned into a pantry.

ing 20 and 16 respectively. After withdrawal, these cars have been remodelled for further service as ordinary coaches.

Wagons-Lits staffed the service only during 1929. The cars have (or had up till 1960) chairs and upholstery almost the same as those found elsewhere in Wagons-Lits equipment and are provided with coupé compartments. They display FV (Ferrocarilles Vascongados) on the waistline in the centre, and they also had a large notice proclaiming *Desunsectado*. The idea that such unpleasant passengers might be travelling without paying their supplementary fares would surely make Lord Dalziel turn in his grave!

This Pullman service is perhaps overshadowed by the other narrow-gauge Pullmans running on the Montreux Oberland Bernois Railway in Switzerland (MOB), which in 1977 celebrated its seventy-fifth anniversary. The WL *Golden Mountain Pullman Express* would probably not have started at all had it not been for the Mitropa expansion on the Rhätian Railway (RhB) described earlier. After the Engadine, the Bernese Oberland was the obvious choice.

For the narrow gauge, Wagons-Lits ordered 4 Pullmans from SIG, or the Schweizer Industrie Gesellschaft of Neuhausen (near Schaffhausen). These had 14 first- and 18 second-class seats. They were numbered 103–106 MOB, and afterwards were sold to the Rhätische Bahn, which still runs them, mostly in special trains. Two MOB cars, Nos. 84 and 83, were rebuilt and renumbered 102 and 101. No. 102 had 36 seats instead of 32. These were all painted in blue and cream, and since they had large bow windows stretching to the roof, the cars carried the Wagons-Lits title below the windows immediately above the badge. *Golden Mountain Pullman Express* was painted in English below the badge, on either side of it. The letters MOB and Roman numerals for the class appeared at the ends of the cars, close to the destination board. The lavatory windows were the famous Pullman type: oval with leaded panes.

Two dining cars on the MOB had been operated by the Swiss Dining Car Co. (SSG) since 1906, the only narrow-gauge ones they had. The Pullman train began service on 14th June 1931 and ended,

157. Plan and sections of Z0-class sleeping car as rebuilt with Y interior, inter-communicating doors and compartment 12 turned into a pantry. For the Italian second class, the Z type appeared in 1926, offering 12 2-berth compartments, with wash-basins alternately next to the entrance door or under the window, and zigzag partitions between compartments. Each compartment had 2 windows like the S (while each R-type double compartment in the S had 3 windows). An ingenious set of moveable glass vanes in a brass frame, outside the main pane, could be turned against the direction of the train to admit air without dirt. This arrangement disappeared with the end of steam traction.

The Y class followed in the 1930s, a pantry taking the place of the twelfth Z-type compartment, with single windows and intercommunicating doors. Their absence made the Z type very suitable for the Orient Express route before World War II, and they remained on the Simplon Orient Express/Direct Orient Express from about 1946 to 1966. Many Y-class vehicles had 3-berth compartments fitted at the ends of the cars for use by 3rd-class passengers. The first newly built YT class appeared in 1949 to pre-war design, as the need to replace wartime losses was too urgent to wait for new designs. The need for 3rd-class berths came when Wagons-Lits succeeded in penetrating across the Kattegat into Sweden and Norway to Stockholm and Oslo, where the railways insisted that some berths be 3rd class. They were all fitted with rings for ferry chains (unlike the Z), and one of them, No. 3916, later used on the Arlberg Express, has been preserved at Peterborough by the BBC for film-making. Later the YT compartments were altered to Universal-type dual-position central-berth compartments (YU), which enable the lower berths to have higher head room when the compartment is used as a 1st-class double compartment instead of a tourist-class triple compartment. Many Y-class cars were later altered to 3-berth throughout (U type).

Up till 1955 only one new type WL sleeper appeared, the LJ, designed by Lopez Jamar, the WL Spanish chief engineer, with 30 compartments within the shell of a Y-class car and alternate double and single compartments with vertical Z-shaped partitions that set back the upper berths in the doubles to give more room in the narrow compartment floors. All 20 cars were withdrawn by 1969, partly because of poor-quality wartime steel used in their construction.

so far as Wagons-Lits were concerned, just three months later, on 15th September. Between Montreux and Zweisimmen, the makeup usually consisted of two Pullmans and a diner. It is sometimes for-

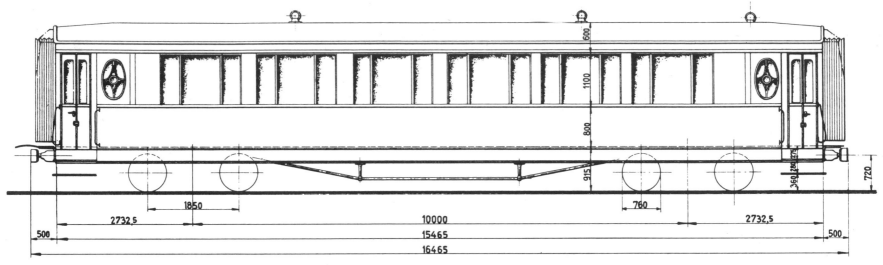

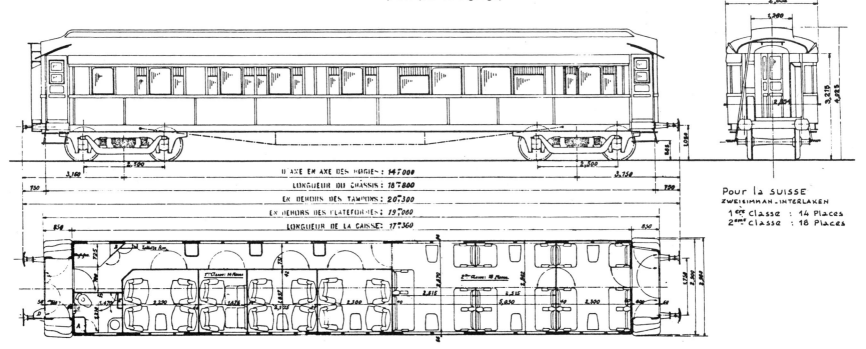

above: 158. Elevation drawing of Pullman Car No. 103 for the MOB portion of the *Golden Mountain Pullman Express* (narrow gauge).

below: 159. Plan, section and elevation of saloon cars Nos. 2444–2446 for the BLS portion of the *Golden Mountain Pullman Express* (standard gauge).

gotten that this express went beyond the Golden Pass on the standard-gauge SEZ line from Zweisimmen to Interlaken via Spiez, part of the Bern Lötschberg Simplon group of private lines owned by the canton of Berne.

In 1932 the MOB sold the two diners to the RhB as ordinary coaches, but retained Nos. 101 and 102. After World War II the company converted No. 101 to an old-style salon-bar car; now both No. 101 and No. 102 are once again running with *Golden Mountain* emblazoned upon them. They can be reserved in advance on payment of 20 first-class tickets with the group reduction offered to groups of 10 to 24 people, while the train leaving Montreaux at 09:28 carries the name *Golden Pass.* Now that privately owned Pullmans are running again in Switzerland (see next section), perhaps there will once again be a *Golden Mountain Pullman Express* extending right through from Interlacken to Zweisimmen and thence to Montreux. But with a difference; for this Train de Luxe will undoubtedly make a long pause at Chamby, where the Chemin de Fer Touristique Blonay-Chamby runs steam trains in the summer. The company also has plenty of steam engines in the Chamby Museum, reached by electric tram from Chamby Station.

IV

THE NEW BATTLE OF THE RAILS

14. The Enemy: The Aeroplane

One of the half-forgotten facts of history is that when Hitler and Chamberlain made their Munich Pact over Czechoslovakia in 1938, Chamberlain flew from London to Munich instead of taking the Orient Express. Hitherto, air travel had never been considered safe enough for use by heads of state.

The age of air travel began after World War I. Since then, Air France has become the largest scheduled network operator in the world, while British Airways, first called 'Imperial Airways' (for in 1918 the word 'Empire' still meant something in Great Britain), have been functioning for half a century. Certain well-tried machines, such as the Douglas Dakota DC3 airliner, which in 1976 celebrated forty years of flying, were still in action in 1979 (for example with Jersey European Airways' services to Dinard and Caen). Such aircraft showed the Americans the possibility of large-scale developments, especially in non-developed countries.

Thus, after World War II the railway had a new competitor, the airliner. Overland air routes evolved somewhat more slowly than did the overseas routes, at any rate in Europe, since airliners were needed for long distances and in places where no roads or railways existed.

Long-distance flying was new, and the development of airliners capable of flying the Atlantic non-stop (instead of refuelling at Newfoundland and Ireland) sent American airlines everywhere in droves, eager to find new customers ready to open new routes.

Very cheap oil supplies, plus the speed of aircraft, had a much more devastating effect on railway passenger traffic in the United States than they did in Europe, and the rising costs of maintaining track in a state suitable for passengers in the USA caused many American railroads to give up passenger carriage altogether. Many railroad presidents saw nothing wrong with this, since they had their hands full competing with road haulage for freight traffic. So the Pullman Co. closed down in 1968, as mentioned earlier, and by 1970 the lack of trains, plus the continued financial plight of the privately owned American railroads, resulted in the creation of Amtrak, as we shall see in Chapter 20.

In Europe, and in most countries outside the United States, the whole pattern of air transport seems to be based on nationalism. Thus, on international routes, traffic rights are almost automatically granted to two operators per route, even where the traffic could probably not support one profitably.

The railways had not been slow to realize the potential of the aeroplane. Indeed, the first airline to carry mail inside Britain belonged to the Great Western Railway, which shortly afterwards combined with its rival, Southern, to form Railway Air Services. Their routes to the Channel Islands were a success, and they resisted nationalization for as long as possible. In 1929, the Pennsylvania and Santa Fe railroads in the USA were among the founders of Transcontinental Air Transport, which later became TWA.

Wagons-Lits, far more conscious of tourism than many railways (but by no means all of them), were early on the scene, serving the first inflight lunch in 1927 on an Air Union plane (now part of Air France) in direct rivalry with their own route—the *Golden Arrow*—which they listed first in the guide to their railway operations.

Wagons-Lits developed their pioneer air catering after World War II. In addition to the bars, restaurants and small transit hotels at Paris Orly Sud, they run a large catering establishment for seventy-five airlines. Supplies for this come from the same Wagons-Lits central kitchens and bulk stores in the new Rungis Market, handily nearby, that serves all Wagons-Lits Paris rail-catering requirements. A special section supplies kosher food to all airlines at Orly, with a separate facility for the rabbi doing the preparatory work. Most airlines, with the exception of Air France, use Wagons-Lits' facilities at Orly for all kinds of passengers. The facilities include a 'marshalling yard', a special sorting area where care is taken to ensure that crockery is returned to the proper airline, and not to a rival. Railway tradition is deeply ingrained in Wagons-Lits thinking! Wagons-Lits have their own fleet of lorries with bodies that can be raised to the level of the aircraft fuselage.

In addition to its services at Orly, Wagons-Lits formerly operated the restaurants and bars at Le Bourget. In collaboration with Roissy Service, they also run the catering and the airport restaurants at Charles de Gaulle and the Arcade Hotel.

Outside Paris, Wagons-Lits manage the Bordeaux Airport bar at Merignac and once had an interest in the restaurants of Marseilles Airport at Marignane. At Schiphol Airport, Holland, they run the restaurants and bars through a Dutch subsidiary, Bredam BV, and also the hotel restaurant 'Luchthaven Eadle' at Gronigen Airport. In Spain Wagons-Lits control, through Eurest España, the restaurant at Palma de Majorca Airport and the airport catering for in-flight meals at Alicante, Las Palmas (Gando) and Ibiza.

If the aeroplane has done considerable harm to rail travel, the trend is finally being reversed as a consequence of several circumstances. Above all, the world-wide oil crisis has so fundamentally altered the long-term international transport outlook that experts seem barely to have grasped its significance. Moreover, a new generation has grown up so familiar with air travel that the experience no longer has an aura of romance about it. The aeroplane, in fact, is as commonplace as a bus, a motor car, a bicycle or a train as a means of transport. Now, ironically, it is the rails that seem exotic. Also benefitting the railways are the difficulties of road-traffic congestion to and from airports, as well as the increasing insecurity of the terminal car-parks. It often takes longer to get to and from your flight than it takes to reach your ultimate destination. Then, upon return from an exhausting (and possible unnecessary) day's trip abroad, you may lose your luggage or find your car damaged or stolen. Airlines also have lost heavily to hijackers. An unsuspecting passenger en route to Nice could well find himself in Entebbe or Algiers, and the 'comforts' of waiting days or hours on boiling tarmac are far removed from the standards of Wagons-Lits. And, finally, there is the unreliability of air travel, with its delays due to weather or its diversions to places where one has no desire to go. With all this in their favour, the railways are at last using some creativity to lure passengers back.

British Rail's creation of Motorail in 1957—or Trains Auto Couchette or Autoreisezuge for Tourists—has done much to help the railways in their battle with airliners. The establishment of special loading stations for motor cars and their passengers, with new, clean toilets and a reception lounge with bar, instead of old-fashioned station facilities, was a major achievement. A whole network of overnight trains of sleeping and couchette cars, with full dining facilities on many of them, has been developed for the specific purpose of carrying passengers with their cars together. Many such services are seasonal and run only at week-ends, but many others run every night.

Another great blow to the airways would be the long-discussed creation of the Channel Tunnel linking Great Britain to the Continent. In 1975 the British Socialist government stopped the tunnel project, which had been planned for completion in 1981. Meanwhile, the Dover Harbour Board maintain that conventional shipping can handle all potential traffic, with large cross-Channel

160. CIWL 'catering' service lorry victualling a British Airways Trident aircraft at Orly Airport in Paris.

steamers leaving the port every 10 minutes throughout the 24 hours, if required. As for the additional costs, the Board say these would be minimal, compared to those for tunnels or bridges. Their assumption, and probably a right one, is that, should Britain complete a single-track tunnel by 1990, the country will wonder how it ever managed without the facility and clamour for a double track.

Today, England favours a tunnel financed by private enterprise, while France has turned Socialist and thus toward public funding. But with many still preferring that public investment be made in the north rather than in the favoured south, it is becoming clearer that the tunnel must be European—that is, paid for by the EEC and immune from nationalization.

Present thinking holds that the first tunnel could be ready about 1990. Meanwhile, British Rail has no international trains for passengers, though motor coaches roll on and off the ferries with their customers on board as though there were nothing to it. The London-Paris and London-Brussels Wagons-Lits ended with the Night Ferry on 31st October 1980.

In France the successful inauguration of the new TGV (high-speed) line from Paris to Lyons has effectively ended Air Inter's Paris-Lyons flights (see Chapter 15). Soon there will be a new TGV Atlantic line running between Paris and Bordeaux. While a TGV service to the north is envisioned, its outcome depends largely on the tunnel. And since 1981 the prospects of that enterprise seem to have risen again, since both France and Britain now tend to agree that it should go ahead. At the same time, the airlines have been publicly warned by the banks that the latter can no longer support the carriers' operating losses. If airlines, like railways, become much more dependent on government subsidies, the governments in-

161. Restored to 1936 CIWL livery, Night Ferry sleeper 3792 was installed in the National Railway Museum at York on 16th January 1980. The RIC plate visible below destination plaque with anchor at far end symbolized the ability to run to England.

162. The Paris-London Night Ferry backing into Dover Marine Station after disembarking from the Train Ferry (behind the signal box, which is now destroyed) in November 1936. The boat had been delayed by bad weather, causing the train to arrive at Victoria at 14:00 instead of 09:10.

volved will think harder about impeding the much-needed—if grandiose—project of direct traffic by rail from England to the Continent. Needless to say, this will delight those with delicate inner ears and turbulent tummies who dread the treacherous Channel but cannot afford the plane.

Of course Europe, compared to the New World, is a cozy group of densely populated countries within a small area, all parts of which are intimately linked by rail. In the United States, the vast distances and the domestic airlines' superb organization and cheap fares continue to challenge any hope for a revival of the great trans-continental rails. In the heavily populated North-Eastern Seaboard, trains could have a brighter future, but needed government subsidies are eternally on the brink of disappearance. Train fares on Amtrak are far from inexpensive, and service is quite haphazard, except in club cars charging a 50 per cent supplement. A family of four travelling from New York to Philadelphia would spend close to $100 for an hour's trip that can be made by car in the same time on a four-lane motorway for $10 worth of gasoline. The railways' older carriages are filthy and dank, and passengers attempting to travel by Greyhound Bus might not survive the central-city terminals aswarm with all sorts of unfortunates. However, as oil prices continue to escalate, perhaps fresh thought will be given to bringing back the railroads that have constituted such an essential part of America's social and economic history.

15. The TEEs and the TGVs

On the initiative of Dr. I. Q. Den Hollander, then president-director of the Dutch State Railways (NS), the six railways of the Common Market and Switzerland decided in 1957 to start a series of international day trains of various types, chiefly diesel multiple-units, all painted in a standard red-and-cream livery.

This was the first time the railways had embarked on running a special network of international day trains with their own rolling stock painted in a common colour. The logo 'TEE' was to be applied to everything: coaches, crockery, glasses, napery, etc. Some twenty years later, certain crack day trains operating entirely within one country, such as the Italian *Settebello* or the French *Mistral,* were added to the network.

The TEE trains offer first class only, with supplement. In most of them, meals are served at every seat, Pullman style. Prior reservation is obligatory, though last-minute places can sometimes be obtained if there is room. Reservations are held on various central computers that also issue seat reservations for ordinary trains. This makes them obtainable either through a travel agent or through the principal seat-reservation offices at stations.

Most countries maintain their own individual computer system for reservations, and, unfortunately, only some of them are directly linked with each other. To minimize the problem, each country's computer booking system is arranged with an international terminal at key centres in other countries.

The fact that the trains are first class only makes them generally cleaner than ordinary ones, and by not conveying parcels, etc., in quantity, the TEE network is rather faster than the 'regular' service, especially since station stops are of very short duration, sometimes just one minute. All TEE trains feature air-conditioning, with double glazing. The public-address system permits a hostess to make announcements in several languages, including English (often in recorded form). As a consequence, the TEE network is very popular with non-European residents from English-speaking countries, who, by paying the supplement and reserving a seat, can travel on them with the First Class Eurailpass. (The Eurailpass is not available to Europeans, including British residents; nor is it honoured in the UK.)

TEE trains have self-operating sliding glass doors between coaches and outer doors that close when the train exceeds 8 kilometres per hour (which, if necessary, permits the doors to be left open on sidings, when the car is being shunted). Each train is run by one particular railway, mostly using the rolling stock that belongs to that railway, though there are also jointly owned trains in which identical coaches belong to different countries.

Many of the TEEs took over the names of famous Pullman trains, such as *Blue Bird, North Star* and (until 1980) *Edelweiss.* Over the years electrification has been extended, and electric engines, able to operate on up to four different kinds of current, have been developed, so that most TEEs in the 1970s ceased to be multiple unit and were hauled electrically.

In 1978 many of the Trans-Europ Expresses were altered to become ordinary trains, following the need for increased second-class accommodation. Some new ones have recently been started, and all are listed in the Appendices. Catering on the TEEs depends upon which railway provides the train. Some have CIWL catering; German trains have DSG catering (see Chapter 11); and in 1951, for the first time since 1903, the Swiss Dining Car Co. (SSG) was permitted to work outside Switzerland to cater for the *Edelweiss.* Among the most famous of the TEEs is the modern *Rheingold.*

The *Rheingold* now makes up at Brig instead of Milan, though one *Rheingold* coach starts its journey from Chur in an ordinary train. A feature of the TEE network is that the trains connect with each other at key points, where certain coaches are sometimes switched to different destinations.

At Brig, the *Rheingold* comprises one car and runs in an ordinary BLS train, usually hauled from Bern by an SBB electric BB class Re 4/4 I or 4/4 II, painted in TEE colours to match the coaches. At the Basle SBB station it collects the dining car and the coach from Chur, which offers connections with St. Moritz, Davos Platz and Pontresina, and then calls at Zurich on its way to Basle. From Basle to Emmerich the engine is a DB class 103 CC electric, which comes onto the rear of the train, propelling one further coach that starts from Basle, where the carriages from the rest of Switzerland reverse direction. The *Rheingold* crosses the Rhine to the Baden Station, as the DB station in Basle is called. Like many stations in Germany, it has high platforms.

The *Rheingold* coaches are partly open saloons and partly compartment stock. Meals are served in the 42-seat diner, and of course the wine includes hock. But the DSG gave up their cellars at Trarbach in 1963 (see Chapter 11).

The Rhine is crossed again between Mannheim and Mainz, and the trip through its beautiful valley past Mainz and Bonn, the German capital, takes up the afternoon. Dinner is served after Cologne. If you look carefully out of the window here, you may see the sumptuously preserved cars of the 1928 *Rheingold*, now the property of the Freundeskreis Eisenbahn Köln. From there, the train proceeds towards Holland. Until 1978, the diner and one coach were detached at Utrecht to run to Hook of Holland, arriving there only 13 minutes before sailing time of the BR overnight ship to Harwich. By contrast there is a 74-minute gap between the ship's arrival at the English port and the departure of the London boat train! Now, however, passengers for England must leave the *Rheingold* at Utrecht and change into the Scandinavia-Holland Express to Hook of Holland.

At Harwich there is also a boat train to Manchester which takes a cross-country route, serving Peterborough, Nottingham and Sheffield on the way. It then returns the same evening in time to connect with the overnight Zealand Shipping Co. vessel (the Dutch member of Sealink) from Harwich to the Hook of Holland. From Hook to Utrecht, passengers for the *Rheingold* must now travel in the Holland-Scandinavia Express.

The Catalan Talgo TEE is quite a different train. It leaves Geneva for Spain, and from 1982 runs again through Grenoble,

163. ETR 300 FS TEE *Settebello* set, between Florence and Rome.

164. DB TEE *Saphir* set in 1957.

with SNCF diesel haulage from Chambéry to Valence. The engine of the Catalan Talgo is an SNCF 7200 BB fitted with specially adapted drawbar gear to handle the light-weight Talgo cars (until 1980, 9300 BBs were used), but apart from the engine, the whole train is entirely Spanish, or perhaps one should say Catalan.

Each of the Talgo cars (except the leading one) has only one axle, the other end of each short-length, low-slung car resting on the car in front. The leading car of later Talgos has an extra axle, but the original ones, running inside Spain, were permanently coupled to their diesel locomotive. Talgos are fixed sets, close-coupled; thus, they had to be built at terminal points on a special turning circle track.

The Talgo conception was developed originally by American Car & Foundry (formerly Jackson Sharp) of Wilmington, Delaware, and was adopted soon after the war by RENFE (Spanish Railways), because the light weight and low centre of gravity enabled the trains to run faster than ordinary ones on track whose condition often imposed slow speed on conventional trains hauled by heavy steam engines.

The Catalan Talgo was the first attempt by RENFE to burst out of the gauge barrier and run their own international trains to France. Service began in 1968–69 when RENFE at first provided its own diesel engines on the standard gauge at Port Bou, the Spanish station on the Franco-Spanish frontier, to haul their train right through to Geneva. This run was made via Grenoble instead of Lyons, and at Culoz it reversed direction. New-generation Talgos

165. Interior of the *Saphir*, 1957.

166. TEE *Rheingold* with DB 103 class CC electric locomotive.

were built to roll in either direction, with engine switching from one end of the train to the other.

Next the Talgo ran via Lyons and was electrically hauled from Geneva as far as Perpignan. Until electrification had been completed in 1982, a SNCF 67400 BB diesel took the Catalan Talgo from Perpignan to Port Bou. There it was detached. A shunting engine pushes the coaches from the rear, slowly, through the wheel-adjusting shed. The bodies of the light cars have their weight taken up by rollers, and the wheels slowly splay out the few inches needed to adjust to the Spanish gauge. The RENFE CC 7600 engine waits just beyond the shed, whence it tows the final cars through, since the shunting engine may not enter the shed. The whole process takes from five to ten minutes, compared to about an hour needed whenever conventional sleeping or couchette cars must change bogies.

Each Catalan Talgo car seats 17. A 48-seat Talgo diner and bar, operated by the Barcelona section of Wagons-Lits, serves lunch in France and dinner in Spain. A Rapide express (with supplement) of sleeping and couchette cars only provides a good overnight connection from Barcelona to Madrid. RENFE hopes one day to build a standard-gauge line from Madrid to Port Bou.

The two other international Talgos use sleeping cars. The berths in the Talgo sleepers align with the direction of travel, which allows them greater length than if they were set transverse. Tourist-class cabins contain four berths. The Barcelona Talgo began overnight service from Barcelona to Paris using the same Port Bou wheel-changing apparatus as the Catalan Talgo. The service eliminated conventional sleeping cars from Paris to Port Bou and the frontier change of train. In 1981, the Paris-Madrid Talgo of similar

sleeping cars replaced the *Puerta del Sol* sleeping cars (see Chapter 13); it changes gauges at Irun. Both trains include a dining car running throughout the journey; but, unlike the *Puerta del Sol,* the Madrid Talgo does not require any special adaptation of the drawbar gear for the BB 9300 SNCF engines that haul it. Its cars are designed to tilt on corners. All Talgos carry a mechanic on board. The Catalan Talgo ceased to be a TEE in 1982.

The *Cis-Alpin* TEE follows the route of the former Simplon Orient Express from Paris to Milan. Beginning in the summer of 1974, it continued on to Venice. Until 1974 this train was operated by a CFF multiple unit TEE set. It interworked with the *Gottardo* TEE from Milan to Basle via Zurich, which involved a rapid change-over by the dining car staffs at Milan, where Wagons-Lits took over the *Cis-Alpin* and SSG the *Gottardo.* This meant changing all the

opposite above left: 167. SNCF TEE *Mistral* (Paris-Nice) on the Côte d'Azur (Riviera) hauled by bi-current BB class 25200 engine, which has replaced the CC 6500 at Marseilles.

opposite above right: 168. SNCF TEE *Aquitaine* hauled by a CC 6500 class engine, the longest TEE non-stop run, in the fastest time.

opposite below left: 169. RENFE TEE Catalan Talgo hauled by SNCF diesel-electric class 67400 BB between Port Bou and Geneva (now electrically hauled for most of the journey).

opposite below right: 170. SNCF/SNCB TEE *North Star* takes its name from a former Pullman Train de Luxe. Hauled by SNCF quadri-current 40100 class CC, it is passing the Compiègne Forest, where the World War I Armistice was signed on 11th November 1918 in CIWL WR No. 2419.

dining cars' stocks as well, and frequently stores got mixed up in the rush.

Nowadays the *Cis-Alpin* is worked by locomotive-hauled SNCF coaches, though CFF owns some cars that are identical. From Paris to Vallorbe a dual-voltage CC 21000 or BB 22200 is used. A CFF Re 4/4 II BB takes over from Vallorbe to Domodossola, where, since 1980, the engine is either an FS 633 BBB 'Tiger' (Tigre) or one of the Mark II type FS 444 BB 'Flying Tortoise' (Tartaruga).

Meals are served both in open saloons and in the Wagons-Lits–staffed TEE diner, which is now detached at Lausanne and then reattached an hour later to the Milan-Paris return *Cis-Alpin*. The bar car in the train runs through to Milan, but to protect the SSG, the car will not serve spirits in Switzerland. Both diner and bar cars are worked by the CIWL Paris 'Inspection de Paris-Lyons'.

In 1980 the *Cis-Alpin* was curtailed in both summer and winter at Milan, owing to a shift in time zoning that made Switzerland one hour behind France and Italy. Now that the future of the train is in doubt, service to Venice has not been reinstated. When the new, triple-voltage TGVs are built, capable of running between Paris and Lausanne over the new line explained in Chapter 9, the *Cis-Alpin* may well be withdrawn.

left: 171. CIWL pocket timetables of the 1970s.

above: 172. Having made its last TEE *Cis-Alpin* run from Milan to Paris, SBB quadri-current TEE set is diesel-hauled by SNCY CC 65507 the 25th May 1974, prior to entering service on the TEE *Edelweiss*. It would run empty from Paris to Brussels.

The TGVs: France's High-Speed Trains

The TGVs—*Trains à Grande Vitesse*—are probably the greatest achievement of the French Railways since the SNCF came into existence in 1937. With the TGVs, the whole concept of rail travel has been transformed, a change that took place within the short span of a mere seven years. The French say the age of the Trains de Luxe is over; yet the TGVs had no place in the French edition of this book, for the simple reason that they did not exist in 1977, a time when much of the brand-new, exclusively TGV track still looked much like any of the fair fields of France between Paris and Lyons—before the arrival of the bulldozers!

The train of the future became today's train on 27th September 1981. No supplement is imposed to pay for comfort or for extra speed, although a TGV cruises at 260 kilometres (160 miles) per hour. Passengers can feel the surge of power as the train enters the new high-speed line and glides forward, rather like a jet plane after take-off—but almost silent! The joints of the long welded rails are nearly inaudible, thanks to the sound-proofing and air-conditioning. Ordinary (Paris-Lyons) fares are $44 in first class and $29 in second class, while on the same route the air fare would be $70 and the cost of making the journey by car about $53.

Each TGV has 386 seats, 275 of them second class, in 10-car formations, comprising a power car at each end with a distinctive polyester-formed nose in front of the driving cabin. In addition, each train includes 3 first-class trailers, 1 with baggage compartment, a bar car with 35 second-class seats and 4 second-class trailers. Six sets out of the total 87 ordered have 287 first-class seats with bar, but no second class. Though often used in pairs, the sets cannot be crossed from one to the other.

All TGVs are bi-current, since the old Paris-Lyons line is 1,500 volts DC and the TGV, called LGV by the SNCF, is 25,000 volts AC. Six of the TGVs, of which just 1 has been built so far, are tri-current, which permits them to run into Switzerland from Vallorbe to Lausanne on the SBB's 16 2/3 AC current. This service will not begin until 1983 when the LGV line is completed throughout. It is 56 miles shorter than the old one, owing to the fact that it bypasses Dijon; instead of following the Yonne River, it climbs up and down hills with gradients as steep as 1 in 28½, unthinkable for freight trains in the days of steam traction. The TGVs have 6,300 kilowatts of power, and 3 driving bogies at each end, with a third powered bogie supporting the trailer at each end next to the power car that drives it. The rest of the train runs on articulated bogies, 1 beneath a pair of trailers, saving weight and friction. The TGVs serving Dijon use a short branch LGV from Pasilly, to rejoin the old line at Aisy, 10 miles (16.4 kilometres) away. There are no tunnels or level crossings throughout the LGV.

Even though only 38 of the 87 TGVs have entered service, by 24th November 1981 they had already carried a million passengers, averaging 13,000 a day. SNCF planners imagined that, since no standing is allowed, about half the clientele would book in advance, and the other half use the 'last-3-minute-booking' machines, which open 1 hour before each train's departure. In fact, 75 per cent book in advance (over 80 per cent for Fridays), partly because the first-class dining service is provided in half of the 2-rake TGVs, unless each half is bound for a different destination once the train reaches Lyons. Unlike Japan's Tokaido trains, which cannot run on older lines because these are all narrow gauge in Japan, the fundamental success of the TGV system lies in its ability to use old lines as well as new ones.

The TGV booking machines, called 'Réséda' (in horticulture, the name of a plant yielding yellow dye) for *Réservation Sud-Est sur Demande d'Admission,* are handily close to the train at Paris' Gare de Lyons and at Lyons' Brotteaux station, a facility that is to be replaced by a new TGV station at Part Dieu. While the machines can assure the passenger a seat, either in first or second class, they do not have the capability to reserve space in the dining half of the train. Nor can they specify smoking or non-smoking seats. Still, the electronic reservation system serves to warn the SNCF operators of the need for running two TGV rakes, or even a supplementary train, for any particular service.

Second class on the TGVs offers no meal service, but the bar car is open to all throughout the journey, and it provides snacks (as well as drinks and magazines) at prices ranging from 13 to 18 francs. The snacks include a TGV cheese speciality called 'Talmouz' and the TGV sandwich, three assorted mini-sandwiches in a box with a picture of various TGV cars. (Children collecting these boxes will eventually have a complete train.) The bar, like the first-class tray-meal service, is run by a brand-new concern called 'Service 260', which refers to the train's cruising speed, the speed announced on the loudspeakers as the sound-proofed and air-conditioned TGV

173. One of France's new TGVs on the special long welded-rail Sud Est line (Paris-Lyons) near Le Creusot, where the bogies for these, the world's fastest, trains are manufactured.

surges forward and glides almost soundlessly over the long welded track. Unfortunately, the intercom also announces the delights of luncheon even to those in the half without service. The latter must put up with a mini-sandwich *à la* TGV, while imagining the delights of a cold entrée such as ham or smoked salmon, a hot *plat du jour* with vegetables or a steak (sometimes a roast is available), followed by cheeses (from the selection of master cheese-maker Claude Anthes) and a patisserie created by M. Bréda, the one-time master-chef at Fauchon, Paris' famous provision shop in the Place de la Madeleine. The price charged for this meal is 95 francs, with a half-bottle of wine available at 16–24 francs. The TGV has a repertoire of 28 different 4-course table d'hôte luncheons, to provide a different one daily, but supper is à la carte at 65 francs for a grill (not the same one served at luncheon), or the luncheon plat du jour may be repeated. A board of 3 cheeses, or a dessert, costs 18 francs.

Modern Frenchmen are supposed to prefer light suppers at low cost to the grand Train de Luxe candlelit dinners. However this may be, Service 260 is limited to 90 minutes, since Lyons will be reached in 2 hours when the whole LGV is open in 1983. It is also limited by the space aboard the TGVs, each of which has a small restaurant store in the end trailer, but deep-frozen food cannot be used. Breakfast (21 francs) happens to be the most popular meal—French or Continental breakfast, of course—but eggs are beyond the scope of the TGV micro-ovens.

Service 260 is staffed by 230 fresh recruits (boys and girls), whose average age is 20.5 years. Eventually, their numbers will swell to 750. A third of those now aboard the trains have hotel-college diplomas, and all bring some catering experience with them.

They work for a brand-new company called Sorenolif (for Société de Restauration de la Nouvelle Ligne Ferroviaire), wearing a green-and-tartan uniform designed by Carven, who won a competition held among various Paris fashion houses. Only the elegance of the service from a trolley, with real china and Christofle silverware, and perhaps some of the wine labels betray the fact that Sorenolif is 100 per cent owned by Wagons-Lits! The wines include a Rosé, a Beaujolais Villages (grown beside the track), a Côtes du Rhône (TGVs will be running through to Marseilles by summer 1982) and a St. Emilion (evocative of President Mitterand's order, at the time he inaugurated the 'TGV South East', that would set in motion the 'TGV Atlantic' linking Paris with Bordeaux).

The Gare de Lyons in Paris has been extensively rebuilt, with new underground platforms to accommodate suburban commuter trains, new raised platforms (symbolic of the new order) and service platforms between them for restocking the TGVs for their next journey. The lines are provided with inspection pits. Villeneuve St. Georges does the overhauls, while running repairs are taken care of at the Conflans sidings just outside the station. Both facilities use existing installations, which were reconstructed for TGV to save the cost of purchasing new land. At Villeneuve a whole train can be raised off its wheels at once. At the Gare de Lyons a new 500-metre-long kitchen is being constructed to service the TGVs, which eventually will be running every 5 minutes. For the time being supplies come from CIWL Orly Catering (see Chapter 14).

The LGV will leave the old line at Combs la Ville, crossing the tracks at St. Florentin, 108 miles from Paris, where the new LGV currently starts, and running past Pasilly to Macon. Only two new stations have been built. One is at Macon, where LGV crosses the old line at right angles, and also where the TGVs leave to join the line that branches off to Geneva. The other new station is at Montchanin, serving Le Creusot, an industrial town that built the TGVs' bogies.

Special moveable high-speed points allow smooth running into the station loops at up to 100 miles per hour, while the cross-overs (which in an emergency allow trains to switch lines) can tolerate even higher speeds. Both lines can be worked in either direction.

TGVs have cab signalling on the new line, and are connected to the Paris Control Centre by radio. On older lines, they use conventional signals.

The new line runs on south and ends at Sathonay, just north of Lyons-Brotteaux. TGVs to St. Etienne (and Avignon-Marseilles in the summer of 1982) go straight on, while those ending their journey at Lyons run round to Lyons-Perrache, where they enter the station from the Marseilles direction.

Two TGVs a day run through from Paris to Geneva, calling at Macon. The Marseilles and Montpellier TGVs will run non-stop from Paris to Avignon, and there divide, which means that they cannot be taken by passengers for Lyons. Nearly half the French population use this artery, and the old line to Dijon, which, as we have seen elsewhere, carries traffic for Italy and Switzerland as well, is only double track, forming a bottleneck shared by passenger and freight traffic alike.

Moreover, TGVs are expected to work through to Le Havre and Lille, using the new lines provided by the recently established Réseau Express Régional (the regional underground suburban network), which joins up the main lines in Paris, directly connecting the Gare de Lyons with Charles de Gaulle Airport.

16. New Zealand's *Silver Star*

The New Zealand Railways operate in two distinct parts. Seventy per cent of the traffic comes from the 2,610 kilometres in the North Island, and the remainder from the 2,187 kilometres in the South Island.

The population of the entire country is only around 3 million, and 4 out of 5 New Zealanders live in towns. Though Wellington is the capital, its population of about 350,000 is only half that of Auckland, the northern port which is New Zealand's fastest-growing city, the growth fueled by both industrial activity and shipping.

The *Silver Star* is an air-conditioned sleeping-car train (with diner) linking Wellington with Auckland. It leaves both cities 6 nights a week, from Sundays to Fridays at 20:00, arriving 12½ hours later. The distance is only 601 kilometres, but the route is hilly. Some 24 kilometres are on a gradient of 1 in 50 or worse and some 240 kilometres at 1 in 100 to 1 in 50. So overnight train travel offers a better solution than fast day rail-cars such as the *Silver Fern,* which takes 10 hours but has difficulty in competing with automobiles. (There is one car to every 2.5 persons in New Zealand.)

The New Zealand Railways' answer to all the motor cars is to own 416 motor coaches and 338 buses, as well as 216 lorries, and engage in massive re-equipment of the freight-wagon fleet, with particular emphasis on handling sea-borne containers.

The *Silver Star,* built in Japan of stainless steel, made its first run in 1971, replacing the *Night Limited,* which had been connecting the two cities since 1924. It has eleven air-conditioned sleeping cars, equipped with showers, offering two types of accommodation: double-berth compartments, called 'twinettes', with bunk rails in the upper berths, because of the sharp curves, and single-berth 'roomettes'.

For many years the New Zealand Railways did not run diners but indulged in meal stops. The staff are clearly very proud of their dining cars of the 1970s, but, whatever the circumstance, New Zealanders are a very courteous, friendly people, eager to show their country to tourists. The air-conditioning for the *Silver Star* is supplied from a generator van with its own diesel engine and baggage compartments. It also has a guard's compartment and one for the train fitter.

Although New Zealand has large supplies of cheap electricity, made by geothermic steam from the country's hot springs as well as by many hydraulic power stations, the railways use diesel engines. In days of steam, the *Night Limited* ran with electric haulage as far as the boundary of the Wellington suburban electrified system, of 1,500 volts DC, but now the powerful DX class Co-Co diesels seem to work right through between Auckland and Wellington and vice versa, instead of stopping to change engines at Paekakariki. The DX class, built in the USA by General Motors, is the most powerful locomotive used in New Zealand, and the original batch of 15 is being augmented by a further 34. So it looks as though the proposal to electrify the whole 'Main Trunk', as the Wellington-Auckland is called, at 2,500 volts AC has been shelved.

The principal junctions on the Wellington-Auckland route are Palmerston North, where the east-coast line to Napier bears to the right, and Merton, where the Auckland line makes a sharp turn to the right into the Rangitakai Valley, leaving the New Plymouth line to continue to that town on New Zealand's western peninsula. A new cut-off involving three viaducts between Utiku and Mangaweka will enable services to be speeded up on the Main Trunk.

The success of the *Silver Star* led in 1975 to the establishment of the *Northerner,* composed of ordinary coaches as well as sleepers and diner/buffet cars. This train takes some 13 hours to complete its journey since it makes more intermediate stops than the *Silver Star,* and it runs nightly, departing at 18:30 from Wellington and

above: 176. The *Silver Star* in the suburbs of Auckland, New Zealand, near the Container Base. Mechanics Bay in the background.

at 17:30 from Auckland except on Saturdays, when it arrives at much the same time as the *Silver Star* did on other days, but starts about half an hour earlier.

The *Silver Star* was withdrawn from service on 10th June 1979, leaving the *Northerner* to take its place. The rolling stock is to be rebuilt so that half of it contains sleeping cars and the other half ordinary coaches. Despite the high cost of oil and the fact that part of the line is electrified, New Zealand Railways say the *Silver Star* will continue to be diesel-hauled throughout, although they do not know when the train will return to service in its new form.

177 DX class Co-Co diesel engine and power car for the *Silver Star* air-conditioning

17. South Africa's *Bloutrein*

The magnificent South African *Blue Train (Die Bloutrein)* is probably the most sumptuous of all the world's most comfortable, regular Trains de Luxe. Everything about the *Bloutrein*—except the narrow-gauge track—is on the grand scale. The South African Railways say the service was planned with only one purpose—to provide the acme of comfort for the traveller.

On the *Bloutrein* you have your name written on the door of your cabin, your very own seat in the dining car and a designated steward to look after you in general. The sleeping-car attendant comes at the touch of a button on the console in your compartment, and will serve you with anything you want. You can, for an extra charge, have all your meals served there. Meals in the diner are included in the fares, which are neither first nor second class, but special 'Luxe', which varies with the type of accommodation selected. The Luxe fare ranges from about $160 to $300.

On the *Bloutrein* there are four different kinds of Luxe service. The grandest is a three-piece suite for two people; it includes a lounge furnished with settee, two easy chairs, refrigerated drinks cabinet, card-table, service telephone and radio. With the bedroom come dressing-table and seat, wardrobes, side-tables for lamps, etc., in addition to private bath and toilet. Then there is a large compartment for three, with a pull-down bed as well as a transverse seat forming a bed, plus a private bathroom with toilet. A smaller, one-person compartment contains a similar transverse seat and, of course, a private bathroom.

Also on the *Bloutrein* are another 29 compartments as well as 20 coupés. The compartments seem more like ship's cabins, in that the beds are often at right angles, not one above the other in line. Each compartment has 3 faucets (taps), for hot, cold or iced drinking water, and the array of knobs on the console will raise, lower or tilt the Venetian blinds between the double glazing of the windows, work the radio or control the temperature of the air-conditioning,

as well as summon the attendant. For shoe-cleaning there is a locker with a door into the corridor, where shoes can be collected for polishing during the night and replaced without disturbing the passengers. Travellers paying an 'A' fare have the use of a shower room at the end of the cars. Those with 'B' fare tickets must make do with the wash-basin in each compartment.

Air-springing and vibration insulation combine to make the entire *Bloutrein* virtually noiseless. Two diesel alternators in the power car work the air-conditioning and refrigeration, with a duplicate set of cables to ensure against failure, since only one alternator is needed at any one time.

The elegant, flower-bedecked lounge car, with a bar at one end, accommodates 34 people in easy chairs. The dining car spaciously seats 46, with tables for 4 on one side of the aisle and only a servery on the other, ablaze with gleaming silverware.

The whole 16-coach *Bloutrein* carries 108 people, of whom 5 may be non-white, though the quality of the accommodation is the same for both whites and non-whites. There is a staff of 26, including train controller, dining-car manager, head chef, chef, scullions, chief stewards, stewards and bedding attendants.

The South African Railways originally created the *Bloutrein* back in the 1930s. They ordered twelve all-steel, fully air-conditioned sleeping cars, following this a month later with an order for two lounge cars and two diners, also fully air-conditioned all-steel vehicles, plus kitchen cars and an all-steel baggage van. The manufacturer was Metro-Cammell of Birmingham, England, often referred to here as a producer of luxury vehicles. All these coaches arrived safely in South Africa at the end of 1939 and the beginning of 1940, after the outbreak of World War II. Though introduced on the *Bloutrein* route to Pretoria from Cape Town, the cars were withdrawn in 1942, along with all the other South African Trains de Luxe, for the duration of the war.

In 1946 the *Bloutrein,* ready and waiting to run, was officially named by the Minister of Transport and sent rolling on its way. Since then the service has become world-famous, which means that it must be booked in advance, especially since in winter it runs only once a week.

Described as a 5-star hotel on wheels, the *Bloutrein* offered a kind of pre-war luxury that by 1972 was 33 years old. So the SAR decided to introduce a new *Bloutrein,* even more sumptuous than the old one, which, repainted green, now runs in the 'Drakensberg' from Johannesburg to Durban. In 1980 the old, rehabilitated train was hired for a Swiss party visiting SAR's steam-locomotive centres; on this occasion it was hauled specially by steam on some of the lines used.

The new *Bloutrein* coaches were all built in South Africa, at Nigel, Transvaal, by the Union Carriage & Wagons Co., and cost five million rands. Perhaps the most impressive aspect of these spacious, luxurious cars is that they run on the narrow (3'6") gauge, made necessary in South Africa by the arduous nature of the wild, mountainous country.

Travel can never be very fast round the tortuous bends of the track, which climbs from sea level at the Cape Town station, with its more than 20 platforms, up to summits of over 4,000 feet. Only the first 36 miles or so are fairly flat and fertile, passing through Paarl, famous for its Cape wines, a copious supply of which is carried on board.

Three electric engines are needed to lift the heavy train up the gradients, mostly 1 in 70 but some as steep as 1 in 50. Electric traction is used between Cape Town and Beaufort West, and between Kimberley and Johannesburg. Diesel serves for the rest of the journey across the dusty Karroo Desert and from Johannesburg to Pretoria. Steam, however, provided the power until 1972, and plenty of steam engines still function in South Africa. Speed av-erages about 60 kilometres per hour on the *Bloutrein,* with a top speed of about 110 kilometres per hour.

Instead of trying to compete with the South African Airways, the South African Railways own them and use planes to bring tourists from all over the world to sample *Die Bloutrein.* SAR also have a statutory monopoly for freight traffic. All this relieves the SAR from the commercial pressures suffered by railways elsewhere, and helps the *Bloutrein* to continue its leisurely, prestigious journey, snaking round one mountain pass after another. A forty-page brochure setting out the train's itinerary and all its facilities is placed in each compartment.

The journey time takes twenty-six hours, leaving in the forenoon prior to luncheon. It occurs twice weekly, in each direction, from August to May and thrice weekly from November to February. The prolific choice on the menus includes a full English-style breakfast. A typical dinner menu is:

Papaw Cocktail	*Roast Turkey with*
Fried Sole and Rémoulade Sauce	*Liver Stuffing St. James*
Crumbled Steak	*Assorted Vegetables*
with Marrow Sauce	*Diplomat Cream Pudding*
Asparagus	*Peach Melba*
with Cream Sauce Princess	*Cheese Biscuits Fruit*

left: 178. The elegant dining car on South Africa's *Bloutrein* in 1980. Note the spacious seating.

right: 179. A super-luxurious bedroom suite on the *Bloutrein.* 1972 stock as used in 1980.

opposite: 180. *Die Bloutrein,* the Afrikaans title of South Africa's famous *Blue Train.*

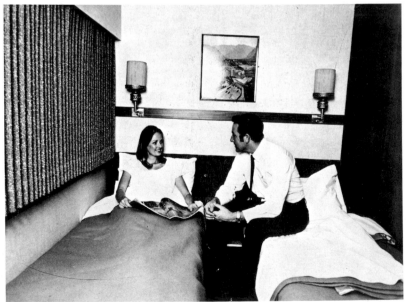

18. Australia's *Indian Pacific*

The *Indian Pacific* takes its name from the two oceans it joins. Its lengthy 2,400 miles across the Australian continent, passing over 267 miles of perfectly straight track through the seemingly endless Nullarbor Desert, make each journey an event. The comfortable air-conditioning of the coaches creates an atmosphere in striking contrast to the stiflingly hot, dusty conditions outside.

The *Indian Pacific* Train de Luxe was started in 1970 to link Perth in Western Australia with Sydney in New South Wales. Never before had Australians been able to enjoy through train travel from one end of their country to the other. Before 1970 they had to change five times, or six times before 1938, a state of affairs that began in 1917, when the Trans-Australian line of the Commonwealth Railways was completed from Kalgoolie, Western Australia, to Port Augusta, South Australia.

The reason for this sorry state of affairs was that the builders of the Australian railways chose several different gauges. Only New South Wales and the Commonwealth Railways adopted the standard gauge of Western Europe (which the Commonwealth Railways extended from Port Augusta to Port Pirie in 1938). Western Australia and parts of South Australia (including Port Pirie–Port Augusta) had 3′6″ gauge, while Victoria and most of South Australia chose the 5′6″ Irish gauge.

In 1975 the Commonwealth Railways evolved into the Australian National Railways and took over the Tasmanian Railways as well as the 'non-Metropolitan' part of the South Australian Railways, including the newly converted standard-gauge line used by the *Indian Pacific* to get from Port Pirie to the end of the New South Wales standard gauge at Broken Hill.

The *Indian Pacific* is a long train of 15 fully air-conditioned, stainless-steel, Budd-pattern coaches, including the baggage car, which contains the air-conditioning plant. Reservation has to be made in advance, since the train is limited to 70 first-class and 68 second-class passengers. Since there were only 2 trains available at first, the service ran only twice weekly. So many passengers booked to go that the waiting list extended a full year. By 1979 trains were usually fully booked 3 months in advance. A third train came into service in 1973, a fourth in 1975 and 2 more by 1979.

Sometimes at peak periods a second relief train is run, coupled to the first one for two days and nights between Perth and Broken Hill. Such a train meets the needs of Australia's vast, sparsely populated area through which it passes, and thirty coaches, which make an impressively long train, simply add to the grandiosity of the luxurious interiors.

The *Indian Pacific* is notable for its courteous service, and the public seem determined to make up for not having had such a service during the 1930s. The tickets are airline style in size and pattern, with detachable coupons headed 'Railways of Australia'.

Fares from Perth to Sydney include meals and sleeper berth for both first and economy classes, as well as free morning tea served in bed and free afternoon tea served in the various lounges. Meanwhile, full English-style breakfast in the dining car is also available. Visitors can obtain various 'Australpasses' that give unlimited travel. They are sold, outside Australia only, by such travel agencies as Thomas Cook, which make the journey even cheaper.

All cars in both classes have hot, cold and iced water in all compartments. First-class passengers have private showers, whereas second-class offers separate showers for men and women at the ends of each car. Passengers with laundry to do can obtain an iron and ironing board from the conductor.

First-class passengers travelling alone occupy roomette single-berth compartments, with private toilet but no shower, or in much

opposite: 181. The *Indian Pacific* crosses Australia from Perth to Sydeny, hauled by various diesel locomotives.

182. Chef in the kitchen of the *Indian Pacific*, Australia's Train de Luxe.

larger 'twinettes' with private shower and toilet, two berths, two chairs, a table and wardrobe, and intercommunicating doors between each pair of twinettes. All compartments have power-operated Venetian blinds between the panes of the double-glazed windows and radios capable of tuning in various programmes.

Like the first Trans-Australia trains of the 1930s, linking Kalgoolie with Port Pirie, the *Indian Pacific* has full air-conditioning. Temperatures can reach 60°C on the Nullarbor Plain, which also has most unpleasant dust storms, while in wintertime there can be snow in the Blue Mountains of New South Wales, whose terrain necessitates gradients as steep as 1 in 33.

The cafeteria car, open to the whole train, serves beer, wine and spirits, as well as hot drinks and snacks. First-class passengers also have the exclusive use of a dining car as well as a lounge car with small cocktail bar, where the piano is a famous 'Trans' tradition. Every passenger receives a twelve-page colour brochure describing all the places passed en route.

The 'Trans' still runs on the three days a week when the *Indian Pacific* does not, going as far as Port Pirie. Both trains leave Perth's Inter State Terminus at 21:20 in the evening.

The 'Westrail' standard-gauge line has branches from Freemantle and from Kwinana, both used for the ore traffic from the mining district of Koolyanobbing. To serve this area, the standard gauge goes 408 miles to Kalgoolie, as compared to the 360 miles of the old narrow gauge, the first railway to reach the gold-mining town.

The sleeping- and dining-car crews change at Kalgoolie at 7 a.m. the next morning. Here the Western Australian Railways hand over to the former Commonwealth, now Australian National Rail-

ways, which use twin Clyde diesels, attached at nearby Parkeston shed. Sanitary inspection is made at Kalgoolie, since the line soon afterwards crosses the state boundary between Western and South Australia. It is forbidden to take fruit or food of any kind across the boundary. Engine crews are next changed at Rawlinna, and after this the line runs straight for 267 miles across the Nullarbor (Latin for 'no trees') Plain.

In the evening of the second day the Train de Luxe reaches Cook and stops for half an hour. Devoid of industry, Cook is purely a railway town, with houses for the railwaymen and their families, a school and a telegraph office. Even the cinema is a mobile railway one.

The next stop is Tarcoola, another enginemen's settlement, where drivers change again during the night. It is also the junction with the new line north to Alice Springs, opened in 1980.

This part of the line is pure desert, with salt pans, until Port Augusta, where the country becomes fertile and civilized again. The line now runs within sight of the sea, to Port Pirie. Here the train reverses, is cleaned and changes sleeping- and dining-car crews again. The stop allows an hour and a quarter in which passengers can explore, or finish reading the newspapers put aboard the train at Port Augusta, before the *Indian Pacific* sets off again, this time via Peterborough to Broken Hill over a line converted to standard gauge, from the 3'6" gauge used in this northerly part of South Australia, laid almost like a light railway. Near Gladstone, before Peterborough, the second *Indian Pacific* coming the other way is met, after the first had been passed near Rawlinna. Sometimes the New South Wales train crew from Sydney would work through to this point, change over and go straight back, a 48-hour stint. In 1979, they worked through to Port Pirie. At Peterborough, there is a broad-gauge connection from Adelaide, and ordinary coaches are added to accommodate local passengers for the run to Broken Hill.

The standard of comfort on the *Indian Pacific* seeks to approach that of the South African *Bloutrein*. The dining-car crew comprises 17 people, one waiter to each table of 4, and meals are served in 3 sittings. Dinner consists of 5 courses and has been completed by the time the train reaches Broken Hill at 19:54. There is a half-hour halt at this frontier point, where a further sanitary inspection occurs. From here to Parkes, the Public Transport Commission for New South Wales, now SRANSW (State Rail Authority), have had to relay their line. It is presently the Trans-Australia main line, instead of a branch to the back of beyond their huge state.

After Parkes, the principal station on this part of the line, the last day presents Australian farming country instead of desert. The line climbs among the hills to Mount Victoria, 1,042 metres or about 3,000 feet above sea level, where eucalyptus forest takes over from the farmland. The train calls at Orange and Bathurst before reaching Lithgow, 97 miles from Sydney and the end of the electrified line from that capital. Double track prevails the rest of the way, some of it 4-track, as the line winds down to sea level at Sydney, which is a huge city, stretching some 50 miles along the coast. The *Indian Pacific* passes non-stop through the suburbs, and after a run taking 65 hours, the sense of eventfulness is suddenly lost, as the world's most recently created long-distance Train de Luxe ends its journey in the bustle of Sydney Central Station at 4 in the afternoon.

19. Japan's Tokaido Bullet Trains

Japan has 21,000 kilometres (12,600 miles) of railway, most of it laid in metre gauge, little suited for fast running. Electrification at 1,500 volts DC prevails throughout many lines, and there are something like 1,000 level crossings. Until the 1960s Japan had no standard-gauge railway at all.

Forty per cent of Japan's dense population (which is expected to reach 64 million by 1985) live between Tokyo and Osaka, the Tokaido route. Here too is concentrated 71 per cent of the country's industry. Needless to say, this was the area through which the Japanese constructed their first long-distance railway. And it was here that they decided to build a brand-new standard-gauge railway, free of level crossings, to take what became the fastest electric trains in the world during the 1960s and 1970s. In the 1980s, however, this distinction has passed to France's TGV.

The first sod of the new railway was cut on 20th April 1959, after which came a great many viaducts, tunnels, bridges and other engineering works, some of which took several years to complete. Electrification is at 60 cycles 25,000 volts AC.

The Tokyo-Osaka high-speed line was opened on 1st October 1964 with thirty trains. These were doubled to sixty by 1966–67, and at that moment the line began to make a profit. The Japanese call the trains *Shinkansen,* or 'Bullet Trains', but Westerners usually refer to them in the collective as the 'Tokaido', since the line serves the Tokaido part of the main island of Honshu.

The trains are all multiple unit, and they do not have locomotives, but power-cars instead. There is no coupling or uncoupling except when the trains are overhauled or, increasingly, made larger. And whereas most of the services described in this book operate once a day, Japan sends off one of its *Hikari* Bullet Trains every quarter of an hour.

Hikari means 'light trains', and indeed the Bullets weigh only 7 tons per axle load. Moreover, cast-iron disc braking is used. Up to 1970 each train set consisted of 12 cars. The Shinkansen Tokaido line had already been extended to Okayama in 1967 but was brought into use only on 15th March 1972. In 1970 the Japanese decided to extend again, this time as far as Hakata, and in March 1974 the 18.7-kilometre (11.59-mile) Shin Kamon Tunnel was completed between the islands of Honshu and Kyushu. The line reached its present Hakata terminus in 1975.

The Hikari trains now have proper diners, as well as a buffet and a Japanese flower-girl who operates a trolley-service, since the 730-mile journey to Hakata from Tokyo takes 6 hours 40 minutes. The fastest of them stop only at Nagoya, Kyoto, Shin-Osaka, Okayama, Hiroshima and Kokura. Another four Shinkansens leave Tokyo each hour, and these stop at all stations. Known as *Kodama* ('echo trains'), the latter are also referred to on occasion as 'Super Express' or 'Limited Express'.

Wherever possible, the Shinkansens run into the same stations as the 3′6″ gauge lines, so as to make connections. At various places like Yokohama (first stop from Tokyo for the Kodamas), this proved impossible, and so a new station has been built, called Shin-Yokohama, Shin-Osaka, etc. (*Shin* meaning 'new').

The rails are welded into 4,920-foot lengths, with tongue-shaped joints to allow for expansion without gaps. Switch points are solid also, with moveable diamonds, permitting top speed over them in the straight direction, and a restriction to 43 miles per hour for turns into loops. The Kodama trains are fitted with equipment to change the points automatically to the loop line.

In 1970 the Hikaris were increased to 16 cars, as were the Kodamas in 1973. The sets now number 133. In 1976 fares rose by 50 per cent. Japan is one of those countries which do not like the term 'first class' or 'second class'. Instead, a 'Green Car' offers luxury travel for a surcharge that amounted to 6,000 yen in 1977, when the Tokyo-Hakata single fare was 14,000 yen. On the narrow

155

183. The last JNR steam train leaving Tokyo Station after the electrification of the line to Takashima Port, in October 1970.

ing there are no trains at all anywhere on the Shinkansen, which permits the line to be maintained by an army of railwaymen. During the day inspection continues on foot and by means of a 6-car train capable of testing track and catenary at the maximum operation speed of 210 kilometres (130 miles) per hour used by ordinary trains. France's TGVs normally run at 260 kilometres (161 miles) per hour.

In 1980 a prototype 961-class Shinkansen attained 304 kilometres (185 miles) per hour, but the Tokaido's record as the fastest electric train in the world was broken by a TGV, which achieved 380 kilometres (235.6 miles) per hour on 26th February 1981, carrying 100 journalists to prove it. This occurred on part of the new Paris-Lyons direct line that is reserved for TGVs only. The first part of this line was opened to public traffic by President Mitterand on 22nd September 1981.

Since all the Tokaido trains travel at about 130 miles (210 kilometres) per hour, their movements and routes are controlled electronically by computers at Central Traffic Control and Automatic Traffic Control.

The rolling stock undergoes running repairs inspection every 30,000 kilometres at Tokyo, Osaka and Hakata. Running gear repairs occur after 300,000 kilometres at Osaka and Hakata, and after 900,000 kilometres the trains go for major overhaul, either at the Hamamatsu works or, in some cases, at Hakata. All kinds of electronic machines are used for detecting metal fatigue.

As on France's TGV line, Tokaido train drivers have a continuous signalling system in the cab, and their speed is limited by signals from control. In Japan control includes details of high winds supplied by anenometers and dangers of earthquakes registered by seismographs installed at every substation.

gauge the Japanese National Railways also have first- and second-class sleeping cars, called 'A' with single- and double-berth, and 'B' with 3-berth compartments. Between midnight and 6 each morn-

opposite: 184. The *Shinkansen* or 'Bullet Train' of the JNR, Japan.

20. Amtrak and VIA's *Canadian*

Amtrak

In 1970, railway passenger traffic in the United States had dropped to a mere 7 per cent of all passengers conveyed by public transport carriers. In 1928 it accounted for some 77 per cent. In 1970 there were some 450 daily passenger trains in the whole of America, running inter-city, compared to 20,000 in the heyday of the 1920s.

The situation caused the Ninety-first Congress to enact legislation bringing the National Railroad Passenger Corporation into existence. Railroads were offered the choice of having a contract with the corporation for the operation of passenger trains on certain 'Basic Routes', or of being obliged by law to continue operating as they were until 1975. The corporation at first thought up the name 'Railpax' for the new services but soon changed this to 'Amtrak'.

Amtrak became law in October 1970 and got under way in May 1971, with 21 routes serving 29 US cities, all with a population of over a million. Operations began with 180-odd trains running over some 22,000 miles of tracks owned by other railways, like Pullman at an earlier time. Unlike Pullman, Amtrak also provides the engine. One hundred sixteen locomotives were either bought or leased. By the following year this had increased to 368.

Amtrak has bought Turbo-Trains from France, as well as new equipment in America. It has also tried out Swedish-built electric engines. But above all Amtrak, by virtue of its marketing, packaging and other efforts, has refurbished the idea of train travel. Moreover, the 'Welcome Aboard' and the projection of the Amtrak image in red, white and blue have greatly helped to raise Amtrak revenue.

This was a major achievement since many railroad presidents did not like Amtrak and hoped it would go away. Instead Amtrak has in some instances started to buy its own track, thereby overcoming difficulties of rough running and enforced speed limits in certain areas. By 1981 Amtrak owned 650 route miles.

The system also retained the famous train names. Thus, there is an Amtrak *Broadway Limited,* an Amtrak *Lake Shore Limited,* an Amtrak *Empire Builder* and so forth. The fast regular-interval electric trains on the New York–Washington run are called 'Metroliners'.

Amtrak's success has been due partly to the introduction of airline-style, electronic reservations systems, and ticket offices are more like travel agencies. In addition, all the pleasures of rail travel, such as relaxing, getting there without unscheduled delays, starting and leaving in city centres, have been exploited fully. Of course, tickets can be bought with credit cards, a feature which is being slowly accepted in Europe, especially on British Rail.

All passenger cars in Amtrak service are air-conditioned. Most needed full overhaul when Amtrak started, owing to lack of maintenance by their previous operators. There are telephones on the Metroliners, and for many people, of course, there is the thrill of going in a comfortable train for the first time.

For longer-distance overnight travel Amtrak offers a variety of accommodations at different prices. Basically the slumber coach comprises double rooms with upper and lower longitudinal berths and single rooms with fold-away bed and private wash-stand. Roomettes, being larger, provide more comfortable accommodation. Bedrooms are even bigger and have private toilets. Finally, the bedroom suites constitute double-sized bedrooms with the intervening walls removed.

Amtrak has Metro club cars, dining cars, tavern lounges and vista-dome cars, offering a variety of food service from snacks to full meals. On the Metroliners, passengers have access to the Metroclub car and a snack bar.

opposite: 185. Dawn over Oregon's Cascade Mountains as the *Coast Starlight/Daylight* Amtrak express from Los Angeles to Seattle leaves Klamath Falls for Portland.

186. Amtrak crossing the Potomac River near the Jefferson Monument in Washington, D.C.

In 1979 Amtrak responded to the need for new coaches, the first for over twenty years on US railroads in any quantity, by ordering double-deck vehicles called 'Superliners'. Like *Pioneer,* they were made by Pullman, though they may be the last order to be fulfilled by the Pullman Standard Car Co., which insists it is going out of the railroad-car-building business. (Perhaps the oil crisis will reverse this decision, which is just the sort that changes— as soon as it has been published in books of this nature!) Also like *Pioneer,* the Superliners are too big for the loading gauge, except on lines west of Chicago. The fleet includes 284 new coaches altogether, some of which started running on 28th October 1979 on the thrice-weekly Chicago-Seattle *Empire Builder.* Gradually they are being used on other trains.

The 70 new sleepers have 5 Deluxe bedrooms and 14 2-berth Economy rooms, 4 of them on the lower deck. These include the usual Pullman 'section' arrangement, that is, 2 chairs pulled together to make the lower berth, with the upper berth folding down from the wall above the window. Each compartment features a wardrobe (closet) and a folding table, space for 2 suitcases, but no washing facilities. In place of the latter there are 5 wash-rooms on the lower deck, called 'restrooms'. Each Deluxe bedroom has a private toilet as well as a wash-basin, two beds, a sofa and a swivel chair, and is twice as wide as the Economy room. On the lower deck there is also a family Economy room for 4 berths (1 extra wide, 1 upper and 2 short children's berths) but no wash-room. There is a special bedroom as well, primarily available for handicapped passengers, with special handles to the toilet, room for wheel chair, etc. The lower deck has full-width rooms with windows on each side, making compartments suitable for families and the handicapped.

Amtrak's Superliner stock is all air-conditioned and heated electrically. The 39 dining cars seat 72, 4 to a side with central gangway, all on the top deck. The 18 tables are divided by a service area for the maître d'hôtel, the waiters and the food lifts. The kitchen, on the lower level, has micro-ovens, ordinary ovens, refrigerators, dishwasher and sinks, coffee-maker, toaster, electric and charcoal grills. The kitchens are enormous compared to those of conventional diners.

Amtrak also boasts 25 sightseer lounge cars each with a 22-seat bar and swivel seats in the end sections set before a screen for closed-circuit TV films, all on the top deck equipped with extra-large windows. On the lower deck there is space for the sale of snacks and beverages, with tables for card-playing or eating, small cocktail tables and an electric piano at one end. The total capacity of the café car is 70.

On the less roomy type of cheaper coaches there are 78 seats, all on the upper deck, whereas the more spacious, 'long-distance' coaches have only 62 seats above, but include an extra 15 seats down below. Leg rests come with this variety of coach.

All the cars have public-address hi-fi systems, which can be used for music, and the usual airline-style overhead luggage racks, attendant call buttons, folding tables and individual reading lights. When the Superliners are coupled to conventional coaches or sleepers, passengers in the latter have no gangway access to them. Thus, west of Chicago, trains of all Superliner double-deck stock will be the feature of long-distance Amtrak service in the 1980s and onwards.

All the Superliner cars have tinted-glass windows and are unpainted, Budd-style aluminium straight-sided vehicles, with, of course, the Amtrak red-white-blue colour-band painted below the

above left: 187. The Superliner's 'economy' bedroom, which can accommodate two adults, features a full-length closet, a folding table, a mirror and storage space for two suitcases.

above right: 188. The *Empire Builder,* equipped with 'bi-level' Superliner cars, prepares to leave Belton, Montana, the western gateway to Glacier National Park. Through the Rockies the train is double-headed.

below: 189. Aboard an Amtrak Superliner before the curtailment of full diner services, dining-car attendants stand ready to serve hungry passengers. Operating on long-distance routes in the West, each 'bi-level' diner has a seating capacity of 72 persons at 18 tables. The dining area is located on the upper level, to which food is transported by dumb-waiters from the lower-level kitchen.

upper-deck windows. The 'long-distance' second-class coaches feature a special lower-deck seat for incapacitated passengers, and all cars fitted for taking wheel chairs include a portable loading ramp for use at stops.

All 284 cars of Amtrak's Superliner were delivered by 1981, and the last one was a sleeping car named 'George M. Pullman' to mark the 150th anniversary of the founder's birth. The Pullman Standard Car Co. says that the Superliners are its swansong. Pullman Inc.'s other former subsidiary, the Pullman Co. of 1899 (which succeeded the Pullman Palace Car Co. of 1867–99), was finally dissolved on 2nd December 1980. As mentioned earlier, it handed over operations to the 59 owner railroads on 30th June 1947, and the last Pullman was run in the United States on 31st December 1968.

Meanwhile, the future of Amtrak is under discussion. Early in 1981, a proposal was made to eliminate all long-distance trains, which would effectively stop the Superliners. But while some services have been curtailed, the demise of the system no longer seems absolutely certain. Already gone, however, is dining in style, and only airline-style snacks are available in the diners just described, the maîtres d'hôtel, waiters, cooks, etc., having been reduced to a staff of two or three attendants.

VIA's *Canadian*

Unlike any US railroad, the Canadian Pacific's tracks extend from the Atlantic to the Pacific as a single entity. And the Canadian Pacific is one of the world's largest and most comprehensive private enterprises involved in public transport. It runs its own airline and until recently had its own large fleet of luxury liners. In 1894 it started the *Imperial Limited* and gave the line all-steel coaches in

1912. In the same year the Canadian Pacific began its far-flung Austrian boat trains, which we met in Chapter 12. Meanwhile, it operates a chain of grand hotels in Canada, Mexico and elsewhere.

The Trans-Canada Limited of 1919 succeeded the *Imperial*. The other Canadian railways, faced with a large private monopoly, then reorganized themselves into the government-owned Canadian National Railways (CNR), whose tracks also stretched right across all Canada. When Amtrak was started after World War II, the CNR bought many discarded cars from the American railroads and endeavoured to expand in Canada. At the same time, the need for the CPR's transcontinental *Canadian* to continue caused the Dominion government to pay a million-dollar (Canadian) annual subsidy, beginning in 1970, to permit the service to compete with CNR's *Super-Continental*.

This need developed because only CPR tracks, on the section from Winnipeg to Vancouver, serve Calgary, which in the last thirty years has become a boom town. It is now the world's third largest centre of the oil industry, though the oil fields are mostly farther north. But by 1978, CPR's other passenger services had become so unprofitable that they were threatened with closure. This prompted the Canadian government to form VIA. Like Amtrak, VIA owns the locomotives and rolling stock, taken over from CPR and CNR but operated on their tracks. Unlike Amtrak, VIA's engines are driven by CPR or CNR engineers, depending on the route taken. VIA assumed control of the former CPR *Canadian* and the former CNR *Super-Continental* on 28th October 1978, and the rest of the passenger services on 1st April 1979. The Ontario government (GO) have their Transit Authority, which also runs some passenger trains in that province. Something comparable is under consideration in Quebec.

VIA's *Canadian* leaves in the evening of day 1 in both directions every 24 hours and arrives on the morning of day 5. It has full dining-car service, unlike Amtrak, and a dome car with buffet. Drinks are served in the diner according to the provincial law of the province the car is running through.

The dome car is particularly enjoyable during the train's daytime passage through the Rockies, going west from Calgary through Banff, where CPR has one of its hotels. VIA organizes all manner of tours for visitors from abroad, to help offset the deficit on domestic operations. It also offers five styles of accommodation, from ordinary coach with no supplement upwards. The 'Dayniter' cars have more luxurious seating with heads and footrests to the seats, which incline, as do those in the coaches. Three other kinds of accommodation are offered in the sleeping cars. A 'section' (a Pullman-style arrangement as described earlier) can be taken as a whole for two or the upper and lower berths rented separately. On VIA trains the upper berth is much cheaper than the lower one. Then there is the roomette, with its single seat and single longitudinal berth that lets down at night. The bedroom, finally, comprises double transverse berths at night (upper and lower) and folding armchairs by day. The last two classes have private toilets and washbasins. All cars are air-conditioned.

The fusion of the CNR and CPR proved difficult and slow. By 1980 some cuts had been made to ease the deficit. Now only the *Canadian* runs from Montreal via Toronto, and the *Super-Continental* has ended. At Sudbury, it no longer joins a Montreal portion serving Ottawa. Formerly, the two trains continued their separate ways to Winnipeg, where the *Canadian* pauses three hours on the third day, and there is a connection from Capreol thrice weekly, via the *Super-Continental*'s former route. But no cars serve Ottawa, whose passengers must change at Toronto. VIA's *Canadian* pulls into Winnipeg's CNR station. The CPR station has closed.

West of Winnipeg the routes divide at Portage La Prairie, where the line to Churchill on Hudson Bay branches off northward. The *Canadian* runs by way of Regina, Calgary and Banff to the Rockies' summit near Revelstoke. It descends to Kamloops and there meets the CNR line from Winnipeg via Saskatoon, Edmonton and Jasper. From Jasper (Red Pass Junction) there is a further line, taken by an express named *Skeena*, to Prince Rupert on the Pacific Ocean. Considerable doubt exists as to whether the *Super-Continental* will run again over its former route either in summer or at all. Since November 1981 passengers have had to change at Winnipeg and proceed by day trains with overnight stops at Saskatoon and Edmonton in order to reach Jasper. The train now being dis-

left: 190. VIA's *Canadian* in the Rockies.

opposite left: 191. Part of the extensive wine list available on VIA's *Canadian*. Note the bilingualism and the reference to provincial regulations.

opposite right: 192. Part of the extensive à la carte menu available on VIA's *Canadian*. Note the bilingualism and the reference to railway tradition.

continued, there would be no passenger service from Red Pass Junction to Kamloops.

VIA's financial difficulties are not eased by the need to buy new trains for use in Eastern Canada, serving Quebec, Montreal, Ottawa, Toronto and Windsor. Called LRC (Light Rapid Comfortable), these new trains are none too light (52 tons, against 36 tons of the heaviest HST car) and none too rapid (90 miles per hour is about maximum speed anywhere in Canada), but certainly comfortable, with airline-style meals at every seat, a club car and floor level nearer the ground than in conventional coaches. They are to be hauled by new power cars.

With these trains VIA has set about attracting summer passengers with a wide range of price reductions, as well as with the tours mentioned earlier. In addition, it offers a series of Canrailpasses, available to all, giving unlimited travel over the whole system or merely on sections of it, for different durations up to thirty days.

21. The Style of Trains de Luxe

There is every sort of light,
You can make it dark or bright,
There's a handle you can turn to make a breeze.
There's a funny little basin,
You're supposed to wash your face in,
And a crank to shut the window if you sneeze.

    T.S. Eliot (Old Possum), 'The Railway Cat'

The style of the Trains de Luxe was designed to create an atmosphere of elegance at least as sumptuous as that to which the high society who used them had long been accustomed at home.

The 1980s image of the pre-World War II Trains de Luxe is of carriages with Art Deco interiors of wood panelling embellished with intricate marquetry. The restoration of these old CIWL or Pullman cars by Sea Containers for their London-Venice train has taken five years; it has also cost over $20 million (£11 million), since many of the vehicles had deteriorated after their withdrawal, while many more had been stripped of their woodwork in the 1950s and refaced with formica. Plastic, of course, would only be abhorrent to lovers of Art Deco (not all of whom are equally in love with trains). Even the advertising posters of the 1930s, by such famous masters as Cassandre and Fixmasseau, have come to enjoy the status of true works of art. Fixmasseau has even produced a new set of Art Deco posters for Sea Containers' Venice Simplon Orient Express (VSOE).

The lore of these Trains de Luxe (thought of in the USA simply as the Orient Express, a consequence of the 1974 British film *Murder on the Orient Express*, which netted $40 million [£19 million]) received new stimulus from the 1976 CIWL centenary run by Intraflug from Milan to Istanbul, as well as from the auction of a few CIWL cars by Sotheby's at Monte Carlo in 1977. (Non-French auction houses may not sell in France itself; hence, the choice of Monte Carlo.) Thirty years ago one could count the people with a knowledge of CIWL history, and an interest in the art of comfortable travel, on the fingers of two hands. In 1982, some seven thousand people booked to journey on the VSOE before it had even made its inaugural trip, thanks to Sea Containers' audio-visual presentation of the work carried out on their glamorous cars in the United States, Japan and parts of Western Europe.

The basis of early European design was the horse-drawn travelling carriage. Small, individual forms with frills were the thing, practicality being relegated to a lesser degree of importance. Because European engines were designed to look beautiful, so as not to frighten people—and preferably not frighten horses either—they ended up too small to pull heavy Pullman cars with ease. Owing to the size limitations imposed by the railways, European designers concentrated on making the interiors of trains luxurious. First came the plush, then lincrusta and fairly soon *brise-bise* ('draught excluder'), a blanketing material that could be folded against the windows inside to increase warmth, absorb condensation and partially deaden noise.

opposite left: 193. Y-type sleeper interior, specially arranged for Turkey. Note fans, double windows with netting blinds, as well as the standard Y-type luggage rack, lamps over the wash-basin (table-top), communicating doors between compartments (not normally on Z types) and the swastika design on the cushions.

opposite above right: 194. Detail of a marquetry panel in Pullman Car No. 4018, originally in No. 4029, the latter destroyed by fire at St. Denis CIWL works during restoration in 1976. Tulip-shaped lights on brass torch stems, fastened where the roof mouldings merged with the sides and supplemented by similar, but stemless lights in the ceiling, were standard features of Birmingham-built diners and Pullmans for both Europe and Great Britain.

opposite below right: 195. Detail of the marquetry in door panel of Lx-type sleeping car No. 3532.

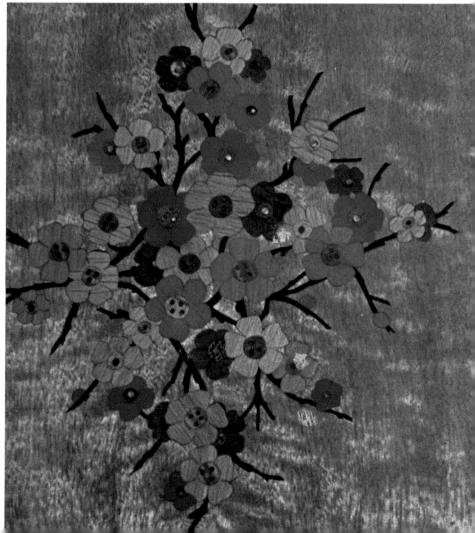

above left: 196. Marquetry details, coat hooks and alarm signal of Lx-type sleeping car No. 3532. Décor by Nelson & Co., built at Aytre (La Rochelle), France.

left and above right: 197, 198. Details of the stainless-steel luggage rack and compartment wall-lamp shade of Lx-type sleeping car No. 3532. (See also Plates 101 and 102.)

The Baker heater, a system of closed-circuit hot-water central heating, generated by an oil-fired coil, came to Great Britain with the bogie Pullman Car. It offered a great improvement over the old foot-warmers, which passengers could only hope might be replaced from time to time at intermediate stations with freshly heated foot-warmers. For years these were considered good enough for ordinary coach heating in Britain.

Odorous whale-oil or colsa-bean-oil pot lamps did not mix with the plush; moreover, they had to be lowered into the compartments from the roof. They yielded poor light and served mainly to give the gaslight that replaced them an acclaim it did not deserve, since gas posed a deadly fire hazard in the event of accident. But a little gaslight reflected beautifully on glass, creating an effect equal to that of large candle-power chandeliers. This made gas economical and above all, light to cart about, unlike electricity. It is sometimes forgotten that Wagons-Lits had a few gas-tank cars, numbered in the same series as sleepers but with the suffix 'R' (for *réservoir à gaz*). They were designed to be run on the rear of Trains de Luxe, as fuel sources at outer termini that had no city gasworks supply.

opposite: 199. *Golden Arrow* Wagons-Lits menu, brass ashtray and reading lamp, white-and-gold china used specially in the *Flèche d'Or* and *Blue Train*. The glass and coffee-pot bear the 1928 monogram.

The first electrically lit Pullman ran in 1881 on the Brighton line (see Chapter 3). But CIWL were also early to illuminate their cars with electricity. The Hensemberger battery system used by the FS and predecessors was made available for Trains de Luxe from Italy to Sicily or within Italy, such as the Rome-Milan Train de Luxe of sleeping cars only, a service not mentioned before in this account. Sometimes Italian-based sleepers with Hensemberger lighting were called into international service. Since replacements for the Hensemberger batteries could not be obtained abroad, standardization was eventually achieved with dynamos and generators (often with shaft drive) mounted on the exterior of one of the bogies. The first CIWL cars with dynamos were Nos. 158–160, designed in 1888 by Mr. Timmins of England for France's Sud Express.

Electricity provided only one of the luxuries found in Wagons-Lits' sleeping cars. The R or Regal class had nine compartments, of which the end ones, intended for servants, were at first without wash-basins, but later fitted with ingenious tip-up basins, round in shape and made of metal.

Each R-type cabin had a settee that revolved into a lower berth, while its back raised to become the upper berth. The cabin boasted three windows, a drop-flap table under the central window (fitted with a wooden louvre to admit air and keep out coal dust) and a tip-up seat facing the settee beyond the table, handy for playing cards or for enjoying the drinks always carried on the cars. The seat was upholstered in the same brushed plush as the panels of the compartment wall and wash-room door.

The wash-room, leading to the next compartment, occupied the centre of the car, its frosted-glass window facing the corridor. Bolting one door automatically turned the bolt in the door opposite. Below the window, the wash-basin (larger than those of 1982) was sunk in a marble-topped shelf, and below this was the cupboard, holding the famous 'vase', shaped like a large sauce-boat. *Sous le lavabo se trouve un vase* is referred to by many a litterateur writing about notices in WL cars. Today, the vessel much more closely resembles a child's 'potty' with a spout, a commonplace object that inspires neither irony nor even comment.

An upholstered strap swung prominently across the compartment roof, from which a further strap hooked to join the upper berth, giving the impression that it supported the weight of the berth, though this was carried on two folding brass stays. The only need for the strap was so the occupant could hoist himself from the top of the three-step, rattle-proof, folding step-ladder, whose ability to pinch the fingers of unwary travellers or tired conductors became famous, or rather infamous, all over Europe.

The celebrated French designer René Prou (1889–1947) decorated the S-class steel cars for the 1922 *Blue Train*. Beaten-leather panels replaced the dust-laden plush of the R class, and blue plush the shiny brown on the seats. Longer than the R cars, the S had eight single-berth and four R-type double compartments, which were in the centre, but newer cars had these at one end, owing to complaints made by single passengers about rough first-class travel over the wheels. The newer cars were called 'S1', the older 'S2', and after World War II the S1 became S3, while on the S4, wider and built for Spanish service, the R-type wash-rooms disappeared altogether when the cars were reconstructed internally. From 1929 to 1939 the S class worked exclusively in the Simplon Orient Express. Two restored S cars provide the single-berth accommodation in the 1982 VSOE.

The new 1929 *Blue Train* Lx10-class sleepers also had René Prou's decoration, though the marquetry for the English-built cars was designed by G.F. Milne of Turner Lord & Morison (London and Edinburgh). Prou's influence in Art Deco was considerable, since he became Professor at the Elisa Lemmonier School in 1921 and at the School of Applied Arts (Paris) in 1926–30, then Professeur/Chef d'Atelier at the École Nationale Supérieure des Arts Décoratifs beginning in 1937. From 1946 until his death in 1947 Prou served as Directeur de l'École de l'Union Centrale des Arts Décoratifs at the Musée Nissim Camondo. Besides four hundred railway cars, he also decorated the dining room of New York's Waldorf-Astoria Hotel, the Mitsubishi department store in Tokyo and the Council Chamber of the Palais des Nations in Geneva.

The décor of *Côte d'Azur* Pullmans Nos. 4141–4147 and 4158–4164 was entrusted to the famous master glazier René Lalique, who perhaps more than anyone else turned a mere comfortable and

200. Illustration from the CIWL Guide at the turn of the century. PLM locomotive with Wagons-Lits cars running above an R-type sleeper wash-room (note marble wash-basin top, carafe and plush door-panel), a typical dining car of 1900 and a sleeping-car compartment of the St. Petersburg–Cannes train in night position (note spitoon, curtain and upper-berth straps). bottom: R-type compartment in day position (note ventilator shutter above central window) and bedroom-saloon compartment of the St. Petersburg–Cannes train in day position (note plush curtains, centre light and mirror).

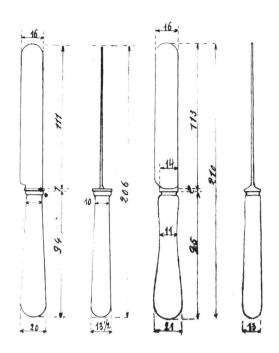

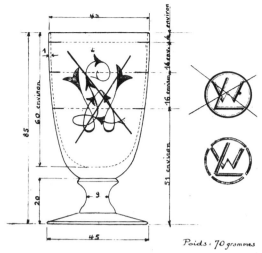

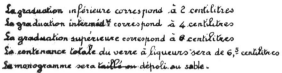

Poids : 70 grammes

La graduation inférieure correspond à 2 centilitres
La graduation interméd.e correspond à 4 centilitres
La graduation supérieure correspond à 6 centilitres
La contenance totale du verre à liqueurs sera de 6,5 centilitres
Le monogramme sera taillé ou dépoli au sable.

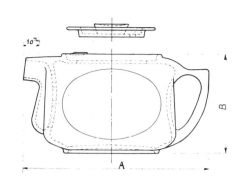

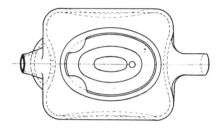

above far left: 201. Christofle-pattern Wagons-Lits table-knife.

above left: 202. English-pattern Wagons-Lits table-knife. (Identical knives were used in the Pullmans of the English *Golden Arrow,* with Pullman monogram instead of the CIWL one.)

above centre: 203. Old-pattern CIWL liqueur glass, larger than the new ones. The monogram was changed in 1928.

above right: 204. Post-war CIWL green china teapot. For the *Côte d'Azur* Pullmans, Christofle designed special cutlery with plain handles, unlike the English type, which had fluted handles, supplied originally with the *Golden Arrow* cars. Special heavy-based carafes, sloping towards the neck without a shoulder, were designed for Pullman service, also salad bowls and fluted flagons for angostura bitters, vinegar, salad oil, etc. Stemmed wine glasses replaced the traditional WL tumbler. In other words, no expense was spared.

luxurious railway car into a work of art. Some vehicles (including No. 4158) had the 'Bacchanalian Maidens' décor; others (including No. 4161) had 'Blue Bird' décor. Nos. 4151, 4161 and 4163 were the Pullman Cars running from 1950 in the original *Mistral,* for which they had new Minden Deutz bogies and air-conditioning (supplied from an SNCF van). Nos. 4160, 4162 and 4164 (1951) were painted blue all over and became the salon-bar cars of the *Blue Train* (see Chapter 9).

205. Upper compartment of the P-type sleeping car. Note the step, fixed seat, tip-up wash-basin (closed), lamps, grid, hook for watch, etc.

Nos. 4131–4140 and 4148–4157 displayed the artistry of René Prou. No. 4152 is now preserved in running order at Nice (L'Escarene) by M. Weiss. All the other preserved Pullman Cars can be found listed in the Appendices.

René Prou also designed the *Golden Mountain* Pullman Cars (see Chapter 13), whose bow windows with small tables on their sills were considered avant-garde, while the *Golden Arrow* style chairs were arranged singly (first class) and in pairs (second class) on either side of the gangway. The same service obtained for first- and second-class passengers alike.

Among the first English-built Pullman Cars of 1908, *Grosvenor* had mahogany panelling inlaid with satinwood, fluted pillars and a green carpet with fleur-de-lys motif, while *Cleopatra* had Indian satinwood inlaid with grey sycamore, blue-velvet upholstery and dark-rose carpeting. For the electric *Brighton Belle* cars, four firms were employed, each decorating two or three interiors, and of course vying with each other to see which might realize the greatest luxury. They were Waring & Gillow, the London furnishers who had been decorating Pullmans since at least 1879; Turner Lord & Morison (mentioned above); Martyn & Co. of Cheltenham and

Maple & Co., the London and Paris furnishers who had supplied most of the WL Grand Hotels in the 1890s.

Waring & Gillow or Morison & Co. built all the *Brighton Belle's* high-backed, upright but spacious chairs, and the chairs for some seventy other Pullmans in the 1920s and 30s. These were known in Wagons-Lits parlance as *Flèche d'Or* type, since they were also supplied in all the British-built *Golden Arrow* cars, such as No. 4018. Largely due to the efforts of Philip Jefford, an Inspector General of the Wagons-Lits, No. 4018 is displayed in 1929 condition at the Mulhouse SNCF Museum.

In the *Golden Arrow* car *Pauline*, Waring & Gillow adopted a floral and ribbon design for the marquetry, the pilasters inlaid with light lines and the moulded cornices cross-banded with light and dark lines. *Pauline's* dove-grey carpet and upholstery also appeared in some of the *Flèche d'Or* cars. The symbol of such Pullman travel was a solid brass, heavy-based reading lamp on each table in the centre of every window. One writer likened a Pullman without these lamps to a Mayor without his chain of office.

All this was duly noted by Mitropa, whose 1928 *Rheingold* saloon-diners were even more sumptuous, employing the very best of German art and architecture. The interior of each car was decorated by a different designer, and even the second-class Salonspeisewagen (see Chapter 11) had chequered marquetry, far superior to the solid mahogany of the *North Star* Pullman seating, or the third-class Pullman Car seating in Great Britain. The *Rheingold* also had a train telephone (see Chapter 10), something not found on European Pullmans. However, the luggage bays and coupé compartments at the car ends were direct copies of Pullman practice.

When in 1937–38 the Americans began streamlining and using light alloys, they introduced an entirely new style of Train de Luxe. Henry Dreyfuss restyled everything on the *Twentieth Century Limited*, from the 4-6-4 Hudsons to the coffee cups (see Chapter 8). The Pennsy retaliated with Raymond Loewy (born in Paris in 1893), who redesigned the *Broadway Limited*. Famous US train features, like the open observation platform or the engine cow-catcher, disappeared in the interest of air-smoothed surfaces. Observation cars displayed rounded, totally enclosed ends, while the cow-catcher became a sheet of metal. Internally, potted plants and heavy drapes were replaced by L-shaped settees, aimed at breaking up the tunnel-like appearance of so many parlour cars into more intimate groupings for four or more people. In the sleeping cars, formica supplanted solid mahogany, and the ever-increasing use of plastics, in place of wood, yielded both lightness and economy. Above all, the Americans wanted air-conditioning.

The American railways had nearly four years' experience in the peace-time use of light-weight Trains de Luxe, since the United States did not enter World War II until 1941. The Pennsy introduced double-deck roomette sleepers on the *General* (but not the *Broadway*), and these, together with the Budd Co.'s aluminium construction, attracted attention in Europe after World War II. Prominent

206. MU-type sleeping-car compartment in night position for tourist class (T3). Note the window-pane crank-handle and the heating control knobs below the window.

207. Poster for the first service of the P-class sleeping cars in Belgium, which began running between Ostend and Milan in 1955. Several years' study under Albert Pillepich, WL chief engineer at the time, resulted in the P-class sleeper. The present WL chief engineer, M. Fontan, spent three months with the Budd. Co., and the P had many features different from previous WL practice. Stainless-steel unpainted body, single vestibule, lavatories in pairs at one end of the car only, full use of the loading gauge, with fixed berths under the roof for the upper compartments. These compartments were arranged in pairs (each with an intercommunicating door), whose partition down the centre of a 'V-shaped trough' floor ended at the two entrance doors leading to three steps down to corridor level. Each upper compartment had a small seat, rectangular tip-up wash-basin and small luggage rack by the bed. The 10 lower of the 20 compartments had the wash-basin by the entrance door, space for luggage under the 'V-trough' and collapsible, moveable armchair for day use when the berth folded against the wall. The compartments were far smaller than in other cars and were designed to offer 2nd-class passengers a single-berth compartment. Eight cars were introduced simultaneously in Belgium, Italy and France in 1955. Abolition of 3rd class in 1956 resulted in these cars' having to be used by 1st-class passengers with a 'special' low supplement. Some were therefore sent to Spain, where three classes lasted a little longer. In 1981 the 39 P-class vehicles in France were downgraded to tourist class, type T2P. Their upper-compartment intercommunicating doors are kept locked open. The lower compartments offer single berth for tourist-class rail fare for the first time.

NATIONALE MAATSCHAPPIJ (B) DER BELGISCHE SPOORWEGEN

nieuwe slaapwagen

speciaal type

met 20 eenpersoonsafdelingen

in dienst tussen Oostende en Milaan

COMPAGNIE INTERNATIONALE DES WAGONS-LITS

among US designers was Otto Kuhler, who restyled almost as many US trains as Prou had created carriages for Europe.

Because Wagons-Lits had lost over eight hundred cars in World War II, the company was obliged to make do and mend in order to keep going, cannibalizing and rebuilding available stock rather than introducing new vehicles with costly air-conditioning. In Germany, however, Mitropa disappeared behind the Iron Curtain (save for joint services from East Germany), and the newly formed DSG had to start from scratch. Smaller than Wagons-Lits, they also proved more progressive. Their sleeping cars had air-conditioning, and shower compartments on some cars, as in the US. DSG's new eleven-compartment sleeper made full use of the European loading gauge, obliterating ventilators and catwalks on the roof, using heavy oil (mazout), instead of coal-fired heating boilers, and heavy rubber gangways, invented by the DB German Federal Railway, rather than the more troublesome bellows-pattern gangways. As reparations, Wagons-Lits received some of these cars, which had three Universal-type berths in each compartment. Belatedly, the traditional coal-fired boilers, supplied even on the P type, were replaced by oil-fired boilers on some Y, F and P as well as on certain other classes.

The lighting in Train de Luxe dining cars provided an appetizing sparkle. The cars were furnished with 42 leather-covered arm chairs, compared to the 56 seats for diners in ordinary services. Some dining cars had panelling inlaid with marquetry between the windows. The earlier models came with smoking saloons whose wicker armchairs were situated at the end opposite to the kitchen. The pantries had plenty of cupboard space, to contain the stock of drinks, etc., that had to be sealed by Customs at each frontier, and opened again by Customs on the return journey. Indeed, several cupboards were

left: 208. YF-type sleeping-car compartment in day position. Used in Spain. Note the control panel for air-conditioning.

right: 209. YF-type sleeping-car compartment in night position. Note the curtain rail fixed to the luggage rack to protect the privacy of the washing area, the cupboard fixed at an angle and the air-conditioning knobs.

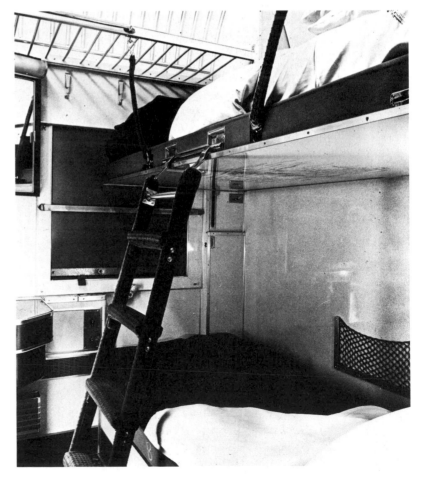

necessary, one for each country the train passed through. Kitchens were equipped with coal ranges on WL diners, while gas served on the vehicles of the Pullman Car Co., which pioneered bottled butane on all British Railways.

Back in 1946, the Pullman Car Co. in England, still safely non-nationalized, wanted something modern for the *Devon Belle*, inasmuch as Devon had had no Pullman service since 1929. So two cars were converted to beaver-tail observation cars, designed by Richard Levin, MSIA. Instead of the formica used by Wagons-Lits,

Pullman adopted Warerite, an obvious choice given the fact that the Chairman of the firm manufacturing this plastic was also Chairman of Pullman, Mr. Stanley Adams, formerly Lord Dalziel's secretary. A feature of the observation cars was the deliberately uncomfortable seating, designed to make passengers wish to return to their Pullman armchairs after ten minutes or so, rather than 'hog' the seats for the whole run. What a sign of the times!

Large numbers of cars were altered to third class for the fourteen-car week-end *Devon Belle* from London (Waterloo) to Ilfra-

left: 210. Lower compartment of T2-class sleeping car (night position), with 1 bed (1st-class 'special'). Note the width of the floor, the upper berth folded back, heat control knob and window crank.

right: 211. Compartment of T2S-class sleeping car (night position). Note the distance between the bed and the wash-basin and the seat back forming a rack for clothes. The growth of tourist-class traffic created a demand for tourist 2-berth

compartment cars. Two thousand drawings were made by a design team under M. Fontan and M. Bugnier (Technical Services Director) for Wagons-Lits' last design, the T2. Interior décor was by Jacques Dumont. The T2 design was adopted by the SNCF, which added full air-conditioning in the later cars. The other members of the Pool of international sleeper operations preferred the T2S, designed by Schlieren of Switzerland. The T2 has 9 lower compartments with two fixed berths under the roof. The T2S has much narrower compartments, 17 on one level, with only 2 seats.

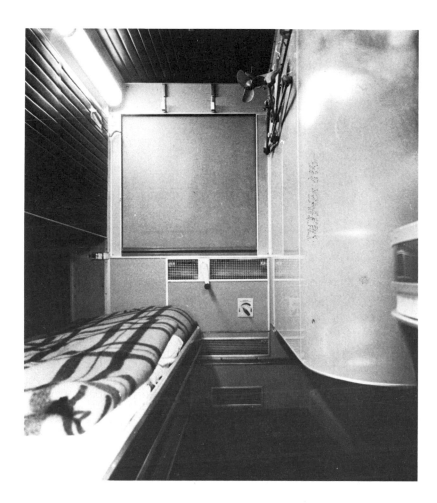

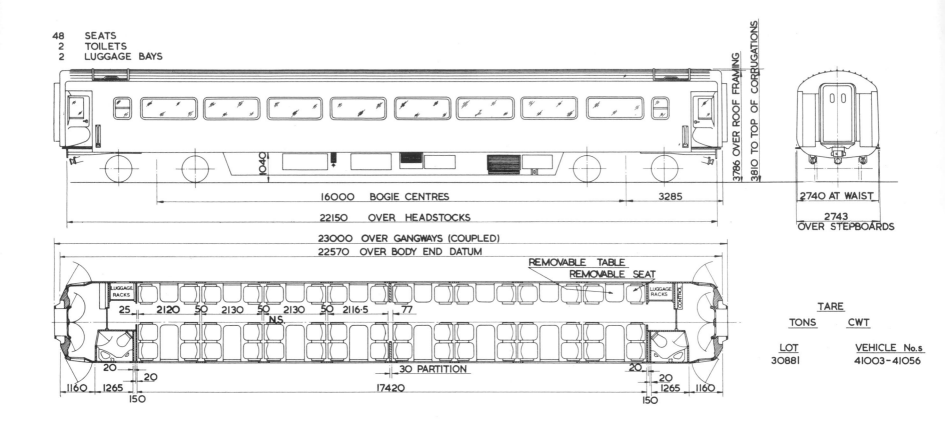

48 SEATS
2 TOILETS
2 LUGGAGE BAYS

3786 OVER ROOF FRAMING
3810 TO TOP OF CORRUGATIONS

1040

16000 BOGIE CENTRES 3285
22150 OVER HEADSTOCKS

2740 AT WAIST
2743 OVER STEPBOARDS

23000 OVER GANGWAYS (COUPLED)
22570 OVER BODY END DATUM

REMOVABLE TABLE
REMOVABLE SEAT

LUGGAGE RACKS

25 2120 50 2130 50 2130 50 2116·5 77
N.S.

30 PARTITION

20 20
20 20
1160 1265 17420 1265 1160
150 150

TARE
TONS CWT

LOT VEHICLE No.s
30881 41003–41056

above: 212. Plan and sections of BR 1st-class Mark III open saloon of HST 125 seats.

below: 213. Ice creams in the *Devon Belle* observation car, with its deliberately uncomfortable seats.

combe and Plymouth, via the now closed SR's tracks. By contrast, the new first-class Pullmans for the *Golden Arrow*, built in 1951 to mark the Festival of Britain, had marquetry bought before the war and stored. *Cygnus* boasted walnut and sycamore marquetry, *Perseus* olive and ash and *Hercules* eucalyptus.

In 1952, Mary Adshead, using lithographed paper scenes of early railways and floral decorations, designed a black-and-silver interior for *Phoenix*, built in Pullman's own Brighton repair shops from the chassis of *Rainbow*, which had burnt out in 1936. White Warerite tables contrasted with jet-black carpet and curtains, the marine-style, opaque-shaded cowls and cupola wall-lights. The car was frequently used for royal journeys, and owing to the death of King George VI in 1952, the black design was considered too mournful. So the Pullman Car Co. substituted a puce-coloured carpet and curtains, effectively ruining Miss Adshead's memorable scheme! This plastic décor did not suit Sea Containers, whose designer, Gérard Gallet of Paris, provided a new one, of walnut with floral marquetry. They rescued the magnifent vehicle from several years' sojourn at the Hôtel Mercure in Lyons, where a photograph of General Charles de Gaulle aboard the car on a state visit to London hung over its bar.

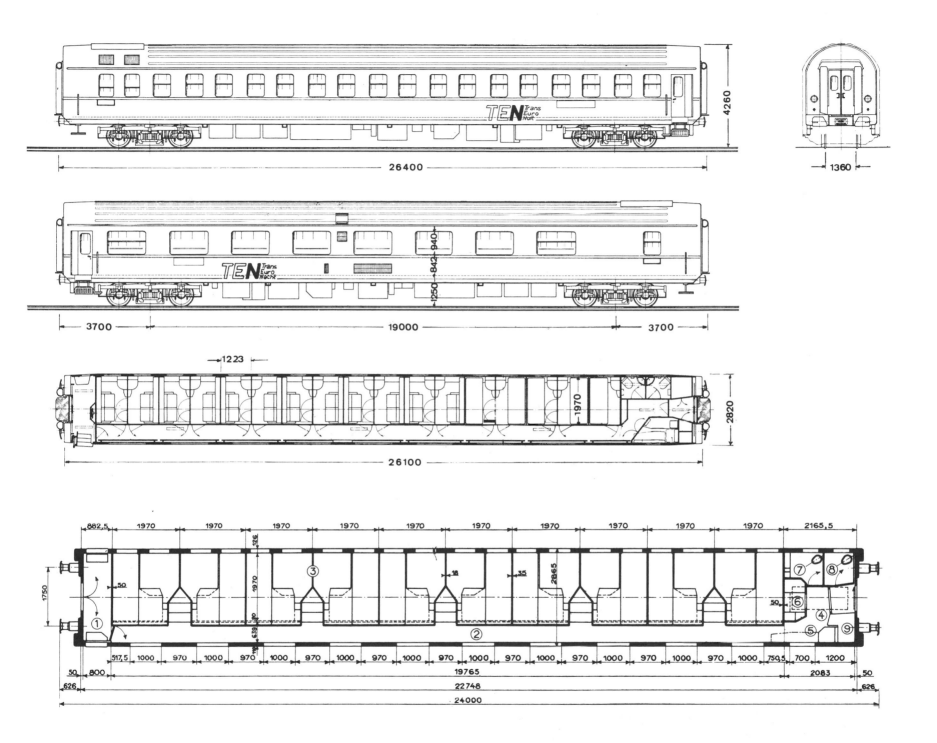

top: 214. T2S-type sleeping car.

above: 215. P-type sleeping car. 1) Entrance vestibule; 2) side corridor; 3) group of 4 compartments; 4) corridor to next coach; 5) conductor's armchair-bed; 6) pantry; 7) WC with clothes cupboard and tip-up wash-basin; 8) WC; and 9) boiler compartment.

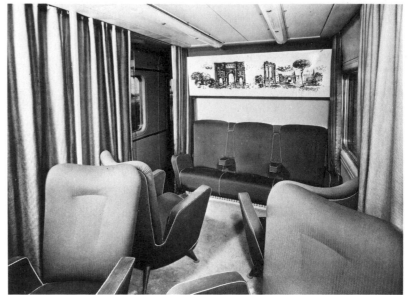

above left: 216. Interior of Pullman Car *Phoenix* of 1952. The tables are covered in white Warerite and the walls decorated in collages of old train and flower motifs by Mary Adshead.

above right: 217. Interior of FS TEE *Settebello*.

below: 218. On the Venice Simplon Orient Express, all 9 compartments of Lx cars are double berth. The décor shown here, in No. 3544, is after René Prou.

Gallet created eight designs for carpets, moquette and curtains in the 1982 VSOE: Carnation (flowers, green, red and black patterns); Flame (gold, mauve and brown abstract); Pink Floral (grey, black and pink); Pink Circles (pink and olive velvet); Art Nouveau (blue and rust); Victorian Tapestry (straw, green and black); Gaufrage (embossed velvet); and Arrowhead (an Art Deco abstract). The materials were expensive, the curtains for *Cygnus* costing £40 per yard and the upholstery £15 per metre. It was also necessary that they be fire-retardant in order to meet the very stringent requirements of BR and SNCF (other railways are less fussy). In the *Golden Arrow* tradition, the same materials are found in some cars on both sides of the Channel.

The cars built in 1951–52 also received classical US-style oval Pullman lavatory windows in place of the square ones originally fitted to break with the past and give the cars a modern look. Instead of plain floors, the lavatories of all the cars were given new mosaic paving, each of the designs, by Margery Knowles of Worcester, England, reflecting the car's name. In the early years of the restoration, other designs for the Venice Simplon Orient Express came from Charles Dorin, FRIBA, and were carried out at Carnforth, Cumbria, for the UK cars. Many craftsmen had developed at Waring & Gillow's nearby factory at Lancaster, which closed before 1977. The Lx-class sleepers were restored by CIWL's Ostend works.

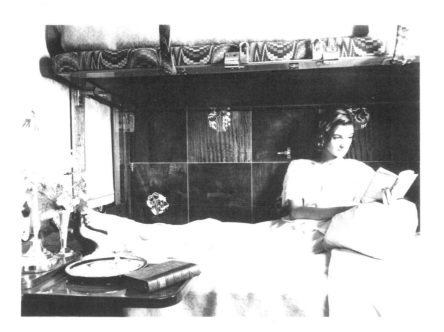

opposite: 219. Pullman Car No. 4018. Note inscriptions in gold leaf, 'P' in a square signifies a privately owned car—a vehicle not belonging to any railway administration. The celebrated Pullman oval lavatory window is very evident in this picture. The car was restored by the CIWL's largest works, the one at St. Denis, which closed in 1978.

ROPEENS

PULLMAN CAR

Nº 4018 E

ESSIEUX | 7   BOGIE | P   8   REV : 21 · 8 · 26

Details of the original décor of Lx cars are given in the Appendices, as are those of all VSOE passenger cars. The other restorations were undertaken at Bremen Waggonbau, formerly Hansa. No. 4095, one of the three former *Golden Arrow* Pullmans used as diners, has Chinese lacquer décor obtained from a scrapped CIWL dining car in Spain. The cars are actually more grandiose than in the 1930s, when high elegance was taken for granted. Such is the allure of old Pullman trains that many Art Deco fans visit CIWL's Astoria Hotel in Brussels just to see the authentic furniture (including the hassocks) adorning the establishment's Pullman Bar.

During the 1960s, the accent was on modernization. At the outset of the decade, the Pullman Car Co. ordered a series of new cars with BR Mark II–style body shells, but with larger windows than in ordinary carriages and inward- instead of outward-opening doors for the *Queen of Scots* Pullman. Décor was by John Carter, FSIA, using chairs taken from earlier cars. In 1961, Jack Howe, FRIBA, FSIA, designed fully air-conditioned Blue Pullman diesel sets for the first-class Midland Pullman (London-Manchester) and first- and second-class Birmingham Pullman. Pullman cars still run between London (Euston) and Manchester (after electrification in

1966), ousting the Midland Pullman, but all the Blue Pullman trains were simply withdrawn following only twelve years' service.

Reclining seats, venetian blinds, double glazing, full air-conditioning and automatic doors are among the features of the Manchester Pullman cars of 1966. They also grace the red-and-yellow or stainless-steel stock of Continental Europe's TEE trains (see Chapter 15).

On the Continent, various types of self-service diner (called 'Gril Express' in France) have replaced the classic waiter service, and some of these find their way into such Trains de Luxe as the *Palatino*. All have service counters, cafeteria and micro-ovens for reheating pre-cooked frozen dishes. The Italian ones offer 39 individual tables facing the window instead of conventional 4-seat tables.

The designs found among Trains de Luxe are much too numerous to be considered within the space of this book, but mention must be made of the *Settebello* ETR 300 TEE with forward observation as well as rearward observation saloons, the Dome cars of the *Rheingold* TEE, now unfortunately withdrawn, and the Barcelona Talgo, with first-class double and four-berth tourist compartments, set at an angle that permits standard-length beds to be used.

Meanwhile, as the illustrations on these two pages reveal, there is scarcely anything in the contemporary world of travel to rival the old Trains de Luxe in the respect they embodied for the civilizing love of good living.

opposite: 220. Pullman Car No. 3544, formerly used by Queen Wilhelmina of The Netherlands (1945–47), has now been restored for the Venice Simplon Orient Express. It is seen here at Ostend—hence, the high platforms. The car is fitted for air-conditioning, unlike the other sleepers in the train.

above: 221. This picture was not taken in 1930—but in 1981! It represents a group of VSOE staff displaying their distinctive uniforms.

right: 222. Luncheon being served in *Cygnus*, on the Venice Simplon Orient Express.

CONCLUSION

Statistics show that the uses of sleeping cars and railway catering vehicles have become more numerous than ever. In 1980 CIWL carried 2,950,000 sleeper passengers overnight in 504 of their own cars, leased to the Pool railways and RENFE, and in 261 railway-owned cars that they staff. They also staff 290 railway couchette cars, which carried a further 2,900,000 people. The trying formalities of the airlines, supplemented by enormous fares and the very real risk of highjacking, have damaged the prestige of air travel, especially since the railways now respond to the new traffic needs with new carriages that are often, though not always, cleaner than before, thanks to the disappearance of steam traction. Diesel haulage, it is true, produces its own brand of dirt and smells, but electric lines, silent and of clinical emaculateness (when properly looked after), as well as fuel-efficient, have brought a considerable traffic back to rail.

Meanwhile, there is a growing mass of people who like travelling by train, not merely to reach their destination but as a pleasure in itself. Usually this has to be catered for by specialized travel agencies, helped by dedicated railwaymen passionately interested in trains, rather than by the railways administrations themselves, though belatedly the latter are starting to respond to demand. In 1977 a great number of old faithful Wagon-Lits cars disappeared from the European railways scene, as had already happened to Pullman Cars in Great Britain. Many of them have been saved, however, notably *Ibis*, a *Golden Arrow* Pullman loaned to Wagon-Lits between 1925 and 1928. If you dream of taking the *Golden Arrow*, you will find *Ibis*, with *Cygnus*, *Perseus*, *Phoenix* and *Minerva*, running weekly in Sea Containers' train from London to Folkestone Harbor, a service that began in 1982. But perhaps you dream of travelling across Europe in a Train de Luxe of Wagon-Lits stock only, where you must don evening dress for candle-lit, gourmet dinners! It is undoubtedly an expensive dream, for Wagon-Lits travel has always been devised for the wealthy, as though everybody who travelled on Trains de Luxe were a millionaire!

One of the best things of life today is that this particular dream can come true, for the 1976, privately sponsored Milan-Istanbul special, run to mark Wagons-Lits' centenary, was such a success that it led to the creation of the Nostalgic Orient Express in 1977, from Zurich via the Arlberg, or from Stuttgart via Salzberg, and taking the Tauern Orient route in spring and autumn. This train is operated by Intraflug A.G. (Taegernstrasse 12A, PO Box 88, 8127 Forch, Zurich, Switzerland) with former Wagon-Lits vehicles displaying their pre-1967 livery, and with Wagon-Lits and SSG staff and victuals. It includes the 'Cantaeuropa' shower car, the former Pullman No. 4013, leased from Wagon-Lits. The rest of the train consists of Intraflug's own Lx16 sleeper Nos. 3472, 3475, 3480, 3487, 3509, 3537, 3540, 3542 and Lx20 No. 3551; Pullman Cars 4149, 4158 and 4161; diner 2741 (bought at the Sotheby Monte Carlo CIWL auction in 1977); *Train Bleu* bar car 4164, with Lalique décor and refurbished leather seating, bought in 1980 from SNCF, and fourgon 1283 (not yet restored to service). All except the fourgon were much too grand to run to Turkey before the war. No. 4158, with Lalique's 'Bacchanalian Ladies' décor, was repainted in 1929 style at WL's Milan works in 1977, with raised gold lettering instead of blue on cream. No. 4161 (bought in 1979) has just been refurbished by WL's Irun works. It has Lalique's 'Blue-Birds' décor, devised for the Blue-Bird Pullman. All the cars have been repainted, many at the WL Vienna works, and by 1981 the diner once more sported its gleaming 1926 Pullman livery. All the cars have the full pre-1967 'Compagnie Internationale des Wagons-Lits et des Grands Express Européens' emblazoned above the windows. (This title in various languages, as carried by different cars, is given in the Appendices.) Intraflug also own two *Rheingold* Salonspeisewagens, one with kitchen.

The Nostalgic Orient Express operates various excursions, such as the annual ones to Bordeaux and Rheims at the end of August, with wine-tasting at prominent châteaux included in the fare. The Tenda Pullman excursions include the newly opened Turin-Cuneo-Breil-Nice line from Zurich over the Lötschberg, the Simplon and the Tenda, which had been closed for forty years; the Gotthard Pullman to Milan with vintage electric and perhaps some steam haulage; and to Vienna for the New Year Schwarzenberg Palace Ball. The Pullmans are often hired for private parties, either as a special train or as one car attached to an ordinary train. The whole Train de Luxe can be hired anywhere in Europe on the UIC (Bern) standard gauge. The SSG provide catering as desired for these trips.

Chiefly, however, the train runs to Istanbul, for that is where the customers wish to go, lured by the mysteries of the Orient, exactly like Nagelmackers' passengers of 97 years ago. Having been on the Simplon Orient Express in 1937 and the Nostalgic Orient Express in 1977, the author knows the service provided by the latter is impeccably authentic. Sometimes the train is run to Athens, via the Simplon Orient route through Venice. There is usually some steam haulage in Yugoslavia, and occasionally in Turkey. The train also forms part of fully inclusive air tours originating in the United States. Details of Intraflug's current programme, including the Trans-Siberian Special Ltd. (see Chapter 6) and the Drakensberg *Bloutrein* (see Chapter 19), can always be found in the Thomas Cook Continental Timetable and the Thomas Cook Overseas Timetable.

Wagon-Lits cars can be admired in all their splendour at the French National Railway Museum in Mulhouse, where sleeper 3532, Pullman 4018 and diner 3348 are on display, while sleeper 3792, just as glamorously restored as the cars in France, is at the (British) National Railway Museum in York. Diner 2975, restored by Thomas Cook in 1979 to mark the Golden Jubilee of their association with Wagon-Lits, serves luncheon on the Nene Valley Railway at Peterborough, within sight of the Thomas Cook headquarters at Thorpe Wood. It is often coupled to sleeper 3916.

But a little trip on a five-mile preserved line is not the same thing as two nights in a row on a once-in-a-lifetime international journey through five countries, crossing the Iron Curtain. And in Switzerland the Nostalgic Orient Express is sure to be hauled by a time-honoured 2D1 AE 4/7 electric train of 1927, perhaps past the Château de Chillon, just as it was in the 1930s (see Plate 129).

V

APPENDICES

Glossary

European terminology and spelling have been used throughout this book. For the benefit of American readers, the US equivalents of European terms are given below. A list of the abbreviations used for the various railways can be found on page 229 of the Appendices.

European term	US equivalent
bellows connection, concertina or gang-way	vestibule
bogie	truck
brigade	crew of dining car
car	luxury railroad carriage
carriage or coach	ordinary railroad carriage
chef de brigade	maître d', or dining-car conductor
chef du train (CIWL)	train captain (CIWL)
CIWL or ISG	International Sleeping Car Co.
conductor/conducteur (CIWL)	porter (sleeping car)
conductor (Pullman Car Co.)	Pullman train captain
couchette car	railroad coach with bunks but no wash-basins, except at ends of coach
CSWR or SSG	Swiss Dining Car Co.
diner	dining car (see WR below)
driver	engineer
DSG	German Sleeping & Dining Car Co.
engine	locomotive
engineer	locomotive designer or railroad builder
fourgon	baggage or luggage van
guard	conductor or railroad train captain
headboard	train nameplate carried on front of engine hauling the train
level crossing	grade crossing
light engine	locomotive with no train
'piano' (CIWL)	Coal-fired kitchen range
points	switch, or switches
Pullman	parlor car, when unspecified as sleeper, diner, etc.
Pullman attendant	steward or waiter
rake	consist
relief train	section (of train)
restaurant car	see WR (below)
section (of train)	relief train
section (Pullman)	two chairs pulled together to make bed
section (CIWL)	smallest independent CIWL rail service unit: running staff, cleaners, fitters, inspectors etc.
shunt (verb)	switch (verb)
shunter	switcher (RR employee)
shunting engine	switcher (locomotive)
sleeper	normally sleeping car; rarely, track tie
sleeping car	luxury car with washrooms in each sleeping compartment
SSG or CSWR	Swiss Dining Car Co.
station	depot
vestibule	end passage inside car, across it
water trough	water troughs laid between the rails enabling steam locomotive tenders fitted with a scoop to pick up water and refill tanks without stopping
WR	diner or dining car

('Diner' or 'dining car' means full restaurant car. 'Buffet car' means light-meal-service car. 'Gril-Express' means self-service diner.)

Pullman trains not described in the text

In Great Britain between World War I and World War II

Thanet Pullman, started 1921. London (Charing Cross)–Margate. Later renamed *Thanet Belle,* still London (Charing Cross)–Margate–Ramsgate.

Sheffield Pullman, 1924–25. London (King's Cross)–Sheffield.

Harrogate Pullman, later Harrogate Sunday Pullman, after 1928. London (King's Cross)–Leeds–Harrogate on Sundays, replacing *Queen of Scots.*

Bournemouth Belle. London (Waterloo)–Southampton–Bournemouth West. Started 1931, Sundays only until 1936. Daily 1936–1939/40. Re-started after the war, it lasted until electrification of the Farnborough-Bournemouth portion of the London-Bournemouth main line in 1966. It was the last steam-hauled Pullman train in Britain.

After the war British Rail extended Pullman services as follows

Thanet Belle, later Kentish Belle, 1948–59.

Devon Belle, London (Waterloo)–Ilfracombe/Plymouth, with observation car, weekends only, 1947–55. Started when petrol and even bread were rationed in England. Fourteen Pullmans in the train, many 3rd class.

Midland Pullman, 1960–66. Blue-and-white, air-conditioned diesel sets, running between London (St. Pancras) and Manchester until electrification of London (Euston)–Manchester inaugurated the present Manchester Pullman by that route, the only two Pullman regular services still running in 1981, Monday to Friday: two trains, London-Manchester-London and Manchester-London-Manchester.

Birmingham Pullman, 1960–66. London (Paddington)–Birmingham–Wolverhampton. Ended with electrification London (Euston)–Birmingham. Air-conditioned diesel sets; connections to Stratford-on-Avon for tourists.

South Wales Pullman, 1955–66. London (Paddington)–Cardiff/Swansea. Classic steam-hauled Pullmans until 1960, then diesel air-conditioned sets.

Master Cutler, London (Marylebone)–Sheffield, 1958; London (King's Cross)–Sheffield, 1959–66. First regularly diesel-hauled Pullman in England.

Hull Pullman, London (King's Cross)–Hull. Originally joined to Yorkshire Pullman.

Tyne Tees Pullman, London (King's Cross)–Newcastle-on-Tyne, 1948–70.

Yorkshire Pullman, London (King's Cross)–Leeds and Bradford. Started 1946, with Hull portion. These two were withdrawn in 1978. HST sets were introduced between London, Leeds and Harrogate.

In 1960 the Pullman Car Co. ordered a new fleet of cars from Metropolitan-Cammell. The chairs for the first class cars were taken from former Pullmans. The cars had a public-address system, double-glazed windows with Venetian blinds between them and forced-draught ventilation. After 1962, most of them were repainted in BR colours. They were built on modified BR Mark II bodyshells with larger windows and of course curved, not straight, sides. Under BR the chairs were removed and a three-a-side seating fixed in all first-class Pullmans. The air-conditioned Pullman diesel sets, painted blue and white, bore only BR numbers. In 1960 also, Pullman streamlined its badge. The Pullman Car Co. contracts having ended in 1962, the staff were integrated fully into British Transport Catering Services, renamed Travellers Fare in 1973.

Continental Europe

The Wagons-Lits Pullman trains not yet mentioned include: Milan-Nice-Cannes Express, December 1925–35. Used British Pullman Car Co. vehicles. 1927 only two Pullmans from Turin-Cannes.

Milan-Venice Express, summer 1926–29. Used stock as above. From Turin 1928 only. *Flèche d'Or* type Pullmans from 1928.

Milan-Genoa-Montecatini Express, 1926–29. Used stock as above. Sometimes ran in Rome Express from Genoa to Montecatini.

North Star (Étoile du Nord), 1927–39, 1946–63. Paris-Brussels-Amsterdam

Blue Bird (Oiseau Bleu). Paris-Brussels-Antwerp, 1929–36; -Amsterdam, 1936–39 and 1947–63. Both these trains became TEE (see Chapter 17).

London-Vichy Pullman Express. 1927–30, Boulogne-Vichy first class, with Paris-Vichy second class. From 1930–39 the Boulogne-Vichy Pullmans ran in an ordinary train.

Calais-Brussels Pullman Express, 1927–39. Ran attached to Nord Express; operated by Wagons-Lits Belgian Division, with SNCB engine working into France right through, usually a Flamand 4-6-0. First class only 1927; 1928 first and second class by request of SR Nord and CIWL. 1929, first class only again, allowing use of

Canterbury (see Chapter 13). 1931–39, first and second class again.

Milan-Ancona Pullman Express, summer 1927–summer 1929. Two Pullmans only; from Milan in the afternoon, back next morning; only one train therefore needed. UK Pullmans used until 1928, then *Flèche d'Or* type.

Deauville Express. A revival of the Paris-Trouville-Deauville that in 1923–24 used *Blue Train* sleepers and one salon. Ran in 1927 with UK Pullmans.

Gothard Pullman Express. 1927–28 autumn; 1929–30 spring and autumn; 1930–31 March to November. One portion Basle-Milan. One portion Zurich-Milan, first and second class, joining at Arth-Goldau. In 1930 and 1931 July–September, one first-class and one-second class car, Paris-Basle-Milan and vice versa. Ended by SBB 1931 due to lack of traffic.

Paris–Côte Belge Pullman Express. Was to have been named *Queen of the Beaches*, but dropped since this applied to Ostend only. Ran only in 1928 and was the last service worked by the UK-type Pullmans, with *Étoile du Nord* second-class cars–couplage Paris-Ostend, 1 couplage Paris-Knokke sur Mer, dividing at Turnhout. After this the UK cars went back in service with the Pullman Car Co. Ltd., among them *Ibis*, now preserved by Sea Containers Ltd. (No. 52 in the CIWL list).

Roma-Napoli Pullman Express, 1929. First class only, one return trip daily.

Ostend-Cologne Pullman Express, 1929–39. The SNCB tried to get this started in 1928 but were turned down. It gave a record-time trip—London dep. 10:00, Cologne arr. 21:50—and was designed to avoid the overnight *Rheingold* arrangement. Operated by the Belgian Division of Wagons-Lits until World War II stopped it.

Carpati-Pullman Express, 1929–31. Bucharest-Brasov. Left Bucharest 17:40 and arrived Brasov at 21:07, returning next morning at 05:40 to reach Bucharest at 08:50. Special adaptation of cars against the cold.

Dunarea Pullman Express, 1929–1939. Bucharest-Galatz. 1932, renamed *Danubiu* (Danube Pullman). Three second-class Pullmans and one first-class Pullman. 1932, a WR added as an experiment for third-class passengers.

Côte d'Zzur Pullman Express, December 1929–May 1939. The inaugural guests of 9th December returned by *Blue Train* to enable the Pullman to enter service both ways at once on 10th December, between Paris and Ventimiglia. Winter 1932 curtailed at Menton, and winter 1933 at Lyons, one rake sufficing in this case. Paris dep. 08:50, Ventimiglia arr. 24:00.

Fulger Regele Carol I ('King Carol I Express'), 1933–39. Bucharest-Constanza. Extended to Constanza Port to meet ships. From 1936, extended in summer to Carmen Sylva and Mangalia in summer. The train averaged 80km/h, very fast for the CFR at the time. The Roumanian contract ended in 1948.

Principal post-war Pullman services (cars in ordinary trains)

Paris-Vichy, 1946–47; Paris–Vichy–Clermont Ferrand (*Thermal Express*), 1947–49; Bucharest-Brasov, 1946; Bucharest-Galatz, 1946–47; Bucharest-Mangalia, 1947; Paris-Brussels, 1947; Vienna-Lindau, 1946–47; Vienna-Innsbruck, (Arlberg Orient Express), 1947–49; Vienna-Basle, 1949; Brussels-Paris (*Blue Bird*), 1948–63; Madrid-Barcelona, 1947–52; Amsterdam-Brussels, 1947–50; Amsterdam-Paris (*North Star*), 1946–63; Paris-Calais (*Flèche d'Or*), 1950–69; Milan-Naples, 1950–70; Turin-Naples 1952–65; Paris-Irun (*Sud Express*), 1947–71; Milan-Nice, 1952–54; Rome-Venice, 1956–57; Paris-Luxembourg, 1956–57; Rome-Syracuse, 1958; Boulogne-Nice, 1964–65; Milan-Rome (last Pullman in service), 1971.

Trans Europ Express (TEE) from 1957

Name	Journey	Type	
North Star	Amsterdam–Paris (Nord)	1	R
Rubens	Brussels (Midi)–Paris (Nord)	1	R
Blue Bird	Brussels (Nord)–Paris (Nord)	1	R
Merkur (X)	Copenhagen–Stuttgart	2	X

Name	Journey	Type	
Gottardo	Basle-Genoa	3	R
Roland (X)	Bremen–Milan/Chur	2	
Van Beethoven (X)	Frankfurt–Amsterdam	2	X
	Amsterdam–Frankfurt–Nurnberg		
L'Aquitaine	Bordeaux–Paris (Austerlitz)	5	R
Blauer Enzian (X)	Hamburg–Klagenfurt	2	X
Helvetia (X)	Hamburg–Zurich	2	X
Parsifal (X)	Hamburg–Paris (Nord)	2	X
Prince Eugen (X)	Hanover–Cologne–Vienna	2	X
Erasmus (X)	Munich–The Hague	2	X
Rembrandt	Munich–Amsterdam	2	
Mediolanum	Munich–Milan	2	
Le Rhodanien	Marseilles–Paris (Lyons)	4	X
Ligure	Milan–Avignon (XX)	6	R
Adriatico	Milan–Bari	6	
Lemano	Milan–Geneva (XX)	6	R
Vesuvio	Milan–Naples (Mergellina)	6	
Settebello	Milan–Rome	7	
Cygnus (X)	Milan–Ventimiglia	6	X
Saphir (X)	Nuremberg–Frankfurt–Brussels	2	X
Ile de France	Paris (Nord)–Amsterdam	1	R
Memling	Paris (Nord)–Brussels (Midi)	1	R
Brabant	Paris (Nord)–Brussels (Midi)	1	R
Stanislas	Paris (Est)–Strasbourg	5	R
L'Arbalete (X)	Paris (Est)–Zurich	5	X
Kleber	Paris (Est)–Strasbourg	5	R
L'Etandard	Paris (Austerlitz)–Bordeaux	5	R
Le Capitol	Paris (Austerlitz)–Toulouse	5	R
Le Mistral	Paris (Lyons)–Nice	4	X
Molière (X)	Paris (Nord)–Cologne	4	X
Ambrosiano	Rome–Milan	6	
Edelweiss (X)	Zurich–Brussels (Midi)	3	R
Iris	Zurich–Brussels (Midi)	3	
Rheingold	Geneva–Amsterdam	2	
Cis–Alpin	Paris–Milan	3 & 5	
Catalan Talgo	Barcelona–Geneva (XX)	8	
Gambrinus	Hamburg–Cologne–Munich	2	
Bacchus (Y)	Dortmund–Munich	2	R
Diamant	Hamburg–Hanover–Munich	2	
Goethe	Dortmund–Frankfurt	2	R
Faidherbe	Paris (Nord)–Lille–Tourcoing	5	
Gayant	Paris (Nord)–Lille–Tourcoing	5	
Watteau	Paris (Nord)–Lille–Tourcoing	5	
Jules Verne	Nantes–Paris (Monparnasse)	5	R
Heinrich Heine	Frankfurt–Dortmund	2	R
Friedrich Schiller	Stuttgart–Dortmund	2	R
Albert Schweitzer	Dortmund–Strassbourg	2	R

R = Train returns same day; X = From 28 May 1978 this named train is an ordinary Express 1st & 2nd cl in some cases with a varied itinerary; XX = Replaced May 1982 by 1st/2nd class Inter City train of same name; Y = Withdrawn 1980, replaced Dortmund–Heidelberg by *Albert Schweitzer*; * Basel–Amsterdam from May 1982.

Type	Railway(s) owning	TEE cars	WR (diner operator)
1	SNCF/SNCB	6–10	CIWL
2	DB	4–9	DSG
3	SBB	5	SSG
4	SNCF	14 with boutique and hair dressing	CIWL
			CIWL
5	SNCF	7	CIWL
6	FS	3–8	CIWL
7	FS	ETR 300 set	CIWL
8	RENFE	Talgo	

Details for the modeller

Principal dimensions of vehicles mentioned (in metres)

CIWL	Length overall	Length of body	Height above rail
MU, T2, P	26,400	25,188	4,260
U Hansa	25,100	24,740	4,260
YF	25,148	23,848	4,260
Y,Z,WR,WP,LJ	23,452	22,200	4,213
F	19,232	16,280	3,934

Dimensions in feet and inches

Pullman Car Co.	Length	Width
USA clerestory	58' (17,6784m)	8'9" (2,667m)
Balmoral and *Culross*	36'3" (11,0490m)	8'7" (2,616m)
The rest of British Pullmans including CIWL 51-60)	63'10" (19,456m)	8'7" (2,616m)
'Hastings' Pullmans (*Barbara*)	57'6" (17,526m)	8'1" (2,463.8m)
'Underground' Pullmans (*Mayflower*)	57'6" (17,526m)	8'7½" (2.629m)
Brighton Belle and SR electric cars	66'0" (20,1168m)	9'0" (2,7432m)
Irish Pullmans	65'11" (20,091m)	8'11" (2.718m)

Colours

Wagons-Lits cars: before 1922, varnished teak (maroon);
after 1922, royal blue with gold lettering and designs

Variations

Wagons-Lits Pullmans had Pullman livery until 1932. In complete Pullman trains, the Fourgons were varied, usually in Pullman colours. After 1932: Pullman blue below waist, cream above, with blue lettering on cantrail over windows instead of raised gold lettering (as in teak cars).
Club trains: green and cream.
Trains de Luxe after 1900: maroon with cream upperworks in certain cases. Cars white in Egypt and North Africa, excepting Pullmans 4171–4176 and 4088.
Certain CIWL cars painted silver all over in Spain in 1958. See LJ class.
Pullman Palace Car Co. cars: maroon, the normal colour of the American Pullmans in the USA.
Pullman Car Co.: chocolate below waist, cream or ivory white above. The cantrail also chocolate after 1929, *excepting:*
—cars running on the Eastern Section of the SR or SE&CR, which were entirely maroon, until about 1930;
—cars running on the Metropolitan Railway, London (1933–39 LPTB), which were also maroon all over, until withdrawn; maroon and cream at first.
The baggage compartments of brake parlour cars, after 1929, also the stores cars *Albatross*, *Thistle* and *Savona*, numbered 11, 15 and 16, were chocolate all over. At stations, metal plates bearing the car number in the train were placed on view beside the entrance doors which opened inwards. The purpose was to identify reservations. They had to be taken down on departure, as they fouled the loading gauge. In Scotland, the Pullman Car Co. diners had seats and décor very similar to those of CIWL diners of the same period. (These diners never ran in Trains de Luxe.)
From an historical point of view, it is interesting to note that scale-model CIWL cars are made by the toy industry producing model railway stock, in a large number of different countries, exactly like the real ones.

Fleet of the International Sleeping Car Co. (CIWL)

The author wishes to acknowledge the assistance of Monsieur G. Coudert, whose list of individual vehicles and numbers is more detailed than space permits here. Opportunity has been taken to correct a number of mistakes in one of the author's earlier books, and to include observations from Mr. J.H. Price, Dr. W.A.C. Wendelaar, Dr. Fritz Stökl, Herr Werner Sölch, Señor Juan Cabrera, and M. Roger Commault.

Abbreviations used in this list and in the Pullman Palace Car list

Type	Meaning	English equivalent or remarks
F	Fourgon	Luggage van
FC	Fourgon-cuisine	Van with kitchen for serving certain WR (or WL in Turkey)
FF	Fourgon-fumoir	Luggage van with smoking compartment for passengers
FP	Fourgon-poste	Luggage van with postal compartment for mails
FT	Fourgon-truck	For the luggage containers used on the *Golden Arrow*
OBS	Observation Car	For the Trans-Siberian
R	Réservoir à gaz	Gas tank wagon
WL	Wagon-Lits	Sleeping car
WLM	Wagon-Lits mixte	Sleeping car with both sleeping and ordinary compartments
WLS	Wagon-Lits salon	Sleeping car with large saloon compartment, with sofa and several beds
WP	Wagon-Pullman	Pullman parlour car with 2 saloons but no kitchen
WPC	Wagon-Pullman cuisine	Pullman kitchen car with 2 saloons
WR	Wagon-restaurant	Dining car with kitchen, unless otherwise stated
WRS	Wagon-restaurant salon	Dining car with saloon portion
WS	Wagon-salon	Saloon car
WSP	Wagon-salon Pullman	Saloon car with one Pullman saloon
WSPC	Wagon-salon Pullman-cuisine	Saloon car with kitchen and one Pullman saloon

Class

Trains de Luxe were originally first class only, with some special servants' compartments. Some WR were built with first- and second-class saloons for use on ordinary trains. Supplementary tickets called 'Bulletins' were needed to travel in WL and WP, but were invalid when not accompanied by the appropriate 'Class Rail Ticket' issued by the railway being traversed. Two supplements and one first-class railway ticket secured a single, but sometimes one and a half supplements sufficed. Later, double compartments could be used with second-class tickets. On some journeys the same sort of accommodation was valid only with a higher-class rail ticket than that required on other journeys. Sometimes there was a railway surtax as well as a sleeper supplement! Some sleeping cars were second class, third class, or second and third class. Except in Russia, the Baltic states, Greece and Turkey, these cars were rarely attached to Trains de Luxe. After No. 1884, sleeping cars were standardized with class letters. After 1919 all had these. After 1956 third class was abolished, and second-class cars with single small compartments were designated 'First Class Special', at a lower fare than that for a first-class single, but higher than that for a first-class double. Some cars with double berths are accessible on second-class tickets, and all triple berths (called 'Touriste') are admissible on second-class tickets.

Classes of Wagons-Lits	(metal bodies unless stated)
A (wooden)	2 saloons + 4 compts. + 2 servants compts.
B (wooden)	1 saloon + 4 compts. + 4 servants compts.

Classes of Wagons-Lits	(metal bodies unless stated)
R (wooden)	16- or 18-berth 'Regal' class
M (wooden)	R class with some 3-berth compartments III cl. (pre-war)
M3 (wooden)	M class but 3-berth throughout III cl.
R3 (wooden)	R class but 3-berth throughout; more compartments than M3
S1 (steel)	8 × I cl. + 4 × II cl. with intermediate toilets in centre of car
S2	8 × I + 4 × II with intermediate toilets, at end of car
S3	6 × I + 6 × II with intermediate toilets at end of car
S3K	S3 but with 1 end double + toilet + end WC remodelled to cafeteria for Spain
S4U (some wooden)	4 × I + 6 × II with intermediate compts. in centre, remodelled later to universal 3-berth and individual toilets for Spain
Lx (Luxe)	10 × I; later Lx 16 4 × I and 6 × II or Lx 20 10 × II
Z (Zigzag)	12 × II; later 11 × II with pantry (Z3 = 12 × III cl.)
Y	11 × II Z-type, but with intercommunicating doors
YT	7 × II Z-type + 4 × III 3-berth III cl. (ZT = YT without intercommunicating doors)
YU	As YT but with universal middle berth I-II-III
F (ferry boat)	9 × II single vestibule
3 (wooden)	6 × II + 6 × III 4-berth, for Baltic states
P	9 × III 4-berth, for Poland (pre-war)
U	11 × 1-2-3-berth Universal
M	12 × 1-2-berth, for Italy (post-war)
LJ	8 × 1-berth + 6 × 2-berth, for Spain
MU	12 × 1-2-3-berth Universal
P	20 × 1-berth special two levels (post-war)
YF	11 × 1-2-berth for Spain
YC	11 × 1-2-berth for Italy
T2	9 × 1 special or 2 tourist + 9 × 2 tourist
T2S	17 × 1 special or 2 tourist

Pullman car classes take their names from the Pullman trains they were originally built for, but of course there were *North Star* and *Côte d'Azur* on the *Flèche d'Or*, and *Flèche d'Or* on the *North Star*. Independent cars ran singly or relied on the WR kitchens. Other cars ran in pairs called *couplages* or in threes (*triplages*) of one or two WP and one WPC, with the kitchen nearest the WP for easier serving. First class (I cl.) had armchairs, one per side, larger chairs in *Côte d'Azur* class. Second class (II cl.) had one and two per side high-backed seats, as in UK Pullmans.

Axles: Where shown, 2 = 4-wheel; 3 = 6-wheel; 4 = 4-wheel bogie; 6 = 6-wheel bogie.

Length excluding buffers: Given where known, for modellers. Height and use of loading gauge was generally similar for S, Lx, Z, Y, LJ, and U, MU, YF respectively.

Seats or berths: Refers to WR seats, Pullman seats, or chairs, salon chairs, and WL berths. WRS seating usually shows the WR seating + places in the salon.

Year: Since it is not possible to show each car separately, unless it was a one-off design, the lot may spread over one or more years. Some lots were allocated numbers but not built until after later lots. Frantic efforts were made to prevent the same number being allocated twice over, after two cars numbered 221 both appeared in Russia and China at the same time. Hence, gaps in numbers.

Builders: These are abbreviated; see list of builders. Three builders who built one lot each are shown in the remarks column. Some builders have more than one works, in more than one country.

Remarks: Cars belonging to the railways or Eurofima which have 'crossed-out, painted numbers' (in the CIWL nomenclature), for reference by the CIWL repair shops, are included. Cars identified as for Russia, for Finland, for Spain or for Portugal could not run on the standard gauge. The Sud Express and the St. Petersburg–Cannes Express ran in two portions, with passengers *and conductors* changing cars at Warsaw. The Nord Express divided at Berlin, for St. Petersburg and for Moscow. Thus, there were two, quite separate Nord Expresses in Russia: St. Petersburg–Wirballen/Eydtkuhnen and Moscow-Warsaw. When cars transferred to Spain (or China), their wheel gauge had to be altered at WL-Irun or WL-Harbin, as necessary. WL-Irun, though fitted with mixed gauge, did not undertake work for the *Direction de Paris* until 1977, when WL–St. Denis and WL–Villeneuve-Prairie were closed and the maintenance of SNCF and French Pool fleets was taken over by the SNCF works. Only the *Puerta del Sol* cars have interchangeable bogies. CIWL's locomotive had no number. Built 1903 for WL Vienna, it was battery electric. Elsewhere shunting was by capstan and transporter. CIWL's wine wagons were numbered in the railway nomenclature for goods vehicles and had no WL number. Railway passenger stock—e.g., TEE restaurants, buffet cars, État Pullmans, railcar buffets, couchette cars, restaurant cars, Talgo restaurants, Talgo sleeping cars, etc.—staffed by CIWL and victualled by them—are not included. The cars of CIWL subsidiaries, built newly for them, in France (CFWB), Germany (DSG) and Switzerland (CSWR/SSG) are not included either, except, for three preserved SSG cars.

Details of WR cars used as temporary stationary restaurants are included. So are WL used as staff sleeping quarters (dortoirs). Many cars were rebuilt and renumbered. Sometimes WL were rebuilt to WR and vice versa. But Pullman cars remodeled to WR were not renumbered.

Every year the company's balance sheet showed the rolling stock on the strength. Decreases in the numbers are due to:
(a) 1920 write off of the Russian fleet, and cars not returned by Mitropa.
(b) Write off in 1947 of cars that disappeared during World War II, a few of which were later found.
(c) Exclusion of 147 WL + 8 WR paid for by the Compagnie Internationale Auxiliaire des Chemins de Fer, including the French-built Lx class, which were not allowed to run in Belgium. These were repurchased by CIWL in 1944, 1949 and 1952.
(d) Exclusion of 114 WR, sold to SNCF in 1961–62 but run in CIWL colours and inscriptions until 1971.
(e) Cars written off but still used, notably WP and Fourgons.

List of builders

Ansaldo	Ansaldo, S.p.a. Stabilimento Ferro-viario, Genoa	ITALY
Arad	Astra, Arad	ROUMANIA
Beasain	Cia Auxiliar de Ferrocarrilles, S.A., Beasain	SPAIN
Bilbao	Sociedad Espanola de Construccion Navales, Bilbao	SPAIN
Birmingham	The Birmingham Railway Carriage & Wagon Co. Ltd., Smethwick, Birmingham	ENGLAND
Blanc Miss.	Ateliers de Construction du Nord de la France, Blanc Misseron Crespin	FRANCE
Braine le Comte	Usines Braine le Comte	BELGIUM
Breda	Società Italiana Ernesto Breda per Construzzione Meccaniche, Milan	ITALY
Bres.	Breslauer Aktiengesellschaft für Eisenbahnwagen, Breslau	GERMANY
Brown Marshalls	Brown Marshalls, Birmingham, absorbed by Metro, 1902	ENGLAND
Brugeoise	Société la Brugeoise, Nicaise & Delouve, Saint Michel-lez-Bruges	BELGIUM
Cardé	Cardé y Escoriaza S.A., Zaragozza	SPAIN

185

List of builders

Carel-Fouché	Carel-Fouché et Cie, Le Mans	FRANCE
Cegielski	H. Cegielski GP, AKC, Poznan	POLAND
CGC	Compagnie Générale de Construction, Saint-Denis, Paris (WL subsidiary)	FRANCE
Credé	Gebrüder Credé, Kassel-Niederzwehren	GERMANY
Desouches	Desouches David et Cie, Pantin, Paris	FRANCE
Diatto	Diatto S.A. Turin (later part of Fiat)	ITALY
Dietrich	Sté. Lorraine des Anciens Ets. de Dietrich,. Reichshoffen, Niederbron-les-Bains	FRANCE
Dyle & Bac	Dyle & Bacalan S.A., Louvain, and Dyle & Bacalan S.A., Bordeaux (2 works, office at Paris)	BELGIUM FRANCE
EIC	Entreprises Industrielles Charentaises Aytré, La Rochelle (today Brissoneau & Lotz)	FRANCE
Eis. Bedarf	Eisenbahn Bedarfs-Atkiengesellschaft, Berlin, Görlitz and Nuremberg (3 works)	GERMANY
El. Ferr	Officine Electro-Ferroviare Tallero, Milan	ITALY
Evrard	Cie Belge pour la Construction de Matériel Chemins de Fer Evrard, Brussels	BELGIUM
Fiat	Fab. Ital. Auto., Turin	ITALY
Ganz	Ganz & Co., Budapest	HUNGARY
Gastell	Gebrüder Gastell, Mainz	GERMANY
Gotha	Gothaer Waggonfabrik, Gotha	GERMANY
Györ	Raab Waggonfabrik, Györ	HUNGARY
Hansa	Hansa Waggonbau, Bremen	GERMANY
Jackson Shp.	Jackson, Sharp & Co. (today American Car & Foundry) Wilmington, Del.	USA
Klett	Klett Machinen Fabrik, Augsburg/Nuremberg	GERMANY
LCDR	Longhedge Works, LC & DR, London	ENGLAND
Leeds	The Leeds Forge Co., Leeds (later part of Metro)	ENGLAND
Linke Hoff	Linke Hofmann Werke, Breslau (later at Salzgitter)	GERMANY
Lyons	Société des Forges de l'Horme, Chantier de la Buire, Lyons	FRANCE
Macosa	Macosa S.A., Valencia	SPAIN
Metro	Metropolitan–Cammell Carriage & Wagon Co. Ltd., Saltley, Birmingham	ENGLAND
Miani	Miani Sylvestri S.A., Milan	ITALY
Midland	The Midland Railway Carriage & Wagon Co. Ltd., Shrewsbury, and later Oldbury, Birmingham (absorbed by Metro., 1902)	ENGLAND
MMCZ	Material Movil y Construccions, Zaragozza	SPAIN

Nesselsdorf	Nesselsdorfer Waggonfabrik, Nesselsdorf and Koprivnice (2 works)	AUSTRIA CZECHO-SLOVAKIA
Nivelles	Les Ateliers de Construction Metallurgiques S.A., Nivelles	BELGIUM
Off. Mech	A. Grondana & Cie, later Officine Mechaniche, Milan (well known as OM)	ITALY
Off. Merid	Officina Meridionale, Naples	ITALY
PLM Algiers	Algiers work of the PLM Rly., Algiers	ALGERIA
Pullman	Pullman Palace Car Co., Inc., Pullman, Ill., and Detroit, Mich.	USA
Pullman, Longhedge	Longhedge Works, ex-LCDR of Pullman Car Co. Ltd., London	ENGLAND
Pullman, Preston Park	Brighton Works of the Pullman Car Car Co. Ltd., opened 1928	ENGLAND
Ragheno	S.A. Ragheno, Malines	BELGIUM
Rathgeber	Waggonfabrik Joseph Rathgeber A.G., Munich	GERMANY
Reggio	Officine Meccaniche Italiane, Reggio d'Emilia	ITALY
Riga	Russian-Baltic Waggon Works, Riga	RUSSIA
Ringhoffer	Ringhofferovy Zavody & Sp. Smichow, Prague	CZECHO-SLOVAKIA
Savigliano	Soc. Naz. delle Officine di Savigliano, Turin	ITALY
Scandia	Vognfabrik Scandia, Randers	DENMARK
Schindler	Schindler Waggonfabrik Pratteln, Basle	SWITZER-LAND
Schlieren	Schweizerische Waggon & Aufzügefabrik Schlieren, Zurich	SWITZER-LAND
SIG	Schweizerische Industrie Gesellschaft, Neuhausen	SWITZER-LAND
Simmering	Waggon Fabriken in Simmering, Vienna, and Hernals, Graz (2 works)	AUSTRIA
St. Petersburg	Russian State Railways works, St. Petersburg (today Leningrad)	RUSSIA
Upper Volga	Upper Volga Works, Twer (today Kalinin)	RUSSIA
Van der Zyp	Van der Zypen & Charlier, Koln-Deutz (today Westwaggon)	GERMANY
Weimar	Waggonfabrik, Weimar	GERMANY
Weyer	Karl Weyer Waggonfabrik, Düsseldorf	GERMANY
WL-Budapest	CIWL works, Budapest	HUNGARY
WL-Greco	CIWL works, Greco, Milan	ITALY
WL-Irun	CIWL works, Irun (Franco-Spanish frontier)	SPAIN
WL–Marly	CIWL works, Marly-les-Valenciennes, Paris (later CGC-Marly)	FRANCE
WL-Neu Aubing (also WL-NA)	CIWL works, Neu Aubing, Munich (today ISG/DSG Werkstäte)	GERMANY
WL-Ost	CIWL works, Slykens, Ostend (today coded WL-OM)	BELGIUM
WL–Saint-Denis (also WL-SD)	CIWL works, Saint-Denis, Paris (different works to CGC Saint-Denis)	FRANCE
WL–Saint-Ouen	CIWL works, Saint-Ouen (only laundry and wine cellars today)	FRANCE
WL-Zossen	CIWL works, Zossen, Berlin	GERMANY

Fleet of the International Sleeping Car and European Express Trains Co. (Wagons-Lits)

Principal abbreviations used in this table. See also the abbreviations given in the tables of car types, car classes and railway companies

MC = Monte Carlo, where the Sotheby auction took place in October 1977; I cl., II cl., III cl. (I-II-II) = first, second and third class; exp. = express; excl. = excluding; no., nos., = number(s); ordy. = ordinary seating, in part of a sleeper; pl., pls. = place(s) (seats or berths); pub = public house or inn; renum. = renumbered; rly. = railway; compt. = compartment; AJECTA = Youth Association for Byegone Trains Preservation (French: Association des Jeunes pour l'Entretien et la Conservation des Trains d'Autrefois), 7 Rue Félix, Vincennes, 94300 France (depots at Longueville, in Provence and at Richelieu [TVT-Touraine Steam Trains]); ARBAC =

Royal Belgian Railway Friends (Association Royale Belge des Amis des Chemins de Fer), Brussels; CFWB = French Buffet Car Co. (defunct CIWL subsidiary); CSWR/SSG = Swiss Dining Car Co., Olten, Switzerland (CIWL associate); Eurofima = European Railways Rolling Stock Finance Co.; Eurovapor = European Steam Enthusiasts Association, c/o Intraflug AG, Taegernstrasse 12A, Forch, 8127 Zurich, Switzerland; Mitropa = German Sleeping Car Co., Berlin, East Germany; Nost. Or. Exp. = Nostalgic Orient Express of Intraflug Ltd.; P&O = Peninsular & Oriental Steam Navigation Co., St. Botolph Street, London EC3A 7DX; VSOE = Venice Simplon Orient Express, operated by Sea Containers Ltd., Suite 2847, One World Trade Center, New York, N.Y. 10048, and Sea Containers House, 20 Upper Ground, London SE 1.

Car no.	Type	Axles	Class	Length excl. buffers	Seats or berths	Year	Builder	Remarks
1–4	WL	2		9,086	12	1872	Simmering	Became fourgons 1023, 1018, 1019 and 1020 in 1888. 3 shown at Vienna in 1873.
5	WL	2		9,086	6	1872	Simmering	Became F 1021 in 1888.
6–10	WL	3		11,588	10	1873	Eis.Bedarf Berlin	For Germany. Rebuilt by Rathgeber in 1886. 6 sold in 1904 for 120 Reichmarks. 7 and 9 became workshops at Vlissingen (Flushing) in 1905. 8 renum. 1 for Liège Exhibition, 1905, withdrawn 1906; became store at WL-Ost. 10 sold 1893 for 520 French francs.
11–14	WL	2			10	1873	Eis.Bedarf Berlin	Rebuilt 1884. 11 sold 1893. 13 renum. 18 in June 1889.
15	WL	3			14	1873	Simmering	First Mann Car. In Paris-Turin in 1878. Became store at Schaerbeek (Brussels).
16	WL	2			12	1873	Evrard	Withdrawn 1893. Chassis became gas transport wagon R 1049 in 1894.
17–19	WL	2			7	1874	Simmering	For Vienna-Prague. 17 sold 1889. 18 and 19 became F 1016 and 1017 in 1888.
20–23	WL	2			12	1874	Simmering	For Roumania Bucharest-Jassy. 23 burnt out at Jassy in 1877.
23		3			12	1878	Simmering	Replaced No. 23. Withdrawn in 1902.
24	WL	3	I-II		16	1874	Eis.Bedarf Nuremberg	For Germany. Became R 1036 in 1891.
25–35	WL	3	I-II		16	1874	Eis.Bedarf Berlin	For Germany. 27 destroyed in 1896.
36–39	WL	2/3			10	1874	Eis.Bedarf Berlin	3rd axle added 1886. 39 named *City of Rouen*. 36 became F 1022 in 1888. 37 became R 1001 in 1889. 38 and 40 destroyed in 1888.
40–41	WL	2			12	1875	Desouches	For Nord Rly., France. Not used on this rly. until 1879.
42	WL	3			12	1874	LCDR	Col. Mann design. Used Britain London-Edinburgh in 1875, Paris-Turin in 1878.
43	WS	3			20	1874	LCDR	Col. Mann design. Mann Co.'s only WS, with honeymoon compt. Used London-Dover (LCDR) in 1874–76. Rebuilt as WL 1888.
44–46	WL	3	I-II		16	1875	Eis.Bedarf Berlin	For Germany, identical to 25–35. 45 burnt at Vienna (Westbhf.) in 1891.
47–52	WL	2		8,000	10	1875	Simmering	For Austria. 47 in Paris-Irun in 1880; withdrawn in 1891. 48 and 49 to Spain in April 1883.
53	WL	3		13,740	14	1876	Eis.Bedarf Berlin	Last Mann Car. Sold in 1910.
54–62	WL	3		10,200	12	1877–78	Evrard	First CIWL order. 54 shown at Florence in 1877. 54–58 for France (PLM), Paris-Turin in 1878–79. 60 in Indian Mail (Calais-Bologna) in 1879. 55 and 59 later in Spain. 61 to Spain in 1902.

Car no.	Type	Axles	Class	Length excl. buffers	Seats or berths	Year	Builder	Remarks
63–64	WL	3		10,200	12	1878	Simmering	For Indian Mail, Calais-Bologna (connection for Brindisi).
65–73	WL	3		10,200	12	1878	Desouches	65 and 66 for Paris-Turin in 1879. 68 in Indian Mail (Calais-Bologna) in 1879. 65, 66 and 68 in Paris-Turin 1879. 72 and 73 to Spain for Madrid-Hendaye 1880. First Spanish gauge cars. 65, 67, 69 and 70 later in Spain.
74	WLM	3		12,940	14	1880	Van der Zyp	First mixed sleeper with ordinary compartments.
75	WL	4		15,080	16	1880	Dyle & Bac.	Louvain works. First CIWL bogie sleeper for Orient Exp. Withdrawn in 1908.
76–106	WL	3		13,025	14	1881–82	Rathgeber	First large standard order, with open platform vestibules and corridor. 76 believed to have been WLM like 94, which was WLM with 10 berths + 9 × I cl. ordinary seats. 78 and 80 to Spain in 1883 for Madrid-Seville and Madrid-Lisbon. 82, 83 and 85 painted white in 1902 in Tunis-Oran Exp. 102 numbered 0102 for I–II cl. service in Hungary and Roumania (perhaps the number got mixed up for cl.!).
107	WR	3		12,410	24	1882	Rathgeber	First CIWL dining car. For Marseilles-Nice.
108–110	WL	3			18	1883	Rathgeber	For Spain. Inaugurated Sud Exp. 3 Nov. 1887.
111–113	WLM	3		13,025	10	1883	Rathgeber	+ 9 × I cl. seats, like No. 94.
114–116	WR	3			24	1883	Rathgeber	Ex-Berlin-Anhalt Rly. 114 for Orient Exp. later in Spain with 116 in 1908–09. 115 burnt out at Oran (Morocco) in 1893.
115	WR	4				1894	WL–Saint-Ouen	Ex-FF 1033. Replaced No. 115 of 1883. Later in Sud Exp. (Spain), 1908–09.
117–120	WL	3			19	1883	Rathgeber	120 for Spain and Portugal. 8 armchairs in the corridor.
121–126	WL	4			25	1883	Rathgeber	Sud Exp. (France) in 1888, first dynamo trial by Mr. Timmins, a British engineer. 122 to Spain in 1893 for MZA (Madrid-Barcelona) as WLM 10 berths + 15 pl. I cl.
127–130	WLM	4	I-II		10	1883	Klett	4 × I cl. + 6 × II cl. berths + 6 × I + 12 × II cl. ordinary seats.
131–137	WL	4		15,620	18	1883	Marly	131 had closed vestibule and no gangway. 133 burnt in 1893; replaced in 1894.
133	WL	4		19,275	20	1894	CGC	Replaced 133 of 1893.

Compagnie Internationale des Wagons-Lits et des Grands Express Européens

Car no.	Type	Axles	Class	Length excl. buffers	Seats or berths	Year	Builder	Remarks (Belgian-French)
138–141	WR	3			24	1883	Rathgeber	138–140 ex-Berlin-Anhalt Rly. 139 inaugurated Sud Exp. (France) 3 Nov. 1887; became R 1101 in 1897. 140 in Sud Exp. (Spain) in 1908–09.
142–144	WL	4		15,620	18	1883	WL-Marly	For Orient Express. 144 had 20 pl. 143 and 144 in P&O Exp. (Calais-Brindisi) in 1891.
145–147	WL	4		14,120	20	1884	Savigliano	For Italy (Calais-Nice-Rome Exp). 147 was 15,620m long. 146 in Spain (MZA Madrid-Barcelona) 1893.
148	WR	4		17,020	37	1883	WL–Saint-Ouen	148–150 rebuilt from Austrian Imperial Train for Deauville Exp. (Paris-Trouville).
149–150	WRS	4			26	1883	WL–Saint-Ouen	+ 12 pl. smoking salon. See No. 148 above.
151–153	WRS	4		17,020	24	1882	WL-Marly	+ 12 pl. salon. For Orient Exp. 151 was 16,780m long. First CIWL production bogie diners.

Car no.	Type	Axles	Class	Length excl. buffers	Seats or berths	Year	Builder	Remarks
154	WL	4		14,120	20	1884–85	Savigliano	For Calais-Nice-Rome-Exp. Later in Spain 1893 (for MZA Madrid-Seville).
155	WS	4		17,994	19	1874	Pullman	Bought in 1884. Ex-*Victoria*. First bogie WS and first ex-Pullman car, for Amsterdam-Rotterdam. Bought from Pullman Palace Car Co. in Italy. Later rebuilt to WR 31 pl.
156–157	WS	4		16,990		1885	Rathgeber	For Amsterdam-Rotterdam. Late delivery. Later rebuilt to: WR 36 pl.
158–160	WL	4		14,120	20	1884	Rathgeber	160 was 15,620m long, 18 pl. In first CIWL dynamo-driven electrically lit train (Sud Exp. France) in 1888, designed by Mr. Timmins of England. 158 and 159 later (1893) in Spain (for MZA Madrid-Seville). 159 sold by auction at Irun in 1911.
161–163	WL	4		15,620	18	1884	WL-Marly	For France.
164–168	WRS	4		17,640	36	1885	WL-Marly	164 sold in 1903 to (CIWL subsidiary) Cie. Française des Wagons-Buffets (CFWB) No. 39.
169–72	WL	4		16,750	18	1885	Rathgeber	For Austria.
173–176	WR	4		16,780	36	1885	Rathgeber	Later in Spain 1893 (for MZA Madrid-Barcelona).
177–179	WR	4			36	1885	Klett	For France. 177 and 178 sold to CFWB in 1908 as Nos. 42 and 43.
180–182	WR	4		17,020	36	1886	WL-Marly	Became WRS in 1894. WR 24 pl. + 8 pl. salon. 182 for Switzerland. Later hired to CSWR/SSG in 1903.
183–186	WRS	4		17,020	24	1886	WL-Marly	+ 8 pl. salon. 183–185 to Spain in 1893 for MZA Madrid-Seville. 186 was WR 36 pl.; sold to CFWB in 1902 as No. 38.
187–188	WL	4		17,440	18	1886	Rathgeber	188 in Sud Exp. (France); electrically lit in 1888; withdrawn in 1911.
189–190	WL	4		17,440	18	1886	Nivelles	For France.
191	WLS	2			107	1878	Chevalier de Grenelle	Bought in 1886 from Duc de Castrie. Ex-Duc de Castrie's salon. Became R 1102 in 1897.
192–194	WR	4		17,020	36	1886	Klett	For Austria.
195–196	WRS	4	I-II	18,750	41	1887	Nivelles	I-II cl. saloons with bar. Reduced loading gauge for Ouest Rly. (France).
197	WR	4		17,240	34	1887	Nivelles	For Belgium.
198–207	WL	4		17,790		1876–77	Pullman	Bought from Pullman Palace Car Co. when services taken over in Italy in 1886. Continued to run with names. 201 built 1883; 202 built 1880. 201–203 were WR from 1888–94; then WL again. 199, 201 and 202 in P&O Exp. in 1891. 198 and 199 became WR in 1894; sold in 1905 to CFWB as Nos. 40 and 41. 207 later rebuilt to WR 30 pl.
208	WR	4		17,240	34	1887	Nivelles	For Belgium. Probably ordered at the same time as 197, but not numbered in sequence, owing to dual CIWL headquarters.
209–210	WS	4		16,474	26	1888	Ragheno	209 later rebuilt WR 30 pl. 210 WS 17 pl. × I, 5 × II ordinary compts.
211–215	WR	4	I-II	18,400	18	1887	Riga	For Russia. First cars with electric lighting. 211 in Trans-Siberian Exp. II cl. 213 Trans-Sib. Exp. I cl.
216–221	WL	4	I-II	17,790		1888	Pullman	Pullman type with 'sections' at first, later rebuilt. Delivered 1888. Milan-Florence in 1888. 218 burnt at Florence Stn. in 1890. Italian Royal Train in 1890. Ostend-Basle 1891–1902. All fitted vestibules in 1902 at WL-Ost. All except 221 withdrawn 1904; bought by a circus. 221 to Russia for China in 1902; dortoir Irkutsk staff 1908–14; to Harbin 1914; dortoir for staff in 1923–32; Sold in 1932.

(Belgian-French)

Car no.	Type	Axles	Class	Length excl. buffers	Seats or berths	Year	Builder	Remarks	(Belgian-French)
221	OBS	4				1913	Chinois	Hired from Chinese Eastern Rly. for Trans-Manchurian in 1923.	
0221	WL	4				1923	Chinois	Hired from Oussouri Rly. (Vladivostok-Kharbarosk).	
222–228	WL	4	I-II	18,400	18	1888	Riga	For Russia. 223 and 224 burnt in 1889; rebuilt at St. Petersburg in 1890. 223 and 228 for Trans-Sib. Exp. II cl.	
229–231	WR	4		17,240	34	1888	Lyons	229 and 231 to Spain in 1893 (MZA Madrid-Barcelona). 230 for Algeria.	
232	WR	4	I-II	17,468	36	1888	Lyons	For Algeria.	
233	WR	4	I-II	17,468		1888	Klett	For Austria.	
234–235	WL	4	I-II	18,400	18	1890	Riga	For Russia. 240 and 241, 10 pl.	
236–241	WL	4		16,300	18	1889	Desouches	236 to Spain in 1893 for MZA Madrid-Seville.	
242–244	WR	4				1889	Desouches	For Club Train (France). No kitchens. 242 in Nord Exp. in 1896 (Liège-Paris)	
245–248	WS	4		18,740	30	1889	Lyons	For Club Train (France). 246 and 247 were WLS, 17,500m long; later WL 15 pl. 245 later in Nord Exp. (Calais-Brussels).	
249–252	WR	4		18,740	30	1889	Lyons	249 sold 1896 to group of French Rlys.; became PR II (French Presidential Train). A second 249 built 1898; renum. 3100 in 1926. 252 later WR 35 pl.	
253–254	WL	4		16,300	18	1889	Rathgeber		
255–261	WS	4		18,740	34	1889	Nivelles	For Club Train (Eng.). 255–258 for LCDR; 259–261 for SER. Painted green. 1893 used for New York Exp. Paris-Cherbourg Trains Trans-atlantiques. 259–261 later WR 35 pl. 261 destroyed, accident at Rambouillet, in 1911.	
262–268	WL	4		17,320	18	1889	WL-Marly	263 in P&O Exp. in 1891. Later in Spain in 1893. 266 for Spain. Last cars built at WL-Marly before works handed over to CGC.	

Internationale Eisenbahn Schlafwagen Gesellschaft

Car no.	Type	Axles	Class	Length excl. buffers	Seats or berths	Year	Builder	Remarks	(German)
269	WS	4		19,600	26	1889	Nivelles	Burnt out at WL, Saint-Denis, in 1893.	
269	WS	4		18,340	26	1894	CGC	Replaced 269 of 1889; sold to group of French Rlys. Became PR I (in French Presidential Train).	
269	WS	4		19,740	26	1899	CGC	Replaced 269 of 1894.	
270	WRS	4		19,600	36	1889	Nivelles	Later became WR 42 pl.	
271	WL	4		17,520	18	1889	Nivelles	At Paris Exhibition in 1889.	
272–275	WR	4		17,440	36	1890	CGC		
276	WS	4			34	1890	CGC	For Russia. Later to China.	
277	WS	4		18,780		1890	Lyons	Used in France and Belgium. Later WR 36 pl.	
278–282	WR	4		18,780	36	1889	Lyons		
283	WRS	4		18,750	18	1890	Nivelles	+ 18 pl. salon.	
284–286	WL	4		17,435	16	1890	Jackson Shp.	For Switzerland (Gotthard Rly.).	
287–289	WL	4		19,255	20	1892	Jackson Shp.	For P&O Exp. (Calais-Brindisi).	

Car no.	Type	Axles	Class	Length excl. buffers	Seats or berths	Year	Builder	Remarks	(German)
290–292	WR	4		17,420	36	1892	Jackson Shp.	For P&O Exp. (Calais-Brindisi). 292 in Nord Exp. in 1896 (Ostend-Berlin).	
293–296	WR	4		17,430	30	1892	Rathgeber	For Austria. 293 later in Algeria.	
297–299	WR	4		17,420	34	1894	CGC	No kitchens. 298 in Spain. 297 and 299 in Algeria.	
300–313	WL	4		17.920	18	1890	Jackson Shp.	For Italy.	
314–322	WR	4		17,240	36	1890	Jackson Shp.	For Italy.	
323–330	WL	4		19,320	16	1892	Jackson Shp.	For Russia.	
331–335	WL	4		16,640	18	1892	Midland	For Spain. Open vestibules at first. First English-built sleeping cars for CIWL.	
336–340	WR	4		17,420	36	1892	Jackson Shp.		
341	WS							No. 341 WS was reserved for the 'Royal Saloon' which was numbered 501 when it emerged from the factory. So. No. 341 was not used for this or any other car.	
342–344	WL	4		19,255	20	1891	Jackson Shp.	For P&O Exp. Rebuilt to WL 16 pl. in 1924.	
345–346	WL	4		19,255	20	1892	CGC	For P&O Exp. Rebuilt to WL 16 pl. in 1924.	
347–349	WL	4		19,255	20	1891	Jackson Shp.	For P&O Exp. Rebuilt to WL 16 pl. in 1924.	
350–352	WRS	4		18,520	30	1892	Brown Marshalls	+ 7 pl. salon. For P&O Exp.	
353–354	WR	4		18,740	40	1891	WL-Irun	For Spain. 354 was 18,760m long.	
355–358	WL	4		17,420		1891	WL-Irun	For Portugal. Ex-CP. Resold to CP in 1913.	
359–366	WR	4		17,420	36	1893	Jackson Shp.	For Italy. 360 renum. 1360 in 1923.	
367–372	WLM	4		19,350	10	1893	Jackson Shp.	For Italy. 370–372 were WL 20 pl. 369–372 rebuilt to WL 16 pl. in 1920.	
373–380	WL	4		18,150	12	1877	WL-St. P'burg.	For Russia. Bought from Russian State Rlys. Reconstructed by WL-St. Petersburg in 1893.	
381–382	WR	4		14,615	30	1897	CGC	Rebuilt from FF 1027 and 1029 in 1897. 381 and 382 in Spain in 1905.	
383–385	WLM	4		18,500	12	1896	CGC	Rebuilt to WL 16 pl. in 1920.	
386–388	WLM	4		18,500	10	1896	CGC	383–388 later all rebuilt to 16 pl.	
389–392	WRS	4		17,640	24	1894	Ringhoffer	+ 8 pl. salon. Renum. 1389–1392 in 1923.	
393–396	WRS	4		17,640	24	1894	CGC	+ 8 pl salon. Renum. 1393–1396 in 1923. 1396 was stores van, Ankara, in 1966.	
397–400	WL	4		18,120	18	1894	CGC	For France.	
401	WR	4		18,130	36	1894	CGC	For France. Destroyed in accident in 1913.	
402–404	WLM	4		18,130	10	1894	CGC		
405–407	WLM	4		19,370	10	1894	CGC	Rebuilt to WL 16 pl. in 1920.	
408–410	WL	4			25	1892	Off. Mech.	For Sicily. Pullman type with US-style 'sections'. Later rebuilt.	
411–413	WL	4		19,500	16	1895	CGC		
414–415	WLM	4		19,370	10	1894	CGC	Rebuilt to WL 16 pl. in 1920.	
416–419	WL	4		19,740	18	1896	CGC	For Nord Exp.	
420–426	WR	4		19,600	42	1896	CGC	425 in Bombay Exp. (Calais-Marseilles) in 1899. 426 built 1897.	
427	WRS	4		17,640	24	1894	CGC	+ 8 pl. salon. Later WR 36 pl.	
428–432	WL	4		19,275	20	1894	CGC	431 destroyed 1922. Rest later in Algeria.	
433	WR	4		18,640	36	1894	CGC	No kitchen. Burnt out at Gourville (France) in 1911.	
434–438	WL	4		19,370	17	1894	Breslau	For Ostend-Vienna Exp. To Mitropa 1916–20 except 436. Renumbered 3101–3105 in 1927.	

Car no.	Type	Axles	Class	Length excl. buffers	Seats or berths	Year	Builder	Remarks (German)
439–442	WL	4		19,370	17	1894	Klett	For Ostend-Vienna Exp. 441 and 442 to Mitropa in 1916–20. Renum. 3106–3109 in 1927.
443–447	WRS	4		17,640	24	1894	Ringhoffer	+ 8 pl. salon. For Ostend-Vienna Exp. Later WR, 36 pl.
448–452	WR	4			16	1894	Russian Rlys.	For Russia. Bought 1894 from Russian State Rlys. Used Moscow-Brest Litvosk.
453–455	WL	4		19,370	18	1895	Ringhoffer	Renum. 3110–3112 in 1927.
456	WL	4		19,740	18	1896	Klett	Renum. 3113 in 1927.

Compagnia Internazionale delle Carrozze con Letti e dei Grandi Treni Espressi Europei

Car no.	Type	Axles	Class	Length excl. buffers	Seats or berths	Year	Builder	Remarks (Italian)
457–467	WL	4		19,740	18	1896	CGC	457–360 and 464 for Nord-Exp. 458 and 460–465 renum. (in 1927) 3115, 3117, 3122, 3119, 3120, 3118 and 3121. 457 built 1895.
468–475	WL	4		20,500	20	1896	CGC	For Russia.
476–478	WRS	4		19,600	24	1896	CFC	+ 12 pl. salon.
479–483	WR	4		19,600	42	1897	CGC	For France.
484–489	WL	4		19,740	16	1896	Ringhoffer	489 to Mitropa in 1916–20. 484–486 renum. 3125–3127 in 1927. 485 and 486 were 18 pl., later 16 pl.
490	WRS	4		19,600	24	1897	CGC	+ 12 pl. salon.
491–494	WR	4		19,600	42	1897	CGC	For France.
495	WR	4		19,600	42	1897	Klett	For Germany.
496–500	WR	4		19,600	42	1897	CGC	497 and 498 were WRS; later WR 40 pl. 497 renum. 10 in Duplicate List in 1898. 500 in Bombay Exp. in 1898.
501	WLS	4		18,620	8	1892	Brown Marshalls	'Royal Saloon' until sold 1896 to group of France Rlys. 8 berths + 9 pl. salon. Became PR III in French Presidential Train.
502–503	WR	4		19,600	42	1897	CGC	502 and 503 renum. 3129 and 3130 in 1927.
507–516	WL	4		19,740	18	1897	CGC	512–514 in Bombay Exp. in 1902. 514 in P&O Exp. in 1901. 515 destroyed in derailment at Sarrebourg in 1922. 507–514 renum. 3131–3138, and 516 renum. 3139 in 1927.
517	WR	4		19,580	42	1897	CGC	For Russia; later in China.
518–532	WL	4		19,740	18	1897–98	Ringhoffer	518–528 for Nord-Sud Exp. Carried name round WL badge on waist. 520 and 522–528 renum. 3142–3149 in 1927.
533–538	WL	3		14,800	14	1899	Ringhoffer	For Vienna-Cracow, later in Turkey.
539	WRS	4		19,600	24	1897	CGC	+ 12 pl. salon. Renum. 3150 (WR 42 pl.) in 1927.
540–543	WR	4		19,600	42	1897	CGC	540 and 541 in Bombay Exp. in 1901–02. 542 renum. 3152 in 1927.
544–549	WL	4		19,740	18	1899	CGC	For Nord Exp. 546 and 547 in Egypt. 545, 548 and 549 renum. 3155, 3158 and 3159 in 1927.

Car no.	Type	Axles	Class	Length excl. buffers	Seats or berths	Year	Builder	Remarks (Italian)
550–552	WR	4		19,580	42	1897	CGC	For Russia. 551 was WRS–WR 24 pl. + 12 pl. salon.
553–567	WL	4		19,740	18	1898	Klett	For Germany. 553–557 and 564–567 to Mitropa in 1916–20. 553–557 and 559–567 renum. 3161–3174 in 1927.
568–573	WRS	4		19,600	24	1897	Klett	+ 12 pl. salon. For Germany. Renum. 3175–3180 in 1927.
574–577	WR	4		19,740	36	1899	CGC	Renum. 3181, 3157 and 3156 in 1928.
578–579	WR	4		19,740	42	1898	CGC	For Switzerland.
580	WR	4		19,720	40	1898	CGC	For Switzerland.
581–587	WL	4		19,740	18	1898	Ringhoffer	582 and 584–587 renum. 3182 and 3184–3187 in 1926–28.
588–591	WLM	4		19,740	8	1898	Ringhoffer	+ 6 pl. I cl. Or + 8 pl. II cl. 590 and 591 renum. 3190 and 3191 in 1926.
592–593	WL	4		19,740	18	1898	CGC	For Egypt. First WL in Egypt. Painted white.
594–597	WR	4		19,740	42	1898	CGC	594 and 595 for Nord Exp. 594 later in Turkey.
598	WRS	4		19,720	24	1898	CGC	+ 12 pl. salon for Nord Exp. (Russia).
599–600	WR	4		19,740	42	1898	CGC	For Nord Exp. 599 later in Turkey.
601–606	WRS	4		19,740	32	1898	CGC	+ 8 pl. salon. 601 for Orient Exp. 604 burnt out at Belgrade in 1928.
607–612	WL	4		19,740	18	1899	Breslau	For Nord Exp. 609–612 acquired by Mitropa 1916–20.
613–614	WL	4		19,740	18	1898	CGC	For Egypt. Painted white.
615–620	WL	4		19,740	18	1899	Eis.Bedarf Görlitz	615 renum. 3195 for Nord Exp. in 1929.
621–630	WL	4		20,500	20	1899	CGC	For Russia.
631–644	WL	4		19,740	18	1899	CGC	For Calais-Méditerannée Exp. 641, 643 and 644 for Nord Exp. 631–636, 639 and 640 renum. 2684–2691 in 1923. 643 renum. 3196 in 1925. 638 later in Algeria; destroyed at Argel.
645–646	WR	4		19,740	42	1899	CGC	645 for Nord Exp. renum. 3197 in 1929.
647–666	WL	4		19,740	18	1900	CGC	660–665 painted brown and cream. 658 in Bombay Exp. in 1902. 662–664 in P&O Exp. in 1903. 663 and 664 in Bombay Exp., accident at Montelimar in 1906. 659 renum. 3194 in 1927. 660–663 renum. 3198–3201 in 1925–26.
667–676	WR	4		19,740	42	1899	CGC	669 in Egypt in 1902. 670 destroyed in Sud Exp. accident at St. Geours in 1900. 672 in Bombay Exp. in 1902. 674 destroyed in 1904.
677	WS	4		19,720	30	1899	CGC	For Portugal (Lisbon-Porto). Later WR 40 pl.
678	WR	4		19,720	40	1899	CGC	For Spain.
679	WR	4		19,740	40	1901	CGC	Later WR 50 pl.
680	WL	4		19,740	18	1900	Ringhoffer	Bombay Exp. in 1909. 680 and 681 believed shown at Paris Exhibition in 1900 (Austrian Pavilion).
681	WRS	4		19,740	22	1900	Ringhoffer	+ 10 pl. salon. See No. 680 (above).
682–691	WL	4		20,480	18	1900	CGC	For Russia. 682, 684 and 686 later in Estonia. 685 later in Latvia.
692–697	WR	4		20,840	42	1900	CGC	For Russia. 693, 695 and 696 later in Finland. Became VR Nos. 2001, 2002 and 2005.
698–712	WL	4		19,740	18	1900	Ringhoffer	For Trains de Luxe. 699, 701 and 711 in Wien-Cannes Exp. 702 in Orient Exp. 707 and 708 in Riviera Exp. 700 to Mitropa in 1916–20.
713–714	WL	4		21,280	18	1900	CGC	For Russia (I cl.). 714 shown at Paris Exhibition, 1900.

Compania Internacional de Coches-Camas
y de los Grandes Expresos Europeos

Car no.	Type	Axles	Class	Length excl. buffers	Seats or berths	Year	Builder	Remarks (Spanish)
715–718	WL	4	II	21,280	26	1900	CGC	For Russia.
719–723	WR	4		19,800	36	1900	CGC	For Russia (Trans-Siberian Exp). 723 shown at Paris Exhibition, 1900. 722 and 723 for Nord Exp. (Wirballen-St. Petersburg).
724	WRS	4		21,280	42	1900	CGC	For Russia (Trans-Siberian). Shown Paris Exhibiton, 1900. Salon de Luxe 6 pl. Became WR later.
725	WLS	4		21,280	12	1900	CGC	For Russia. I cl. salon with barbershop and gymnasium. Shown Paris Exhibition, 1900.
726–740	WR	4		19,740	42	1900	Ringhoffer	726–728 were 40 pl. 728 for Switzerland. 729–734 in Nord Exp. (Ostend-Wirballen).
741–744	WS	4		17,650	30	1889	Dyle & Bac.	+ 12 pl. salon. Ex-French Line (CGT) saloons built in 1889. 744 became FC 1177 in 1907.
745–746	WR	4		17,640	36	1889	Dyle & Bac.	Ex French Line (CGT) saloons built in 1889. Sold to CFWB in 1913 as Nos. 44 and 45.
747–752	WL	4		19,740	18	1900	Breslau	For Riviera Exp. (Berlin-Ventimiglia). 747 renum. 3151 in 1927. 748 renum. 3207 in 1928. 752 to Mitropa in 1916–20.
753–756	WR	4		19,740	42	1900	Breslau	753 for Russia.
757–758	WR	4		16,300	40	1900	WL-Irun	For Spain.
759	WR	4		19,740	40	1900	Miani	For Meridionale Rly. Shown at Paris Exhibition, 1900 (Italian Pavilion).
760–762	WLM	4		20,810	12	1900	Miani	+ ordinary compts. For Italy.
763–765	WR	4		19,830	36	1899	Ringhoffer	For Egypt. Double roof, etc., and air-conditioning with ice blocks.
766–768	WL	4		19,830	16	1899	Ringhoffer	For Egypt.
769	WLM	4		19,350	14	1900	Miani	For Berlin-Constantinople. Ordinary compts. Marked 'CO C*' (Oriental Rlys.). Later rebuilt WL 16 pl.
770–773	WS	4		19,740	30	1903	CGC	For Sud Exp. (France). Later Vichy Exp.; later Trouville Exp.
774–777	WR	4		19,740	56	1902	CGC	774 and 777 in Bombay Exp. in 1915. Renum. 3202–3205 in 1929.
778	WL	4		19,830	16	1900	CGC	For Egypt. Shown at Paris Exhibition, 1900 (French Pavilion).
779–788	WL	4		19,740	18	1900	Ganz	For Berlin-Budapest Orient Exp. Berlin-Constantinople in 1900–02. 779, 782 and 786–788 later in Riviera Exp. Berlin-Ventimiglia. 786 destroyed in 1927.
789–793	WRS	4		19,740	24	1900	Ganz	+ 12 pl. salon 792 in Nord Exp. (Jeumont-Liège).
794–795	WR	4		19,740	40	1900	Miani	794 renum. 3214 in 1928.
796–800	WL	4		21,280	18	1900	CGC	For Russia. 799 had compt. for 6 servants.
801–803	WL	4	II	21,280	26	1900	CGC	For Russia.
804	WR	4		19,800	36	1900	CGC	For Russia.
805–810	WR	4		20,840	42	1900	CGC	For Russia. 806 and 807 for St. Petersburg–Warsaw (-Cannes) Exp.
811–812	WR	4		19,830	36	1900	Ringhoffer	For Egypt. Air-conditioning like 763–765.
813–814	WR	2		15,440	32	1902	PLM	PLM Algiers works. For Algeria.
815–817	WR	4		19,740	40	1902	CGC	816 renum. 3206 in 1927.

Car no.	Type	Axles	Class	Length excl. buffers	Seats or berths	Year	Builder	Remarks	(Spanish)
818–820	WR	4		19,740	40	1902	CGC	With guard's 'birdcage' lookout for Sud Exp. (France). 818 renum. 3208 in 1925.	
821–825	WL	4		19,740	18	1902	Breslau	For Riviera Exp. (Amsterdam-Ventimiglia). Later WL 16 pl. 822 to Mitropa in 1916–20.	
826–830	WL	4		19,740	18	1902	Klett	For Riviera Exp. (Berlin-Ventimiglia).	
831–837	WL	4		19,740	18	1902	Ringhoffer	834 renum. 3213 in 1928. 835 withdrawn 1931 (accident, Port Bou).	
838–839	WR	4		16,300	40	1902	WL-Irun	For Sud Exp. (Spain) 839 had 32 pl.	
840–842	WS	4		19,740	30	1903	Ringhoffer	With guard's 'birdcage' lookout for Sud Exp. (France). 842 was WRS (R 26 pl.); sold in 1918; repurchased in 1921; withdrawn in 1930.	
843–848	WL	4		19,740	18	1903	CGC	For Sud Exp. (Spain). Later WL 16 pl. Sold to MZA as WLM Nos. AAC 45–50, RENFE Nos. 345–350; used in film *Dr. Zhivago*. No CIWL emblem.	
849–860	WR	4		21,280	36	1903	Upper-Volga	For Russia.	
861–866	WLM	4	I-II	21,280	10	1905	Upper-Volga	+ 10 × II cl. berths. For Russia.	
867–883	WL	4		21,280	17	1905	Upper-Volga	For Russia. 867–869 and 871–872 in Nord Exp. (Russia). 874 and 875 in St. Petersburg–Warsaw (-Cannes) Exp. 877 later in China (Manchuria). 882 later in Estonia.	
884–890	WL	4	II	21,280	26	1905	Upper-Volga	887 later in China (Manchuria).	
891–900	WLM	4		21,280	10	1905	Upper-Volga	+ 10 × II cl. for Russia. 896 later in China.	
901–904	WL	4	R	19,740	18	1903	CGC	'Calais Peninsular & Oriental Express Brindisi' on cantrail, not CIWL name, for P&O Exp. Later R Cl. 16 pl. 901 rebuilt to R3 for Portugal in 1921. All to Spain in 1922. Later all sold to Norte Rly. as WLM (904 as WL), retaining CIWL emblem.	
905–908	WL OBS	4		19,740	26	1903	CGC	Wagons-salons (observation cars) for Berlin-Karlsbad Exp. 905 and 906 in Tzar Nicholas II Special Paris-Berthelon (Loudun), in 1912.	
909–910	WR	4		19,740	52	1903	CGC	For Sud Exp. (France). 909 in Bombay Exp. Montelimar Accident in 1906 (survived). Renum. 3209 and 3210 in 1927 and 1926.	
911	WS	4		19,740	30	1904	CGC	With guard's 'birdcage' lookout and Sud Exp. (France) in 1903–04. In Simplon Orient Exp. in 1921 (Milan-Trieste).	
912	WS	4		19,740	26	1904	CGC	For special services. Used by US General Pershing in Berlin-Karlsbad Exp. in 1918.	
913–918	WL	4		19,740	18	1903	CGC	913 in Portugal. 914–917 in Bombay Exp. in 1906–09. 916 in Montelimar accident, in 1906. 914–918 to Spain in 1922.	
919–921	WR	4		19,740	40	1904	CGC	919 renum. 3219 in 1928.	
922–932	WR	4		21,280	36	1905–06	Upper-Volga	For Russia. 922 in St. Petersburg-Warsaw (-Cannes) Exp. 928 and 932 later in China.	
933–941	WL	4		21,280	17	1905	Upper-Volga	For Russia.	

Det Internationale Sovevogns- og de Store Europaeiske Eksprestogs-Selskab

Car no.	Type	Axles	Class	Length excl. buffers	Seats or berths	Year	Builder	Remarks	(Danish)
942–943	WLM	4		21,280	10	1905	Upper-Volga	10 × II cl. For Russia.	
944	WR	4		19,830	36	1903	Ringhoffer	For Egypt.	
945	WL	4		19,830	16	1903	Ringhoffer	For Egypt.	
946–947	WL	4		20,490	20	1903	Bres	For Denmark. Bought from Mecklenburg Rlys. in 1906 (previously staffed by CIWL). To Mitropa 1916–20.	
948–949	WR	4		19,740	52	1904	CGC	Renum. 3222–3229 in 1929.	
950–955	WR	4		19,740	40	1904	CGC		
956–965	WS	4		19,740	30	1904	CGC	For Sud Exp. (France). Also used for Savoy Exp. (Paris–Aix-les-Bains). 958 and 959 later in Spain. 957, 960 and 961 in Simplon Orient Exp. (Vinkovci-Bucharest) in 1921. 960–965 renum. 2983–2988 in 1927.	
966	WL	4		20,490	20	1904	Bres	For Denmark. Bought from Mecklenburg State Rlys. in 1906.	
967–976	WL	4		20,320	18	1904	CGC	For France. 967 and 969–975 in Bombay Exp. in 1909–19. 973 and 974 painted brown and cream. 973 destroyed Buchs (Switzerland) in 1931. 974 renum. 3234 in 1928.	
977–986	WL	4		20,320	18	1905	Diatto	For Italy, 977 disappeared 1917; 'withdrawn' in 1923. 986 destroyed in 1919.	
987	WR	4		19,830	36	1904	Ringhoffer	For Egypt. Air-conditioned like 763 and 765.	
988–992	WL	4		20,320	18	1905	CGC	For France. 992 in Bombay Exp. in 1919.	
993–995	WR	4		16,300	40	1905	WL-Irun	For Spain. Withdrawn in 1940, 1925 and 1933.	
996–997	WR	2		13,550	32	1905	Ringhoffer	For Tunisia. Bogies added in 1916.	
998–999	WR	6		21,150	46	1905	CGC	999 painted brown and cream, shown at Liège Exhibition in 1905.	
1000	WL	6		21,150	17	1905	CGC	Painted brown and cream; shown at Liège Exhibition in 1905.	
1001–1004	F	2		8,160		1883	WL-Marly	1001 built in 1883; destroyed at Paris Austerlitz in 1888; number reused in 1889. 1002–1004 in P&O Exp. (Indian Mail) in 1892–1903.	
1001	R	3				1889	WL-Marly	Chassis of WL 37.	
1005–1007	F	3		12,160		1884	Rathgeber	For Orient Exp.	
1008–1015	F	3		12,160		1885	Ragheno	1011 destroyed in Orient Exp. accident in 1910.	
1016–1017	F	3				1885	Klett	Ex-WL 18 and 19. 1016 in Sud Exp. with electric light.	
1018	F	2		9,600		1888	WL–Saint-Ouen	Ex-WL 2 destroyed Sud Exp. (France) accident at St. Geours in 1900 (near Dax).	
1019–1021	F	2		9,600		1888	Klett	Ex-WL 3, 4 and 5. 1020 first fourgon with Timmins dynamo in 1888, Sud Exp. (France).	
1022–1023	F	2		900		1888	WL–Saint-Ouen	Ex-WL 36, 1 for Spain. Believed in Sud Exp. (Spain).	
1024–1026	FC	2		8,345		1889	WL-Marly	For Club Train (France) FC for WRS 242–244.	
1027–1028	FF	4		16,615		1889	Ragheno	Fourgons-fumoirs for Club Train (England) LC & DR train. Painted green. 1027 and 1029 rebuilt as WS 381 and 382 in 1894.	
1029–1030	FF	4		16,615		1889	Braine le Comte	For Club Train (England). For the SER Club Train.	
1031–1033	FF	4		16,615		1889	Ragheno	Chassis of 1033 became WR 115 in 1894, in place of WR 115, destroyed at Oran in 1893.	
1034–1035	F	2		8,520		1892	Brown Marshalls	For P&O Exp. (Calais-Brindisi).	
1036	R	2				1891	WL-Marly	Ex-WL 24.	

Car no.	Type	Axles	Class	Length excl. buffers	Seats or berths	Year	Builder	Remarks	(Danish)
1037–1040	F	3		12,400		1892	Jackson Shp.	1037 and 1039 in P&O Exp. 1038 in Orient Exp.; later in P&O Exp.	
1041–1044	F	2		8,520		1892	Brown Marshalls	For P&O Exp.	
1045–1048	F	2		8,520		1894	CGC		
1049	R	2				1894	WL–Saint-Ouen	Ex-WL 16.	
1050–1053	F	2		8,520		1894	Dyle & Bac	Louvain works. For P&O Exp.	
1054–1058	F	3		12,520		1894	Dyle & Bac	Louvain works. For P&O Exp.	
1059–1065	FP	3		12,520		1896	Klett	1060 and 1061 for Wien-Cannes Exp. 1065 for Nord-Sud Exp. (painted on waist centre); destroyed 1933. 1062 in Bombay Exp. in 1909; repainted blue in 1922 for Train Bleu. 1059, 1063 and 1065 in Bombay Exp. in 1915.	
1066–1068	F	3		12,520		1896	Klett	Open platform at one end. 1066 in Bombay Exp. in 1915. 1067 for Wien-Cannes Exp. in 1896.	
1069–1072	F	3		12,520		1896	Ringhoffer	1071 and 1072 for Vienna-Cannes Exp.	
1073–1077	F	4		19,740		1898	CGC	For Riviera Exp. 1073–1076 repainted blue for Train Bleu inaugural journey in 1922.	
1078	F	4		19,740		1898	CGC	For Russia (Trans-Siberia Exp.). Barbershop, gymnasium, etc. Later in Nord Exp. (Russia, Wirballen–St. Petersburg).	
1079–1082	F	4		19,740		1898	CGC	For Nord Exp. 1080 and 1082 renum. F 1306 and 1307 in 1929.	
1083–1085	F	3		12,520		1898	CGC	For Bombay Exp. 1083 and 1084 in Tzar Nicholas II Special Train to watch manoeuvres (3 days) at Berthelon (Loudun), from Paris in 1912.	
1086–1088	F	4		19,740		1899	CGC	For Nord Exp. Renum. F 1308, 1303 and 1304 in 1928–29. 1304 in Spain.	
1089–1094	FP	4		19,740		1898	Ringhoffer	1094 in Nord Exp. 1089–1094 renum. 1297, 1299, 1300, 1301, 1298 and 1302 in 1929, without postal compartment.	
1095–1100	F	3		12,520		1896	Ringhoffer	1095 and 1097 painted blue for Train Bleu inaugural journey in 1922.	
1101	R	3				1897	Dyle & Bac	Bordeaux works. Ex-WR 139 withdrawn 1927.	

Companhia Internacional das Carruagens-Camas e dos Grandes Expressos Europeus

Car no.	Type	Axles	Class	Length excl. buffers	Seats or berths	Year	Builder	Remarks	(Portuguese)
1102	R	2				1897	Dyle & Bac	Bordeaux works. Ex-WL 191. Withdrawn in 1927.	
1103	F	4		19,740		1898	CGC	For Russia (Trans-Siberian). Barbershop and gymnasium like 1078.	
1104–1108	F	4		19,740		1898/1900	CGC	1105–1108 for Nord Exp. (Paris-Warsaw, and Ostend-Wirballen). 1105 and 1106 were FP. 1108 in Sud Exp. (France) in 1926. 1104, 1106 and 1108 renum. 1309–1311 in 1929. Believed painted chocolate and cream Pullman colours for Sud Exp. until 1932.	
1109–1110	F	4		21,280		1900	CGC	For Russia. Trans-Siberian Exp. Generator, showerbath, and 8-berth WL staff compt.	
1111	R	2				1900	Ringhoffer		
1112	F	4		13,600		1900	Ringhoffer	For Wien-Cannes Exp. In Bombay Exp. in 1919.	
1113–1115	F	4		13,600		1900	CGC	For Wien-Cannes Exp. 1113 and 1115 repainted blue for Train Bleu in 1922.	

Car no.	Type	Axles	Class	Length excl. buffers	Seats or berths	Year	Builder	Remarks (Portuguese)
1116–1118	F	4		12,600		1900	Weimar	1116 was 12,520m long and FP. In Bombay Exp. in 1919.
1119	FP	4		19,740		1900	Weimar	Renum. 1305 in 1928.
1120–1124	F	4		19,740		1900	Ganz	For Berlin-Budapest-Orient Exp. in 1900–1902. Later in Ostend-Vienna-Orient Exp. 1120 and 1122–1124 renum. 1312–1315 in 1929.
1125	F	4		19,740		1900	Weimar	For Nord Exp. (Paris-Wirballen). Renum. 1316 in 1929.
1126–1128	F	4		21,280		1900	CGC	For Russia. 1126 in Nord Exp. (St. Petersburg-Wirballen); 1127 and 1128 in St. Petersburg-Warsaw (-Cannes) Exp. All with generator, showerbath, etc., like 1109–1110.
1129–1130	R	2				1901	CGC	
1131–1133	F	4		17,640		1902	CGC	Renum. F 1317–1319 ±n. in 1930. 1133 in Sud Exp. (France) in 1926.
1134–1135	F	2				1902	PLM	Bought from PLM (Algiers) for Tunis-Oran Exp. Painted white. Resold later to PLM (Algiers).
1136–1145	F	3		13,600		1902	Klett	1145 in Bombay Exp. in 1909. 1138, 1139 and 1142–1145 were FC in Turkey for Simplon Orient Exp. in 1930.
1146–1154	F	4		21,280		1904	Upper-Volga	For Russia. With generator. 1148, 1149 and 1152 for Nord Exp. (Warsaw-Moscow).
1155	F	3		10,560		1902	WL-Irun	Ex-WL 61. For Spain.
1156–1162	F	4		21,280		1905	Upper-Volga	For Russia. With generator for Trans-Siberian Exp.
1163	F	4		17,640		1906	CGC	In Bombay Exp. in 1933–35.
1164–1176	F	4		19,740		1906–07	Ringhoffer	1165 was FP. 1170–1172 and 1176 were 17,640m long. 1164 and 1166–1168 for Riviera Exp. (Berlin-Ventimiglia). 1173–1175 for Orient Exp. 1164 and 1167 used in Paris-Calais Pullman trial trip in 1925 (see Chap 13). 1170 and 1176 later in Spain. 1170 chassis used for 1244 in 1926. 1171 in Spain; stores van WL-Irun in 1959.
1177	FC	4		16,500		1907	CGC	For Club Train (France). Ran with WRS 245. Ex-WRS 744. Later in Trains Transatlantiques.
1178–1187	FP	4		19,740		1908	Ragheno	For Ostend-Vienna Exp. 1185 was FP in Yugoslavia in 1945.
1188–1198	F	4		19,740		1908	Weyer	1196–1198 for Denmark. 1190 in Bombay Exp. in 1933–35.
1199–1200	F	4		19,740		1907	Ringhoffer	For Orient Exp. 1200 was FP with one open platform.
1201–1202	F	4		19,740		1908	Weyer	
1203–1207	F	4		19,740		1908	Ringhoffer	1202 for Riviera-Exp. 1204–1207 for Warsaw-Wien-Cannes Exp.
1208–1211	F	4		19,740		1910	CGC	
1212–1221	F	4		19,740		1909	Crede	
1222	F	4		17,640		1911	Beasain	For Spain. Stores Van WL-Aravaca (Madrid) in 1959.
1223–1235	F	4		19,740		1912–13	Credé	
1236–1243								Series not built due to World War I. So nos. not used.
1244	F	4		17,640		1926	Beasain	For Spain. Ex-1170. Stores van WL-Irun in 1959.
1245–1256	F	4		23,452		1926–27	CGC (Marly)	With 8-berth staff compts. 1245–1252 for Nord Exp. (Paris-Riga). All sold to *Paris Presse* in 1956.
1257	F	4		20,400		1926	CGC	Ex-WR 2092.
1258	F	4		20,360		1926	WL-Greco	Ex-WL 1772.
1259	F	2		7,425		1926	Beasain	For Spain.
1260–1262	FT	4		17,512		1927	Blanc Miss	For *Flèche d'Or*. Container trucks, centre staff/guard's compt. painted blue and cream (chocolate and cream to 1932). Carried 4 British SR containers. 1260 and 1261

Car no.	Type	Axles	Class	Length excl. buffers	Seats or berths	Year	Builder	Remarks (Portuguese)
								withdrawn 1955. 1261 and 1262 stored WL–Villeneuve-Prairie in 1959. 1262 became axle transport wagon; WL-VP (not permitted to run over SNCF) until withdrawn in 1965.
1263–1276	F	4		20,800		1928–29	Metro	Steel body. Some originally blue and cream for Pullman trains. 1272 in P&O Overland Exp. (Calais-Marseilles Joliette) in 1937–39. 1271–1276 to Spain for Sud Exp. Portugal as FP Irun-Lisbon. 1272 still running in Sud Exp. in 1980 in WL livery, though WL-Postman's service ended in 1976.
1277–1296	F	4		20,800		1929	Metro	Steel body. With showers for Simplon Orient and Rome Exp. 1283 used in film *Murder on the Orient Exp.* 1974 sold to Intraflug for Nost. Orient Exp. in 1978 (stored WL-Vienna). 1295 stores van WL–Villeneuve-Prairie in 1959.
1297–1304	F	4				1927–30	CGC	WL-SD old fourgons renum. For details see above. 1303 in Bombay Exp. 1933–35.
1305–1319	F	4				1927–30	CGC	1308 stores van WL-Rome in 1959. 1311 stores van WL-SD in 1959. 1312 in Yugoslavia in 1945.
1320–1325	RF	4		23,452		1939–40	CGC Marly	For Taurus Exp. Ex-WL 1893–97 and 1902. 1 baggage and 3 postal compts. for Turkey, Syria/Egypt and Iraq. Also 1 sleeping compt. for the WL-Postman.
1326–1359								Nos. not used.
1360	WR	4		17,420	42	1923	WL-NA	Ex-WR 360 of 1893.

ΔΙΕΝΘΗΣ ΕΤΑΡΙΑ ΤΩΝ ΚΛΙΝΑΜΑΞΩΝ ΚΑΙ ΤΩΝ ΤΑΧΕΙΩΝ ΕΥΡΩΠΑΙΚΩΝ ΑΜΑΞΟΣΤΟΙΧΙΩΝ

Car no.	Type	Axles	Class	Length excl. buffers	Seats or berths	Year	Builder	Remarks (Greek)
1361–1388								Nos. not used.
1389–1396	WR	4		17,640	42	1923	WL-Neu Aubing	Ex-WR 389–396. 1396 store for PR (running repairs) Ankara in 1966.
1397–1500								Nos. not used.
1501–1510	WS	4		19,740	41	1898	Nivelles	For Belgium. CIWL title in Flemish on 1 side obligatory. To replace I cl. SNCB coaches on internal trains, also Amsterdam-Mons Exp. (Note: The Nord refused this Train de Luxe of WS and WR between Paris and Mons [in Belgium the Nord Belge subsidiary ran to Mons, from Maubeuge]). 1515 shown at Paris Exhibition in 1900 (Belgian Pavilion). 1536, 1537, 1539–1541 in Sud Exp. (France) in 1899–1900 (borrowed). In Belgium the WS had buffets, removed for use in Sud Exp. 1537 and 1552 in Sud Exp. accident at St. Geours in 1900. 1501–1541 and 1543–1545 sold to SNCB in 1901 but continued to be staffed and run by CIWL. 1542 sent back to France, became WR 48 pl. in 1905. 1546 and 1550 became WR 44 pl. in 1910. 1547–1549 and 1553 to Spain and Portugal.
1511–1515	WS	4		19,740	41	1898–99	Ragheno	
1516–1520	WS	4		19,740	41	1898	Braine le Comte	
1521–1530	WS	4		19,740	35	1899	Miani	
1531–1545	WS	4		19,740	34	1899	CGC	
1546–1553	WS	4		19,740	35	1899	Miani	
1554–1599								Nos. not used.
1600–1605	WR	4		19,740	40	1905	CGC	1603 for Riviera Exp. in 1909.
1606–1611	WR	4		19,740	40	1905	Ringhoffer	1606 later in Algeria. 1608–1610 for Riviera Exp. in 1909. 1609–1611 became WR bar 24 pl. in Latvia.

Car no.	Type	Axles	Class	Length excl. buffers	Seats or berths	Year	Builder	Remarks	(Greek)
1612–1618	WL	4		20,320	18	1905	Ringhoffer	For Wien-Cannes Exp.	
1619–1632	WL	4		20,320	18	1905	CGC	1620 renum. 3246 in 1928. 1624 and 1625 later in Morocco. 1624 and 1626–1632 in Bombay Exp. in 1919.	
1633–1637	WR	4		19,740	40	1905	CGC	Painted brown and cream. 1635 in Morocco later.	
1638–1642	WR	4		19,740	40	1905	Van der Zyp	For Germany. 1638–1641 'acquired' by Mitropa (Nos. 901–904) in 1916. 1642 in Finland; renum. 2019; sold in 1959.	
1643–1647	WR	4		19,740	40	1905	Weyer	For Germany. 1643–1645 and 1647 'acquired' by Mitropa (Nos. 905–908) in 1916. 1646(?) in Estonia.	
1648–1649	WR	4		19,830	36	1905	Ringhoffer	For Egypt. Air-conditioned like 987.	
1650	WRS	4		19,740	34	1907	Nesseldorf	+ 12 pl. salon. For Orient Exp.	
1651–1653	WR	4		20,320	40	1906	Ringhoffer	1651 was special design.	
1654–1656	WR	4		16,300	40	1906	WL-Irun	For Spain.	
1657–1661	WL	4		20,320	20	1906–07	Off. Mech.	For Italy. 1657 shown at Milan Fair. Pullman type with 'sections'; later rebuilt.	
1662–1669	WR	4		20,320	40	1906–07	Off. Mech.	For Italy.	
1670–1673	WLM	4		20,320	12	1906	Diatto	+ ordinary comps.	
1674–1676	WLM	4		20,320	12	1906	Ringhoffer	+ ordinary compts.	
1677–1678	WS	4		19,740	30	1906	CGC	For France (Sud Exp. Paris-Biarritz portion) and Paris-Trouville Exp. Later in Simplon Orient Exp. (Milan-Trieste) in 1921. To Spain in 1927.	
1679–1682	WR	6		20,400	40	1906	Van der Zyp	For Holland. 1681 'acquired' by Mitropa in 1916 (No. 909).	
1683–1685	WR	4		19,740	40	1906	Ringhoffer	For Austria.	
1686–1691	WR	6		20,400	40	1906	Klett	For Germany. 'Acquired' by Mitropa in 1916 (Nos. 910–915).	
1692–1697	WL	4		19,740	18	1906	Ringhoffer	For Spain. Later rebuilt to 16 pl. with salon in compts. 13–14 for customs personnel, etc.	
1698–1705	WR	6		20,400	40	1906	Van der Zyp	1703–1705 for Holland (Riviera Exp. Amsterdam-Zevenaar). Later in Dutch internal services. 1698–1700 'acquired' by Mitropa in 1916 (Nos. 916–918).	
1706–1708	WR	4		19,740	40	1906	Ringhoffer	For Spain.	
1709–1714	WL	4		20,320	18	1907	Ringhoffer	1709–1711 for Orient Exp. 1711–1714 for Ostend-Vienna-Orient Exp.	
1715–1718	WL	4		20,320	18	1907	Klett	For Denmark.	
1719–1721	WL	4		20,320	18	1907	Rathgeber	For Austria.	
1722–1724	WL	4		20,320	18	1907	CGC	For France. 1724 later in Morocco.	
1725–1734	WR	6		21,150	46	1907	CGC	1732 for French Presidential Train. 1728 in Tzar Nicholas II Special, Paris-Berthelon in 1912. 1728–1732 painted blue in 1922–23 for Calais-Méditerrannée Exp. (*Blue Train*).	
1735–1742	WR	4		19,740	40	1907	CGC	1737 for Riviera Exp. (Besançon-Ventimiglia). 1738–1742 later in Algeria.	
1743–1750	WL	4		20,320	18	1907	Scandia	For Denmark. 1746 and 1747 rebuilt to M class 22 pl. Later ZS. Last teak cars.	
1751–1752	WL	4		20,390	30	1906	?	I-II-III cl. Bought from DSB in 1906. For Denmark.	
1753–1754	WL	4		20,490	20	1906	Linke Hof.	For Germany-Denmark service. Bought from Mecklenburg State Rlys. in 1908.	
1755–1761	WL	4		20,320	18	1907–08	CGC	For France. In Bombay Exp. in 1915. Later in Morocco.	
1762–1764	WL	4		20,320	18	1908	Klett	For Hungary and Romania.	

Internationale Maatschappij der Slaapwagens en Groote Europese Sneltreinen

Car no.	Type	Axles	Class	Length excl. buffers	Seats or berths	Year	Builder	Remarks	(Dutch/Flemish)
1765–1766	WR	4		20,320	40	1908	Györ	For Hungary.	
1767–1771	WL	4		20,320	18	18	Ringhoffer	1770 and 1771 for Ostend-Vienna-Orient Exp.	
1772–1783	WL	4		20,320	18	1908	Klett	For Ostend-Vienna Exp. 1772 became F 1258 in 1926. 1774 and 1778 later in Palestine. 1775 later rebuilt to M class. 1777 and 1780 later in Egypt. 1779 to Spain in 1924. 1781–1783 rebuilt in France (CGC?) for Spain in 1924.	
1784–1790	WRS	4		20,320	22	1908	Ringhoffer	+ 12 pl. salon. 1785–1790 for Ostend-Vienna-Orient Exp.; later in Greece.	
1791–1798	WL	4		20,320	18	1908	Van der Zyp	For Lloyd-Exp. (Berlin-Genoa). 1791 destroyed (fire) at Levadia (Greece) in 1932.	
1799–1802	WRS	4		20,320	22	1908	Ringhoffer	+ 12 pl. salon for Lloyd Exp. Berlin-Trieste (Austrian Lloyd Line).	
1803–1814	WL	4		20,320	18	1908	Miani	All in Bombay Express in 1915. 1812 and 1813 later rebuilt to M class.	
1815–1818	WL	4		20,320	18	1908	Scandia	For Denmark.	
1819–1822	WL	4		20,320	18	1908	Van der Zyp	For Denmark.	
1823–1828	WR	6		20,400	40	1908	Van der Zyp	For Holland. Amsterdam-Basle and internal services. 1828 at Prague in 1959.	
1829–1834	WR	4		20,320	40	1908	Ringhoffer	For Wien-Cannes Exp. 1829, 1831, 1833 and 1834 later WR bar (24/36 pl.). 1831 at Prague in 1931. 1832 stores van WL-NA in 1959.	
1835–1837	WL	4		20,320	18	1908	Bres	For Wien-Cannes Exp. 1837 painted green for use by German High Command during World War II.	
1838	WL	4		19,740	16	1909	Behovia	For Spain. Built by Behovia, Irun. Conveyed over metre-gauge Bidassoa Rly. Bridge to main line, for which parapet had to be removed. Only car built by Behovia.	
1839–1858	WL	4	I-II	21,280	10	1909	Upper-Volga	For Russia. 1841 later in China.	
1859	WR	4		20,320	30	1908	Ringhoffer	For Egypt. Air-conditioned like 1648 and 1649.	
1860–1865	WR	6		20,400	40	1908	Van der Zyp	1861, 1863 and 1864 later became WL 24 pl.	
1866	WL	4		20,320	18	1908	Ringhoffer	For (St. Petersburg-) Warsaw-Cannes Exp. Later rebuilt to M class.	
1867	WRS	4		20,320	22	1908	Ringhoffer	+ 12 pl. salon. For (St. Petersburg-) Warsaw-Wien-Cannes Exp.	
1868–1870	WL	4		20,320	18	1908	Bres	For (St. Petersburg-) Warsaw-Wien-Cannes Exp.	
1871–1876	WR	4		20,320	40	1908	Ringhoffer	For Austria.	
1877–1880	WR	4		20,320	40	1907	Miani	For Italy.	
1881–1883	WR	4		20,320	40	1908	Klett	For Germany. 'Acquired' by Mitropa in 1916 (Nos. 919–921).	
1884–1890	WLS	6 A		23,452	12	1908	CGC	For PO and Midi Rlys. (France). 6-wheel bogies at first. With 2 large sleeping saloons. 1887 and 1889 in Tzar Nicholas II Special, Paris-Berthelon. 1888 in Marshal Foch's Train, at Compiègne 11 Nov. 1918 with 2419 (Armistice Car). All sold to Mitropa in 1940. (On Mitropa Cologne-Berlin service in 1954.)	
1891–1903	WLS	6 B		23,452	11	1908	CGC	For PO and Midi Rlys. With 1 large sleeping saloons, 3 berth, 2 washrooms and 1 WC. Used in Switzerland; then stored. 1893–1897 and 1902 became F 1320–1325 for Taurus Exp. in 1939–40. Rest sold to Mitropa in 1940. 6-wheel bogies at first.	

Car no.	Type	Axles	Class	Length excl. buffers	Seats or berths	Year	Builder	Remarks (Dutch/Flemish)
1904–1925	WL	4	I-II	21,280	10	1908–09	Upper-Volga	+ 10 berths II cl. for Russia.
1926–1928	WL	4		21,280	17	1908	Upper-Volga	For Russia. St. Petersburg–Warsaw (-Cannes) Exp.
1929–1935	WL	4		20,320	18	1908	Ringhoffer	For (St. Petersburg-) Warsaw-Wien-Cannes Exp. 1930–1933 and 1935 later rebuilt to M cl. 22 pl.
1936–1940	WRS	4		20,320	22	1909	Ringhoffer	+ 12 pl. salon. For Orient Exp. 1938 became WR bar 24 pl. Rest rebuilt as WR 36 pl. for Spain in 1925. 1939 stores van (PR) Lisbon in 1959.
1941–1943	WRS	4		20,320	22	1908–09	Nesselsdorf	+ 12 pl. salon. For Orient Exp. Later in Spain as WR 40 pl.
1944–1950	WR	6		20,400	40	1909	Van der Zyp	1944–1946, 1949 and 1950 later WR bar 24 pl. 1947 later WR 50 pl. 6-wheel bogies at first.
1951–1956	WL	4		20,320	18	1909	Van der Zyp	For Orient Exp. 1951 later rebuilt M3 (III cl.) 27 pl. 1955 and 1956 rebuilt to M cl. 22 pl.
1957–1965	WL	4		20,320	18	1909	Klett	1959 broad gauge for Russia. 1957, 1958 and 1960–1965 for Orient Exp. 1957 rebuilt to M cl. 22 pl. 1958 and 1962 to M3 27 pl. (III cl.).
1966–1971	WL	4		20,320	18	1908	Upper-Volga	For Russia. Later 21 pl.
1972–1974	WR	4		16,300	40	1909	WL-Irun	For Spain. Later WR 24 pl.
1975–1977	WR	4		20,320	40	1911	Van der Zyp	For Denmark.
1978	WRS	4		20,300	40	1913	Brugeoise	+ 12 pl. salon. Later WR 40 pl. In Estonia (Russian gauge) in 1927.
1979	WRS	4		20,300	22	1913	Nivelles	+ 12 pl. salon.
1980–1981	WR	4		21,280	36	1909	Upper-Volga	For Russia, Nord Exp. (Warsaw-Moscow).
1982–1985	WL	4		21,280	17	1909	Upper-Volga	For Russia, Nord Exp. (Warsaw-Moscow).
1986–1988	WL	4		20,320	18	1909	Van der Zyp	For Roumania.
1989	WL	4	I-II	21,280	10	1909	Upper-Volga	+ 10 berth II cl. for Russia.
1990–1996	WL	4		20,300	18	1910	Van der Zyp	Later all rebuilt to M cl. (I-II-III) 22 pl.
1997–2005	WR	4		20,400	40	1910	Van der Zyp	For Germany. 2002–2005 'acquired' by Mitropa (Nos. 922–925) in 1916. 2002 (922) returned to CIWL in 1920.
2006–2007	WL	4		20,300	18	1910	Ringhoffer	For Hungary. 2007 later rebuilt to M cl. 23 pl.
2008–2009	WL	4		20,300	18	1910	Nesselsdorf	For Hungary. Rebuilt later to M cl. 23 pl.
2010–2015	WR	4		20,300	40	1910	Györ	For Hungary.

Avrupa Surat Katalari ve Beynelmilel Yatakli-Vagonlar Sirketi

Car no.	Type	Axles	Class	Length excl. buffers	Seats or berths	Year	Builder	Remarks (Turkish)
2016–2019	WR	4		20,300	40	1910	Breda	For Italy.
2020–2030	WR	4		20,300	40	1909	CGC	For France. 2023–2050 50 pl. 2020–2026 later in Algeria.
2031–2043	WL	4		21,280	16	1909	Upper-Volga	For Russia. 2031–2037 were I-II cl. for Trans-Siberian Exp. to 1918. 2038 and 2043 were 8 pl. I cl. 2033 and 2035 were rebogied in China to standard gauge. 2033 was shipped (perilously on a raft) down Yangtse and across it to Shanghai (for Shanghai-Nanking service).
2044–2049	WL	4		20,320	18	1911	CGC	For Spain.

Car no.	Type	Axles	Class	Length excl. buffers	Seats or berths	Year	Builder	Remarks	(Turkish)
2050	WR	6		20,300	40	1911	Gotha	For Germany. To Mitropa (No. 926) in 1916–20. 6-wheel bogies. Later WR bar 24 pl.	
2051–2056	WR	4		20,300	40	1911	Ringhoffer	For Austria. 2054 later WR bar. 2052 in Yugoslavia in 1945; to JZ.	
2057–2061	WR	4		20,300	40	1911	Nesselsdorf	For Austria. 2057 was WR bar 24 pl. in 1932. 2059 was WR supplying Canadian Pacific Rlys. parlour cars in Trieste-Vienna boat trains, 1912 (connecting with CPR liners to Canada). 2060–2061 in Yugoslavia in 1945; to JZ.	
2062–2086	WL	4	R	20,300	18	1910	Van der Zyp	2067 later in Greece; 2072 in Palestine; 2082 in Lithuania; 2083 in Latvia. 2062–2065, 2069 and 2075–2080 rebuilt to M cl.; 2084 to R3 cl. 2076 and 2080 in Lithuania as M cl. 2079 in Yugoslavia in 1943; transferred to Spain.	
2087–2108	WR	4		20,400	40	1910–11	Van der Zyp	For Belgium and Germany. 2093, 2099 and 2104 in Yugoslavia in 1945; to JZ. 2103–2108 'acquired' by Mitropa. 1916–1920 (Nos. 927–932) except 2107 (931), which was never returned. 2087 later WR bar 24 pl. 2092 became F 1257 in 1926. 2101 at WL-Ostend, in 1980, for ARBAC or some other rly. museum. (Rebuilt WR 50 pl. before preservation.)	
2109–2116	WR	4		20,300	40	1910	Györ	For Hungary. 2109–2111 became WR bar 24 pl. 2109 painted green in World War II for German High Command train with 2417.	
2117–2119	WR	4		20,300	40	1910–11	Miani	For Italy. 2118 in Yugoslavia in 1945; to JZ.	
2120–2123	WL	4	R	20,300	18	1911	Miani	For Italy. 2120–2121 in Yugoslavia in 1945; to JZ.	
2124–2126	WL	4	R	20,300	18	1911	CGC	For France.	
2127–2132	WR	4		20,300	40	1911	CGC	For France.	
2133–2135	WL	4	R	20,320	18	1911	CGC	For Spain.	
2136–2144	WR	4		20,300	40	1911	Gotha	2139–2141 'acquired' by Mitropa (Nos. 933–935) in 1916. 2137 in Yugoslavia in 1945; to JZ.	
2145–2150	WR	4		19,740	40	1912	Beasain	For Spain. 2147 later rebuilt to WR bar. Stores van WL-Aravaca (Madrid) in 1959.	
2151–2154	WR	4		20,300	40	1911	Miani	For Italy.	
2155–2157	WR	4		19,240	40	1911	Klett	For Germany. 'Acquired' by Mitropa (Nos. 936–938) in 1916.	
2158–2159	WL	4	R	20,300	18	1911	Miani	For Italy.	
2160–2161	WR	4		20,300	40	1911–12	Ringhoffer	For Hungary.	
2162–2166	WR	4		20,300	40	1911	Györ	For Hungary. 2162 built in 1912.	
2167–2176	WL	4	R	20,300	18	1911	Van der Zyp	For Germany and Poland. 2168 later in Palestine. 2167 and 2171 later rebuilt R3 (III cl.). 2169 and 2173–2176 rebuilt to M cl. (I-II-III cl.).	
2177–2178	WR	4		20,400	40	1911	Van der Zyp	2177 later WR 50 pl.	
2179	WRS	4		20,300	22	1911	Van der Zyp	Later became WR 40 pl.	
2180–2185	WL	4	R	20,300	18	1912	Eis. Bedarf Görlitz	For Austria. 2180 without guard's lookout; 2181–2185 with guard's lookout. 2184 in Austrian Red Cross Train in 1917; later in Greece. 2181 rebuilt to M cl. for Greece; 2182 and 2185 rebuilt to R3 cl., 2185 in Greece as R3. 2184 and 2185 in Yugoslavia in 1945; to JZ. 2183 in Yugoslavia in 1943; transferred to Spain; painted blue about 1949.	
2186–2188	WR	4		20,300	40	1912	Eis. Bedarf Görlitz	For Austria. 2188 in Yugoslavia in 1945; to JZ.	
2189–2198	WL	4	R	20,300	18	1911–12	CGC	Rebuilt to cl. R3 in 1933. 2191 was dortoir for staff, Hook of Holland, in 1959. 2196 was stores van WL-Villeneuve-Prairie in 1959.	

Car no.	Type	Axles	Class	Length excl. buffers	Seats or berths	Year	Builder	Remarks (Turkish)
2199–2206	WR	4		20,300	50	1912	CGC	For France.
2207–2212	WL	4		20,300	18	1913	Cardé	For Spain.
2213	WR	4		20,300	36	1911	Ringhoffer	For Egypt with air-conditioning like 1859.
2214–2255	WL	4		21,280	18	1911–13	Upper-Volga	For Russia. 2217 and 2218 8 × I cl. berths + 18 × II cl. berths. Rest had 8 × I cl. + 10 × II cl. berths 2224, 2235 and 2252–2255 for Trans-Siberian Exp. 2226 and 2249 later in China.
2256–2265	WR	4		21,280	36	1911–13	Upper-Volga	For Russia.
2266–2269	WR	4		19,740	40	1912	Nesselsdorf	For Spain.
2270–2281	WL	4		19,850	16	1912	Ringhoffer	For Spain. 2277 stores van WL-Aravaca in 1959.
2282–2289	WR	4		20,300	40	1911	Györ	For Hungary. 2284 and 2289 in Yugoslavia in 1945; to JZ. 2287 rescued from Hungary in 1977, restored in NS Museum Utrecht (Holland).
2290–2293	WL	4	R	20,300	18	1911	Nesselsdorf	Later rebuilt to M cl. 22 pl.
2294–2296	WR	4		20,400	40	1912	Van der Zyp	For Germany. 'Acquired' by Mitropa (Nos. 942–944) in 1916. 2296 (No. 944) returned in 1920. 2294 and 2295 finally sold to Mitropa in 1922.
2297–2301	WR	4		20,400	40	1912	Miani	For Italy. 2300 later rebuilt to WR 50 pl. 2298–2301 in Yugoslavia in 1945; to JZ.
2302–2304	WR	4		20,400	40	1912	Ringhoffer	2302 later in Palestine. 2303 and 2304 rebuilt to WR 50 pl.
2305–2310	WR	4		20,400	40	1913	Györ	For Hungary and Roumania. 2305 and 2307 in Yugoslavia in 1945; to JZ.
2311–2322	WL	4	R	20,300	18	1913	Ringhoffer	Later in Poland.
2323–2330	WL	4	R	20,300	18	1913	Nesselsdorf	2326–2330 later in Turkey.

Nemzetkozi Vasuti Halokocsi Tarsasag

Car no.	Type	Axles	Class	Length excl. buffers	Seats or berths	Year	Builder	Remarks (Hungarian)
2331–2338	WL	4	R	20,300	18	1912–13	Ringhoffer	2333–2338 became M cl. later. 2332 and 2334 to Mitropa in 1916–20. 2331 to Spain in 1943 from Yugoslavia.
2339–2343	WL	4	R	20,300	18	1913	Nesselsdorf	2343 to Mitropa in 1916–20. 2340–2342 became R3 čl. later. 2343 in Yugoslavia in 1945; to JZ.
2344–2353	WR	4		20,300	40	1912–13	Ringhoffer	2347 preserved Budapest Museum. 2346 and 2351 later in Palestine. 2348–2350 became WR bar 24 pl.
2354–2360	WR	4		20,300	40	1913	Nesselsdorf	2357 later WR bar 24 pl.
2361–2367	WR	4		20,300	40	1913	Miani	For Italy 2367 later WR 50 pl.
2368–2373	WR	4		19,740	40	1913	Van der Zyp	For Spain.
2374–2399	WR	4		20,400	40	1912	Van der Zyp	For Germany. 2374–2384, 2388, 2390, 2394 and 2397 'acquired' by Mitropa in 1916 (Nos. 945–959). 2375–2380 (946–951), 2384, 2388 and 2394 (954, 955, 958) returned in 1920. 2374, 2381, 2382, 2390 and 2397 bought by Mitropa in 1922. 2376–2379, 2382 and 2383 hired to CSWR/SSG for a period in 1920s. 2393–2396 and 2398 later in Turkey. 2399 later WR 50 pl. in Greece. Stores van WL–Neos Iannos (Athens) in 1959. 2377 later in Spain.

Car no.	Type	Axles	Class	Length excl. buffers	Seats or berths	Year	Builder	Remarks	(Hungarian)
2400–2402	WL	4	R	20300	18	1913	Van der Zyp	2401 and 2402 later M cl.	
2403–2424	WR	4		20300	40	1913–14	CGC	For France. Etat Rly. narrow loading gauge I and II cl. saloons. 2403, 2405, 2407, 2409–2411 and 2421–2423 later WR bar 32 pl. 2406, 2408, 2416 and 2417 later WR 48 pl. 2418 WR in Marshal Foch's train in 1914–18. 2419 became office car for Marshall Foch's train in 1918; Armistice Car in 1918. Rebuilt WR 48 pl. in 1919; presented to France and rebuilt as office car in 1921, for Invalides, then Rethondes in 1921–40. Removed by road to Berlin; then destroyed at Ohrdruf by SS in 1944 at Hitler's special order. 2404, 2405 and 2410 later in Turkey. 2407 destroyed in 1944; 2408 later in Morocco. 2409, 2412–2415, 2418, 2421 and 2422 to China in 1923. 2416 and 2423 requisitioned; disappeared during World War II. 2420 destroyed in 1924; 2424 later in Finland, renum. 2020 c. 1958; sold to VR in 1959. 2405 at Ankara in 1959.	
2425–2428	WR	4		20,300	40	1913	CGC	For France. 2425–2427 later in Finland; renum. 2016–2018 c. 1958. Sold VR in 1959. 2428 destroyed at Pont-sur-Yonne in 1919. 2431–2433 and 2435–2438 became WR bar 34 pl. 2439 renum. 2419 in 1945; preserved at Compiègne Museum; Rethondes as Armistice Car; rebuilt as office.	
2429–2439	WR	4		20,300	50	1913	CGC		
2440–2442	WL	4	R	20,300	18	1913	Miani	For Italy.	
2443–2446	WS	4		20,300	26	1913	Ringhoffer	For Sud Exp. 2443 WS in Marshal Foch's train in 1914–18. 2444 for French Min. of War in 1914–18; for Pres. Clémenceau in 1918–21. 2445 and 2446 in Paris-Warsaw Exp. (Strasbourg-Munich) in 1919–21. 2444–2446 painted blue and cream for Golden Mountain Pullman Exp. (Montreux-) Zweisimmen-Interlaken (BLS portion) in 1931.	
2447–2452	WL	4	R	20,300	16	1913	Van der Zyp	2447–2449 in Turkey for Anatolia Exp. (Istanbul-Ankara) in 1925. 2552 later rebuilt to M 19 pl. I-II-III.	
2453–2456	WL	4	R	20,300	16	1914	Credé	2455–2456 in Turkey for Anatolia Exp. in 1926.	
2457	WL	4	R	20,300	16	1921?	Ringhoffer?	Built 1914? Built Credé? In Turkey in 1926.	
2458–2460	WL	4	R	21,240	16	1914	Credé	To Mitropa in 1916–20. In Turkey, Anatolia Exp., in 1926.	
2461–2470	WR	4		20,400	40	1914	Credé	2463, 2467 and 2470 'acquired' by Mitropa in 1916–20 (Nos. 960–964). 2461–2467 to Spain in 1929. 2463–2466 returned to France in March 1931. 2468 later WR bar.	
2471–2476	WR	4		20,400	40	1914	Györ	For Hungary.	
2477–2480	WR	4		20,400	40	1914	Van der Zyp	For Belgium.	
2481–2484	WR	4		20,400	40	1914	Ringhoffer	For Austria.	
2485–2489	WL	4	R	20,300	16	1920	CGC	Also dated 1913–14. 2485 later rebuilt to M for Yugoslavia; to JZ in 1945.	
2490–2495	WL	4	R	23,452	16	1913–20	Ringhoffer	For Austria.	
2496–2500	WL	4	R	20,300	16	1914	Nesselsdorf	2497–2498 later rebuilt to R3 III cl. 2497 to Spain in 1943 from Yugoslavia.	
2501–2509	WR	4		20,300	50	1916	CGC	2505 and 2506 renum. 4250 and 4251 in 1943. 2507 painted blue for Bombay Exp. in 1923; sold in 1969 to OBB as bath car in construction train.	
2510–2517	WL	4	R	20,300	16	1916/21	CGC	CGC 2510 and 2513 from WL-SD to Shanghai in 1935. 2516 and 2517 later rebuilt to M cl. for Yugoslavia; to JZ in 1945.	
2518–2525	WL	4		21,280	16	1914	Upper-Volga	Also shown as built CGC. Last cars for CIWL-Russia. For Trans-Siberian Exp. Some later in China.	

Car no.	Type	Axles	Class	Length excl. buffers	Seats or berths	Year	Builder	Remarks *(Hungarian)*
2526–2536	WR	4		20,300	50	1915/16	Miani	For Italy 2527–2529 and 2531 in Yugoslavia in 1945; to JZ.
2537–2540	WR	4		20,400	50	1922	Credé	For Roumania.
2541–2555	Cars to which nos. allocated not built due to World War I. Nos. not used.							
2556–2560	WL	4	R	20,300	16	1923	Gyor	For Hungary. Later rebuilt to M cl. 19 pl. 2558 and 2559 in Yugoslavia in 1945; to JZ.
2561–2605	Cars to which nos. allocated not built due to World War I. Nos. not used.							
2606–2630	WL	4	S2	23,452		1922/3	Nivelles	Wooden bodies. 2606–2614 in Paris-Méditérranée. Exp. in 1922–23. All series for Rome Exp. in 1922–23. All, except 2618–2622, rebuilt to ST. 2625 and 2629 sold in 1969. OBB dortoirs in construction train. 2623, 2626 and 2627 in Yugoslavia in 1945; to JZ. 2630 at WL-VP in 1959.
2631–2640	WL	4	S2	23,452		1923/4	WL–Neu Aubing	Wooden bodies. Rebuilt to ST cl. 2638 sold to OBB; dortoir like 2625.
2641–2674	WL	4	S1	23,452		1922	Leeds	First all-steel cars. 2641–2646 without inter-compt. wash-rooms for Bombay Exp. 2649–2677 for Calais-Méditérranée Exp. Painted blue and gold, hence *Train Bleu* in 1922–23. 2644 to Spain in 1958 as S4U. 2657 to Spain in 1958; rebuilt WL-Irun as S3K 13 pl. + cafeteria in 1961. 2660–2663 and 2677–2679 later in Turkey; all rebuilt to SGT; except 2660 and 2663 transferred to Spain in 1958. 2673 later in Greece.
2675–2680	WL	4	S1	23,452		1923	Leeds	
2681–2683	WL	6		20,405	26	1908	Gastell	Wooden bodies. Ex-Alsace-Lorraine Rly. Nos. 169–171. Bought in 1921 for Baltic States. In Latvia in 1922.
2684–2691	WL	4	R	19,740	16	1923	CGC	Ex-WL 631–636 and 639–640.

Mezinarodni Spolecnost Luzkovych Vozu a Velkych Evropskych Expresnich Vlaku

Car no.	Type	Class	Length excl. buffers	Seats or berths	Year	Builder	Remarks *(Czech)*
2692	All cars below have steel bodies and 4 axles unless otherwise stated. 2692 no. not used.						
2693	WR		23,452	56	1926	Dyle & Bac	Bordeaux works. First all-steel WR. For Bombay Exp. in 1933–35. Sold to SNCF in 1962.
2694	WL	S2	23,452		1926	CGC	First French all-steel S2. Later rebuilt to ST cl. for Algeria.
2695–2699	WL	ST	23,452		1926	Savigliano	For Italy. 2695 and 2698 to Spain in 1958. 2698 rebuilt to S3K 13 pl. + cafeteria in 1961. 2699 rebuilt and renum. 3861 in 1949.
2700	WR		23,452	42	1926	Birmingham	WR for French Presidential Train. Later became ordinary WR, for Night Ferry (Dunkerque-Paris); for Paris–St. Malo in 1966. Sold to SNCF, retaining CIWL name, in 1962. This no. allotted to first all-steel WL, the X cl., ordered from Pullman Chicago in 1913; cancelled in 1916 due to World War I.
2701–2711	WL	S2	23,452		1926	Savigliano	For Italy. Some for sale in 1965 at 23 lire per kg. 2706 to Spain 1958.
2712–2715	WL	Z	23,452		1926	Breda	2714 renum. 3872 in 1949. For Arlberg Orient Exp.
2716–2719	WL	Z	23,452		1926	Miani	2716, 2717 and 2719 renum. 3884, 3871 and 3876 in 1949. For Arlberg Orient Exp.
2720–2721	WL	Z	23,452		1926	El Ferr	2720 renum. 3879 in 1949. For Arlberg Orient Exp.

Car no.	Type	Class	Length excl. buffers	Seats or berths	Year	Builder	Remarks	(Czech)
2722–2731	WL	Z	23,452		1926	Reggio	2727 renum. 3874 in 1949. For Italy and Arlberg Orient Exp.	
2732–2736	WL	Z	23,452		1926–27	Off. Merid	2736 renum. 3880 in 1949. For Italy.	
2737–2742	WSP	Sud Exp.	23,452	24	1926	Dietrich	Sud Exp. WP had 1 saloon and several coupes. Painted chocolate and cream in 1926–32. 2737 and 2739 rebuilt to WR 52 pl. To Spain in 1939. 2741 rebuilt to WR 46 pl; in Portugal in 1939–77; M-C; in 1977 bought by Intraflug for Nostalgic Orient Exp.; repainted chocolate and cream in 1980. 2742 rebuilt to WR 41 pl.; in Algeria 1939–53; then Spain. 2740 rebuilt WR 46 pl. in 1939; at WL-Villeneuve-Prairie in 1959.	
2743–2748	WSP	Sud Exp.	23,452	18	1926	Dietrich	2743 and 2744 rebuilt WR 48 pl.; later in Algeria. 2745–2747 rebuilt to WR 46 pl.; in Spain by 1939. 2748 sold to Holland 1946 as Dutch Royal Saloon (1946–59).	
2749–2773	WR		23,452	56	1926	Reggio	2749 preserved Zurich, Eurovapor (Glaser). 2750 and 2752 with telephone compt. for Inter City Plus services, Holland, in 1979–81. 2757 became Denham Express pub, Denham, Bucks (England), in 1969. 2753 and 2772 sold to CSWR/SSG in 1965. 2758 and 2765 sold to SNCF 1962. 2770 became WL 3878 in 1949.	
2774–2788	WL	S2	23,452		1926	Blanc Miss	2774–2784 later rebuilt to ST. cl. 2783 to Spain in 1958; rebuilt to S3K 13 pl + cafeteria in 1960. 2787 to Spain in 1958; sold to SNCF as departmental vehicle in 1968.	
2789–2818	WL	S2	23,452		1926	Nivelles	2789–2796 and 2799 for Nord Exp. (Ostend-Bucharest). All rebuilt to ST, except 2789, 2792, 2793, 2796, 2799 and 2812–2815. 2796, 2800 and 2803 to Spain and Portugal in 1958. 2800 and 2803 sold to CP 1977. 2798 rebuilt and renum. 3873 in 1949. 2788, 2790 and 2797 in *Chopin* (Vienna-Warsaw) in 1963. 2808 in Prague-Vienna in 1962. 2804 and 2813 in Greece in 1961.	
2819–2838	WR		23,452	56	1926	Dyle & Bac	Bordeaux works. Series sold to SNCF 1962 (retaining CIWL title and colour) except 2837. 2835 later to 5th French Army Engineers (1968).	
2839–2841	WSPC	Compl.	23,452	32	1926	Dyle & Bac	Bordeaux works. Sud Exp. complementary cars. Became WR 42 pl. in 1930.	
2842–2851	WL	S2	23,452		1926	Breda	2846–2848 and 2850 became S3K, 13pl + cafeteria in Spain in 1960.	
2852–2866	WR		23,452	56	1925–26	Birmingham	2852 and 2859–2866 sold to SNCF in 1962. 2866 Libre-service ('self-service') 1967–68, rest withdraw in 1967–68. 2853, 2856 and 2857 sold to CSWR/SSG in 1963. 2856 later laboratory car, Brown Boveri Co. Baden. 2855 in 6-nation diner SSG 75th-year Diamond Jubilee train; CSWR, in 1978.	
2867–2880 2881	WR WR		23,452 23,452	42 36	1925–26 1926	Birmingham Birmingham	For Simplon Orient Exp. (Paris-Istanbul, later Lausanne-Svilengrad). 2867 and 2878 sold to CSWR/SSG in 1963. In service in CIWL livery until 1969. 2877 in Direct Orient Exp. Turkey in 1966; sold to TCDD in 1967. 2876 became snack-bar car. 2869 in *Palatino* (Rome-Turin) in 1969. 2868, 2872, 2874 and 2876 sold to TCDD in 1967. 2881 WR for French Presidential Train. Later WR 40 pl. on hire to FS.	
2882–2891	WL	S2	23,452		1926	Miani	2885 and 2890 to Spain in 1958; Became S3K in 1960. 2883–2885, 2888 and 2890 rebuilt to ST.	
2892–2901	WL	S2	23,452		1926	Ringhoffer	2894, 2896, 2898, 2900 and 2901 became ST. 2893 to Portugal in 1958; sold to CP in 1979. 2895 lost during World War II. 2899 in Greece in 1961. 2898 preserved by AJECTA Longueville (France).	
2902–2911	WL	S1	23,452		1926	CGC	2904–2911 later in Algeria. 2911 destroyed at Attafs (Algeria) in 1938 attack by bandits.	

Car no.	Type	Axles	Class	Length excl. buffers	Seats or berths	Year	Builder	Remarks	(Czech)
2912–2913	WL	S2	23,452			1926	Savigliano	For Italy.	
2914–2917	WSPC	Ind.	23,452		21	1926	Birmingham	For Egypt. Wooden body, painted white with names (see list). Never ran in Europe.	
2918–2932	WL	S1	23,452			1926	Birmingham	2918, 2922, 2928 and 2931 rebuilt to ST 24 pl. 2922, 2923, 2926, 2927, 2928, 2931 and 2932 to Spain in 1958.	
2933–2942	WL	S1	23,452			1936	Metro	2933–2939, 2941 and 2942 to Spain in 1956; 1958 as S3 cl. 2933, 2934 and 2942 became ST cl.	
2943–2967	WL	S1	23,452			1926–27	Credé	For Nord Exp. (Calais-Warsaw-Niegoeloje). 2947, 2951, 2961 and 2964 became ST cl. 2943, 2945, 2946, 2949–2960, 2962, 2963 and 2965–2967 to Spain in 1956–58.	
2968–2982	WR		23,452		56	1927	Reggio	For Italy and Switzerland. 2969–2971 2973, 2976 and 2982 remodelled in 1965–66 with full air-conditioning by Soc. Pistoesi, Pistoia (Italy). 2977 at Munich Transport Fair in 1965 (stationary diner, Austrian brigade); 2974 bought by Sea Containers in 1979; rebuilt to bar for VSOE in 1981. 2975 sold to Thomas Cook in 1978, to mark 50 years of WL/Cook assn. In service on Nene Valley Rly., Peterborough (England). 2970 and 2971 in Rome-Turin and Rome-Genoa in 1981–82.	
2983–2988	WR		19,740		48	1927	CGC	Ex-WS 960–965 wooden bodies.	
2989–3000								2991–3000 reserved for UK. Pullmans Nos. 51–60 in Duplicate List (q.v.) so nos. not used.	
3001–3004	WL	3	23,452		38	1923	Nesselsdorf	Wooden body for Baltic states. 4-berth III cl. compts. No wash-basins. Russian-gauge bogies.	
3005–3009	WL	3	23,452		38	1923	Ringhoffer	Wooden body like 3001. For Baltic states and Poland.	
3010–3017	WL	ZS	23,452		30	1925	Scandia	For Denmark. Wooden bodies, originally M3. 3015–3017 later in China. Last teak cars in service in 1962 (Copenhagen-Esbjerg).	
3018–3020	WL	3				1926	Nivelles	For Baltic states. Russian-gauge bogies; broad-gauge services all withdrawn in 1941.	
3021–3026	WL	P	23,452		36	1926	Nivelles	For Poland, 4-berth III cl. compts. without wash-basins.	
3027–3032	WL	P	23,452		36	1926	Ringhoffer	For Poland. 4-berth III cl. compts. without lavabo (basin). 3026, 3029 and 3032 later rebuilt without III cl. Do not confuse with post-war 'P' class.	
3033–3042	WL	Z	23,452			1926	Nivelles	3033 renum. 3883 in 1949. 3036 became Z3 III cl. in Greece (3-berth compts.). 3035 became Z3 also.	
3043–3052	WL	Z	23,452			1926	CGC	3043–3049 ZT (end compts. 3-berth) except 3047 later.	
3053–3099								Nos. not used. Nos. 3100–3246 had wooden bodies. Not mentioned elsewhere due to lack of space.	
3100	WR		19,740		52	1926	CGC	Ex-WR 249.	

Miedzynarodowe Towarzystwo Wagonow Sypialnych i Ekspresów Europejskich

Car no.	Type	Class	Length excl. buffers	Seats or berths	Year	Builder	Remarks	(Polish)
3101–3109	WI.	R	19,370	20	1925/6	WL–Saint-Denis	Ex-WL 434–442	
3110–3113	WI.	R	19,370	20	1926/7	CGC	Ex-WL 453–456	
3114–3116							Nos. not used.	
3115	WI.	R	19,740	16	1927	CTC	Ex-WL 458	

Car no.	Type	Class	Length excl. buffers	Seats or berths	Year	Builder	Remarks	(Polish)
3117–3122	WI.	R	19,740	16	1927/8	CGC-Mary	Ex-WL 460, 464, 462, 463, 465, 461	
3123–3124							Nos. not used.	
3125	WL	R	19,740	16	1926	CGC	Ex-WL 484	
3126	WL	R	19,740	16	1928	CGC Marly	Ex-WL 485	
3127	WL	R	19,740	16	1926	WL-Prague	Ex-WL 486	
3128							Nos. not used.	
3129–3130	WR		19,600	52	1926	CGC	Ex-WR 502–503	
3131	WL	R	19,740	16	1925	WL–Saint-Denis	Ex-WL 507	
3132–3134	WL	R	19,740	16	1925	CGC	Ex-WL 508–510	
3135	WL	R	19,740	16	1925	WL–Neu Aubing	Ex-WL 511	
3136	WL	R	19,740	16	1926	O. Moncen.	Ex-WL 512. Built by Officina Moncenisio. Turin.	
3137–3139	WL	R	19,740	16	1926	CGC	Ex-WL 513, 514, 516	
3140–3141							Nos. not used.	
3142	WL	R	19,740		1925	WL–Saint-Denis	Ex-WL 520	
3143–3144	WL	R	19,740		1927/5	CGC	Ex-WL 522–523	
3145–3146	WL	R	19,740		1924	WL–Neu Aubing	Ex-WL 524– 525	
3147–3149	WL	R	19,740	16	1926	CGC	Ex-WL 526–528	
3150	WR		19,600	50	1926	WL–Saint-Denis	Ex-WRS 539	
3151	WL	R	19,740	16	1927	CGC	Ex-WL 747	
3152	WR		19,600	52	1927	CGC	Ex-WR 542	
3153–3154							Nos. not used	
3155	WL	R	19,740	16	1925	CGC	Ex-WL 545. In Turkey	
3156–3157	WR		19,740	48	1927	CGC	Ex-WR 576 and 575. 3156 in Spain, and 3157 in Portugal.	
3158–3159	WL	R	19,740	16	1925/6	WL-NA/SD	Ex-WL 548–549	
3160							Nos. not used.	
3161	WL	R	19,740	16	1924	WL–Neu Aubing	Ex-WL 553	
3162	WL	R	19,740	16	1926	CGC	Ex-WL 554	
3163	WL	R	19,740	16	1924	WL–Neu Aubing	Ex-WL 555	
3164	WL	R	19,740	16	1924	WL–OST	Ex-WL 556	
3165–3167	WL	R	19,740	16	1924	WL–Neu Aubing	Ex-WL 557, 559, 560	
3168	WL	R	19,740	16	1925	CGC	Ex-WL 561	
3169–3174	WL	R	19,740	16	1924/5	WL–Neu Aubing	Ex-WL 562–567	
3175–3181	WR		19,600	40	1926/7	CGC	Ex-WRS 568–574. 3181 was 19,740m long. WR 48 pl.	
3182	WL	R	19,740	16	1927	CGC	Ex-WL 582	
3183	WR		19,740	48	1927	CGC	Ex-WR 577	
3184–3185	WL	R	19,740	16	1925/6	WL-NA/CGC	Ex-WL 584–585	
3186–3187	WL	R	19,740	16	1927	CGC	Ex-WL 586–587	
3188	WL	R.	19,740	16	1927	WL-NA/SD	Ex-WL 588	
3189	WL	R	19,740	16	1926	WL-NA/CGC	Ex-WL 589	
3190–3191	WL	R	19,740	16	1928	CGC/WL-SD	Ex-WL 590–591	
3192–3193							Nos. not used	
3194–3196	WL	R	19,740	16	1927/5	CGC	Ex-WL 659, 615, 643. 3194 later in Turkey.	
3197	WR		19,740	52	1927	CGC	Ex-WR 645	

Compania Internationala a Vagoanelor cu Paturi si a Marilor Exprese Europene

Car no.	Type	Class	Length excl. buffers	Seats or berths	Year	Builder	Remarks	(Roumanian)
3198–3201	WL	R	19,740	16	1925–26	CGC	Ex-WL 600–663. 3198–3199 in Algeria. 3200–3201 in Syria.	
3202–3206	WR		19,740	48	1927	CGC	Ex-WR 774–777 and 816.	
3207	WL	R	19,740	16	1928	CGC (Marly)	Ex-WL 748.	
3208	WR		19,740	50	1925	WL–Saint-Denis	Ex-WR 818.	
3209	WR		19,740	48	1927	CGC	Ex-WR 909.	
3210	WR		19,740	48	1926	WL–Saint-Denis	Ex-WR 910.	
3211–3212							Nos. not used.	
3213	WL	R	19,740	16	1928	CGC/WL-SD	Ex-WL 834	
3214	WR		19,740	40	1928	CGC	Ex-WR 794.	
3215–3218							Nos. not used.	
3219	WR		19,740	40	1928	CGC/WL-SD	Ex-WR 919.	
3220–3223							Nos. not used.	
3222	WR		19,740	40	1928	WL–Saint-Denis	Ex-WR 948.	
3223	WR		19,740	40	1927	CGC	Ex-WR 949.	
3224–3229	WR		19,740	40	1928	CGC/WL-SD	Ex WR 950–955 with Russian gauge bogies. 3224 and 3229 for Baltic states (Estonia). 3225–3228 for Finland, later renum. VR 2012–2015. Sold to VR in 1959.	
3230–3233							Nos. not used.	
3234	WL		20,320	18	1928	WL–Saint-Denis	Ex-WL 974. Sold to SNCF (departmental vehicle) after World War II.	
3235–3245							Nos. not used.	
3246	WL		20,320	18	1928	WL–Saint-Denis	Ex-WL 1620.	
3247–3300							Nos. not used. The following cars have all-steel bodies unless otherwise stated.	
3301–3310	WL	S1	23,452		1926–27	Nivelles	3301 and 3304 later ST cl. 3309 for Sea Containers Venice Orient Exp. 1982.	
3311–3340	WL	Z	23,452		1927	E.I.C.	3325, 3329, 3332 and 3323 in Greece in 1961. 3329, 3332, Z3.	
3341–3360	WR		23,452	56	1928	E.I.C.	3352 in P&O Overland Exp. in 1937–39. 3353, 3355 and 3358 new Schlieren bogies for Mistral c. 1950. 3354 and 3360 WR in French Presidential Train. All cars sold to SNCF in 1962, retaining CIWL name and livery. 3345 bought by 141R Society; preserved at Ury, France. 3348 restored WL-SD for SNCF for Mulhouse Museum in 1977.	
3361–3380	WL	S4	21,550		1928	Metro	For Spain, Norte Rly. Sud Exp. 3369 badly damaged at Aravaca in Civil War; rebuilt in 1939 with commemorative plaque by WL-Irun. Series in Lusitania Exp. in 1943. Double compts.; later became triple with reduced cl. supplement. In service until 1981.	
3381–3390	WL	S4	21,580		1928	Nivelles	For Spain, MZA Rly. Wooden bodies, since metal considered too hot for So. Spain. Last WL car series with wooden bodies to be built. Withdrawn in 1964 with all other wooden-bodied stock on RENFE.	
3391–3405	WR		23,452	42	1929	Metro	For Trains de Luxe. 3394–3396 to Spain in 1964. 3396 modernized in 1980 like 3568. 3398 at WL-SD in 1959. Rest sold to TCDD in 1967.	
3406–3415	WL	S1	23,452		1929	Nivelles	3406 later SG; sold to TCDD in 1967. 3407 damaged in war; became 3875 in 1949. 3410 at Brussels Exhibition in 1935. 3409–3412 to Egypt as ST in 1950s. 3412 staff coach at Cairo in 1959.	

Car no.	Type	Class	Length excl. buffers	Seats or berths	Year	Builder	Remarks	(Roumanian)
3416–3431	WL	S1	23,452		1929	Birmingham	3416, 3419 and 3421 later ST cl. 3418 rebuilt to SGT; later again rebuilt with 3423 as SG for Turkey. 3417 to Portugal; sold CP (in service) in 1979. 3419, 3421 and 3422 to Egypt in 1950s as ST. 3425 bought by Sea Containers in 1979 for Venice Orient Exp.	
3432–3455	WL	SG	23,452		1929	Birmingham	For Turkey. Later ST for Egypt. 3433 sold to TCDD in 1967. 3435–3438, 3440–3443 and 3448–3449 rebuilt by WL-Hayderpasa as SGT II-III cl.	
3456–3465	WL	S1	23,452		1930	Simmering Graz	3456 and 3457 later to Egypt as ST cl. 3459 and 3462 rebuilt as SGT II-III cl. for Turkey.	
3466–3495	WL	Lx	23,452	10	1929	Metro	For *Blue Train*, Rome Exp. and P&O Overland Exp. (Calais-Marseilles). Later Lx 16/Lx 20. 3469 and 3493 sold to CH (in service with WL conductors) c. 1973. 3472, 3475, 3480 and 3487 bought by Intraflug in 1977 for Nostalgic Orient Exp. 3489 M-C bought in 1977 by Sea Containers, and 3473, 3482 and 3483 bought by Sea Containers in 1978–79. In 1982 converted Lx 18, 9 compts, at WL-Ost for Venice Orient Exp. 3484 and 3486 sold to CP in 1979.	
3496–3555	WL	Lx	23,452	10	1929	E.I.C.	For *Blue Train*, Pyrénées–Côte d'Argent Exp., etc. 3509–3515 Nord Exp. (Paris-Riga). 3540–3555 were Lx 20; rest later Lx 16/20. Some owned by Cie. Int. Aux. de Ch. de Fers; not to run in Belgium before 1949. 3507 at Paris Exhibition in 1937. 3538 for Duke of Windsor in 1936; rebuilt with salon and shower, 13 pl.; derailed by Maquis into Loire in 1944–1945; rebuilt to Lx 20 WL-SD in 1945–46 (20,000 hrs. work!). To Spain and Portugal in 1973–24 with 3470, 3471, 3473, 3478–3480, 3483–3486, 3489, 3492, 3497, 3498, 3500, 3501, 3507, 3509, 3511, 3515, 3517, 3523, 3523, 3526, 3527, 3529, 3531, 3539, 3540, 3541, 3543, 3546–3548 and 3552–3555. 3504 in film *Vivre pour Vivre* in 1967 and *Murder on Orient Exp.* in 1977. 3544 in Dutch Royal Train in 1945–48. 3537, 3542 and 3551 bought in 1977 by Intraflug Zurich for Nostalgic Orient Exp. 3519 preserved AJECTA (for Ajeca-Provence) as of 1977. 3532 restored to Lx 10 by WL-SD in 1976; preserved at Mulhouse Museum. 3543 M-C bought in 1977 by Sea Containers. 3548 M-C bought in 1977 by Paccard; preserved at Annecy (?). 3525, 3539, 3544, 3552, 3553 and 3555 bought by Sea Containers in 1978–80; converted by WL-Ost in 1981–82 to 9 compts. Lx 18 with conductor's compt. or Lx 18, but no showers or air-conditioning, for Venice Simplon Orient Exp. (Boulogne-Venice), starting 28th May 1982. 3517 sold to CP in 1979. 3509 and 3540 bought by Intraflug in 1981 for Nost. Or. Exp. 3514 sold to CH (in service with WL conductors) in 1974. 3468, 3521, 3524, 3550 destroyed in war. 3466, 3467, 3474, 3476, 3477 and 3488 'disappeared' in war; some used by Mitropa until 1971.	
3556–3561	WR		21,550	48	1928	Beasain	For Spain, MZA Rly. Last WR cars with wooden bodies. Withdrawn in 1964.	
3562–3569	WR		21,550	36	1930	Bilbao	For Spain. 3567–3569 48 pl. for *Puerta del Sol*. Rest for Trains de Luxe, Sud Exp. 3562 and 3563 later in Portugal. 3563 destroyed (fire) on 10 Feb. 1956.	
3750–3577	WL	S			1928	Birmingham	For Egypt. Painted white. Never ran in Europe. Order not subcontracted to Metro. 3573 and 3577 staff coaches at Cairo (1959).	
3578–3587	WR		23,452	42	1928	E.I.C.	3478–3583 and 3587 to Spain in 1941. 3584 destroyed (accident) in 1968. 3565, 3567, 3568 and 3587 modernized; 1 saloon fitted with Spanish TV receiver sets in 1980. 3587 became WR bar in 1980.	
3588–3607	WL	Y	23,452		1930	Dietrich	3588–3594 for Nord Exp. (Paris-Copenhagen). Rest for	
3608–3627	WL	Y	23,452		1930	E.I.C.	ordinary trains with pantry. 3624 at Paris Exhibition in	

Car no.	Type	Class	Length excl. buffers	Seats or berths	Year	Builder	Remarks *(Roumanian)*
							1937. 3588–3607 later had metal doors to compts. Most rebuilt to U Ord. or YU cl. Used in last Direct Orient Exp. on 19th May 1977 (Paris-Istanbul). 3604, 3606 and 3608 sold to CH (in service with WL conductors).
3628–3647	WR		23,452	56	1930	E.I.C.	Series sold to SNCF in 1962, except 3641, 3643, 3645, and 3647.
3648–3662	WL	Z	23,452		1930	Reggio	3655 rebuilt to WL 3882 in 1949. 3662 bought AJECTA 1975; preserved at Richelieu (TVT), France.

Medunarodno Drustvo Kola za Spavanje i Velikih Europskih Ekspresa

Car no.	Type	Class	Length excl. buffers	Seats or berths	Year	Builder	Remarks *(Yugoslav)*
3663–3682	WR		23,452	56	1931	E.I.C.	All sold to SNCF in 1962, retaining CIWL name and livery. 3670 and 3676 became Libre-Service ('Self-Service') in 1960. 3676 SNCF departmental vehicle (brake instruction car) at Saintes (1982). 3674 bought by Sea Containers in 1980. Rebuilt to bar in 1982.
3683–3692	WL	Y	23,452		1930	E.I.C.	3684 destroyed WL-VP (Paris) in 1944 (37 bombs). Some converted to U Ord. in 1950s.
3693–3702	WR		23,452	56	1932	Ganz	3696 and 3697 sold to SNCF in 1962.
3703–3742	WL	Y	23,452		1931	Credé	Some converted to U Ord. in 1950s.
3743–3767	WL	YT	23,452		1932	Birmingham	Last sleepers built by Birmingham.
3768–3777	WL	Z	23,452		1931	Reggio	3768 damaged; became 3877 in 1949.
3778–3787	WR		23,452	56	1932	Cegielski	3779 and 3787 sold to SNCF in 1962.
3788–3799	WL	F	19,232		1936	Blanc Miss.	For England (ferry). Dual vaccuum and air brakes. Vac. brakes removed in 1962. 3789 used by German Ahty. in France. Rest 'acquired' by Mitropa in 1940. 3788 and 3795 lost during war. 3793, 3796 and 3799 never returned. After damage in air raid near Dresden, 3793 rebuilt to Mitropa WR. 3789 cannibalized for parts in 1970s; bought by Sea Containers in 1979 as baggage stores van VSOE; exchanged for 3801 in 1981. 3790 sold to SNCF (Nancy) as departmental vehicle. 3791 scrapped in 1978. 3792 restored in 1980 by WL-Ost for National Rly. Museum at York. 3794, 3797 and 3798 in service; leased by SNCF in 1971 (BR conductors since 1977); for sale since 1980.
3800–3805	WL	F	19,232		1937–47	CGC	For England. Ready for Hitler's visit to 'conquered' GB, but stored at Saint-Denis incomplete until 1945–46 to prevent requisition. Leased to SNCF in 1971 (BR conductors since 1977). 3801 repainted SNCF livery in 1978. Bought by Sea Containers in 1981. All withdrawn in Oct. 1980. For sale.
3806–3809	WL	Y	23,452		1939	Linke Hof.	3808 converted to U Ord. in 1949.
3810–3842	WL	Y	23,452		1939	Nivelles	3835 preserved as restaurant of Orient Exp. at St. Cyr (France) by Azoulay. 3815 preserved AJECTA, Longueville.
3843–3860	WL	Y	23,452		1940–41	Breda	For Italy. 3847 and 3854 damaged; renum. 3886 and 3887 in 1949 (rebuilt).
3861–3870	WL	YT	23,452		1940	Ganz	For Hungary.

Car no.	Type	Class	Length excl. buffers	Seats or berths	Year	Builder	Remarks	(Yugoslav)
3871–3887	WL	Y	23,452		1950	Ansaldo	New construction incorporating parts of 2717, 2714, 2798, 2727, 3407, 2719, 3768, 2770, 2720, 2736, 2699, 3655, 3033, 2716, 4236, 3847 and 3854, all badly war-damaged.	
3888–3902	WL	Y	23,452		11948	Nivelles	For Turkey. Ankara Exp./Anatolia Exp. Double windows originally. No elec. heat circuits. 3893 remodelled with elec. heat circuits, etc., for film *From Russia with Love;* later in France. 3894, 3898 and 3901 in Turin-Rome in 1981 (Oct.).	
3903–3931	WL	YT	23,452		1949	Nivelles	3908, 3911, 3920, 3930 and 3931 preserved at Hotel Koyo Paradise, Kyoto (Japan). 3907, 3912 and 3915 bought by Sea Containers (for VSOE staff/baggage) in 1979–81. 3916 bought by BBC in 1980 for film *Caught on a Train.* In 1981 presented to Nene Valley Rly., Peterborough (England). 3929 preserved VVM Hamburg at Schonbergerstrand, Kiel (Germany) in 1977. 3904 3921 and 3925 sold to CH.: 1978 (in service in Greece, with WL conductors). For Venezia-Athens Exp. in 1980. 3922 destroyed by accident in 1963.	
3932–3947	WL	YT	23,452		1950	E.I.C.	3933 and 3938 preserved at Hotel Koyo Paradise, Kyoto (Japan). 3932, 3934 and 3937 sold to CH in 1978 (in service with WL conductors). 3940 and 3941 preserved Ch. de Fer du Doller, Mulhouse, since 1980.	
3948–3962	WL	Y	23,452		1950	E.I.C.	Some later converted to YU.	
3963–3982	WL	LJ	23,452		1952–53	Bilbao	For Spain. 20 pl. 3968, 3969, 3971, 3972, 3975, 3976 and 3978–3981 painted white with blue inscriptions (3975 red) for Int. Rly. Congress in 1958. Repainted blue later. Withdrawn in 1967–69, owing to small compts. and defective, rusty-steel bodywork. Some bogies reused in 4641–4668.	
3983–3989	WL	F	19,232		1952	CGC	For England. 3985 at BR rolling stock exhibition, Old Oak Common (Paddington Carriage sheds) in 1965, promoting London-Basle service (1965–67). Series sold to SNCF in 1971 (BR conductors since 1977). 3986 withdrawn (cannibalized) in Nov. 1978. Some repainted in SNCF livery after 1978. All withdrawn on 31 Oct. 1980. Last WL in UK service.	
3990–4000							No. series beginning 4000 originally for Pullman cars. So nos. not used.	
4001–4015	WPC	I cl. *Flèche d'Or*	23,452	24	1926	Birmingham	4001–4004 became II cl. 31 pl. *North Star* type in 1932; rebuilt WR 35 pl. in 1953. 4001 and 4004 in Greece. 4005 and 4006 became WR bar 32 pl. in 1936. 4006 bar exp. in 1954 (long counter); sold to SNCF in 1962. Rest became WR 40 pl. (4008, 41 pl). In 1967 4013 rebuilt WL-Rome as cruising service for Cantaeurope Exp. (La Scala Opera Tour) with 7 shower compts., laundry, 2-berth staff compt., 1-berth director's compt., 3 pl. staff seat in corridor. Now used in Nostalgic Orient Exp., hired from CIWL.	
4016–4030	WP	I cl. *Flèche d'Or*	23,452	32	1926	Metro	Type *Flèche d'Or.* 4016–4019 became II cl. 41 pl. in 1932. 4016 burnt in 1936. Rest, except 4029 and 4030, became WR 41 pl. (4026–4028, 36 pl.). 4025 damaged; rebuilt as WR 4270 in 1955. 4029 burnt at WL-Saint-Denis while being restored in 1975. 4018 and 4019 became bar-dancing in 1965. 4018 restored by Saint-Denis in 1976 for Mulhouse Museum, with marquetry and furnishings from 4029. In 1961 4024 became snack-service van for Italy (2-berth staff compt.). Sold in 1962 to SNCF. 4026 sold to TCDD in 1967.	
4031–4040	WPC	I cl. *Flèche d'Or*	23,452	24	1927–28	CGC	Type *Flèche d'Or.* All became WR 40 pl., except 4036 WR bar 32 pl. 4037–4040 remodelled to WR bar 32 pl. 4032 preserved at Telfs Hippological Museum, Austria.	

Car no.	Type	Class	Length excl. buffers	Seats or berths	Year	Builder	Remarks	(Yugoslav)
							4038 sold to SNCF in 1962; preserved at AJECTA. 4039 lost during war. 4033 later (1961) snack-service van (2 pl. staff compt.) for Italy CIT train Rimini-Boulogne.	
4041–4050	WP	I cl. *Flèche d'Or*	23,452	32	1927–28	CGC	4042 lost during war. Rest became WR 41 pl. 4047 and 4048 sold to SNCF in 1962. 4049 converted to technical service car in 1964, with bar, workshop and 2 berths.	
4051–4065	WPC	I cl. *Flèche d'Or*	23,452	24	1926	Leeds	4062 and 4065 for China in 1937; stored in Hong Kong; sold at Hong Kong in 1948; in 1980 seen running in Kowloon-Canton Rly. (III cl. coach). 4053 destroyed during war. 4051, 4052 and 4055–4057 became WR 34–40 pl. for Turkey. Sold TCDD in 1967. In 1961 4054 became snack-service van in Italy, like 4024. 4059 became WR in 1948, used in Dunkirk Ferry as stationary WR.	
4066–4080	WP	I cl. *Flèche d'Or*	23,452	32	1926	Leeds	4069, 4073 and 4076 destroyed during war. 4066–4071 and 4078 became WR 41 pl. 4073 and 4076 chassis for WR 4265 and 4266. 4077 was staff coach for WL-Ost. in 1959.	
4081–4085	WPC	I cl. *Flèche d'Or*	23,452	24	1927	Birmingham	All became WR 41 pl., except 4085, 4081, 4082 and 4084, which were lost during war.	
4086–4090	WP	I. cl. *Flèche d'Or*	23,452	32	1927	Metro	4088 to Egypt in 1938 (with name); air-conditioned. 4087 lost in war. 4086 became WR 41 pl.	
4091–4110	WPC	II. cl. *North Star*	23,452	38	1927	Birmingham	Type *Etoile du Nord*, became WR 38 pl. 4094, 4095, 4096, 4100, 4101, 4104 and 4110 to Portugal (Sud Exp.). 4104 withdrawn in 1973 (Sud Exp. accident). 4102, 4105, 4107, 4108 and 4109 in Greece since 1961. 4103 in Ostend-Herbesthal (Nord Exp.), with blue colour but Pullman seating, for Railtour special trains(?). 4106 destroyed during war; rebuilt to WR 4267 in 1955. 4095, 4104 and 4110 bought by Sea Containers in 1979–80 as WR for Venice Simplon Orient Exp. (Boulogne-Venice).	
4111–4130	WP	II cl. *North Star*	23,452	51	1927	Metro	4112, 4114, 4116, 4117 and 4124 destroyed during war. Chassis used for WR 4268, 4269 and 4272–4274. 4111, 4119, 4120, 4125 and 4130 plus all above except 4117, became WR (?) pl. In 1978 4121 became WR bar-dancing for Railtour special trains in Belgium. Bought by Sea Containers in 1980 for Venice Orient Exp., to start in 1982.	
4131–4147	WPC	I cl. *Côte d'Azur*	23,452	20	1929	E.I.C.	4144 became WR 52 pl.; used in King George VI Calais-Paris Special for state visit in 1938. 4141 bought by Sea Containers in 1981; rebuilt at Bremen as WP 36 pl. for VSOE WR service; Lalique décor.	
4148–4164	WP	I. cl. *Côte d'Azur*	23,452	28	1929	E.I.C.	4154 destroyed during war; chassis for 4271 in 1955. 4160, 4162 and 4164, painted blue all over, became WS bar for *Blue Train* in 1951; sold to SNCF 1962; withdrawn in 1975. 4160 damaged by fire in 1974. 4164 bought by Intraflug in June 1980 as WS bar for Nostalgic Orient Exp. In 1957, 4151 (150km/h), 4161 and 4163 (160km/h) fitted with new Schlieren bogies and air-conditioning for *Mistral*. 4163 used in film *Murder on Orient Exp.* (1974) and *Julia* (1977); then sold to M-C in 1977; bought by Paccard for preservation at Annecy. 4155 preserved at AJECTA (TVT), Richelieu. 4159 became 21 pl. with 1 saloon WR for Drapeau; later (1976) remodelled to Pullman; used CIWL Dutch Div. centenary train, Maastricht-Zandfoort; then used by SNCF for *Azur 2000* and *Alpes 2000*, for which 4148 remodelled as bar-dancing car. 4149 in Mulhouse Mus. (1969–75); then bought by Intraflug 1977. 4158 (Lalique 'Maidens') bought by Intraflug 1976, and 4161 (Lalique 'Blue-birds') bought by Intraflug 1980 for Nost. Or. Exp. 4152 preserved at Nice (Weiss).	

Kansainvalinen Makuuvaunu-Ja Euroopan Pikajunayhtio

Car no.	Type	Class	Length excl. buffers	Seats or berths	Year	Builder	Remarks	(Finnish)
4165–4170	WP	I cl. Independent	21,552	24	1930	Cardé	For Spain. Wooden bodies. 4165 later converted at Barcelona to cinema coach. 4165, 4167 and 4168 staff coaches at WL-Aravaca (Madrid). 4169 and 4170 staff coaches at WL-Irun in 1959. (All Pullmans withdrawn by 1971.) 4165 to be preserved.	
4171–4173	WPC	I cl. Egyptian	23,452	24	1928	Birmingham	For Egypt. Painted blue and cream; CIWL badge at each end of car. Never ran in Europe. For car names, see separate table.	
4174–4176	WP	I cl. Egyptian	23,452	28	1928	Birmingham	For Egypt. Painted blue and cream; CIWL badge at each end of car. Never ran in Europe. For car names, see separate table.	
4177–4200							Nos. not used.	
4201–4218	WR		23,452	46	1940	Nivelles	4201, 4205, 4207–4210, 4217 and 4218 sold to SNCF in 1962, retaining CIWL title and livery. 4202 sold to Mitsui, Japan, in 1978. 4206 destroyed in war. 4208 sold to Soc. Pioner; preserved at Vélizy, Versailles. 4217 and 4218 in *Train Bleu* in 1951. In 1979, 4217 bought by Azoulay; restaurant Orient Exp., St. Cyr. 4207 preserved AJECTA.	
4219–4224	WR		23,452	42	1939	Cegielski	4223 and 4224 never entered service, owing to war. 4223 became I cl. PKP coach, Polish Rlys.	
4225–4241	WR		23,452	56	1940/1	Reggio	4236 damaged, became WL 3895 in 1949. 4227, 4228 and 4234 destroyed in war. 4225–4231 and 4235 painted in WP colours as carrozza-buffet-bar cars for Rome-Ventimiglia in 1960s; withdrawn 1976. 4229 preserved at Vichy (France) works canteen.	
4242–4249	WR		23,452	46	1943	Arad	For Roumania. Later in Denmark. 4243 in Nord Exp. (Nyborg-Osnabruck) in 1961. 4246 in NS Inter City Plus service, with telephone compt., in 1979 (free coffee and newspapers); Withdrawn in 1981. 4249 preserved at Utrecht Museum (Holland) since 1981.	
4250–4251	WR		20,300	50	1944	WL-Budapest	For Hungary, rescued to Austria. Rebuilt from 2506 and 2505. Metal panelling imitating the original teak. In Ostend-Vienna Exp. (Stuttgart-Wien) until 1954. 4250 preserved Eisenbahnfreunde Oesterreich (Austrian Rly. Friends) since 1979. 4251 preserved Hippomobile Museum, Telfs (Austria) since 1966.	
4252–4254	WR						In process of rebuilding from WR nos. 2502, 2501 and 2503 at WL-Budapest when Russian invasion took place. Never completed, so nos. not used.	
4255–4264	WR		23,000	46	1950	Simmering	For Austria. Last new WRs.	
4265–4274	WR		23,452	52	1955	Breda	New WRs built from parts of damaged 4073, 4076, 4106, 4112, 4114, 4025, 4154, 4116, 4117 and 4124. Vestibule and outer doors at one end only. 4271–4274 sold to SNCF in 1962. 4271 in film *Murder on Orient Exp.* Last WRs built for CIWL.	
4275–4500							Nos. not used.	
4501–4525	WL	P	24,000		1955–56	Nivelles	Stainless-steel unpainted Budd-patent body shell with 20 small compts. for II cl., single, but used as I cl. since III cl. abolished before entering service. 'Special' low supplements. Single vestibule one end only. 4501–4520 to Spain in 1967–68. 4518 destroyed (fire) in 1980. 39 P class in France became II cl. tourist T2P with single lower and upper pairs kept locked open as doubles. All in service except 4518.	
4526–4550	WL	P	24,000		1955–56	Carel-Fouche		
4551–4565	WL	P	24,000		1955–56	Ansaldo		
4566–4580	WL	P	24,000		1955–56	Fiat		
4581–4600	WL	U	25,100		1957	Hansa	War reparations cars. First cars with oil heat. 'Universal' cars with 2-position middle berth. 4589, 4590, 4593, 4594,	
4601–4620	WL	U	25,100		1957	Donauwörth		

215

Car no.	Type	Class	Length excl. buffers	Seats or berths	Year	Builder	Remarks	(Finnish)
							4596, 4604, 4607, 4609 and 4614 for *Puerta del Sol* in 1969, with new Minden-Deutz bogies for Spanish portion; sold to Wasteels Travel Agents, Brussels, in 1980, but still in SNCF service in France, after replacement of *Puerta del Sol* by RENFE Pendular Talgo in 1981.	
4621–4640	WL	Y	25,100		1958	Fiat	For Italy. Air-conditionned. Same size as Hansa U, but with single or double compts. only (I cl.). Later called 'YC' (climatized).	
4641–4668	WL	YF	25,148		1963–65	MMCZ	For Spain. Identical layout to YC with some Fiat patents (hence YF). Air-conditionned with diesel generator. Bogies from WL 3693–3982 on some cars.	
4669–4690	WL	YF	25,148		1969–70	MMCZ	For Spain. Air-conditionned as 4641–4668.	
4691–4700							Nos. not used	
4701–4740	WL	MU	26,400		1964–65	E.I.C.	Universal type, 1, 2 (I cl.) or 3 (II cl.) berths, single vestibule, 12 compts. 147 MUs in service in 1982.	
4741–4760	WL	M	26,400		1964	Fiat	For Italy. Air-conditioned. Identical to MU but I cl. single or double compts. only.	
4761–4775	WL	MU	26,400		1964–65	Fiat	For international services from Italy. Air-conditioned.	
4776–4785	WL	MU	26,400		1963–64	Donauwörth	For Switzerland. Plated 'Propriété CFF' (SBB property) lower waist end, but carried full CIWL livery and title in 1964–72. 4780 damaged in *Wiener Walze*; withdrawn in 1968 (accident).	
4786–4790	WL	MU	26,400		1964	Donauwörth	4786 SBB-owned, in place of 4780, in 1968. 4787 at Munich Exhibition in 1965.	
4791–4805	WL	MU	26,400		1966	Donauwörth	Rented from Eurofima by CIWL in 1969. Owned by Eurofima until 1981.	
4806–4820	WL	MU	26,400		1968–70	Fiat	Owned by Eurofima for TEN Pool. Air-conditioned.	
4821–4840	WL	MU	26,400		1970–71	Fiat	Owned by Eurofima for TEN Pool, except 4821 and 4822 and 4826–4828, which are owned by CIWL for Italy. Air-conditioned.	
4841–4868	WL	MU	26,400		1972	Fiat	Owned by Eurofima for TEN Pool, except 4856–4858 and 4862–4865, which are owned by CIWL for Italy. Last CIWL MU cars.	
4869–5000							Nos. not used.	
5001–5020	WL	T2	26,400		1968	Donauwörth	For France. 5003 and 5004 for *Palatino* (Rome-Paris) in 1969. Last CIWL design. Forced-draught ventilation. I cl. Special; II cl. Tourist Double, 18 compts.	
5021–5300							Nos. reserved for SNCF-owned T2. 82 built, plus 6 T2 for SNCB, but because SNCF maintain own cars at Romilly, since 1977, nos. not used.	
5301–5320	WL	T2	26,400		1977–79	Beasain	For Spain. Last CIWL-owned cars. Air-conditionned with diesel generator.	
5321–5400							Nos. not used.	
5401–5445	WL	T2	26,400		1977–79	Macosa	For Spain. Supplied to RENFE. Air-conditionned. 5431 destroyed (accident) in 1981.	
5446–6000							Nos. not used.	
6001–6012	WL	YF	25,150		1971–72	MMCZ	For Spain. Last YF CIWL-owned cars.	
6013–6100							Nos. not used.	
6101–6110	WL	YF	25,150		1974	MMCZ	For Spain. Supplied to RENFE.	

Internationella Sovvagns-och Europeiska Expresstagsbolaget

Car no.	Type	Class	Length excl. buffers	Seats or berths	Year	Builder	Remarks	(Swedish)
6111–6400							Nos. not used.	
6401–6416	WL	T2S	26,400		1975	Schlieren	Eurofima-owned for the TEN Pool. Schlieren (Swiss), not CIWL design. 17 compts. on 1 level, II cl. double, I cl. 'special'. 6401–6411 painted red for DB. 6412–6416 (painted blue) for FS.	
6417–6449	WL	T2S	26,400		1975	Casaralta	Builder is Casaralta, S.p.A., Bologna, Italy. Eurofima-owned for the TEN Pool, and for Italy (FS)	
6450–6454	WL	T2S	26,400		1975	Schlieren	Eurofima-owned for SBB. For Switzerland.	
6455–6463	WL	T2S	26,400		1975	Schindler	Eurofima-owned for the TEN Pool: 6455–6457 for OBB; 6458–6459 for NS; 6460–6461 for DSB (in Copenhagen-Frederikshavn, 1981); 6462–6463 for OBB.	

Blue Train décor

1929 Art Deco marquetry of the Grand Luxe (Lx) class sleeping cars

Car nos.	Decorator	Design		Car nos.	Decorator	Design
(built in England)				3498–3500	Prou	'Grey and Rose'
3466, 3467, 3473, 3477, 3480	Morison	'Garland'		3501, 3503, 3505, 3507, 3509	Prou	'Grey and Pink'
3481, 3483, 3487, 3489, 3491	Morison	'Flower Basket'		3502, 3504, 3506, 3508, 3510	Prou	'Green'
3468–3472	Maple	'Acacia Ice'		3511–3515	Prou	'Red Shell Pattern'
3474–3476, 3478, 3479	Maple	'Woodtrellis Blue-Green'		3516–3520	Prou	'Finnish Wood'
3482, 3484–3486, 3488	Maple	'Trapeze Style', upper portion		3521–3525	Prou	'Sapelli Pearl'
3490, 3492–3495	Maple	'Encrusted Lacquer'		3529–3531, 3534, 3535	Prou	'Cuban Unified'
(built in France)				3526–3528, 3537, 3538	Prou	'Red Square Transparent'
3496, 3497	Prou	'Grey and White'		3532, 3536, 3539–3555	Nelson	See Plates 101 and 102

Fleet of the International Sleeping Car Co.

Duplicate List (Does not include the cars with the same number which are in the principal list)

Car no.	Type	Class	Year	Builder	Remarks (Palestine and China used English)
10	WR		1898	CGC	Ex-WR No. 497. Reason not known
51–60	WP/WPC		1925	Birmingham	Ex-Pullman Car Co. cars with names. Returned to Pullman Car Co., except Nos. 54 and 58, sent to Egypt with new names.
101–106	WP		1931	SIG	For *Golden Mountain*. 101 and 102 belonged to MOB, ex-Nos. 83 and 84 (MOB.). Rest sold to Rhatische Bahn and used on that line. Metre gauge (Switzerland).
351–373	WR		1931	EIC	Ex-Etat Pullmans of Trains-Transatlantiques, leased after the war. (France.)
578, 579, 583, 584	WL	AC*	1936	Decauville	Ex-PLM couchette cars, leased 1945–60. Co.'s title under the windows. (France.)
586, 591–599	WL	AC*	1931	Lyons	Ditto.

*AC = *ancienne couchette*.

Sleeping cars of the Oussouri Railway (Chap. 6), which, beginning in 1923, ran with Wagons-Lits

0111	I. cl.	
0171	I. cl.	
0172	I-II cl.	
0221	II cl.	Not the same as those bearing the no. 221 mentioned in the principal list. 3 cars in all carried the no. 221
0222	II cl.	
0223	II cl.	
0351–0355	III cl.	

Sleeping cars of the Chinese Eastern Railway (Chap. 6) taken on charge by Wagons-Lits

I-II cl. mixed nos.: 302, 304, 308, 310–314;
II cl. nos.: 411, 412, 414, 415, 421, 426, 433, 708;
III cl. nos.: 422, 427, 714, 733, 734, 741, 742, 744, 747

SBB dining car fleet of CSWR/SSG

22 teak diners were all built by Ringhoffer between 1906 and 1914, of which two (No. 22 of 1914 and No. 14 of 1907) are preserved respectively at the Lucerne Swiss Transport Museum and by the Oensingen Balsthal Railway. The latter run their car in their vintage steam train and describe it as a Simplon Orient Car, in as much as it once substituted for a CIWL diner, failed at Lausanne, and is believed to have run to Istanbul in the train. More likely it ran to Trieste. Nos. 11–13 and 17 were metre gauge for MOB. These cars were absorbed into SBB in 1947, with 102 prefixed to their numbers for such standard-guage cars as were in service. For special trains, No. 25, built by Schlieren in 1930, has been restored to traffic by SSG since 1981 and fitted with gas cooking for working off electric lines and on special steam-hauled trains, etc. Its rather drab wooden body is to be decorated internally with marquetry from old CIWL stock.

Space precludes a listing of all SSG dining cars used at the present time by SSG, who are getting 4 new dining cars in 1982.

Mixed sleepers and diners in Spain

In addition to the CIWL sleepers sold to Norte and MZA as WLM staffed by CIWL, the Norte had 15 teak WLM Nos. 15–30 (later 615–630) and 8 mixed I cl. bar cars (WR 13 pl.) Nos. 601–608. The Ouests (West) had 5 teak WLM Nos. 301–305 (RENFE 201–205) and 6 steel WLM Nos. 601–606 (RENFE 1201–1206), also 2 bar cars (II cl.) WR 12 pl. Nos. 261–262. All these were disguised as CIWL cars with badge. CIWL also staffed 14 teak WLM and 8 II cl. (MZA) mixed bar cars (WR 13 pl.) and 3 steel WLM for the Central Aragon, none of which had CIWL markings.

List of Pullman Car names

I. Cars of the Wagons-Lits Co.

No.	Type	Name	Remarks
54 2994	WPC	Karnak	Formerly *Hermione*, name removed for CIWL service. New name added when car was sent to Egypt. 2994 was allocated but never used, since car remained on Duplicate List.
58 2998	WPC	Cleopatra	Formerly *Rainbow*, name removed for CIWL service. New name added when car was sent to Egypt. 2998 was allocated but never used, since car remained on Duplicate List.
2914	WPC	Luxor	
2915	WPC	Assuan	
2916	WPC	Fayoum	
2917	WPC	Siwa	
4088	WP	Le Sphinx	Only Pullman cars in Egypt had names. No. 4088 was named on transfer to Egypt. For details of builders, see list of CIWL cars or Duplicate List. For details of the services operated, see Chap. 8.
4171	WPC	Edfou	
4172	WPC	Bendera	
4173	WPC	Rosetta	
4174	WP	Tutank Amen	
4175	WP	Nefertari	
4176	WP	Rameses	

II. Cars of the Pullman Palace Car Co. in Great Britain and Italy

All the cars were built by Pullman, USA, and erected at Derby, Turin or Brighton

Schedule No.*	Name	Type	Year	Remarks
	Midland	WL	1/1874	Sold to Midland Rly. in 1888 (MR No. 20); body preserved by the city of Derby at Midland Rly. Trust Butterley.
	Excelsior	WL	2/1874	Sold to MR in 1888: MR No. 21.
	Enterprise	WL	1874	Burnt out at Hunslet, Leeds, in 1882; renamed *Alexandra* in 1880; sent to Italy in
	Victoria	WP	1874	1883; sold to CIWL in 1884 (WL No. 155, see list above); no name while in CIWL service; ran on LSWR in 1880.
	Britannia	WP	1874	Rebuilt with 6-wheel bogies as WR *Windsor* in 1882; sold to Midland Rly. in 1883: MR No. 15.
	Leo	WP	1874	Rebuilt with 6-wheel bogies as WR *Delmonico* in 1882; sold to MR in 1883: MR No. 14.
	St. George	WL	1875	Sold to MR in 1888: MR No. 22.
	Jupiter	WP	1875	Used on LCDR in 1882–84; sent to LBSCR in 1884; became III class No. 1 in 1915 (see Part III below).
	Saturn	WP	1875	Sold to MR in 1883: MR No. 1.
	Transit	WL	1875	Sold to MR in 1888: MR No. 24.
	Ocean	WL	1875	Ran on GNR in 1875–80; in Italy in 1883; sold to CIWL in 1886 (see Nos. 216–221 in list above); no name in CIWL service.
	Saxon	WL	1875	Sold to MR in 1888: MR No. 25.
	Ohio	WP	1875	Ran on GNR; became WR *Prince of Wales* in 1879 (first WR in Great Britain); sold to GNR in 1885: GNR No. 2992.
	Mars	WL	10/1875	On LBSCR until 1883, used permanently in day position; in Italy in 1884; sold to CIWL in 1886 (see Nos. 216–221 above); no name in CIWL service.
	Mercury	WP	1876	Sold to MR in 1883: MR No. 2.
	Juno	WP	1876	Ditto: MR No. 3.
	Bart-Bona	WL then WRS	1876	Sold to CIWL in 1886 (No. 198); name carried in CIWL service.
	Piemonte	WL then WRS	1876	Ditto: No. 199.
	Toscana	WL then WRS	1876	Ditto: No. 200.
	Australia	WL	1876	On MR to 1883; in Italy in 1883; sold to CIWL (No. 201) in 1886; name carried in CIWL service.
	Castalia	WL	1876	On MR to 1883; in Italy in 1883; burnt out at Riate in 1884.
	Germania	WL	1876	On MR in 1876–78, then GNR 1878–80; in Italy in 1883; sold to CIWL in 1886 (No. 201); name carried in CIWL service.
	Scotia	WL	1876	Sold to MR in 1888: MR No. 26.
	Italia	WL	1876	Later became WR; sold to CIWL in 1886 (No. 203); name carried in CIWL service.
	Venus	WP	1876	Sold to MR in 1883: MR No. 4.
	Vesta	WP	1876	Sold to MR in 1883: MR No. 5.
	Norman	WL	1876	Sold to MR in 1888: MR No. 27.
	India	WL	1876	On MR in 1876–78; then GNR in 1878; destroyed at Thirsk in 1892 (collision).
	Minerva	WP	1876	Sold to MR in 1883: MR No. 6.
	Crotona	WL	1876	Later WR; sold to CIWL in 1886 (No. 204); name carried in CIWL service.
	Metaponto	WL	1876	Later WR; sold to CIWL in 1886 (No. 205), name carried in CIWL service.
	Heraclea	WL	1876	Later WR; sold to CIWL in 1886 (No. 206); name carried in CIWL service
	Sybaris	WL	1876	Later WR; sold to CIWL in 1886 (No. 207); name carried in CIWL service.
	Planet	WP	1876	Sold to MR in 1883: MR No. 7.
	Albion	WP	1876	Sold to MR in 1883: MR No. 8.
	Comet	WP	1876	Sold to CIWL MR in 1883: MR No. 9.

Schedule No.*	Name	Type	Year	Remarks
	Apollo	WP	1876	Sold to MR in 1883: MR No. 10.
1	Ariel	WP	8/1876	On MR in 1876–81; renamed *Louise* in 1881 for LBSCR; withdrawn 1929; became bungalow in Sussex.
	Adonis	WP	1876	On MR in 1876–81; renamed *Victoria* in 1881 for LBSCR; became WPC; later became III class No. 2 in 1915.
	Aurora	WP	1877	Sold to MR in 1883: MR No. 11.
	Ceres	WP	1877	On MR in 1877–81; renamed *Maud* in 1881 for LBSCR; became WR in 1884; scrapped in 1899 after accident at Wivelsfield.
	Eclipse	WP	1877	Sold to MR in 1883: MR No. 12.
	Alexandra	WP	1877	Sold to MR in 1883: MR No. 13.
	Alexandra	WP	1877	On LBSCR; became III class No. 3 in 1915.
	Albert Edward	WP	1877	On LBSCR; became III cl. No. 4 in 1915.
2	Globe	WP	1877	On MR in 1877–81; renamed *Beatrice* in 1881 for LBSCR; first Pullman car with electric lighting; derailed at Lovers Walk, Brighton, in 1914; withdrawn in 1918.
	Columba	WL	1880	For GNR in 1880; sold to GNR & NER in 1895.
	Iona	WL	1880	For GNR in 1880; sold to GNR & NER in 1895.
	St. Andrew	WL	1882	Sold to MR in 1888: MR No. 28.
	St. Mungo	WL	1882	Sold to MR in 1888: MR No. 29.
3	Balmoral	WL	1882	3-axle 6-wheel car; rebuilt as bogie WL in 1895; on GNR 1883–85; to Highland Rly. 1885–1907; ended its life running in mixed passenger/goods trains in 1907; stored 1907–18.
4	Culross	WL	1882	As *Balmoral,* but renamed *Dunrobin* in 1885 for service on Highland Rly.
	St. Louis	WL	1882	As *Balmoral;* rebuilt with bogies in 1885; sold to MR in 1888: MR No. 30.
	St. Denis	WL	1882	As *Balmoral;* rebuilt with bogies in 1885, sold to MR in 1888: MR No. 31.
	Missouri	WL	1883	Sold to MR in 1888: MR No. 32.
	Michigan	WL	1883	Sold to MR in 1888: MR No. 33. Derby Pullman assembly works closed in 1888.
	All cars below entered service on LBSCR (SR after 1923) unless shown otherwise			
6 5 7	Princess Prince Albert Victor	WP WP WP	12/1888 12/1888 12/1888	First cars for England with vestibules and gangways. Erected at Brighton, not Derby. Built for Pullman Ltd. (Chap. 3) as multiple unit. Originally *Prince* did not have buffers, since it ran in the centre of the rake. Buffers added in 1915. *Princess* became WPC in 1920, withdrawn with *Albert Victor* in 1929. Became studio of celebrated writer on and painter of trains, C. Hamilton Ellis, at Partridge Green, Sussex. *Prince* withdrawn in 1932.
8	Duchess of Albany	WP	3/1890	On LSWR from 1890 to 1907–12. Became WPC in 1913 (Pullman Longhedge). On LBSCR 1912–23, SR 1923–29. Withdrawn 1929 to Partridge Green with *Princess.*
9	Duchess of Fife	WP	3/1890	On LSWR from 1890 to 1907–12. Became WPC in 1912 (Pullman Longhedge). On LBSCR/SR 1912–29, when withdrawn.
10	Empress	WP	5/1890	Withdrawn in 1932. Used as bungalow at Lancing, Sussex, by J.S. Marks on retirement as General Manager of Pullman.
76	The Queen	WP	11/1890	Became III cl. car No. 9 in 1920 as WPC (Pullman Longhedge).
11	Pavilion	WP	2/1893	Last Pullman with high windows and clerestory roof to remain in service LBSCR/SR. Became WPC in 1923 (Pullman Longhedge). Withdrawn in 1934.
12	Princess Mary	WP	3/1893	Became WPC in 1909. Scrapped in 1932.
13	Duchess of Connaught	WP	3/1893	Became WPC in 1914 (Pullman Longhedge). Scrapped in 1932.
14	Princess Margaret	WP	3/1893	On LSWR from 1890 to 1907, then LBSCR. Became WPC in 1913 (Pullman Longhedge). Withdrawn in 1932; became bungalow at Lancing, like *Empress.*
15	Prince Regent	WP	3/1893	Became II cl. No. 3 in 1921 as WPC.
16	Princess of Wales	WP	10/1895	Became III cl. No. 19 in 1915 as WPC.
17	Duchess of York	WPC	10/1895	Became III cl. No. 17 in 1915.
77	Her Majesty	WP	10/1895	Became III cl. No. 10 in 1922 as WPC.

Schedule No.*	Name	Type	Year	Remarks
19	The Arundel	WP	7/1899	6-wheel bogies like all cars below. Renamed Majestic as WPC in 1905, since its name was confused with a destination board. Withdrawn in 1932; became bungalow at Lancing.
18	The Chichester	WP	7/1899	Renamed Waldemar, as WPC in 1905, since its name was confused with a destination board. Withdrawn in 1932; became a bungalow at Lancing.
20	Devonshire	WPC	8/1900	Withdrawn in 1931. Canteen at Preston Park Pullman Works until 1964.

*The last three Pullman Cars built in USA were delivered after the sale of the Pullman Palace Car Co. had started. They are listed later on. The Schedule Nos. in this list were added after 1908.

III. Cars of the Pullman Car Co. Ltd.: 1908–62

This table, which groups the cars in the order of names used by the staff and cites the dates of the batches built, recaptures the flavour of the British company. Thus, Pearl, Diamond and Onyx rolls off the tongue, twenty years after the firm's demise, whereas in today's tidy, computerized world Diamond, Onyx, Pearl would be better appreciated! Sometimes a bar car had a name different from that of the car.

Each Car was identified by a Schedule Number, mounted on a plate or painted on the car end. Only first class (and non-supplement dining cars in Scotland) bore names. Third-class cars carried 'Car No. 00 Third Class' in the name panel. No third class ran in Britain after 1956, and the terms 'Third Class' or 'Second Class' disappeared. Before 1956 second class existed only on 'Continental Expresses' from London to the Channel Ports. Pullmans on these trains bore the words 'Car No. 00 Second Class' (also on the Golden Arrow when second-class Pullmans ran in it). The cars were identical to third class. The numbers bore no relation to the Schedule Number in many cases, and identification became even more problematic with the change of some Schedule Numbers in 1960 (here ignored). Cars frequently changed status, but not all changes are recorded for reasons of space. Names often recurred, but no two cars with the same name ran at the same time during this period. The abbreviations for the car types enployed elsewhere are inappropriate for this quintessentially British firm, whose own abbreviations are:

P = Pullman Parlour Car, usually two saloons and two end coupés;
K = Pullman Parlour Car with kitchen, two saloons and one coupé;
GP = Parlour Car with hand-brake wheel in one end vestibule, tip-up seat for the guard and 'Guard' painted on the vestibule doors, used on SR;
BP = Parlour Car with luggage van, hand brake and seat of guard inside the van (known as Brake Parlour);
MBP = Brake Parlour with driving compartment at one end instead of vestibule, used at each end of 5-car Brighton Belle electric sets;
OBS = Parlour Car with small buffet, large rear window and no vestibule at one end;
D = Non-supplement dining car in Scotland, with kitchen, chairs in the saloons similar to CIWL diners (WR), not Pullman armchairs;
RC = Some non-supplement buffet cars in SR service in England bore the title 'Refreshment Car' in the name panel, others painted green, with no name;
CC = Withdrawn Pullman Cars transferred to BR ownership, with BR Regional Number, converted to 'Camp Coach' ('Holiday Coach' on SR), stationary, at country stations; numbers are BR Regional Nos.

Schedule No.	Names	Type	Bogies	Year	Builder	Remarks
21–23	Duchess of Norfolk,	K	6	1/1906	Pullman USA	For LBSCR. Last cars built in USA, reaching England after takeover; withdrawn in 1932; became bungalow at Lancing (Sussex). Scrapped in 1932.
	Princess Ena,	K	6			
	Princess Patricia	P	6			Rebuilt to K by Pullman Longhedge in 1925; scrapped in 1934.
24–30	Verona, Alberta,	BP	6	11/1908	Metro	All except Princess Helen rebuilt to K by Pullman Longhedge in 1914. Verona withdrawn in 1930; became wood and marquetry store, Preston Park. Rest withdrawn in 1935.
	Belgravia, Cleopatra,	P	6			
	Bessborough, Princess Helen,	P	6			
	Grosvenor	K	6			Rebuilt to bar car in 1936 by Pullman Preston Park; withdrawn in 1960; CC BR (E) No. CC 169.
35–40	Sorrento, Corunna, Savona,	P	4	3/1910	Birmingham	Sorrento and Corunna rebuilt to K in 1924; withdrawn in 1962; CC BR(S) Nos. P63 and P62. Savona became K in 1924; mobile stores supply car in 1933; rebuilt to I cl. in 1951; withdrawn in 1960; CC BR (Sc) No. SC44.
	Valencia, Florence,	K	4			Valencia and Florence withdrawn in 1962; CC BR(S) Nos. P54 and P53.
	Clementina	K	4			Clementina withdrawn in 1960; CC BR(E) No. CC166.
32–34	Galatea, Mayflower,	K	4	6/1910	Birmingham	Galatea and Mayflower without gangways for Metropolitan Rly. in 1910; London Transport in 1933–39; withdrawn in 1939; became wood merchant's store/office; scrapped in 1948.
	Emerald	K	4			Burnt out in 1955; became Instruction Car No. 101; preserved as Emerald at Conway Valley Museum, Bettws-y-Coed, Wales/Cymru.
42–44	Regina,	K	4	10/1910	Birmingham	Withdrawn in 1962; CC BR(S) No. P55.
	Sapphire, Palermo	P	4			Became Army (NAAFI) Canteens Nos. 37 and 21 in 1942–48; withdrawn in 1962; CC BR(S) Nos. P51 and P64. Sapphire preserved at SE Steam Centre, Ashford.
78	Shamrock	D	4	3/1911	Birmingham	Renamed Duchess of Gordon in 1918; sold to LMS in 1933 (No. 210).

Schedule No.	Names	Type	Bogies	Year	Builder	Remarks
31 46	Vivienne, Myrtle	P K	6 6	7/1911	Cravens	Built by Cravens Ltd., Darnall, Sheffield. Vivienne scrapped in 1935. Myrtle rebuilt in 1936 to bar car by Pullman Preston Park; withdrawn in 1962; CC BR(Sc) No. SC47.
48	Cosmo Bonsor	K	4	5/1912	Cravens	Named after SE & CR chairman; renamed Rainbow in 1948; withdrawn in 1962; CC BR(Sc) No. SC46.
41 45, 47	Leghorn, Seville, Alicante	P K	4 4	12/1912	Cravens	Withdrawn in 1962; CC BR(S) No. P61. Seville became Army (NAAFI) Canteen No. 3 in 1942–48; withdrawn in 1962; CC BR(S) No. P47. Alicante withdrawn in 1962; CC BR(W) No. W 9874.
49–53	Glencoe, Scotia, Hibernia, Orpheus	P K	6 6	1/1914	Cravens	All in War Office Special Train, London-Dover, in 1914–18. Scotia used by King George V, Lloyd George and other VIPs. Glencoe scrapped at Shoreham in 1955. Scotia withdrawn in 1960; CC BR(E) No. CC167. Hibernia and Orpheus withdrawn in 1960; became CC BR(S) No. P46 and BR(E) No. CC164.
56, 58, 59, 50 60	Ruby, Daphne, Hawthorn, Mimosa Topaz	K P	4 4	3/1914	Birmingham	Ruby was last composite ½ cl. car in Le Havre boat train, London (Waterloo)-Southampton Docks until rebuilt to I cl. in 1956. All withdrawn in 1962; CC BR(S) Nos. P45, P60 and P58. Mimosa BR(W) No. W9869. Withdrawn in 1960; preserved at NRM York (armchairs removed for 1960 cars); ran in Travellers Fare Centenary Exp. in 1979 and Rainhill Rocket 150 Cavalcade in 1980.
55, 57, 64, 67, 63, 66, 61, 62, 52, 65	Mary Hamilton, Mary Beaton, Mary Seaton, Mary Carmichael, Annie Laurie, Helen McGregor, Flora Macdonald, Fair Maid of Perth, Lass O'Gowrie, Maid of Morven	D OBS	6 4	5/1914– 8/1914 7/1914	Cravens	For Scotland, Caledonian Rly., G&SWR & Highland Rly. All sold to LMS in 1933 (Nos. 200–208). Maid of Morven for Glasgow-Oban; delayed by World War I from entering service until 1923; sold to LMS in 1933 (No. 209).
72–75, 17, 19	Car Nos. 1–4 III cl.; Car Nos. 17 and 19 III cl.	K	4	1915	Pullman USA	Converted to III cl. at Brighton LB&SCR in 1915. Scrapped in 1932 except '4'; which became store Preston Park, then scrapped in 1950.
68–71	Car Nos. 5–8 III cl.	K	6	1917	Pullman Longhedge	'5' became 'New Century Bar' in April 1946, and then 'Trianon Bar' from July 1946 to 1955. '6' and '8' withdrawn in 1962; CC BR(S) Nos. P57 and P56. '7' scrapped (Shoreham) in 1955.
79	Tulip	P	4	3/1919	Jackson Ship.	Ex-SER I cl. 'Folkestone Vestibuled Ltd.' built in 1897; No. 171; scrapped in 1930.
80, 87, 84, 86, 83, 82, 85, 81	Dorothy, Stella, Dora, Mabel, Venus, Hilda, Albatross, Thistle	P P K	4 4	1919	Metro	Ex-SER 'Folkestone Vestibuled Ltd.' cars, built in 1897; Nos. 205/4/2/3/6. All scrapped in 1930 except Venus, which was scrapped in 1929. Ex-SER 'Folkestone Vestibuled Ltd.', built in 1897; Nos. 201/8/7; rebuilt at LBSCR Brighton in 1919. Albatross and Thistle became mobile stores supply cars in 1931–38; withdrawn in 1938; became office at Lancing SR Carriage Works in 1940. Hilda scrapped in 1930.
17, 106. 173, 107, 108, 109	Car Nos. 45 and 47 III cl. Car Nos. 56 and 57 II cl. Ansonia, Arcadia	D D K	6 6 6	2/1920	Clayton	Built at Clayton Wagon Works, in Lincoln. '45' and '47' rebuilt with 'left-handed' kitchens as D by Pullman Longhedge in 1923 (opposite side corridor and kitchens to other standard Pullmans). Later III cl. K. Withdrawn in 1962; CC BR(Sc) No. SC45 and BR(S) No. P50. For 'Hook Continental' London-Harwich GER, in 1920–23; rebuilt to III cl. K and III cl. BP by Pullman Longhedge in 1923; withdrawn c. 1938 Remodelled to BP I cl. in 1924 by Pullman Longhedge; became III cl. BP Nos. '94' and '95', at Pullman Preston Park in 1934. '94' scrapped at Shoreham in 1955. '95' withdrawn in 1962; CC BR(Sc) No. SC50.
88–90, 105, 103, 104	Carmen, Constance, Figaro, Diana, Dolphin, Falcon	K P	4 4	1920	Gilbert	Rebuilt LBSCR Brighton in 1920; ex-SER, 'Hastings Car Train' cars built by Gilbert Car Co., Troy, NY, in 1891. Carmen destroyed in derailment at Sevenoaks in 1927. Rest withdrawn in 1928–30.

Schedule No.	Names	Type	Bogies	Year	Builder	Remarks
99,	*Padua,*	P	6	10/1920	Birmingham	*Padua* became 'No. 99 II cl.' in 1946; GP II cl; GP '99' in 1947; withdrawn in 1962; CC BR(S) No. P59; preserved by Flying Scotsman Enterprises, Carnforth, as *Padua*.
101	*Portia*	K	6			*Portia* withdrawn in 1960; CC BR(E) No. CC163.
76	Car No. 9 III cl.	K	4	11/1920	Pullman USA	Formerly *The Queen*; scrapped in 1932.
119, 120, 126	*Cambria, Catania, Corsair*	K	6	11/1920	Clayton	For 'Hook Continental' London-Harwich GER. *Cambria* rebuilt to BP in 1924 by Pullman Longhedge. All withdrawn in 1938. *Cambria* preserved at Tenterden; K & ESR (Dine).
97, 98,	*Calais, Milan,*	P	6	1/1921	Birmingham	For SE&CR London-Dover boat trains and trains to Kent coast. Became 'Nos. 97 and 98' III cl. in 1947; withdrawn 1962; CC BR(W) No. W9870 and BR(S) No. P52.
100, 102	*Palmyra, Rosalind*	K	6			*Palmyra* withdrawn in 1960; CC BR(E) No. CC168. *Rosalind* became Army (NAAFI) Canteen No. 18 in 1942–48; withdrawn in 1960; CC BR(S) No. P47. Preserved at Steamtown, Carnforth, by Flying Scotsman Enterprises.
110	Car No. 46 III cl.	D	6	2/1921	Clayton	For London-Harwich boat trains LNER; rebuilt to BP in 1924 by Pullman Longhedge; scrapped in 1932.
91, 96, 95,	*Cadiz, Sylvia, Sunbeam,*	P	6	1921	Pullman Longhedge	For SR Continental Exp. *Cadiz* and *Sylvia* became 'Nos. 294 and 96' II cl. P in 1947. *Cadiz* and *Sunbeam* withdrawn in 1960; CC BR(E) No. CC170 and BR(Sc) No. SC41. *Sylvia* withdrawn in 1962; CBR(S) No. P48.
92–94	*Malaga, Monaco, Neptune*	K	6			*Monaco* and *Neptune* withdrawn in 1960; CC BR(Sc) No. SC43 and BR(E) No. CC162. *Malaga* bought by Ian Allan; preserved at Shepperton, Surrey (boardroom), in 1962; refurbished for Ian Allan in 1981 by Sea Containers.
121–125	Car Nos. 40 and 41 III cl. Car Nos. 42–44 III cl.	BP D	6 6	8/1921	Birmingham	40 destroyed by air raid on Preston Park in 1943. '41' withdrawn in 1962; CC BR(Sc) No. SC42. '42–44' became K; remodelled by Pullman Longhedge in 1924. All withdrawn in 1939. For LNER services.
15	Car No. 3 II cl.	K	4	9/1921	Pullman USA	Ex-*Prince Regent*; rebuilt at Brighton LBSCR; became No. 18 III cl. in 1925; scrapped in 1932.
118, 138, 174 199, 201	*Albion, Alexandra, Nevada, Atlanta, Columbia*	K	6	9/1921	Birmingham	*Albion* and *Alexandra* scrapped in 1935–36. Rest rebuilt to D in 1927 by Pullman Longhedge for LMS (Scottish) services. *Nevada* renamed *Jenny Geddes*; *Atlanta* renamed *Diana Vernon*; *Columbia* renamed *Jeannie Deans*. Sold LMS in 1933 (Nos. 212, 213, 211).
132–137	*Anaconda, Erminie, Coral, Elmira, Formosa, Maid of Kent*	K	4	11/1921	Clayton	All ex-LNWR ambulance coaches of 1918 hospital train; composite cars rebuilt at Pullman Preston Park in 1934. *Anaconda, Erminie, Elmira* and *Maid of Kent* became III cl. 'Nos. 132, 133, 135 and 137' in 1948. *Formosa* became *Maid of Kent* I cl. in 1948 for Thanet Belle. All withdrawn in 1960; CC BR(LM) No. 0222260; BR(Sc) No. SC 40; BR(S) No. P43; BR(LM) No. 022261; BR(E) No. CC161; BR(LM) No. 022262. *Elmira* and *Maid of Kent* preserved as 'Nos. 135 and 137 (non-runners) by Ravenglass & Eskdale Rly., Ravenglass, Cumbria.
111–116 113, 114	Car Nos. 11–16 III cl. (Pullman, on waist)	K OBS	4 4	1921 1947	Clayton Pullman Preston Park	All ex-LNWR ambulance coaches of 1918 hospital train, 1918. All except '12' became bar cars in 1937 at Pullman Preston Park; '12' scrapped in 1943 after damage in air raid. '11, 15 and 16' rebuilt in 1949 to BP by Pullman Preston Park; withdrawn in 1960; CC BR(S) Nos. P40, P42, and P41. '13 and 14' rebuilt to OBS with 'Pullman Observation Car' in cream below windows, which rose to roof. Sold to BR in 1957; Nos. SC281 and M280. '13' preserved at National RR Museum, Green Bay, Wisc. (USA). '14' preserved by Torbay Rly., Paignton, Devon; originally as BR 280, later repainted in Pullman Observation livery.
127–129	Car Nos. 18, 20 and 21 III cl.	K	4	2/1922	Midland	All ex-GWR ambulance train of 1918. '18' became 'Car No. 3 II cl.' in 1925 and 'No. 30' III cl. in 1927; withdrawn in 1960; CC BR(S) No. P 44. '20 and 21' scrapped in 1943 after damage in air raid at Preston Park.
131, 130, 139, 140, 141	Car No. 23 III cl. Car Nos. 22, 24 III cl. Car Nos. 25, 26 III cl.	K P BP	4 4 4	1922	Pullman Longhedge	All ex-Lancs & Yorks Rly. ambulance train of 1918. '25 and 26' scrapped in 1935; rest scrapped in 1938.

Schedule No.	Names	Type	Bogies	Year	Builder	Remarks
142, 143	*Lady Nairn, Bonnie Jean*	D	4	6/1922	Midland	Ex-GWR ambulance train of 1918. For LMS (Scottish) services. Sold to LMS in 933 (Nos. 214 and 215).
77	Car No. 10 III cl.	K	4	12/1922	Pullman USA	Ex-*Her Majesty*; scrapped in 1932.
153–156	*Aurora, Flora, Juno, Montana*	GP	4	3/1923	Birmingham	End cars of 1924 'White Pullman'; *Golden Arrow* from 1929. *Flora* became 'No. 154' in 1946–48. *Aurora* and *Juno* became 'Nos. 503 and 502' in 1950–52. All III cl. GP for *Devon Belle*; nos. screwed on board over names. *Montana* withdrawn in 1960; CC BR(E) No. CC165. Rest withdrawn in 1962; CC BR(W) Nos. W9873, W9871 and W9872.
148, 149, 151 152	Car Nos. 48, 49, 52 and 53 III cl.	D	6	6/1923	Clayton	For LNER Scottish services. Sold to LNER in 1939.
147, 150	Car Nos. 50 and 51 III cl.	K	6			Rebuilt by Pullman Longhedge to 'Nos. 2 and 1' II cl. 1923; renumbered '17 and 19' II cl. in 1927. '17' withdrawn in 1962; CC BR(Sc) No. SC48. '19' scrapped at Shoreham in 1955.
157, 158	Car Nos. 54 and 55 III cl.	K	4	7/1923		'54' rebuilt to BP by Pullman Preston Park in 1937; withdrawn in 1963; preserved at Birmingham Museum Tyseley; sold to Sea Containers in 1981 for London-Folkestone portion of Venice train. '55' became D I cl. (no name) in 1925; rebuilt to BP by Pullman Preston Park in 1937; withdrawn in 1963.
161–163, 164	*Fortuna, Irene, Iolanthe, Rosemary*	K P	4	6/1923	Midland	*Fortuna* and *Irene* rebuilt by Pullman Preston Park to BP 'Nos. 161 and 162' in 1946; III cl. for *Devon Belle*. All withdrawn by 1966.
159, 144,	*Meg Dods, Lass O'Ballochymyle,*	D	4	1923	Clayton	For LMS Scottish services. Sold to LMS in 1933 (Nos. 217, 216, 218).
145,	*Mauchline Belle,*	D	4			Renumbered '27' in 1928; rebuilt to BP by Pullman Preston Park in 1937.
146	Car No. 80 III Cl.	K	4			Withdrawn by 1966.
165–171	*Argus, Geraldine, Marjorie, Sappho, Viking, Medusa, Pauline*	K K K	4 4 4	1924 11/1924 11/1924	Midland	For 'White Pullman' (*Golden Arrow* from 1929). *Geraldine, Marjorie, Viking* and *Pauline* remodelled to III cl. 'Nos. 166, 167, 169 and 171' for *Devon Belle* in 1947–48. All withdrawn about 1964–66.
160, 172, 175 179, 00,00,00, 00,00 00,00,00, 00,00,	*Rosamund, Aurelia, Fingall, Cynthia, Adrian, Ibis, Hermione, Lydia, Rainbow, Leona, Minerva, Niobe, Octavia, Plato*	K K K P P	4 4 4 4 4	10/1924 7/1925	Birmingham	For 'White Pullman' (*Golden Arrow* from 1929). *Cynthia* built in 1925 after those in batch without schedule numbers, which were all sold to CIWL (Nos. 51–60; see Duplicate List). Withdrawn in 1962–63. *Fingall* preserved by Bluebell Rly., Sheffield Park, Sussex. Cars sold to CIWL; returned 1928 (below), except *Hermione* and *Rainbow*. See CIWL Pullman Car names list. *Ibis* preserved by Sea Containers (below).
186,	Car No. 58 III cl.	K	4	7/1925	Midland	Remodelled to II cl. D in 1928–36; then III cl. K. Withdrawn in 1962; CC BR (Sc) No. SC49.
187, 188	Car No. 65 I cl. Car No. 66 III cl.	D P	4 4			'65' rebuilt to III cl. BP in 1937 by Pullman Preston Park. '65 and 66' withdrawn about 1964.
180, 181, 182, 183, 184, 185	*Camilla, Latona, Madelene, Pomona, Theodora, Barbara*	K K K	4 4 4	1/1926	Metro	For London-Tonbridge-Hastings line. Narrow bodies. *Madelene, Pomona* and *Barbara* renamed 'RC' in 1946. All repainted green, no names, 1958. Sold to BR(S) in 1960; Nos. S 7872/3/5/6/4/7S for ocean liner boat trains Waterloo–Southampton Docks. Withdrawn by BR(S) in 1964. *Theodora* and *Barbara* preserved by K&ESR; used in 'Wealden Pullman' wine and dine special, Tenterden, Kent.
189–191 195–198	Car Nos. 31–33 III cl. Car Nos. 100–103 III cl.	K K	4 4	8/1926 6/1926	Birmingham	Withdrawn about 1963. For Ireland. Bogies supplied by LMS (NCC) for Irish Pullmans Ltd. Used only in Southern Ireland; sold to GSR in 1937; Nos. 100–103. Chassis of 100 used in 1981 of Inchicore works as mobile rail/timber store, CIE (Irish Rlys.)
192–194	Car Nos. 34–36 III cl.	P	4	7/1926		'35–36' became II cl. in 1946. All II cl. in 1951, with square lavatory windows, remodelled for *Golden Arrow*. All withdrawn in 1962–63. '35' preserved at Haven Street, Isle of Wight. '36' preserved by H.P. Bulmer Ltd., Hereford, for 'Cider Train'.
200 176–178	*Cassandra, Rainbow, Plato, Octavia*	K K	4 4	11/1926 1/1927	Metro	*Rainbow* burnt out at Micheldever, Hampshire, in 1936. Chassis used for *Phoenix* in 1952. Rest withdrawn about 1963.
202–204	*Queen Margaret, Kate Dalrymple, Helen of Mar*	D D D	4 4 4	1927	Metro	For LMS (Scottish) services. I and III cl. saloons. Sold to LMS in 1933 (Nos. 219–221).

Schedule No.	Names	Type	Bogies	Year	Builder	Remarks
205–209	Cecilia, Chloria, Zenobia, Leona, Niobe	K K P	4 4 4	11/1927 11/1927 1927	Midland	For LNER Pullman trains. *Leona* rebuilt at Pullman Preston Park as III cl. GP 'No. 208' in 1947; withdrawn in 1967; preserved at Cressing, Essex. *Niobe* rebuilt at Pullman Preston Park as III cl. GP 'No. 209' in 1948; renamed *Niobe* GP I cl. in 1959. All withdrawn in 1967. *Minerva* rebuilt by Pullman Preston Park in 1951 as GP I cl. with square lavatory windows for *Golden Arrow;* withdrawn in 1965; preserved at Lytham St. Annes; bought by Sea Containers in 1981 for VSOE (UK portion).
213	Minerva	K	4	12/1927		
210–212	Marcelle, Sybil, Kathleen	K	4	1927	Metro	For LNER Pullman trains. Became III cl. 'Nos. 105, 106 and 107' for Yorkshire Pullman in 1946; withdrawn in 1966.
214–216, 218	Car Nos. 59 60, 61 and 63 III cl.	K D	4 4	1928	Midland	For LNER services. '59' rebuilt in 1948–61 by Pullman Preston Park as 'The Hadrian Bar' for *Queen of Scots;* sold to BR(S) No. S7879S. '63' rebuilt to BP by Pullman Preston Park 1950. '62 and 64' for London-Harwich boat trains; rebuilt to P III cl. by Pullman Preston Park in 1937. '62' rebuilt to BP by Preston Park c. 1950. All withdrawn by 1966. '64' preserved at Hereford by Bulmer Ltd. for 'Cider Train'.
217, 219	Car Nos. 62 and 64 II cl.					
220–225 226–229 230–233 234, 235, 237 236, 239 238, 240, 241 242, 243	Car Nos. 67–72 III cl. Car Nos. 73–76 III cl. Car Nos. 77–80 III cl. Nilar, Belinda, Thelma Sheila, Agatha, Phyllis, Penelope, Philomel Ursula, Lucille	K P BP K P K P	4 4 4 4 4 4 4	1928	Metro	For *Queen of Scots* (Chap. 8). All-steel cars. *Agatha, Sheila* and 'Nos. 75–80' in LNER colours as LNER Nos. 468, 469, 481, 482, 485–488 in 1942–48. *Phyllis* and *Lucille* in *Bournemouth Belle* in 1963–66; withdrawn in 1966; preserved at SE Steam Centre, Ashford, Kent. All withdrawn c. 1966. '75' preserved as 'Spot Gate' (pub), Hilderstone, by Ind Coope (Allied Breweries). '76' preserved by Bulmer Ltd., Hereford, for 'Cider Train'. '79' preserved at Grosmont for North Yorks Moors Rly.'s 'Yorkshire Pullman'. *Agatha* bought Sea Containers for London-Venice train reserve, UK portion (at Steamtown, Carnforth, 1978–82).
244–246 247 248 249, 250 251	Adrian, Ibis, Lydia Princess Elizabeth Lady Dalziel Pearl, Diamond Onyx	K K GP K P	4 4 4 4 4	1928 1928 1928	Midland Birmingham Midland	All built by Birmingham in 1925 (see above); bought back from CIWL in 1928. Only *Adrian, Ibis* and *Lydia* bore their old names. In *Golden Arrow* in 1946. *Princess Elizabeth* rebuilt to GP *Isle of Thanet* by Pullman Preston Park, 1950(?), for *Thanet Belle.* In inaugural electric-hauled *Golden Arrow* in 1961, and with *Lydia* in Sir Winston Churchill's funeral train in 1965. Both withdrawn in 1966; believed preserved at National RR Museum, Green Bay, Wisc., USA. *Lady Dalziel* became III cl. GP 'No. 248' for *Devon Belle* in 1948. *Pearl* became III cl. P 'No. 249' in 1947 for *Devon Belle. Diamond* became 'Trianon Bar' for *Golden Arrow;* then 'One Hundred Bar' for RTM Belgian Marine Ostend-Dover service *Centenary;* then 'New Century Bar'—all three renamings in 1946! Renamed 'Diamond, Daffodil Bar' in 1955. All withdrawn in 1966–67. *Ibis* preserved at Birmingham Rly. Museum, Tyseley; bought by Sea Containers; restored in 1981 for Venice Simplon Orient Exp. (UK portion, London-Folkestone) in 1982. (*Ibis* did not run in Sir W. Churchill's funeral train as stated on car.)
252–254 255–258	Eunice, Juana, Zena Ione, Joan, Loraine, Evadne	P K	4 4	1928	Metro	For GWR London-Plymouth ocean liner boat trains and Torquay Pullman (1929). Later in 'Cunarder' boat train, London (Waterloo)-Southampton Docks, and in LNER Pullman trains. All-steel cars. *Joan* used by Gen. Eisenhower during World War II, now preserved at National RR Museum, Green Bay, Wisc., USA. All withdrawn by 1967. *Zena* preserved by Steamtown, Carnforth, and *Ione* by Birmingham Rly. Museum, Tyseley, in 1967–80; both bought by Sea Containers for Venice Simplon Orient Exp. (UK portion).
259, 260 261, 262	Car Nos. 81 and 82 III cl. Car Nos. 83 and 84 III cl.	K P	4 4	1931	Birmingham	For ocean liner boat trains and LNER Pullman trains. 'Nos. 81 and 82' rebuilt by Pullman Preston Park to II cl. GP in 1959–60 for *Bournemouth Belle.* 'Nos 83 and 84' in LNER colours in 1942–48 as LNER Nos. 483 and 484. All withdrawn c. 1967. '83' preserved by Bulmer Ltd. for 'Cider Train'. '84' preserved by Keighley & Worth Valley Rly., Yorks.
263–278	Ida, Ruth, Rose, Violet, May, Peggy, Clara, Ethel, Alice, Gwladys, Olive, Daisy, Anne, Naomi, Lorna, Bertha	K	4	1932	Metro	Composite I and III cl. 'electric' cars for SR '6-Pull' rakes of 5 SR coaches and 1 Pullman per rake. For London-Brighton, Eastbourne, Hastings, Worthing and Littlehampton services. *Ruth* preserved at Hereford by 6,000 Loco. Assn. *Bertha* preserved by Bluebell Rly., Sheffield Park, Sussex, by Mr. R. Martin. All withdrawn in 1965–68.

Schedule No.	Names	Type	Bogies	Year	Builder	Remarks
279–293						For *Southern Belle* of 1933; renamed *Brighton Belle* in 1934. SR '5-Bel' sets: 5-Bel Set 2051 (later 3051) '88-Hazel-Doris-86-89'; 5-Bel Set 2052 (later 3052) '90-Audrey-Vera-87-91'; 5-Bel Set 2053 (later 3053) '92-Gwen-Mona-85-93'. All withdrawn in 1972.
279	Hazel	K	4	1932	Metro	Preserved as Black Bull Inn (pub), Moulton, Yorks.
280	Audrey	K	4			Preserved by Mr. D. Lowther. Ran in Rainhill 1980 'Rocket 150' Cavalcade with *Brighton Belle* roofboards. Bought by Sea Containers in 1981 and altered for loco-haulage with dynamo, etc., for London-Venice train, UK portion (London-Folkestone Harbour), in 1982.
281	Gwen	K	4			Preserved on Colne Valley Rly., Castle Hedingham, Essex.
282	Doris	K	4			Preserved at Finsbury Park BR (London) by City Industrial Ltd.
283	Mona	K	4			Preserved at Brighton Belle Inn (pub), Winsford, Cheshire.
284	Vera	K	4			Preserved at Westleton, Suffolk, by Mrs. Amadée Turner, Member of European Parliament.
285	Car No. 85 III cl.	P	4			Preserved at Nags Head (pub), Mickleover, Derbyshire.
286	Car No. 86 III cl.	P	4			Bought by Sea Containers in 1980 for London-Venice train, UK portion; to be altered for loco-haulage, I cl., for London-Folkestone train.
287	Car No. 87 III cl.	P	4			Preserved at North Norfolk Rly., Sheringham, by Allied Breweries.
288	Car No. 88 III cl.	MBP	4			Preserved at Stour Valley Rly., Chappel, Essex.
289	Car No. 89 III cl.	MBP	4			Preserved as 'Derbyshire Belle', Little Mill Inn (pub), Raworth, Stockport.
290	Car No. 90 III cl.	MBP	4			Preserved by Travellers Fare (BR Catering Dept.), on Nene Valley Rly., Peterborough.
291	Car No. 91 III cl.	MBP	4			Preserved at North Norfolk Rly., Sheringham, by Allied Breweries.
292	Car No. 92 III cl.	MBP	4			Preserved at Preston Park, former Pullman works, by Brighton Pullman Assoc.
293	Car No. 93 III cl.	MBP	4			Preserved at Preston Park, former Pullman works, by Mr. M. Allen.
294–300	Brenda, Elinor, Enid, Grace, Iris, Joyce, Rita	K	4	1932	Metro	Composite I and III cl. 'electric' cars for SR '6-Pull' sets, like *Ida* above. All withdrawn in 1963–68.
301–310						This series built in 1951 for *Golden Arrow* 'Festival of Britain 1951' train and for royal trains. Used marquetry bought pre-World War II and stored. Last Pullmans built before majority shareholding of Pullman Car Co. acquired from CIWL by BR in 1954. They had square lavatory windows. All cars withdrawn by 1972.
301	Perseus	P	4	1951	Birmingham	Bought by Sea Containers in 1978 for Venice Simplon Orient Exp., UK portion. Oval lavatory windows restored, for London-Folkestone service, starting 30th May 1982.
302	Phoenix	P	4	1952	Pullman Preston Park	Built of *Rainbow* chassis (1927, see above). Used for royal trains. Preserved at Hôtel Mercure, Dardilly, Lyons (France), in 1972–80. Bought by Sea Containers in 1980 and restored in 1982 to run in London-Venice train (UK portion).
303	Car No. 303 II cl.	K	4			In *Golden Arrow*, 1951–65; used also in special trains; withdrawn in 1967.
304	Aries	K	4	1952	Pullman Preston Park	Withdrawn c. 1967; preserved as Yew Tree Inn (pub), Rochdale, Lancashire.
305	Aquila	K	4	1951	Birmingham	Preserved by H.P. Bulmer Ltd., Hereford, in 'Cider Train'.
306	Orion	K	4			Preserved by Peco Ltd. (Pritchard), Beer, Seaton, Devon.
307	Carina	K	4			Preserved as Hôtel Mercure, Dardilly, Lyons, France; bought by Sea Containers in 1980 for Venice Simplon Orient Exp., UK portion (London-Folkestone).
308	Cygnus	P	4			Bought by Sea Containers in 1979 for London-Venice train, UK portion. Restored, with oval lavatory windows in 1981, to start 30th May 1982.
309	Hercules	P	4			Believed preserved at National RR Museum, Green Bay, Wisc., USA.
310	Pegasus	Bar	4			Named 'Trianon Bar' in *Golden Arrow* to 1965; preserved at Birmingham Rly. Museum, Tyseley.
311–331						This I cl. series had BR Mark II type curved-side body shells, with public-address and single-side armchairs taken from old Pullmans, for BR(E) Pullman trains, viz. Yorkshire Pullman, Tees-Tyne Pullman, Hull Pullman, etc. All withdrawn in 1978 following

Schedule No.	Names	Type	Bogies	Year	Builder	Remarks
						introduction of HST BR trains. Seating altered by BR to II cl. style, and names painted out after c. 1965, when BR livery substituted.
311	Eagle	K	4	1960	Metro	Preserved at National Rly. Museum, York, with *Emerald* (below). In Travellers Fare Centenary Exp., 1979, and Rainhill 'Rocket' Cavalcade, 1980.
312	Falcon	K	4			To King, Snailwell, scrap; bogies removed in 1980.
313	Finch	K	4			Preserved by West Somerset Rly. (Bailiss) for Quantock Pullman (Minehead-Bishops Lydeard, Somerset).
314	Hawk	K	4			To King, Snailwell, scrap in 1979; no bogies.
315	Heron	K	4			No name; in service with BR in 1979; withdrawn in 1980; for sale, no bogies; believed scrapped by King, Snailwell.
316	Magpie	K	4			No name; BR staff coach in 1979; withdrawn in 1980; for sale without bogies; believed scrapped by King, Snailwell.
317	Raven	K	4			Preserved by West Somerset Rly. (Bailiss) for Quantock Pullman (Minehead-Bishops Lydeard).
318	Robin	K	4			Privately preserved in 1980 on North Yorks Moors Rly., Grosmont. For NYMR 'Yorkshire Pullman' (Grosmont-Pickering) in 1981 with '79', *Opal*, *Garnet* and '332'.
319	Snipe	K	4			Preserved by West Somerset Rly. (Bailiss) for Quantock Pullman.
320	Stork	K	4			No name; BR staff coach in 1979; withdrawn in 1980; for sale without bogies; believed scrapped by King, Snailwell.
321	Swift	K	4			No name; in service with BR in 1979; withdrawn in 1980; for sale; no bogies; believed scrapped by King, Snailwell.
322	Thrush	K	4			To King, Snailwell, scrap; bogies removed in 1980.
323	Wren	K	4			No name; BR staff coach in 1979.
324	Amber	P	4			Preserved by West Somerset Rly. (Bailiss) for Quantock Pullman.
325	Amethyst	P	4			Preserved by Strathspey Rly., Aviemore, Scotland, 1978.
326	Emerald	P	4			Preserved at NRM, York. In Travellers Fare Centenary Exp., 1979.
327	Garnet	P	4			Preserved by North Yorks Moors Rly., Grosmont, for Yorkshire Pullman NYMR.
328	Opal	P	4			Preserved by North Yorks Moors Rly. NYMR.
329	Pearl	P	4			Preserved by West Somerset Rly. (Bailiss) for Quantock Pullman.
330	Ruby	P	4			Believed preserved privately.
331	Topaz	P	4			Pres. by West Somerset Rly. (Bailiss) for Quantock Pullman (as a bar).
332–354						The series below had body shells identical to those of I cl. but with 3-a-side seats for II cl. Nowadays BR consider that suitable for their Manchester Pullman cars, which are I cl. All withdrawn by 1980. All have vaccuum brakes retained.
332	Car No. 332	K	4	1960	Metro	Preserved by North Yorks Moors Rly., Grosmont, for NYMR 'Yorkshire Pullman' (Grosmont-Pickering).
333	Car No. 333	K	4			Preserved at Castleton Motel (pub), Stamford, Lincolnshire.
334	Car No. 334	K	4			To King, Snailwell, scrap; bogies removed in 1980.
335	Car No. 335	K	4			Preserved by Strathspey Rly. as mess van 1979; bought by SLOA in 1981 for SLOA Pullman train. Kitchen converted to boutique for BR running.
336	Car No. 336	K	4			To King, Snailwell, scrap; bogies removed in 1980.
337	Car No. 337	K	4			Preserved privately at Wansford, Nene Valley Rly.
338, 339	Car Nos. 338, 339	K	4			To King, Snailwell, scrap; bogies removed in 1980.
340	Car No. 340	K	4			In BR stock; for Sale in 1979; believed bought privately and preserved in Bournemouth, Hants, area.
341–345	Car Nos. 341–345	K	4			To King, Snailwell, scrap; bogies removed in 1980.
346	Car No. 346	K	4			Preserved at Castleton Motel (pub), Stamford with 'No. 333'.
347–353	Car Nos. 347–353	P	4			In service with BR on football specials, etc., until 1980. Bought by Steam Locomotive Operators Assoc. (SLOA) for their steam-hauled specials on BR. Details from SLOA Marketing, 104 Birmingham Road, Litchfield, Staffs. WS 14 9 RW. The train can be hired with steam, or with BR traction, when not running SLOA specials. It is based at Carlisle Upperby, maintained by BR for SLOA. The train includes '335' (above) and 'The Hadrian Bar' (below).
354	'The Hadrian Bar'	Bar	4			For Tees-Tyne Pullman; replaced No. 214; name removed later; renamed 'The Nightcap Bar' and used in 'Night Limited' all-sleeper BR London-Glasgow train, until 1979; withdrawn in 1980; bought by SLOA.

IV. Blue Pullmans (painted light blue and cream)

These were the first new services introduced by British Rail, after that agency had acquired the shares of the Pullman Car Co. Ltd. in 1954, to use diesel power cars and permanently coupled trailer cars as all-Pullman trains. On the London Midland Region the trains, which began running in 1960, offered first class only and operated between London (St. Pancras) and Manchester via the former Midland Railway main line, while the main line from Euston to Machester was being electrified. Once completed in 1966, the Manchester Pullman transferred to the Euston route, with new electrically hauled cars (below), built by BR after the Pullman Car Co. had wound up in 1962. The Manchester Pullman is the only BR Pullman service still running, and the cars, which run coupled to an ordinary locomotive-hauled train, have the same double glazing with Venetian blinds between inner and outer glass as the diesel Pullman sets. Similar diesel Pullman cars went into service for the Bristol and Birmingham Pullmans on the Western Region, but with eight-car formation and second-class accommodation. After twelve years, they were withdrawn in 1972. The diesel sets carried no names, only their BR numbers. The cars were too new ever to need overhaul at Preston Park before that works was closed, and the Pullman Car Co. Schedule Numbers were simply book entries and never appeared on the cars.

Builder	Schedule No.	British Rail No.		
		6-car Midland Region set		
Metro	PCC 355–358 =	M60090–60093	1st & 6th car	Power car with I cl. saloon
Metro	359–362 =	M60730–60733	2nd & 5th car	I cl. saloon with kitchen
Metro	363–366 =	M60740–60743	3rd & 4th car	I cl. saloon
		8-car Western Region set		
Metro	367–372 =	W60734–60739	3rd & 6th car	I cl. saloon with kitchen
Metro	373–378 =	W60744–60749	4th & 5th car	I cl. saloon
Metro	379–384 =	W60094–60099	1st & 8th car	Power car with II cl. saloon
Metro	385–390 =	W60044–60049	2nd & 7th car	II cl. saloon

V. British Rail Pullman Cars built in 1966

The Manchester-London Pullman, began in 1980, is the last supplementary-fare Pullman train in Europe, running Mondays to Fridays in both directions. Each rake consists of two Pullman brakes, two Pullman parlours and two Pullman kitchen cars, all built at Derby to BR Mark II specifications, with three-a-side seating, blinds between the double glazing, pressure ventilation and vacuum brakes. These arrangements make it impossible for the cars to run with Mark III air-conditioned, air-braked stock; thus, the days of the train are sometimes said to be numbered.

Full lists of BR coaching and carriage stock, including HST sets and such Pullman cars as remain in service, are given in the Railway Correspondence and Travel Society's publication, *BR Coaching Stock 1980:*

Pullman Kitchen Cars BR Class PFK* Nos. M.500–506 (B.5 Bogies);
Pullman Parlour Cars BR Class PFP* Nos. M.540, 543–546 and M.548–553 (B.4 Bogies);
Pullman Parlour Brake Cars BR Class PFB* Nos. M.581–584 and 586 (B.4 Bodies).

Various Pullman Cars have been preserved by the privately operated museum railways in Great Britain, which have renamed some of the cars. Moreover, certain non-Pullman vehicles have been painted in colours matching those of the Pullmans they run with. Catering vehicles—bar cars in particular—are very popular on these museum railways. The name changes that are not historic have been ignored in this list. For instance, the car called *Mary* by the Keighley & Worth Valley Railway, after the wife of the late Bishop Eric Treacy, is not shown here as *Mary*. Details of these preserved lines may be obtained from any office of the British Tourist Authority: 64 St.

James's Street, London, SW1W.ODU; 680 Fifth Avenue, New York, N.Y. 10019; 151 Bloor Street West, 460 Toronto, Ontario M5S.IT3; 171 Clarence Street, Sydney, N.S.W. 2000; P.O. Box 6256, Union Castle Buildings, 36 Loveday Street, 2000 Johannesburg, South Africa; Box 3655 Wellington, New Zealand. The British Tourist Authority maintains other offices at Oslo, Stockholm, Copenhagen, Sao Paulo, Buenos Aires and Mexico City. In the United Kingdom, details may also be obtained at the offices of English, Scottish and Welsh Tourist Boards and Regional English Tourist Boards.

*PFK = 18 seats; PFP = 36 seats; PFB = 30 seats. First class only. Present Pullman supplement = £2.

Suffixes used until 1940

Now restored on the Nostalgic Orient Express and Venice Simplon Orient Express cars

A	Bogie sleeping car
B	Bogie sleeping car with some ordinary seats compartments
C	Rigid sleeping car, 3-axle 6-wheelers
D	Dining car
DE	Dining car with saloon compartment, or Pullman kitchen car
F	Saloon car, or Pullman parlour car
L	Rigid luggage van, 2- or 3-axle, 4- or 6-wheelers
M	Bogie luggage van
MP	Bogie luggage van with postal compartment
R	Gas tank wagon

Plaque RIC

(*Regolamento Internazionale Carrozze*)

All 'international' rolling stock can now run everywhere, except on the rail systems of those countries identified by the plaque mounted on the individual car. The plaque also cites the country responsible for the car's conformation to the RIC rules (Austria: A; Belgium: B; France: F; Italy: It; other countries: initials of the railway). Formerly, the plaque set forth all the countries across which the car could run.

UIC numbers

Only the UIC number must be shown. The first two digits mean: interior service (50); international service (51); special international service vehicle, e.g., TEE or sleeping car of national fleet (61); International Pool Sleeping Car (71); car able to circulate on British gauge and use train ferries to Great Britain (66).

The second pair of digits indicates the administration operating the car concerned. The number 66 is only used by CIWL cars that are neither leased nor sold to another owner/operator.

The third pair of digits indicates the type of car, the first digit being 0 for privately owned cars, or 8 for national railway ownership. The second digit means: 6 for a sleeping car mixed first and second class; 7 for a second-class-only sleeping car; 8 for a dining car; 9 for a saloon or dancing car. Thus, 09 indicates a Pullman, since virtually all Pullmans are privately—i.e., not railway—owned.

The fourth pair of digits is technical, indicating the permitted maximum speed, type of heating, etc. The three following digits make up the individual number of the car, and the last digit is the control number for computers. Thus, a sleeping car of the Wagons-Lits Co. matriculated 51 66 06 becomes 61 83 86 when it is allocated to the Italian national fleet, or 71 85 86 if allocated to the Swiss Federal Railways part of the Pool. Since the UIC regulations say nothing about crossed-out numbers, while strictly forbidding that any non-UIC numbers be painted on the cars, the CIWL numbers of the cars can be seen, neatly and legibly crossed out!

The cars of the CIWL carry only the numbers of one of the following railway-car operators:

66 = CIWL	80 = DB	83 = FS	85 = SBB	87 = SNCF
71 = RENFE	81 = OBB	84 = NS	86 = DSB	88 = SNCB

Initials of railway administrations

A. National railways

Initials logo	Full name	Country	Remarks
Amtrak	National Railroad Passenger Corp.	USA	Created in 1970; trains mostly run on private companies' tracks
ANR	Australian National Railways	AUS	Fusion in 1975 of Commonwealth, Tasmanian & South Australian Railways (except South Australian urban lines)
BR	British Rail	GB	Fusion in 1947 of GWR, LNER, LMS & SR
CH	Greek Railways	GR	
DB	Deutsche Bundesbahn	D	German Federal Railways, created in 1920; DR (Deutsche Reichsbahn) before 1945; DR now in East Germany
DSB	Danske Statsbaner	DK	Danish State Railways
ERR	Egyptian Republic Railways	ET	ESR (Egyptian State Railways) before 1950
FS	Ferrovie dello Stato	I	(Italian) Railways of State; created in 1905; fusion in 1885 of successors to SFAI, SFM, etc.
JZ	Jugoslovenske Zeleznice	YU	Yugoslav Railways; JDZ before 1945
NS	N.V. Nederlandse Spoorwegen	NL	Dutch Railways
NZR	New Zealand Railways	NZ	
OBB	Oesterreichische Bundesbahn	A	Austrian Federal Railways (DR 1938–45); B.B. Oesterreich before 1938
RENFE	Red Nacional de los Ferrocarriles Espanoles	E	Spanish National Railways; fusion in 1941 of MZA, Norte, Andalusian Rlys, etc. (sometimes shown as Renfe)
SAR/SAA	South African Railways/Suid Afrikaans Spoorwegen	ZA	
SBB/CFF	Schweizerische Bundesbahn/Chemins de Fer Fédérales	CH	Swiss Federal Railways
SJ	Statens Jarnvagar	S	Swedish State Railway
SNCB	Société Nationale des Chemins de Fer Belges	B	Included Nord Belge only after World War II. Belgian National Railways
SNCF	Société Nationale des Chemins de Fer Français	F	French National Railways; fusion of private companies and État in 1937
TCDD	Türkiye Cumhürriyet Devlet Demiryolari	TR	Turkish State Railways; fusion of CO, SCP, etc., c. 1924
VR	Valtionrautatiet	SF	Finnish State Railways

B. Railway companies mentioned

Initials logo	Full name	Country	Remarks
BLS	Berne-Loetschberg Simplon*	CH	Includes BN (Neuchatel) and SEZ (Spiez-Zweisimmen)
CR	Caledonian Railway	GBS	Includes Carlisle-Glasgow-Perth
CO	Chemins de Fer Orientaux	TR	CO = Oriental Railways; private railway co. in European Turkey that has been part of Greece since 1918
CP	Caminhos de Ferro Portugueses E.P.*	P	Portuguese Railways
EST	Chemin de Fer de l'Est	F	Est = East; includes Paris (Est)-Strasbourg and Paris-Belfort-DELLE
ETAT	Chemin de Fer de L'État	F	State Railway; ex-Ouest (West); bought before 1937
GER	Great Eastern Railway	GBE	Includes London (Liverpool Street)–Harwich
GNR	Great Northern Railway	GBE	Includes London (Kings Cross)–York, London–Leeds
GSWR	Glasgow & South Western Railway	GBS	Includes Carlisle-Glasgow via Kilmarnock
GWR	Great Western Railway	GBE/CY	Includes London (Paddington)-Reading–Exeter–Plymouth– Torquay; also London–Cardiff, London–Birmingham
HR	Highland Railway	GBS	Includes Perth-Inverness
K&ESR	Kent & East Sussex Railway	GBE	Light Railway until 1947; partly restored*
LBSCR	London, Brighton & South Coast Railway	GBE	Includes London (Victoria)–Brighton, London–Newhaven
LCDR	London Chatham & Dover Railway	GBE	Fusion with SER in 1899
LMSR	London Midland & Scottish Railway	GB	Created in 1923 by fusion of Midland, LNWR, Caledonian Rly., GSWR and Highland Rly.
LNER	London & North Eastern Railway	GB	Created in 1923 by fusion of GER, GNR, NER, NBR and Great North of Scotland Rlys.
LNWR	London & North Western Railway	GBE	Includes London (Euston)–Crewe–Carlisle
LSWR	London & South Western Railway	GBE	Includes London (Waterloo)–Salisbury–Exeter–Illfracombe–Plymouth; also London–Southampton– Bournemouth
MR	Midland Railway	GBE	Includes London (St. Pancras)–Derby–Leeds–Carlisle
Midi	Chemin de Fer du Midi	F	Midi = Southern; includes Bordeaux–Irun, Bordeaux–Toulouse-Cerbere; fusion with PO in 1934.
MOB	Montreux-Oberland Bernois*	CH	Narrow gauge
MZA	Madrid Zaragoza & Alicante Railway	E	Includes Madrid–Barcelona–Port Bou
NBR	North British Railway	GBS	Includes Carlisle–Edinburgh–Aberdeen, Edinburgh–Berwick

Initials logo	Full name	Country	Remarks
NER	North Eastern Railway	GBE	Includes York–Newcastle–Berwick
NORD	Chemin de Fer du Nord	F	Nord = Northern; includes Paris (Nord)–Calais; also Paris (Nord)–Mons on line to Brussels and Paris–Charleroi on line to Liège (Nord Belge subsidiary in Southern Belgium)
NORTE	Northern Railway	E	Includes Madrid–Irun
NYC	New York Central System	USA	Now Penn Central
PLM	Paris–Lyon–Méditérranée	F	Includes Paris–Dijon–Vallorbe and Paris–Dijon–Modane
PO	Paris–Orleans	F	Includes Paris (Orsay)–Bordeaux and (with Midi) Paris–Toulouse–Cerbere

Initials logo	Full name	Country	Remarks
RhB	Rhätische Bahn*	CH	Grisons Railway (narrow gauge)
SCP	Smyrne, Cassaba & Prolonguements	TR	Asiatic Turkey, based on Izmir
SER	South Eastern Railway	GBE	Includes London (Charing Cross)–Folkestone–Dover
SE&CR	South Eastern & Chatham Railway	GBE	Fusion in 1899 of SER and LCDR
SFAI	Strade Ferrate Alta Italia	I	Upper Italian Railway; includes Modane–Turin–Genoa, Ventimiglia–Genoa
SFM	Strade Ferrate Meridionale	I	Central Italian Railway; includes Bologna–Brindisi
SR	Southern Railway	GBE	Created in 1923 by fusion of LSWR, LBSCR and SE&CR

* = Still running.

Bibliography

Beebe, Lucius. *Mansions on Rails*. Berkeley (Calif.), 1950.
——. *Twentieth Century Limited*. Berkeley (Calif.), 1962.
Behrend, George. *History of Wagons-Lits*. London, 1959.
——. *Pullman in Europe*. Shepperton (England), 1962.
——. *Grand European Expresses*. London, 1962.
——. *Railway Holiday in France*. Newton Abbot (England), 1964.
——. *Yatakli-Vagon (Turkish Steam Travel)*. With Vincent Kelly. Isle of Jersey, 1969.
——. *Hof Steam (Souvenirs of DB Steam)*. Isle of Jersey, 1971.
Brandt, Walter. *Schlaf- und Speisewagen der Eisenbahn*. Stuttgart, 1968.
Des Cars, Jean. *Sleeping Story*. Paris, 1976 (French text).
Commault, Roger. *La Compagnie Internationale des Wagons-Lits à 75 ans*. In collaboration with Maurice Mertens. Paris, 1951.
——. *Georges Nagelmackers*. Uzès (France), 1966.
Compagnie International des Wagons-Lits. *Guide Wagons-Lits*. Biannual until 1976. Paris.
——. *Swift Services to the South*. Paris, 1929.
Cookridge, E.H. *Orient Express*. London, 1979.
Dekobra, Maurice. *The Madonna of the Sleeping Cars*. Paris, 1925 (English trans. London, 1927).
Dubin, Arthur D. *More Classic Trains*. Milwaukee, Wisc. (USA), 1974.
Ernst, Friedhelm. *'Rheingold': Luxuszug durch fünf Jahrzehnte*. Dusseldorf, 1970.

Grunwald, Kurt. *Türkenhirsch*. Jerusalem, 1966.
Hamilton-Ellis, C. *The Royal Trains*. London, 1975.
Harris, Michael. *Preserved Railway Coaches*. Shepperton (England), 1976.
Hasenson, A. *The Golden Arrow*. London, 1970.
International Sleeping Car Co. *The International Traveller and Continental Sportsman* (Wagons-Lits Guide in English!). Paris, 1894–1914.
Kalla-Bishop, P. *Hungarian Railways*. Newton Abbot (England), 1973.
Page, Martin. *The Lost Pleasures of the Great Trains*. London, 1975.
Pullman Car Co. Ltd. *The Golden Way*. Monthly until 1939. London.
——. *The Princely Path to Paris*. London, 1926.
Solch, Werner. *Orient Express*. Dusseldorf, 1974 (German text).
——. *Jules Vernes Express*. Dusseldorf, 1980 (German text).
Stockl, Fritz. *Rollende Hotels*. Vienna/Heidelberg, 1967.
——. *Komfort auf Schienen*. Basle, 1970.
Swinglehurst, Edmund. *The Romantic Journey* (story of Thomas Cook). London, 1974.
TEN. *International Sleeping Car Timetable*. Biannual ORC (Organisme Répartiteur Central du Pool), Paris.
Thomas Cook. *Continental Timetable*, ed. by J.H. Price. Monthly. Peterborough (England).
——. *Overseas Timetable*, ed. by P. Tremlett. Bimonthly. Peterborough (England).
Ustinov, Peter. *God and the State Railways*. London, 1960.
Westcott-Jones, Kenneth. *Romantic Railways*. London, 1971.
Whitehouse, Patrick. *Great Trains of the World*. London/New York/Sydney/Toronto, 1975.

Index

Photographic credits

The numbers cited in the credits are plate numbers. Amtrak, United States Travel Service: 186, 187, 188, 189; George Behrend, Fliquet, St. Martin: 138; Coll. George Behrend, Fliquet, St. Martin: 33, 45, 47 (bill #14092: photo Schweiz. Verkehrsmuseum, Lucerne), 70, 81, 105, 130, 148, 153, 171; Bisagno (Coll. G. Behrend): 35; British Rail, London: 72–74, 78, 79, 212; British Rail, London (Coll. J.H. Price): 76, 152; CIWLT, Paris: 9–11, 22–24, 26–28, 36, 39, 41, 43, 48–55, 57–59, 92–94, 96, 97, 99–102, 109, 110, 114, 124, 128, 129, 132, 133, 135, 137, 139, 140, 145, 154–156, 158, 159, 160–162, 174, 193–195, 199, 205, 207, 208, 215, 219; CIWLT, Paris (Coll. Coudert): 107, 108, 159; R.O. Coffin, Briston (Coll. H.P. Bulmer Ltd., Hereford): 3; Roger Commault, Serquigny:66; Coll. Roger Commault, Serquigny: 91; Thomas Cook & Son Ltd., Peterborough: 103; Thomas Cook & Son Ltd., Peterborough (Coll. J.H. Price): 80, 142, 143, 149, 163, 217; Gerard Coudert, Paris (Coll. J.H. Price): 98, 172; Crown Copyright, National Railway Museum, York: 61; DB/E. Below (Coll. J.H. Price): 127, 159; DB, Frankfurt-am-Main:164–166; DSG Frankfurt-am-Main: 125; Coll. Arthur Dubin, Chicago: 16–18, 62, 63 (photo Riad Shehata, Cairo), 67, 68, 83, 88, 89, 112; Coll. Arthur Dubin, Chicago, with the gracious permission of the Chicago, Milwaukee & St. Paul Railroad: 111; Coll. Arthur Dubin, Chicago, with the gracious permission of the New York Central Railroad: 84–87; Coll. Arthur Dubin, Chicago, with the gracious permission of Pullman-Standard, Chicago: 5–7; M.W. Earley, Reading: 2, 75, 77, 150, 151; EMI Film Distributors, London (with their gracious permission): 31, 32; Friedhelm Ernst, Cologne: 118, 119, 126; Evans (Coll. G. Behrend): 46; FS, Rome: 40; N.N. Forbes (Coll. J.H. Price): 56; Georg Gerster, Zurich: 184; Wentworth Gray (Coll. J.H. Price): 19, 71; Billy Hamilton Public Relations Ltd., London: 218, 220-222; Linke-Hofmann-Busch, Salzgitter-Watenstedt: 113; Intraflug A.G., Forch: 1, 134; Kunstgewerbemuseum der Stadt Zurich (photo Werner Hauser, Altikon): 25, 34; Meissner (Coll. Friedhelm Ernst, Cologne): 122; MOB, Montreux: 158; Douglas Morriss (Coll. R. Spark/European Railways): 213; National Publicity Studios, Wellington, through the High Commissioner for New Zealand: 176; New Zealand Government Railways, through Railway Gazette International, London: 69; New Zealand Railways, through Railway Gazette International, London: 177; Horace W. Nicholls, Ealing (Coll. J.H. Price): 4, 141; J.H. Price, Peterborough: 106, 117, 131; Coll. J.H. Price: 21, 64, 65, 116; PTC, through the Australian Tourist Commission, London: 181, 182; Publicity and Travel Department, South African Railways, Johannesburg: 180; Pullman Car Co. (Coll. BR, London): 20; Pullman Car Co., with the gracious permission of Mary Adshead: 216; Pullman-Standard, Chicago (with their gracious permission): 8; SATOUR (South African Tourist Corp.), Pretoria: 115, 178–180; SBB (Coll. R. Spark, Surrey): 123; Schindler: 90; Schlieren: 211, 214; Coll. Sedgwick and Marshall: 136; J.L. Smith: 82; SNCF, Paris: 37, 104, 144, 173 (photo Patrick Olivain), 175 (photo Jean-Claude Dewolf); F. Scholz (Coll. Werner Sölch, Munich): 44; Werner Sölch, Munich: 30, 38; Werner Sölch (Coll. CFF, Berne): 29; Walter Studer, Berne: 196-198; Takenda, Tokyo: 183; "Topical" (Coll. J.H. Price): 95; VIA Canada: 190-192; *la Vie du Rail*, Paris: 167 (photo Imbert), 168 (photo Breton), 169 (photo B.D.), 170 (photo Pilloux), 206, 210; P. Ransome Wallis: 146, 147; Ed. Wotjas, United States Travel Service: 185. Illustration 120 (painting by A.J. Jöhnssen) is taken from the work *Le Monde des Locomotives à Vapeur*, by Gustavo Reder, Fribourg, 1974.